SHOW-HA SHOTEN!

3

Story by **Akinari Asakura**

Art by **Takeshi Obata**

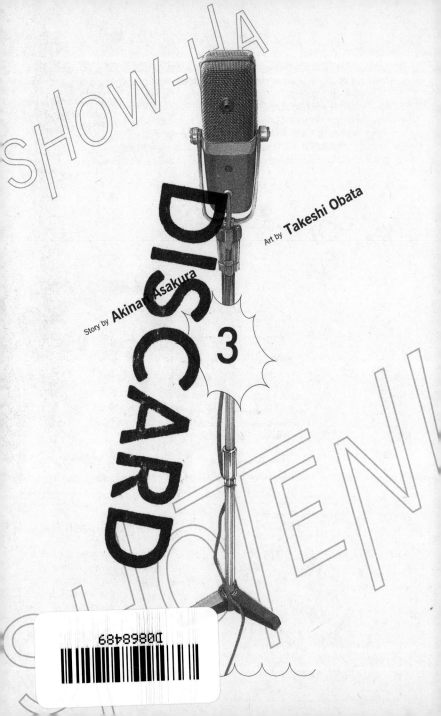

Story

OH GI RI
DYNAMICS
OH GI RI
DYNAMICS

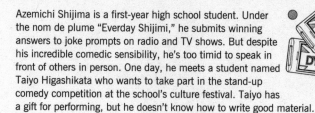

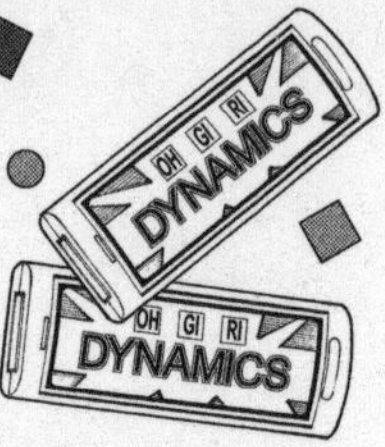

Azemichi Shijima is a first-year high school student. Under the nom de plume “Everday Shijimi,” he submits winning answers to joke prompts on radio and TV shows. But despite his incredible comedic sensibility, he’s too timid to speak in front of others in person. One day, he meets a student named Taiyo Higashikata who wants to take part in the stand-up comedy competition at the school’s culture festival. Taiyo has a gift for performing, but he doesn’t know how to write good material.

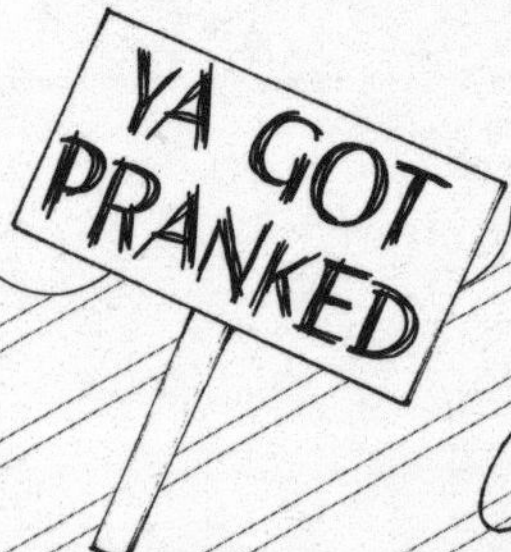

YA GOT PRANKED

Character

Azemichi Shijima

JOKE IDEAS No. 162

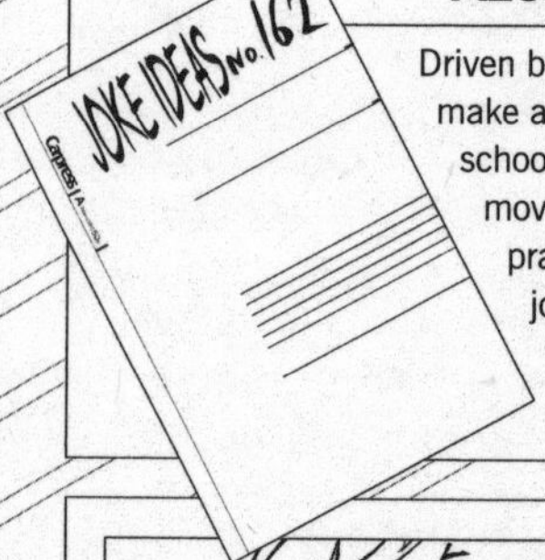

Driven by regret that he couldn’t make a girl from middle school laugh when she was moving away, he started practicing comedy. Writes jokes under the name “Everyday Shijimi.” Gets stage fright.

Everyday Shijimi

Taiyo Higashikata

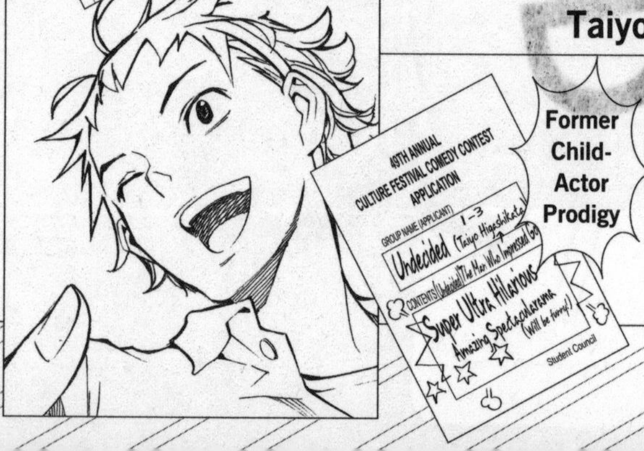

49TH ANNUAL
CULTURE FESTIVAL COMEDY CONTEST
APPLICATION
GROUP NAME (APPLICANT)
1-3
Undecided (Taiyo Higashikata)
Super Ultra Hilarious
Amazing Spectacularama
(Will be funny!)
Student Council
Former Child-Actor Prodigy

A former child-actor prodigy with a gift for performing. After his previous comedy partner passed away, he inherited the dream of rising to the top of the comedy world.

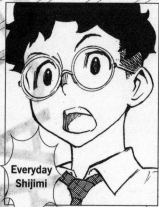

When Taiyo learns that Azemichi is Everyday Shijimi, he invites him to be his partner in the contest. Despite having been written on the fly, their sketch is a hit, and the duo experience the elation of their first true wave of laughter. For Azemichi, it's the motivation he needs to finally dedicate himself to being a comedian. Next, they're setting their sights on rising to the very pinnacle of comedy!

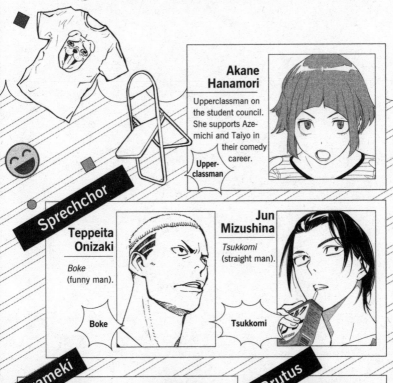

Akane Hanamori

Upperclassman on the student council. She supports Azemichi and Taiyo in their comedy career.

Upperclassman

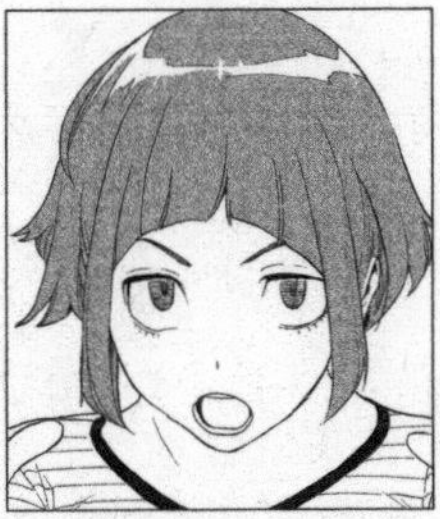

Sprechchor

Teppeita Onizaki

Boke (funny man).

Boke

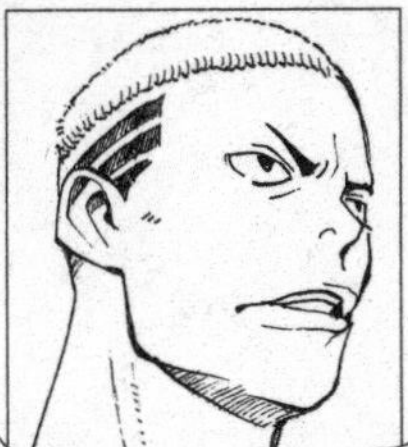

Jun Mizushina

Tsukkomi (straight man).

Tsukkomi

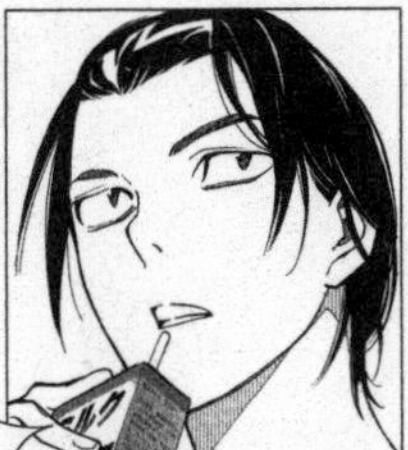

Kirameki Confections

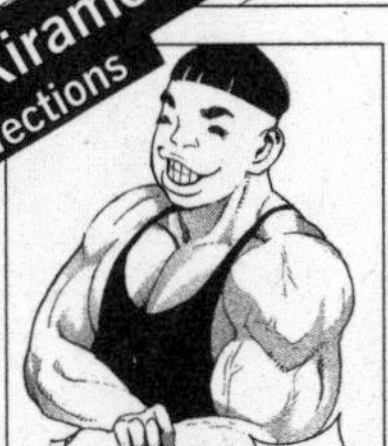

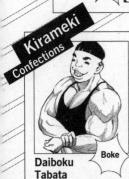

Boke

Daiboku Tabata

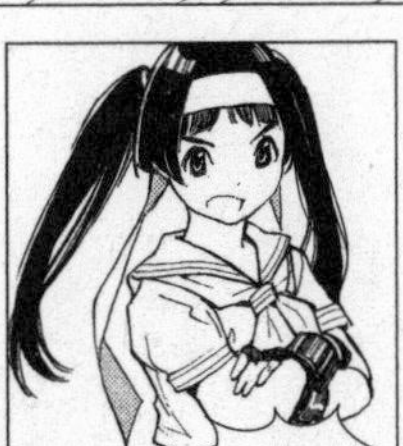

Tsukkomi

Suzume Kanade

Brutus

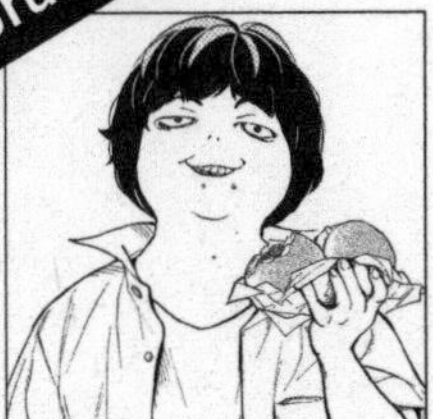

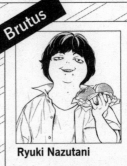

Ryuki Nazutani

Contents **3**

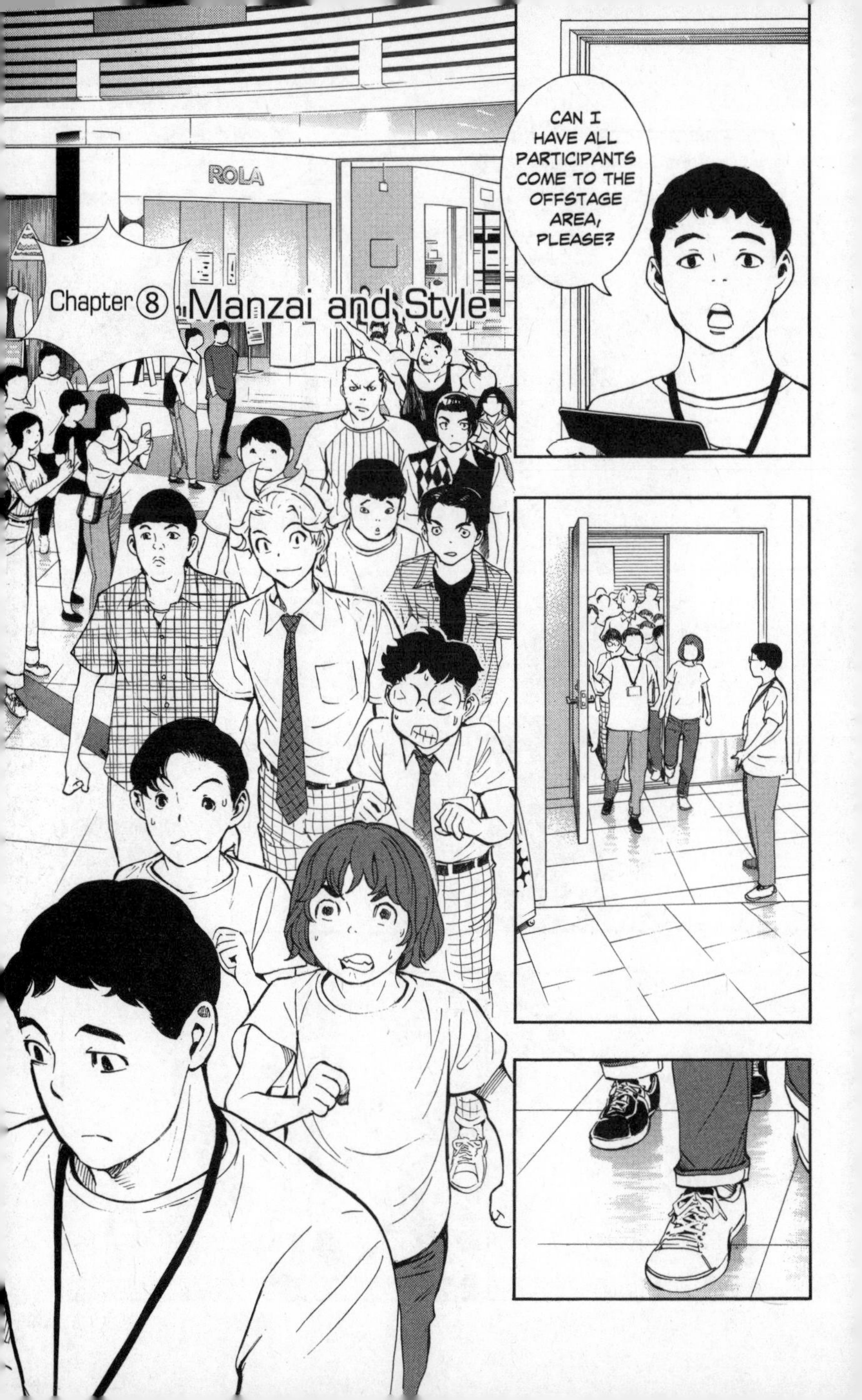
CAN I HAVE ALL PARTICIPANTS COME TO THE OFFSTAGE AREA, PLEASE?
Chapter 8 Manzai and Style
ROLA

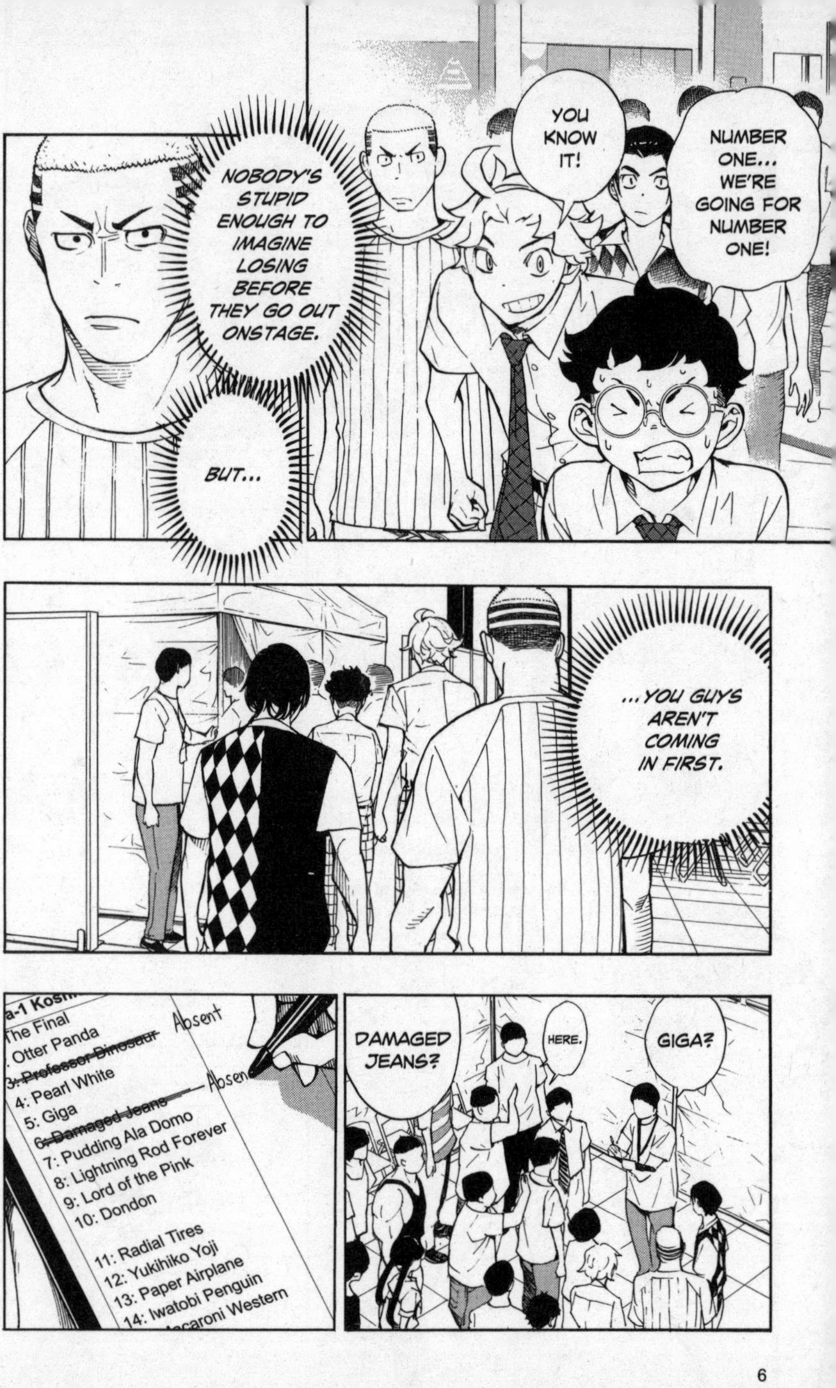
NUMBER ONE... WE'RE GOING FOR NUMBER ONE!
YOU KNOW IT!
NOBODY'S STUPID ENOUGH TO IMAGINE LOSING BEFORE THEY GO OUT ONSTAGE.
BUT...
...YOU GUYS AREN'T COMING IN FIRST.
GIGA?
HERE.
DAMAGED JEANS?
a-1 Kosh
The Final
. Otter Panda
3: Professor Dinosaur
Absent
4: Pearl White
5: Giga
6: Damaged Jeans
Absen
7: Pudding Ala Domo
8: Lightning Rod Forever
9: Lord of the Pink
10: Dondon
11: Radial Tires
12: Yukihiko Yoji
13: Paper Airplane
14: Iwatobi Penguin
acaroni Western

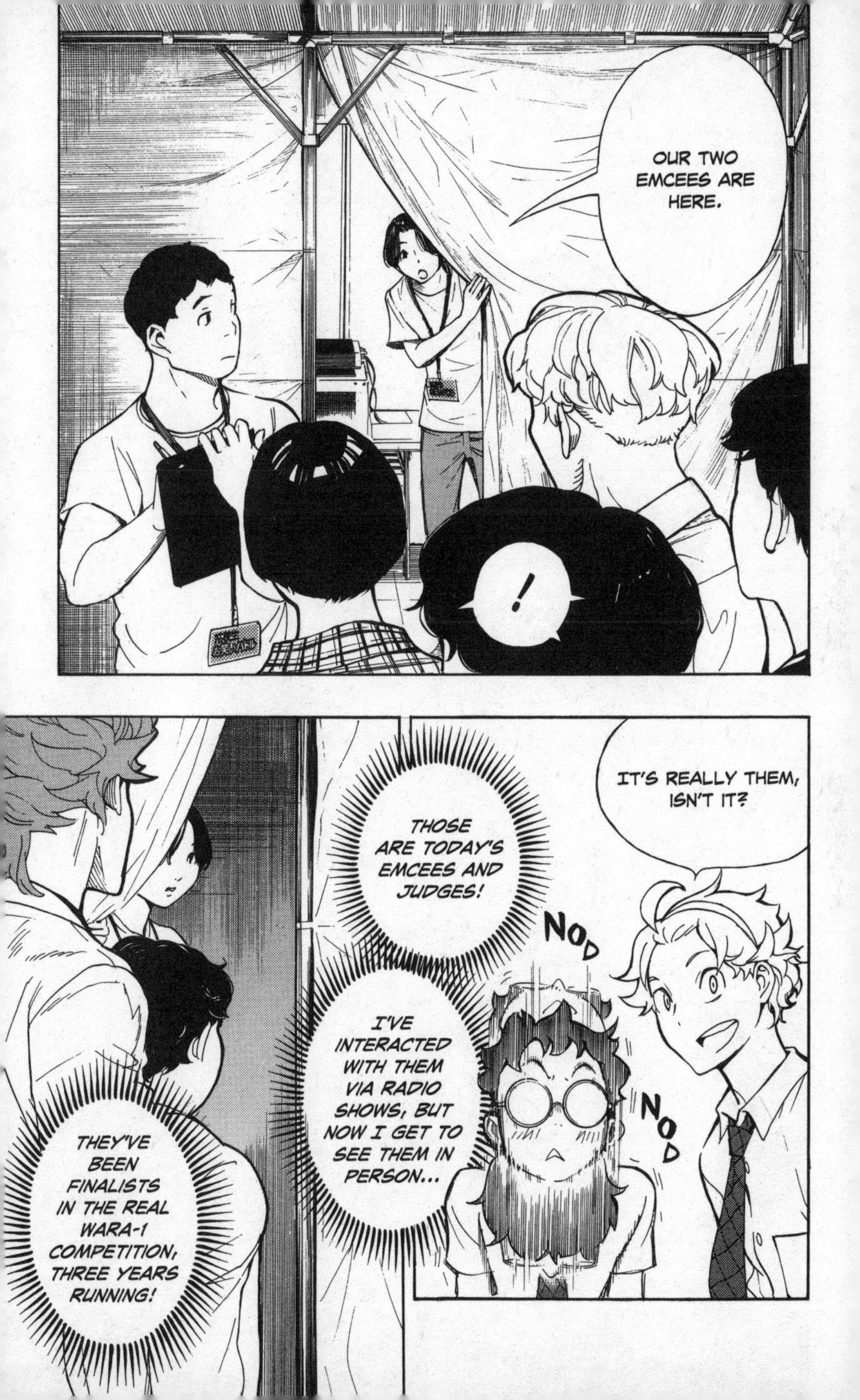
OUR TWO EMCEES ARE HERE.
!
IT'S REALLY THEM, ISN'T IT?
NOD
NOD
THOSE ARE TODAY'S EMCEES AND JUDGES!
I'VE INTERACTED WITH THEM VIA RADIO SHOWS, BUT NOW I GET TO SEE THEM IN PERSON...
THEY'VE BEEN FINALISTS IN THE REAL WARA-1 COMPETITION, THREE YEARS RUNNING!

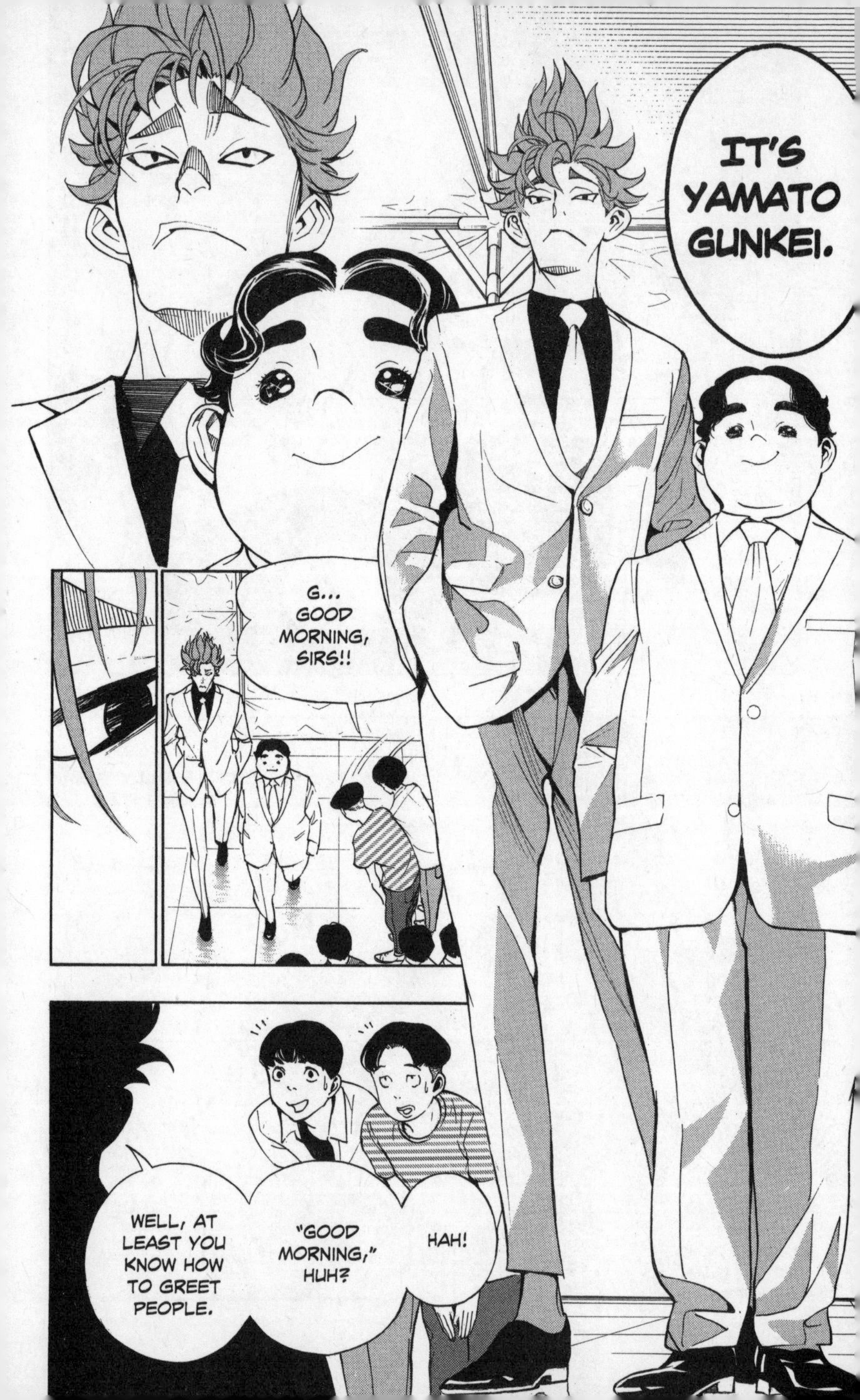
IT'S YAMATO GUNKEI.
G... GOOD MORNING, SIRS!!
HAH!
"GOOD MORNING," HUH?
WELL, AT LEAST YOU KNOW HOW TO GREET PEOPLE.

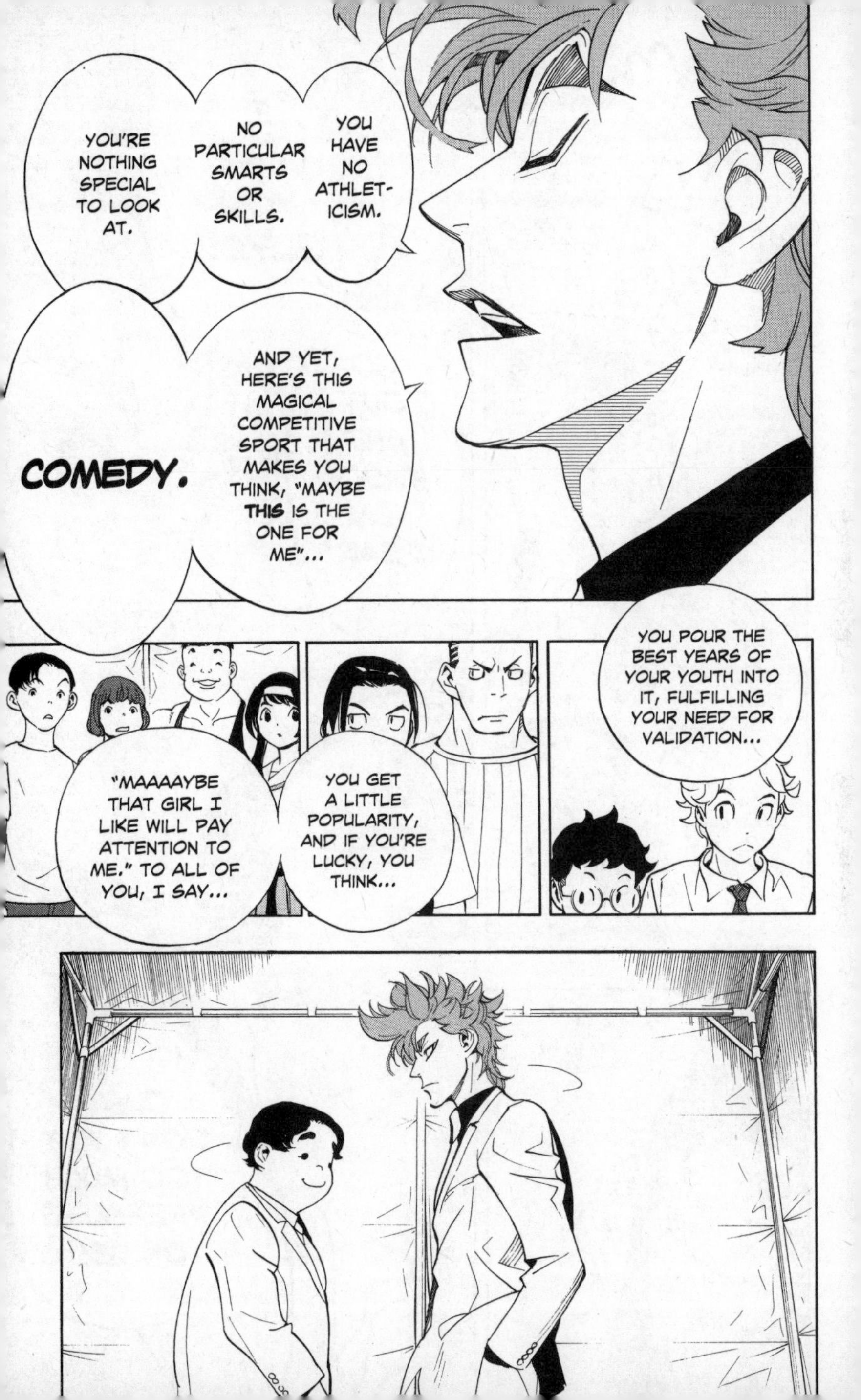
YOU HAVE NO ATHLETICISM.
NO PARTICULAR SMARTS OR SKILLS.
YOU'RE NOTHING SPECIAL TO LOOK AT.
AND YET, HERE'S THIS MAGICAL COMPETITIVE SPORT THAT MAKES YOU THINK, "MAYBE THIS IS THE ONE FOR ME"...
COMEDY.
YOU POUR THE BEST YEARS OF YOUR YOUTH INTO IT, FULFILLING YOUR NEED FOR VALIDATION...
YOU GET A LITTLE POPULARITY, AND IF YOU'RE LUCKY, YOU THINK...
"MAAAAYBE THAT GIRL I LIKE WILL PAY ATTENTION TO ME." TO ALL OF YOU, I SAY...

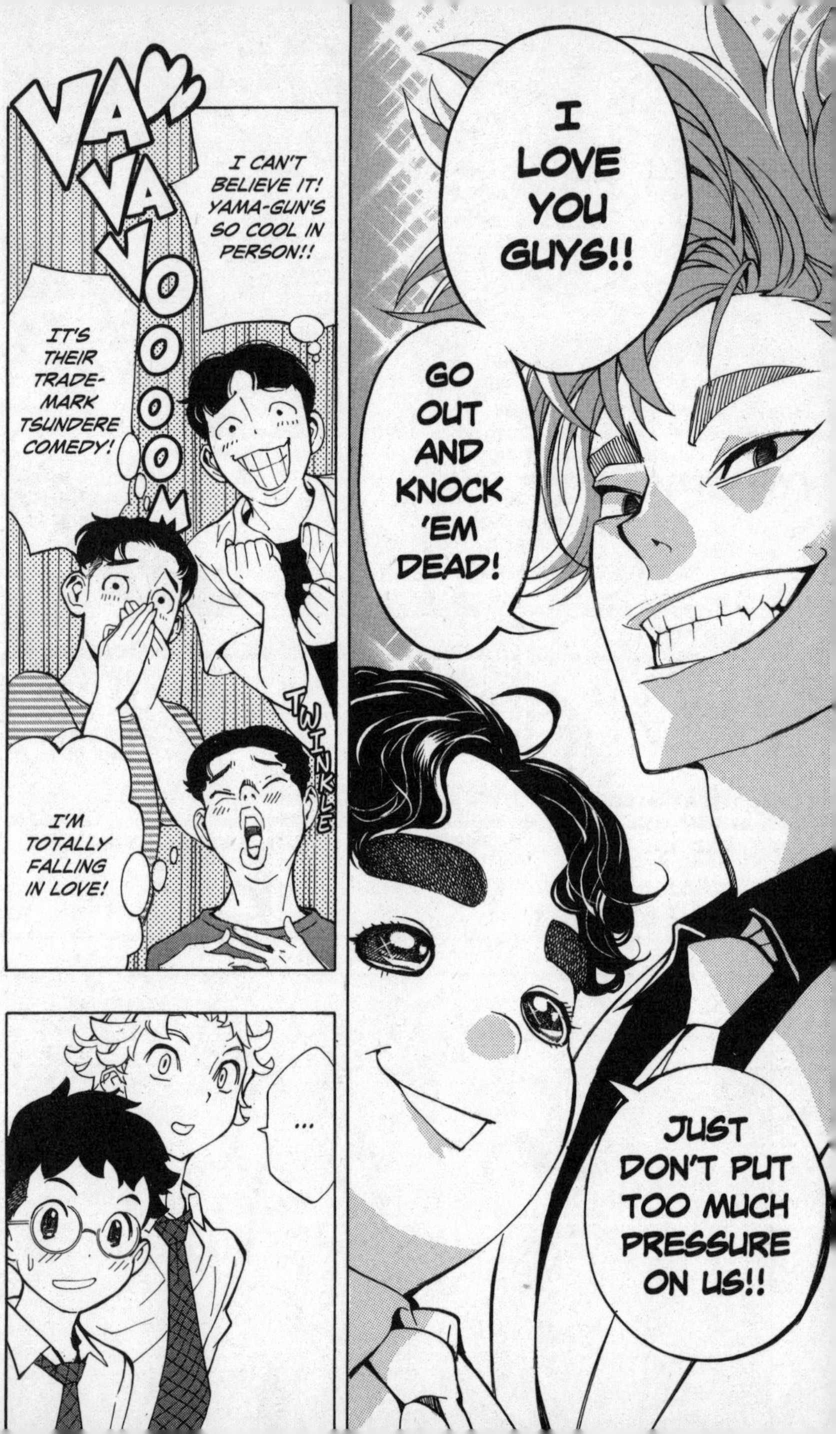
I LOVE YOU GUYS!!
GO OUT AND KNOCK 'EM DEAD!
JUST DON'T PUT TOO MUCH PRESSURE ON US!!
VA VA VOOOOOOOM
I CAN'T BELIEVE IT! YAMA-GUN'S SO COOL IN PERSON!!
IT'S THEIR TRADEMARK TSUNDERE COMEDY!
TWINKLE
I'M TOTALLY FALLING IN LOVE!
...

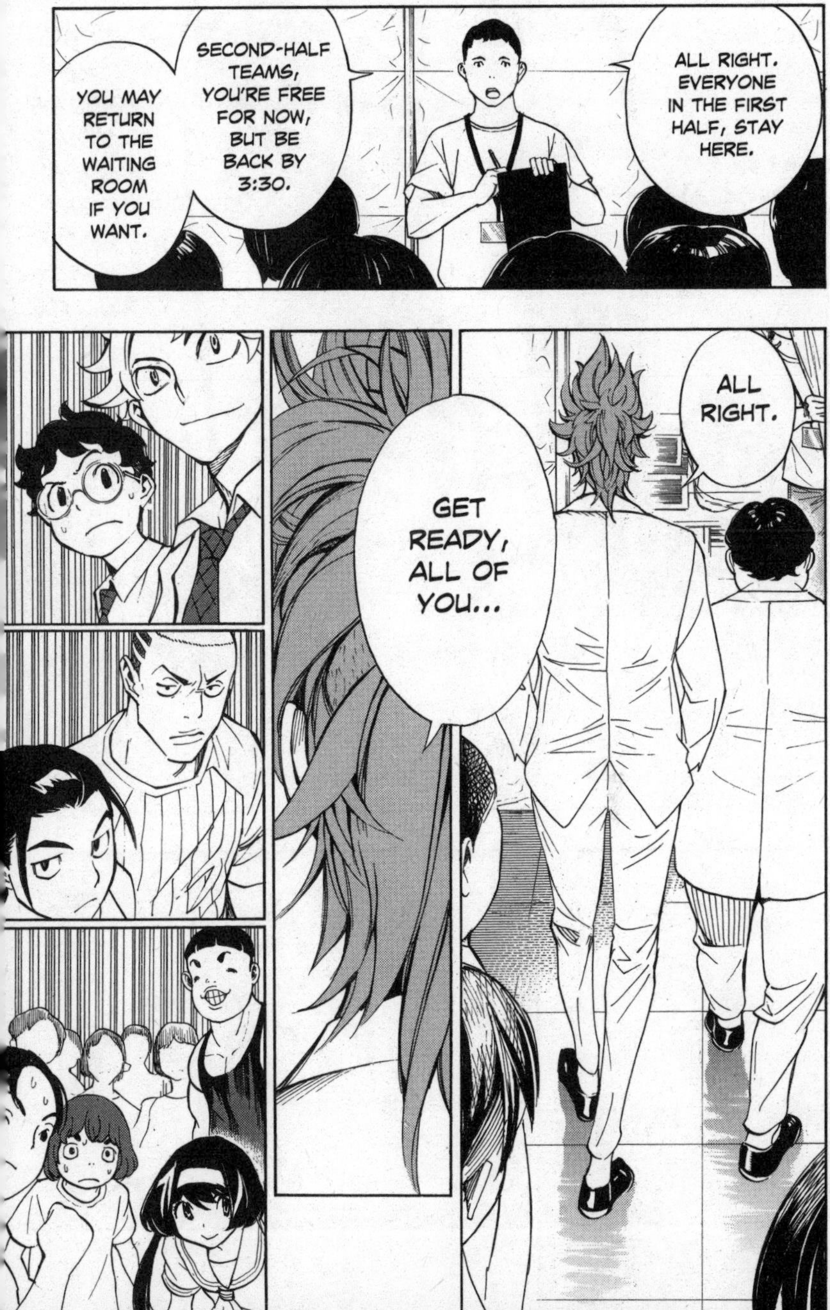
ALL RIGHT. EVERYONE IN THE FIRST HALF, STAY HERE.
SECOND-HALF TEAMS, YOU'RE FREE FOR NOW, BUT BE BACK BY 3:30.
YOU MAY RETURN TO THE WAITING ROOM IF YOU WANT.
ALL RIGHT.
GET READY, ALL OF YOU...

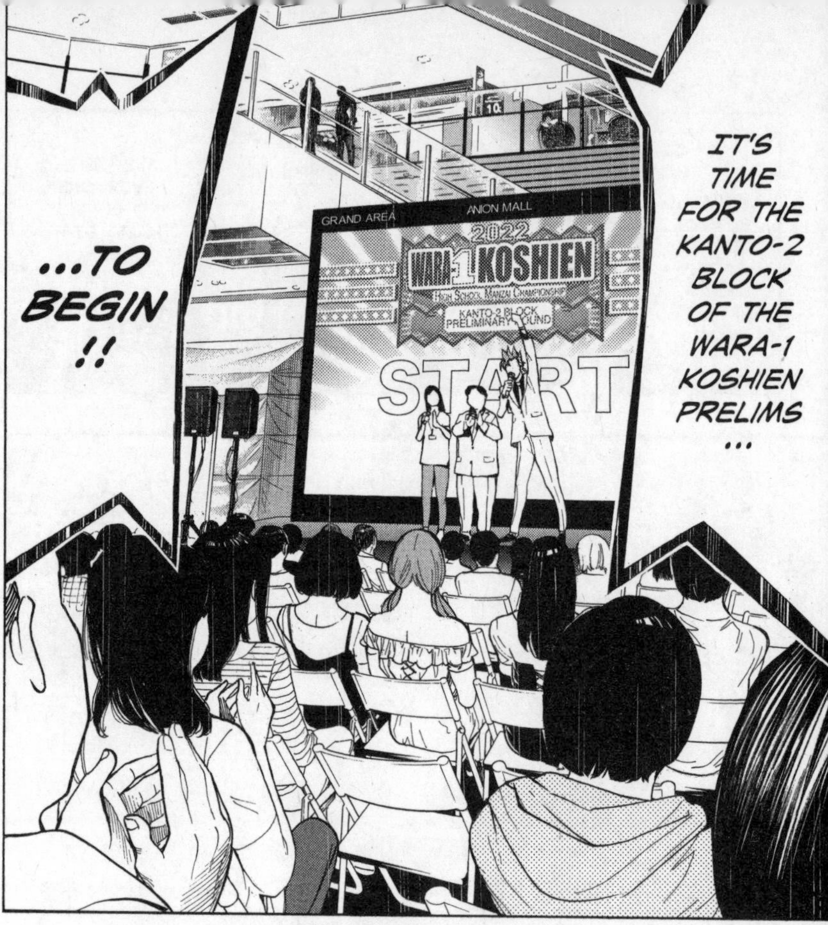
IT'S TIME FOR THE KANTO-2 BLOCK OF THE WARA-1 KOSHIEN PRELIMS...
...TO BEGIN!!
GRAND AREA
ANION MALL
2022
WARA-1 KOSHIEN
HIGH SCHOOL MANZAI CHAMPIONSHIP
KANTO-2 BLOCK PRELIMINARY ROUND
START

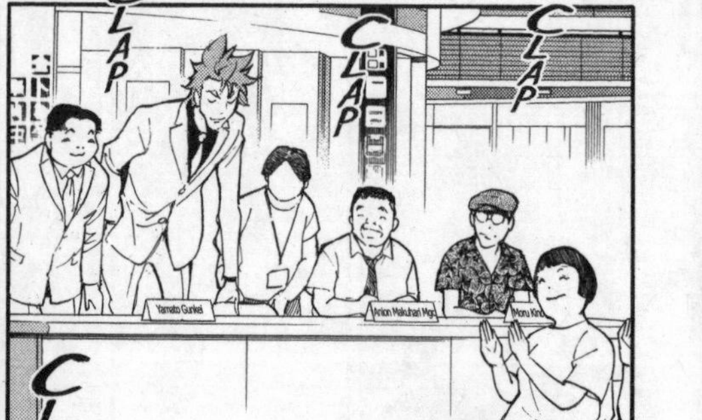
CLAP
CLAP
CLAP
Yamato Gunkei
Anion Makuhari Mgr.
CLAP

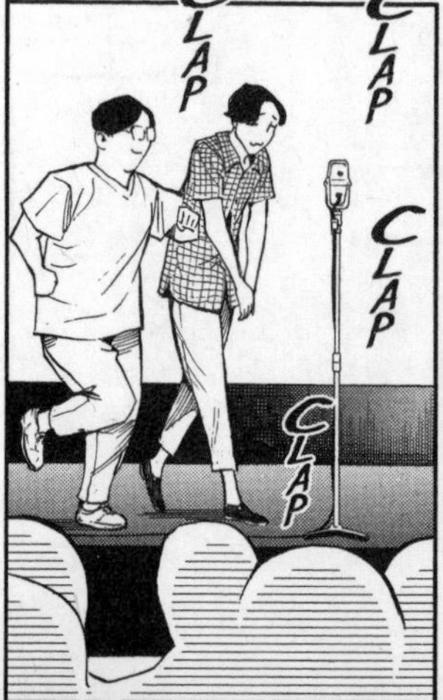
CLAP
CLAP
CLAP
CLAP

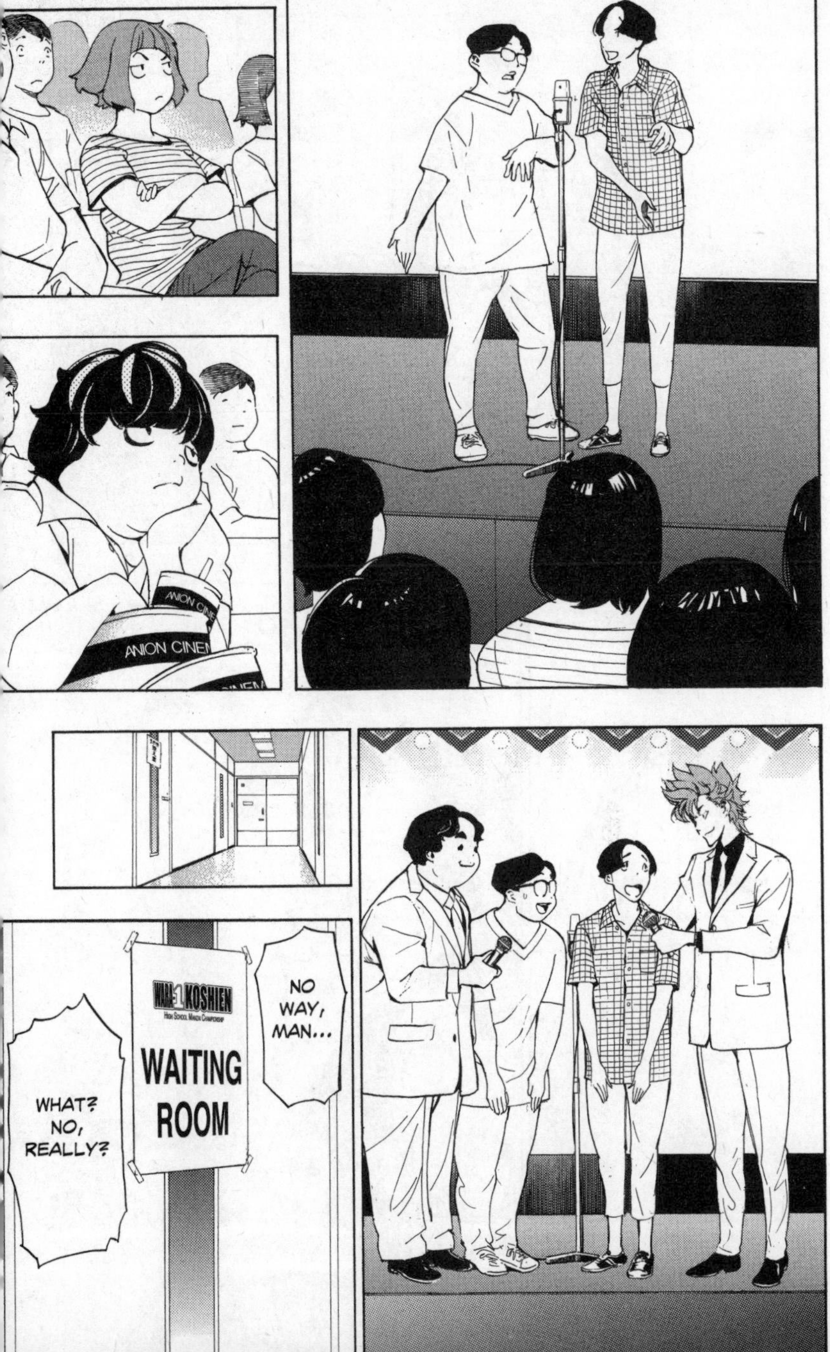
ANION CINEM
ANION CINEM
NO WAY, MAN...
WARA-1 KOSHIEN
HIGH SCHOOL MANZAI CHAMPIONSHIP
WAITING ROOM
WHAT? NO, REALLY?

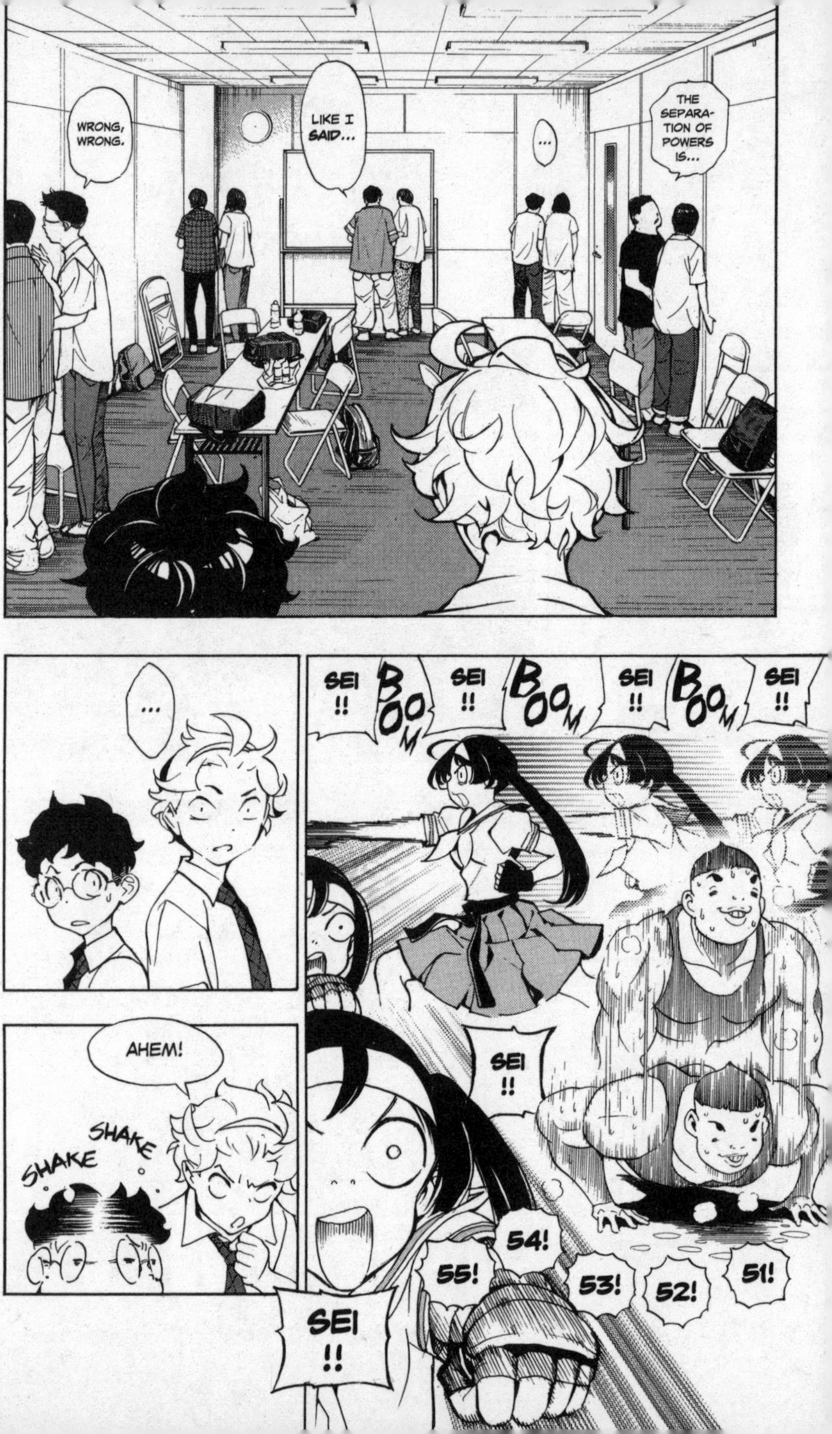
THE SEPARATION OF POWERS IS...
...
LIKE I SAID...
WRONG, WRONG.
SEI!!
BOOM
SEI!!
BOOM
SEI!!
BOOM
SEI!!
SEI!!
51!
52!
53!
54!
55!
SEI!!
...
AHEM!
SHAKE
SHAKE

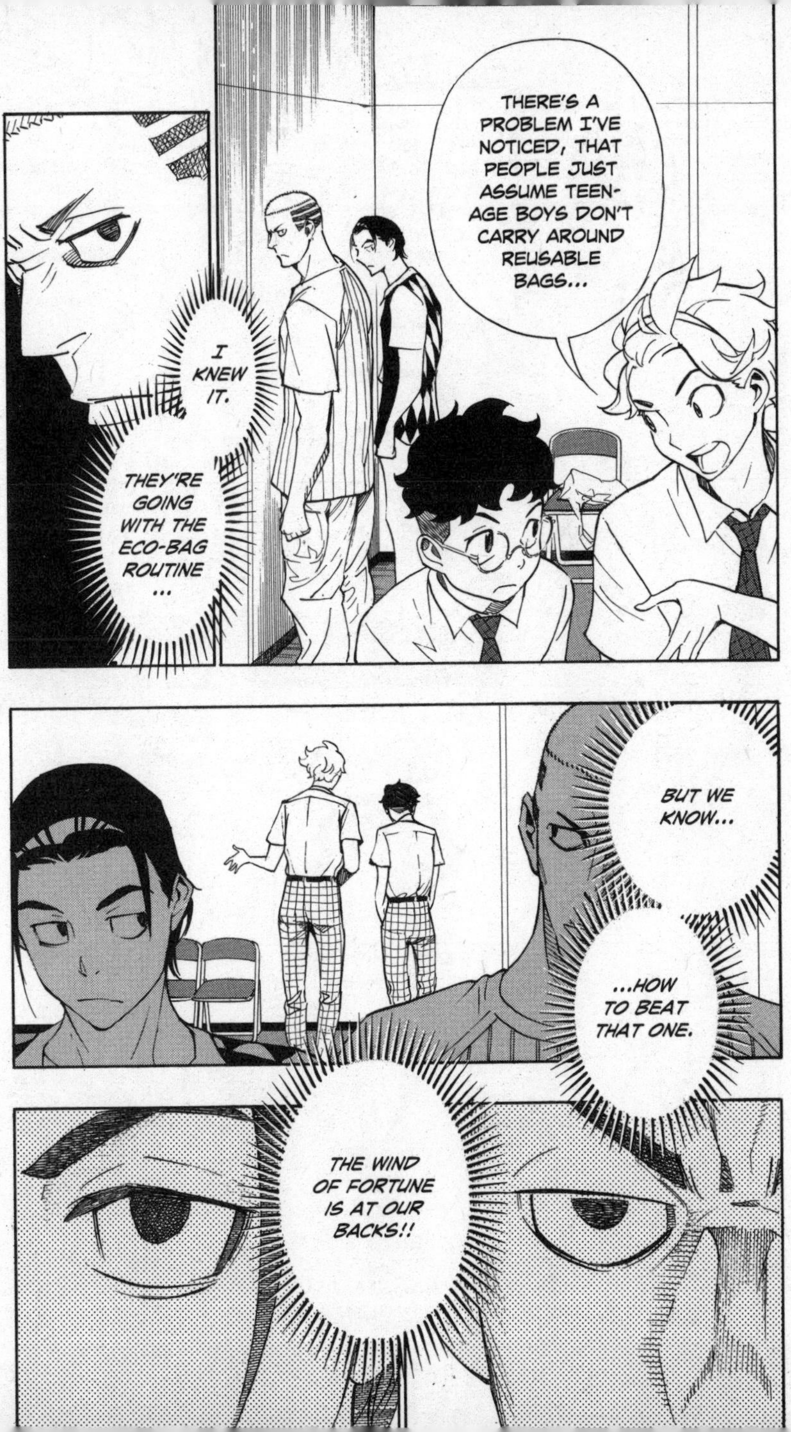
THERE'S A PROBLEM I'VE NOTICED, THAT PEOPLE JUST ASSUME TEEN-AGE BOYS DON'T CARRY AROUND REUSABLE BAGS...
I KNEW IT.
THEY'RE GOING WITH THE ECO-BAG ROUTINE...
BUT WE KNOW...
...HOW TO BEAT THAT ONE.
THE WIND OF FORTUNE IS AT OUR BACKS!!

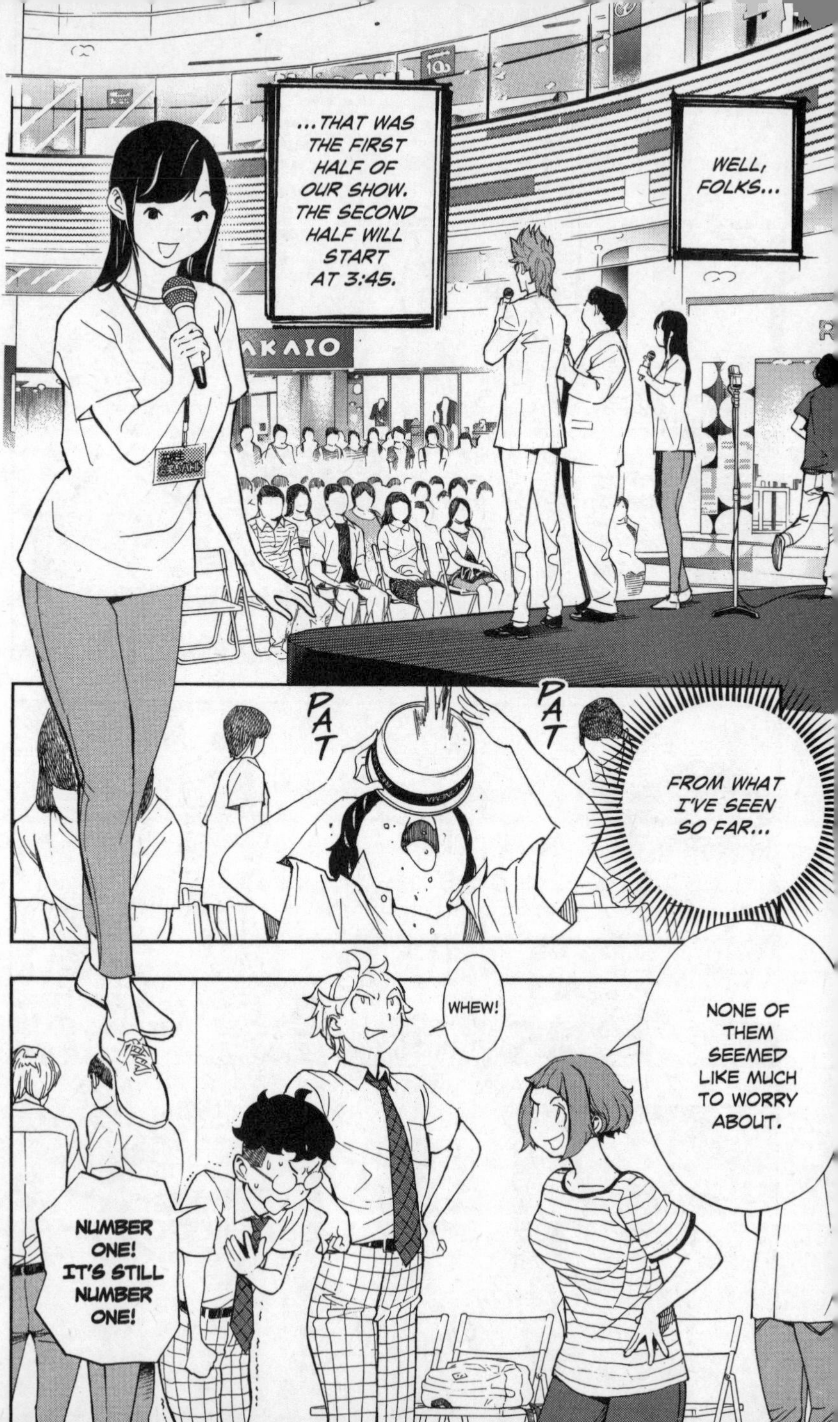
WELL, FOLKS...
...THAT WAS THE FIRST HALF OF OUR SHOW. THE SECOND HALF WILL START AT 3:45.
PAT
PAT
FROM WHAT I'VE SEEN SO FAR...
NONE OF THEM SEEMED LIKE MUCH TO WORRY ABOUT.
WHEW!
NUMBER ONE! IT'S STILL NUMBER ONE!

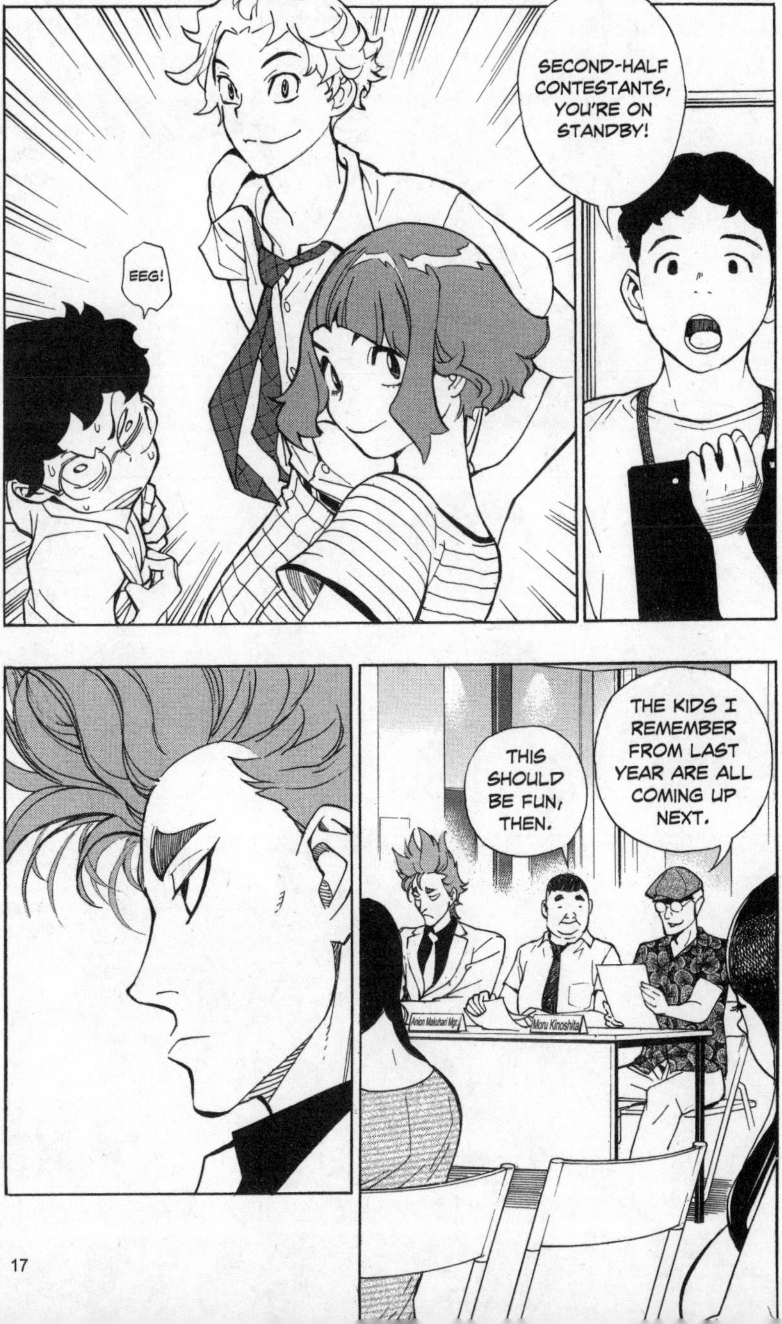
SECOND-HALF CONTESTANTS, YOU'RE ON STANDBY!
EEG!
THE KIDS I REMEMBER FROM LAST YEAR ARE ALL COMING UP NEXT.
THIS SHOULD BE FUN, THEN.
Moru Kinoshita
Anion Makuhari Mgr.

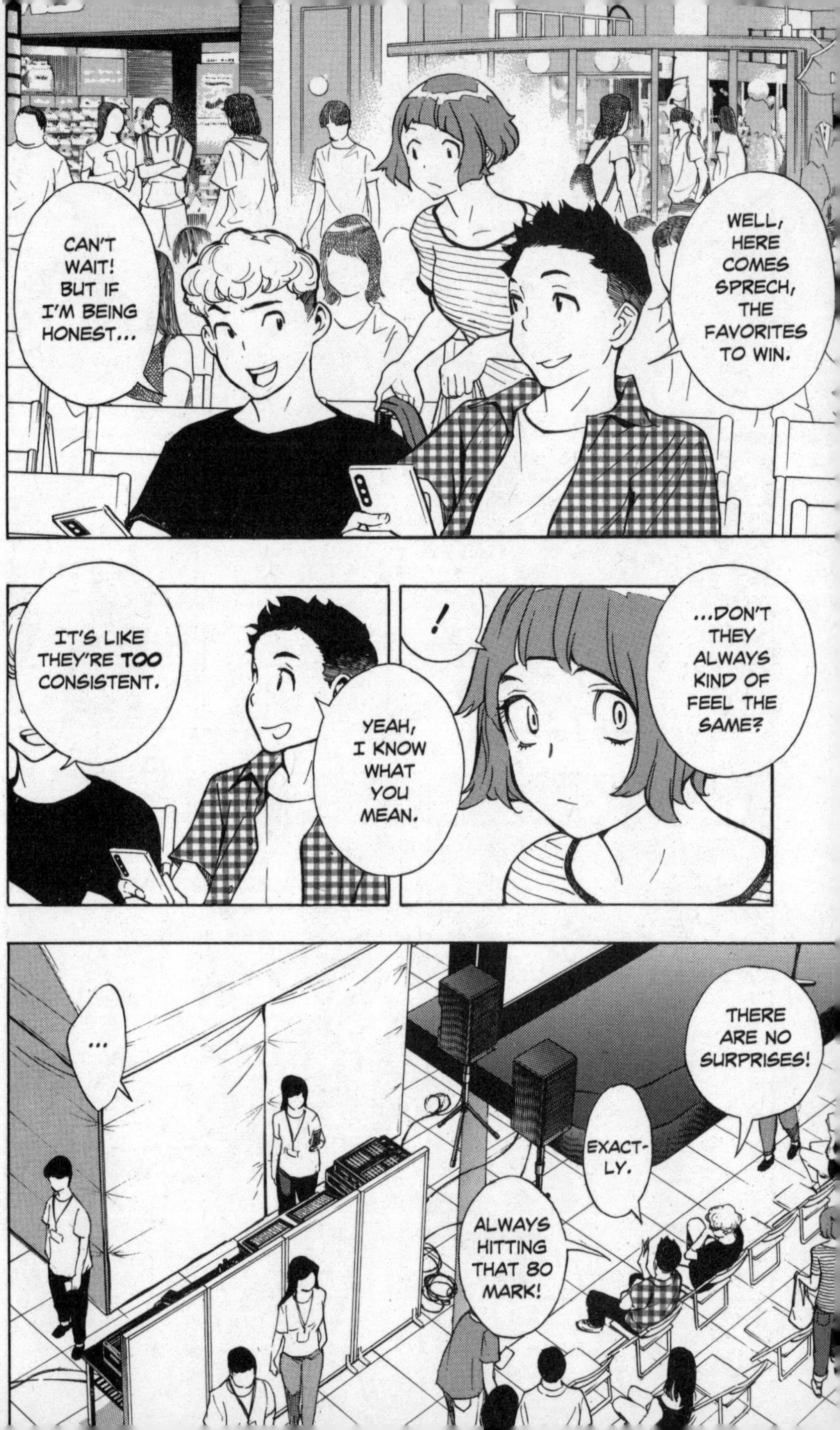
WELL, HERE COMES SPRECH, THE FAVORITES TO WIN.
CAN'T WAIT! BUT IF I'M BEING HONEST...
...DON'T THEY ALWAYS KIND OF FEEL THE SAME?
!
IT'S LIKE THEY'RE **TOO** CONSISTENT.
YEAH, I KNOW WHAT YOU MEAN.
THERE ARE NO SURPRISES!
EXACT-LY.
ALWAYS HITTING THAT 80 MARK!
...

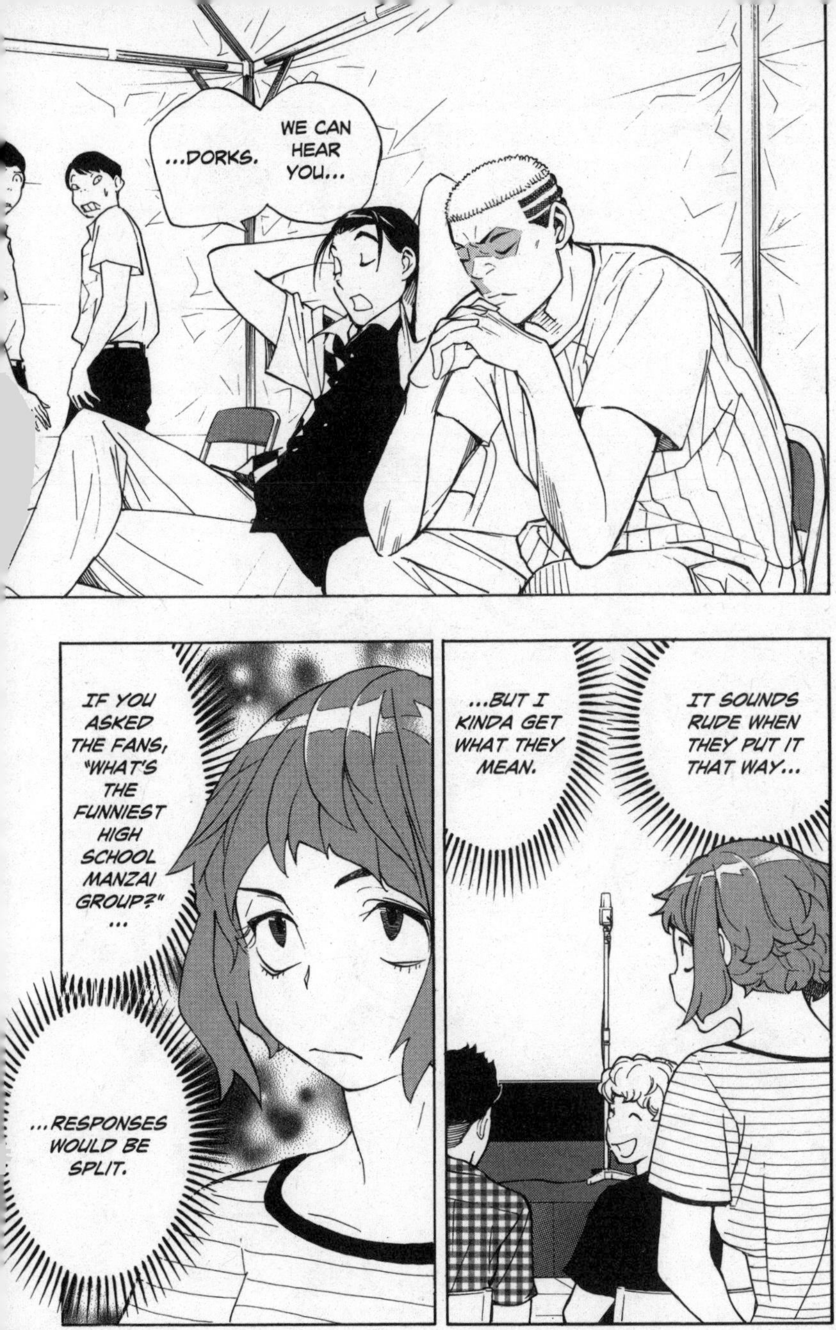
WE CAN HEAR YOU...
...DORKS.
IT SOUNDS RUDE WHEN THEY PUT IT THAT WAY...
...BUT I KINDA GET WHAT THEY MEAN.
IF YOU ASKED THE FANS, "WHAT'S THE FUNNIEST HIGH SCHOOL MANZAI GROUP?" ...
...RESPONSES WOULD BE SPLIT.

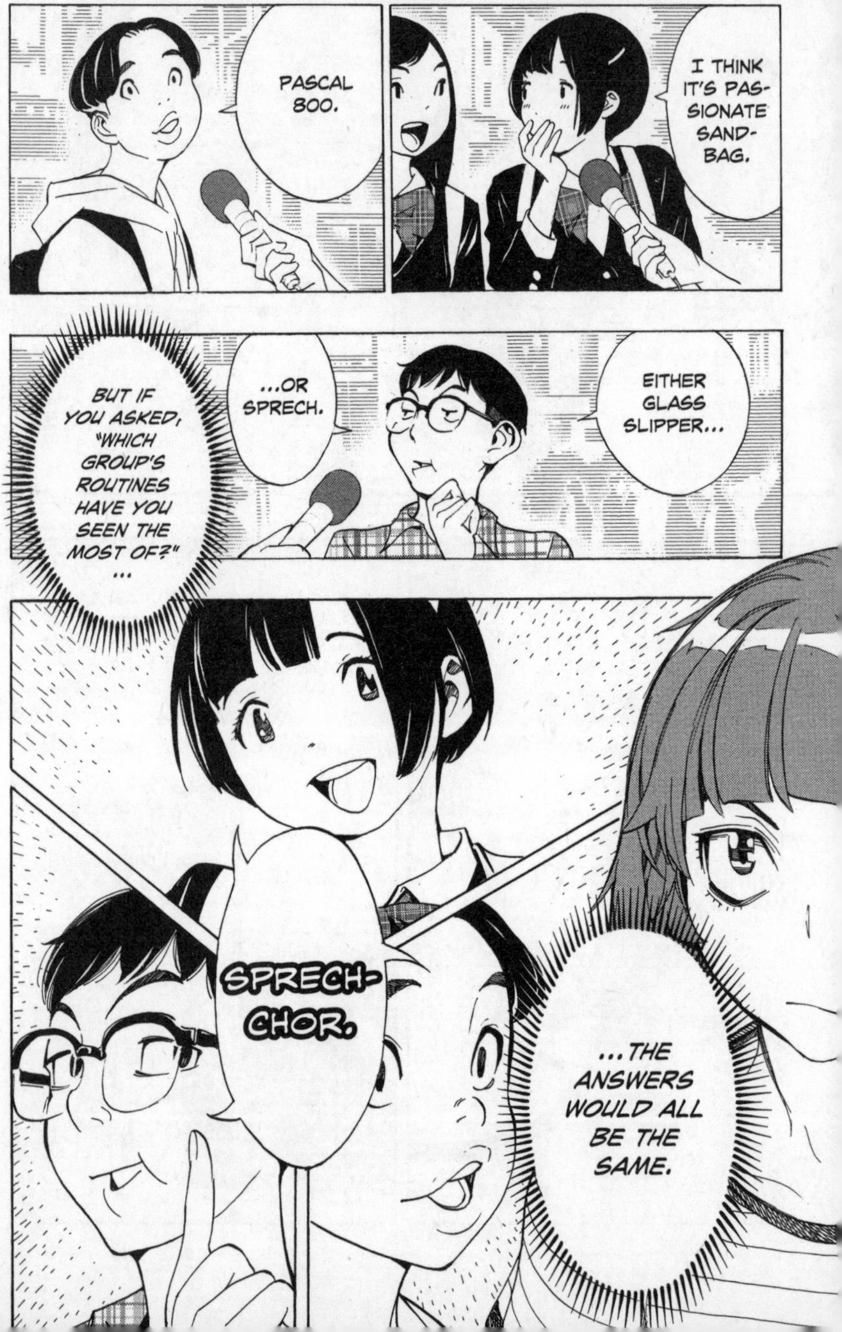
I THINK IT'S PAS-SIONATE SAND-BAG.
PASCAL 800.
EITHER GLASS SLIPPER...
...OR SPRECH.
BUT IF YOU ASKED, "WHICH GROUP'S ROUTINES HAVE YOU SEEN THE MOST OF?" ...
...THE ANSWERS WOULD ALL BE THE SAME.
SPRECH-CHOR.

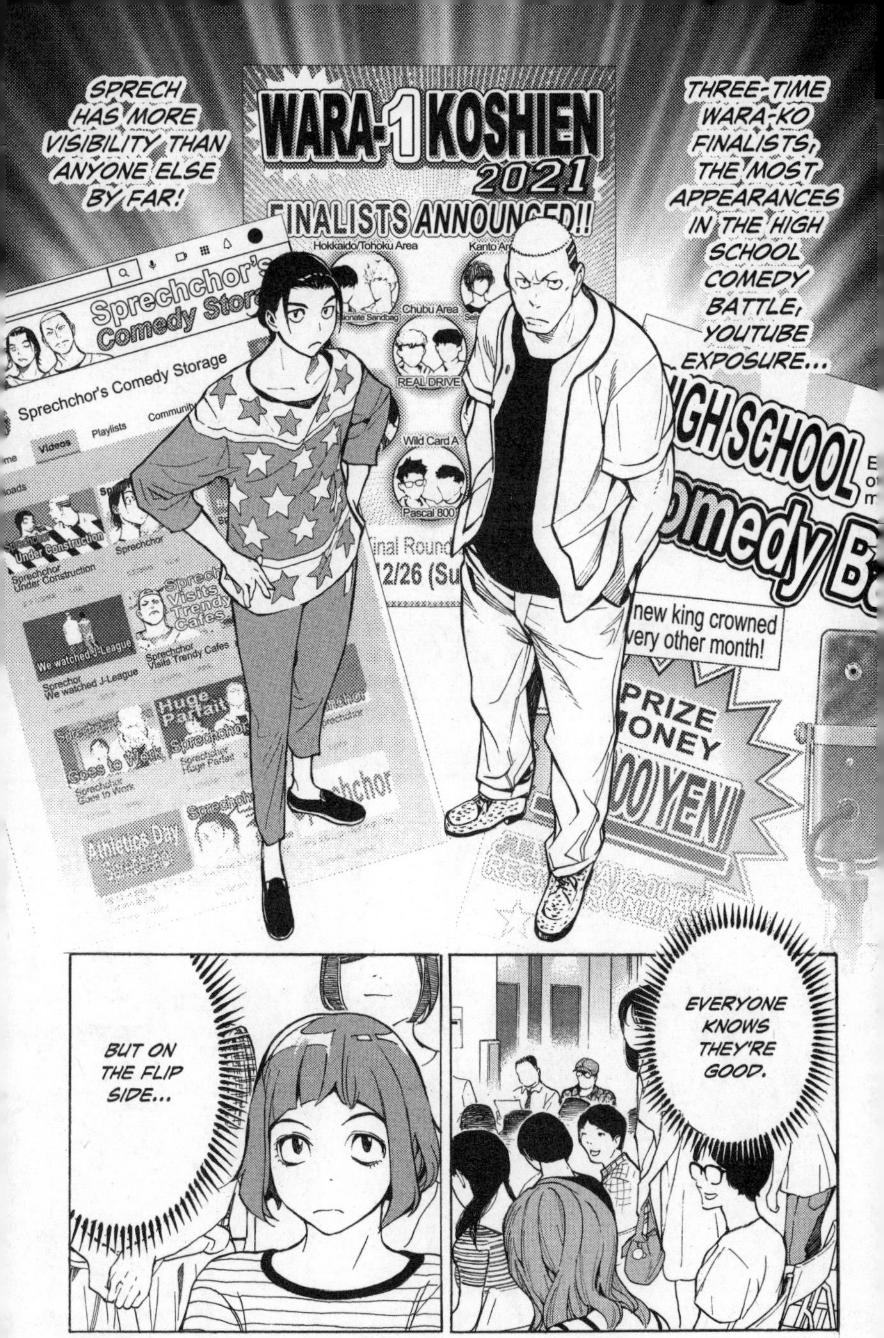
THREE-TIME WARA-KO FINALISTS, THE MOST APPEARANCES IN THE HIGH SCHOOL COMEDY BATTLE, YOUTUBE EXPOSURE...
WARA-1 KOSHIEN
2021
FINALISTS ANNOUNCED!!
Hokkaido/Tohoku Area
Chubu Area
REAL DRIVE
Wild Card A
Pascal 800
SPRECH HAS MORE VISIBILITY THAN ANYONE ELSE BY FAR!
Sprechchor's Comedy Storage
Playlists
Videos
Sprechchor Under Construction
We watched J-League
Sprechchor Visits Trendy Cafes
Huge Parfait
PRIZE
EVERYONE KNOWS THEY'RE GOOD.
BUT ON THE FLIP SIDE...

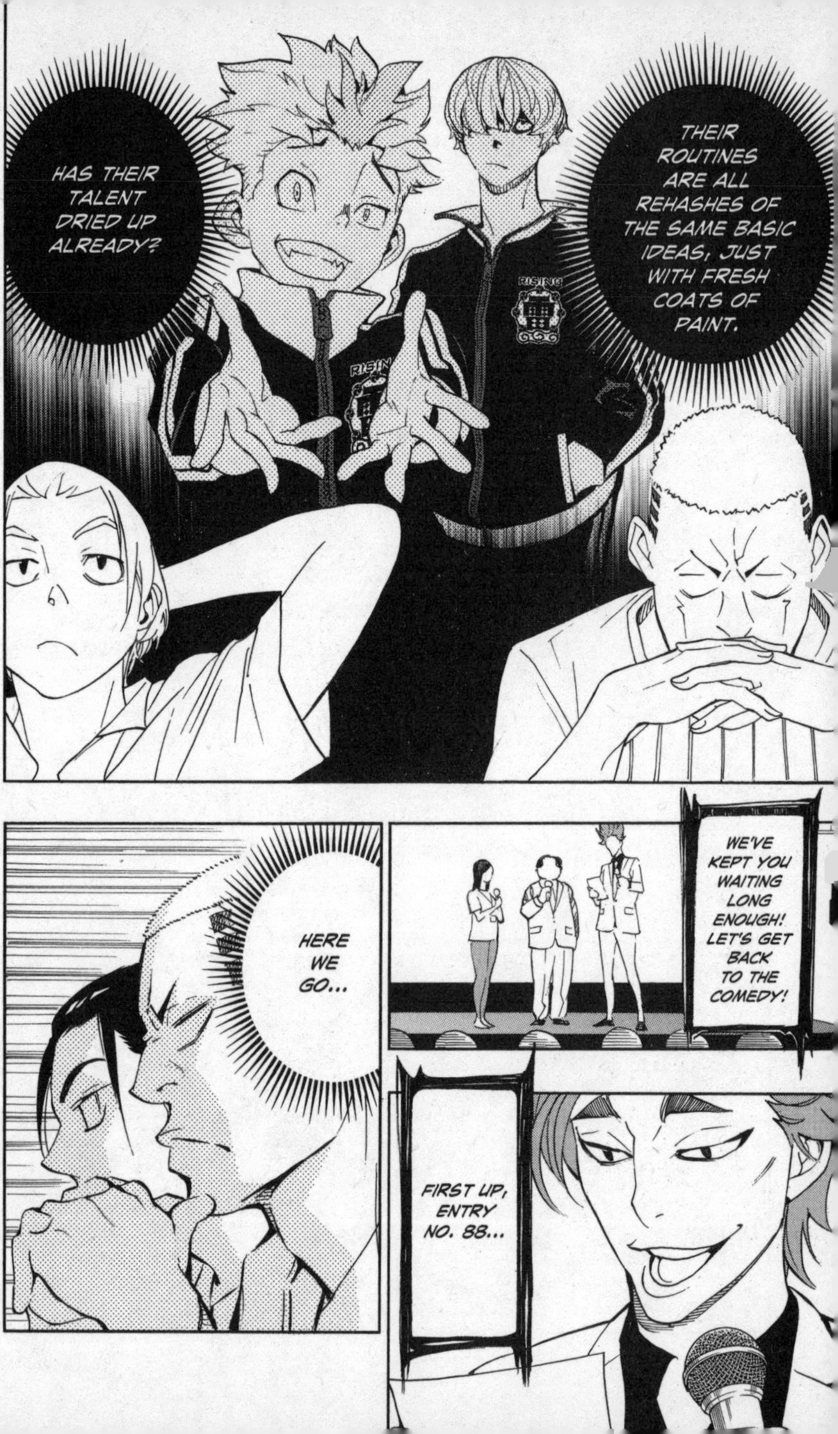
THEIR ROUTINES ARE ALL REHASHES OF THE SAME BASIC IDEAS, JUST WITH FRESH COATS OF PAINT.
HAS THEIR TALENT DRIED UP ALREADY?
RISING
WE'VE KEPT YOU WAITING LONG ENOUGH! LET'S GET BACK TO THE COMEDY!
FIRST UP, ENTRY NO. 88...
HERE WE GO...

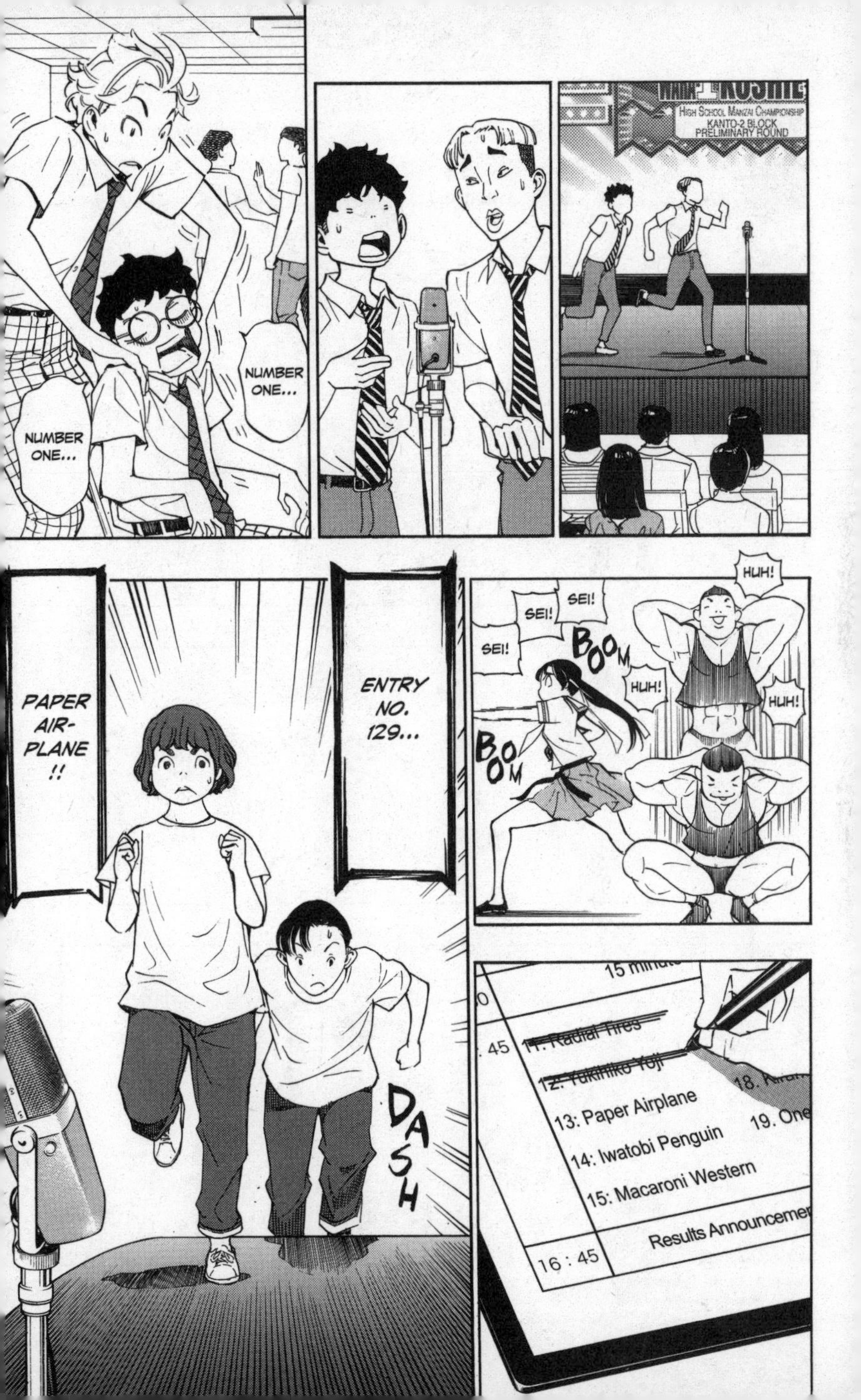
HIGH SCHOOL MANZAI CHAMPIONSHIP
KANTO-2 BLOCK
PRELIMINARY ROUND
NUMBER ONE...
NUMBER ONE...
HUH!
SEI!
SEI!
BOOM
HUH!
HUH!
SEI!
BOOM
11. Radial Tires
12. Yukihiko Yoji
13: Paper Airplane
14: Iwatobi Penguin
15: Macaroni Western
16 : 45
ENTRY NO. 129...
PAPER AIR-PLANE !!
DASH

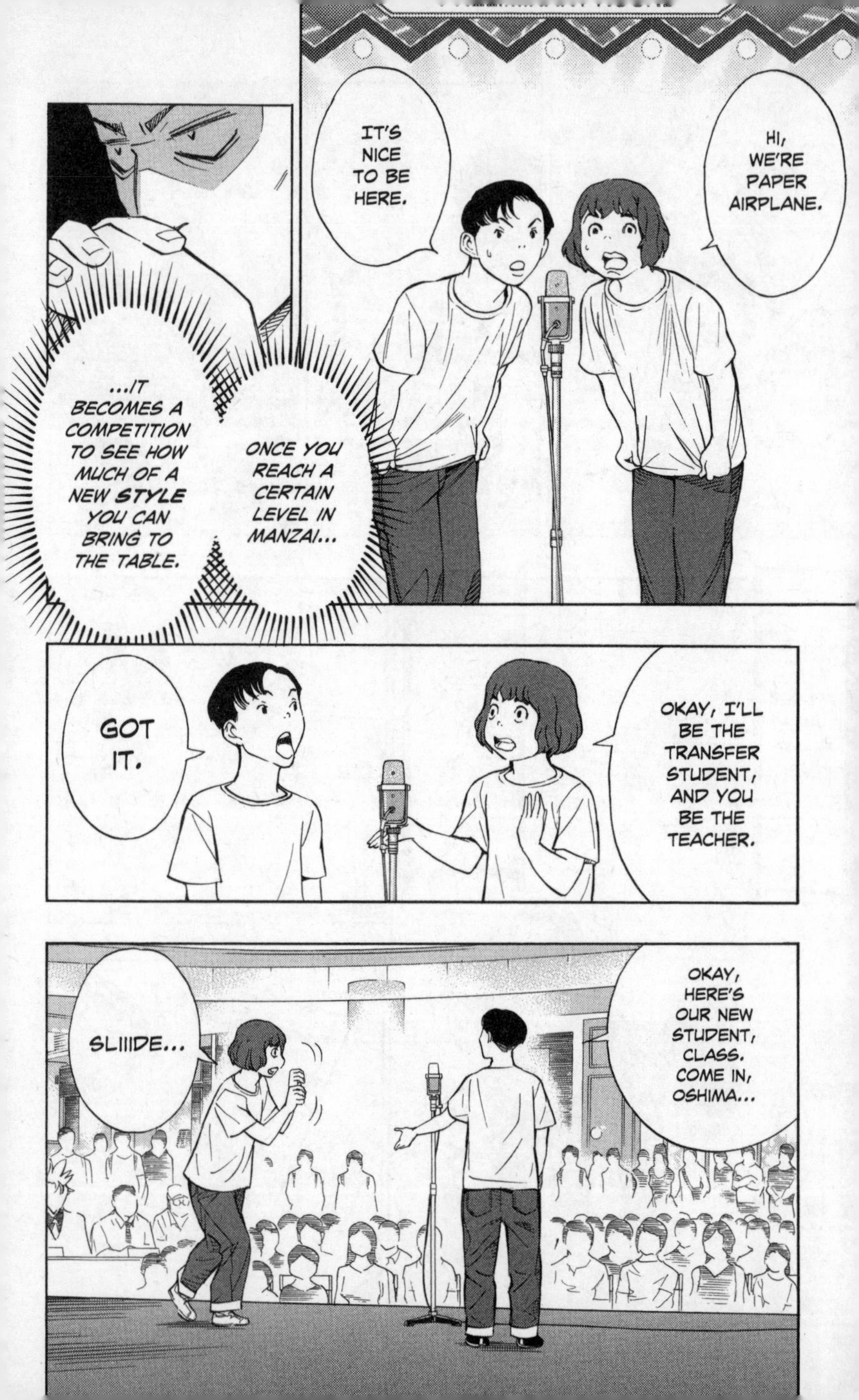
HI, WE'RE PAPER AIRPLANE.
IT'S NICE TO BE HERE.
ONCE YOU REACH A CERTAIN LEVEL IN MANZAI...
...IT BECOMES A COMPETITION TO SEE HOW MUCH OF A NEW STYLE YOU CAN BRING TO THE TABLE.
OKAY, I'LL BE THE TRANSFER STUDENT, AND YOU BE THE TEACHER.
GOT IT.
OKAY, HERE'S OUR NEW STUDENT, CLASS. COME IN, OSHIMA...
SLIIIDE...

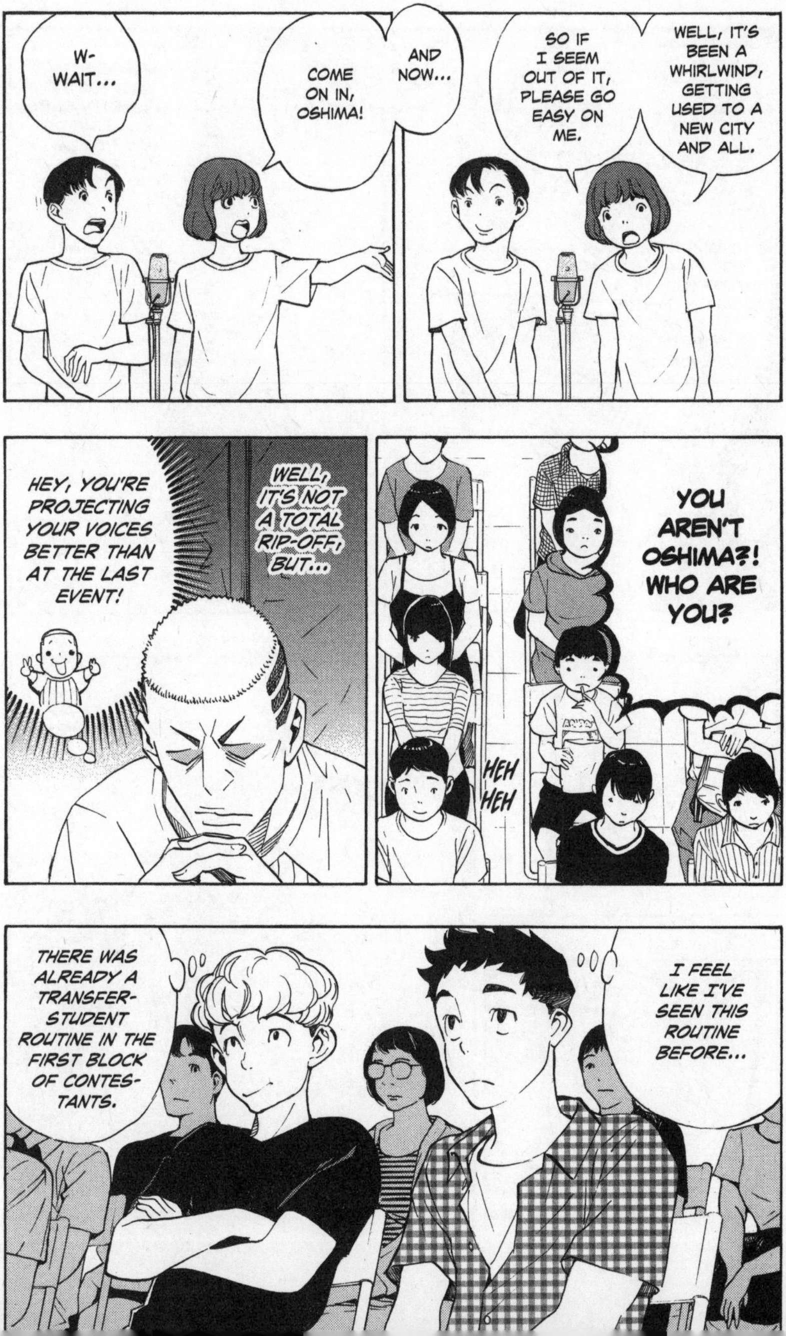
WELL, IT'S BEEN A WHIRLWIND, GETTING USED TO A NEW CITY AND ALL.
SO IF I SEEM OUT OF IT, PLEASE GO EASY ON ME.
AND NOW...
COME ON IN, OSHIMA!
W-WAIT...
YOU AREN'T OSHIMA?! WHO ARE YOU?
HEH HEH
WELL, IT'S NOT A TOTAL RIP-OFF, BUT...
HEY, YOU'RE PROJECTING YOUR VOICES BETTER THAN AT THE LAST EVENT!
I FEEL LIKE I'VE SEEN THIS ROUTINE BEFORE...
THERE WAS ALREADY A TRANSFER-STUDENT ROUTINE IN THE FIRST BLOCK OF CONTES-TANTS.

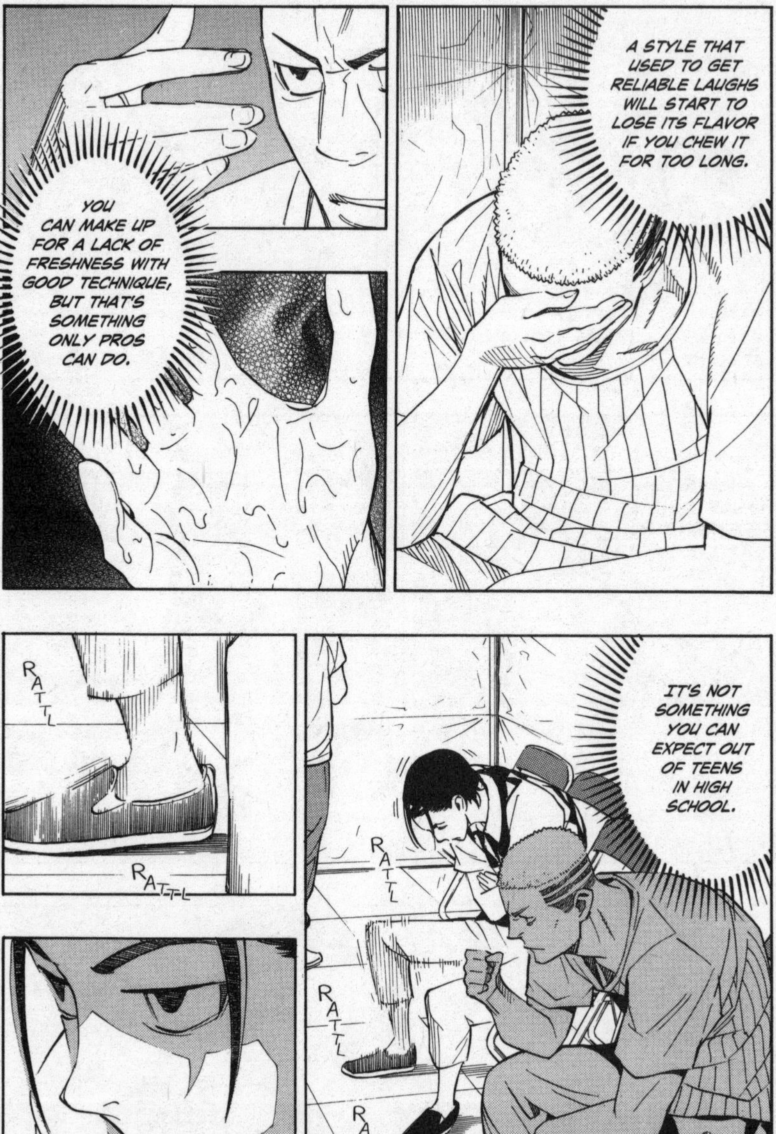
A STYLE THAT USED TO GET RELIABLE LAUGHS WILL START TO LOSE ITS FLAVOR IF YOU CHEW IT FOR TOO LONG.
YOU CAN MAKE UP FOR A LACK OF FRESHNESS WITH GOOD TECHNIQUE, BUT THAT'S SOMETHING ONLY PROS CAN DO.
IT'S NOT SOMETHING YOU CAN EXPECT OUT OF TEENS IN HIGH SCHOOL.
RATTL
RATTL
RATTL
RATTL
RATTL
RATTL

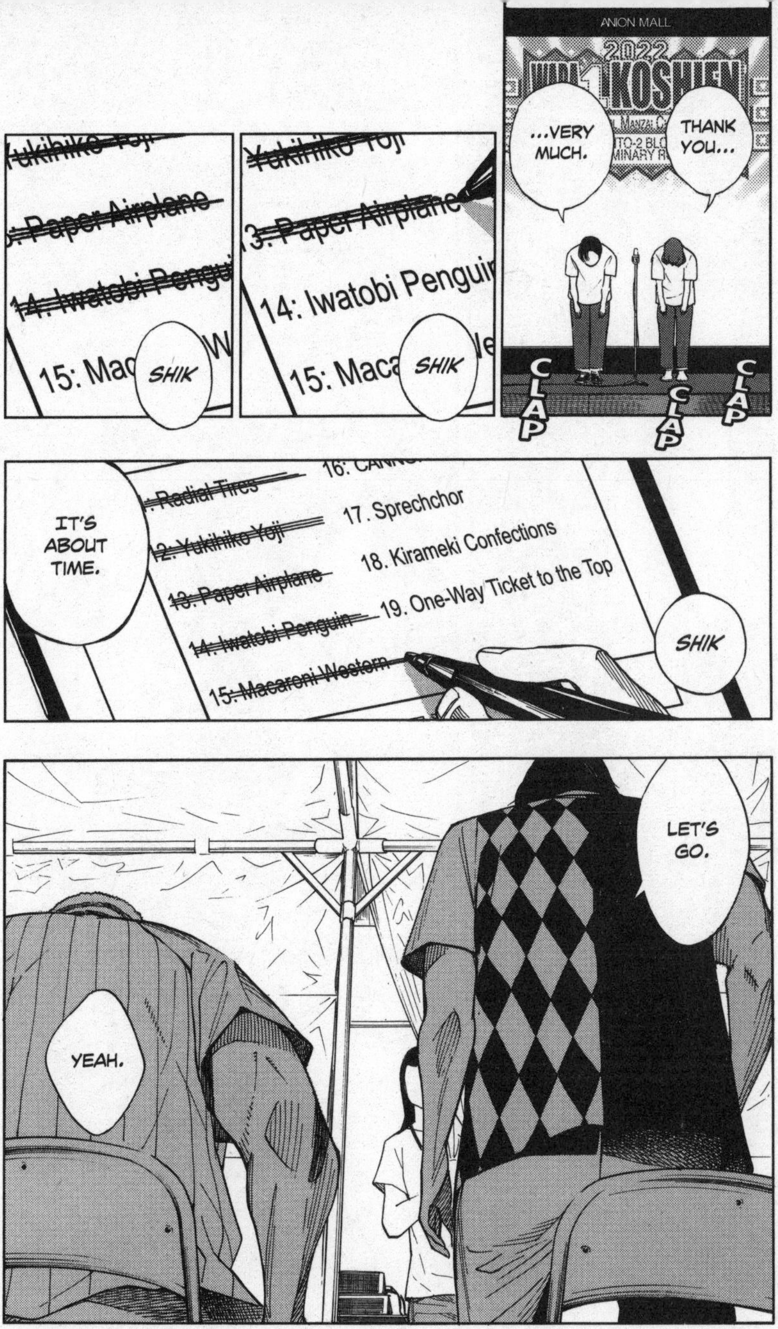
ANION MALL
2022
KOSHIEN
THANK YOU...
...VERY MUCH.
CLAP
CLAP
CLAP
Yukihiko Yoji
13: Paper Airplane
14: Iwatobi Penguin
15: Maca
SHIK
SHIK
Radial Tires
12. Yukihiko Yoji
13. Paper Airplane
14. Iwatobi Penguin
15: Macaroni Western
17. Sprechchor
18. Kirameki Confections
19. One-Way Ticket to the Top
SHIK
IT'S ABOUT TIME.
LET'S GO.
YEAH.

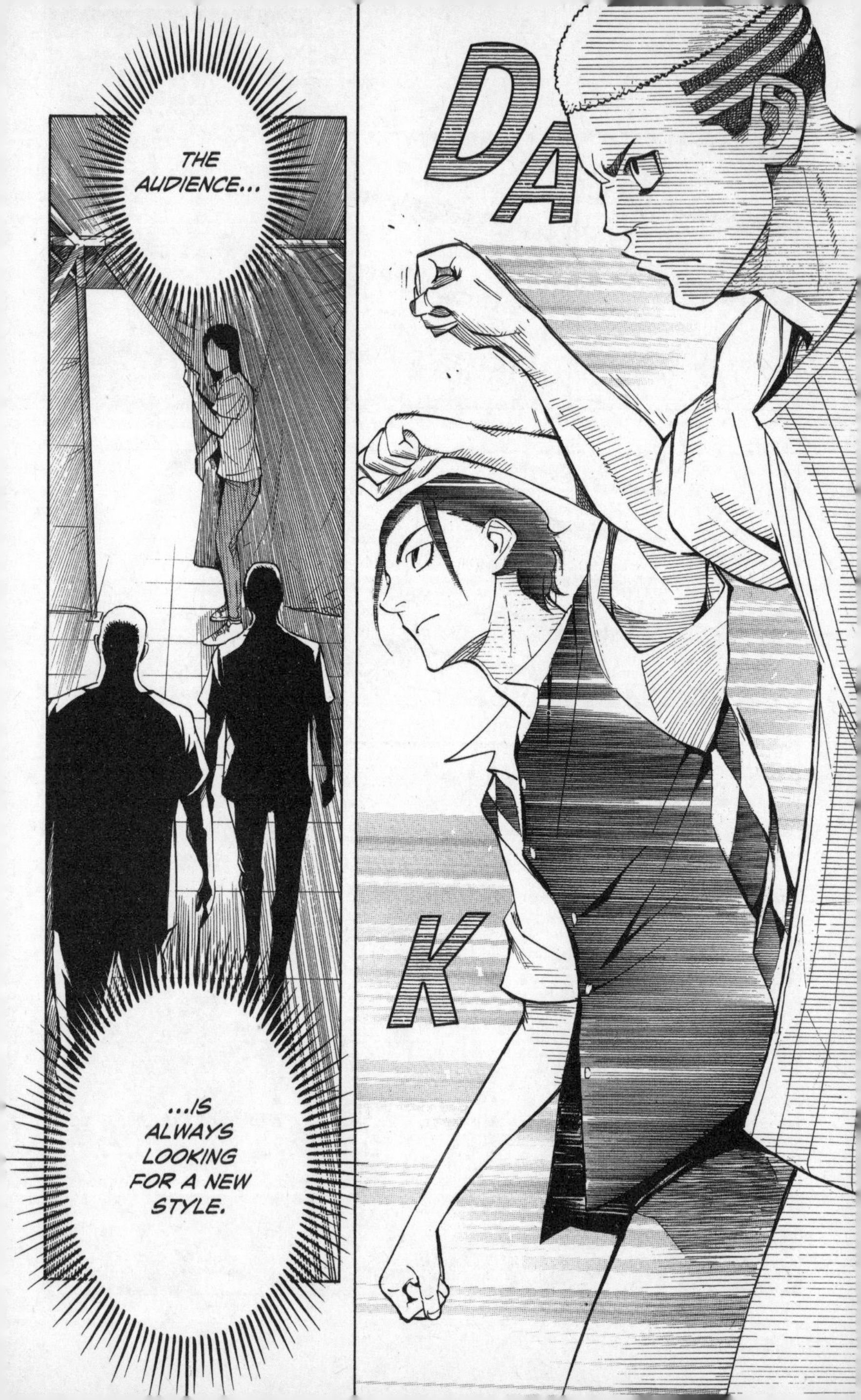
DAK
THE AUDIENCE...
...IS ALWAYS LOOKING FOR A NEW STYLE.

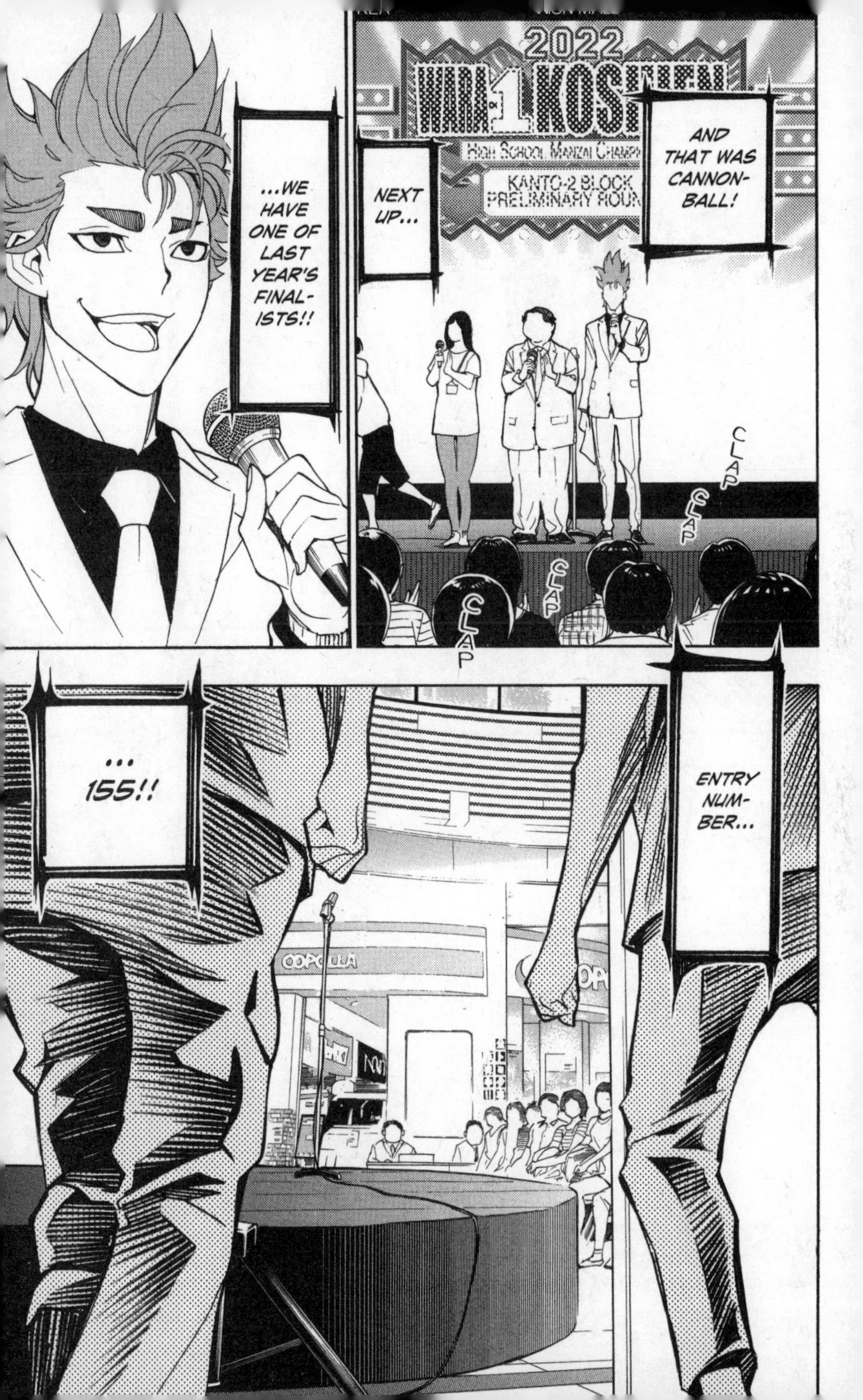
2022
KANTO-2 BLOCK
AND THAT WAS CANNON-BALL!
NEXT UP...
CLAP
CLAP
CLAP
CLAP
...WE HAVE ONE OF LAST YEAR'S FINALISTS!!
ENTRY NUMBER...
...155!!

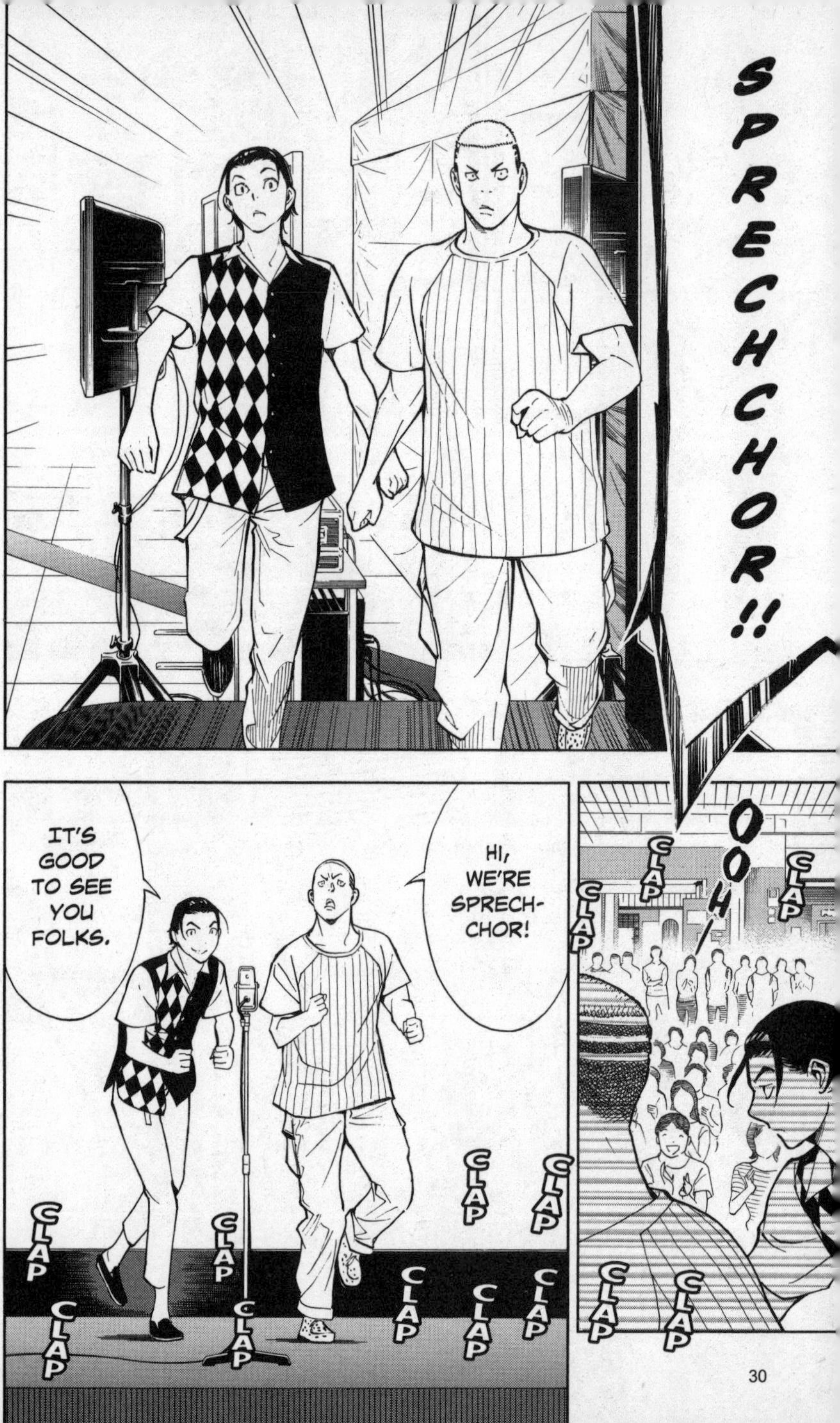
SPRECHCHOR!!
OOH!
CLAP CLAP CLAP CLAP CLAP
HI, WE'RE SPRECH-CHOR!
IT'S GOOD TO SEE YOU FOLKS.
CLAP CLAP CLAP CLAP CLAP CLAP CLAP CLAP CLAP

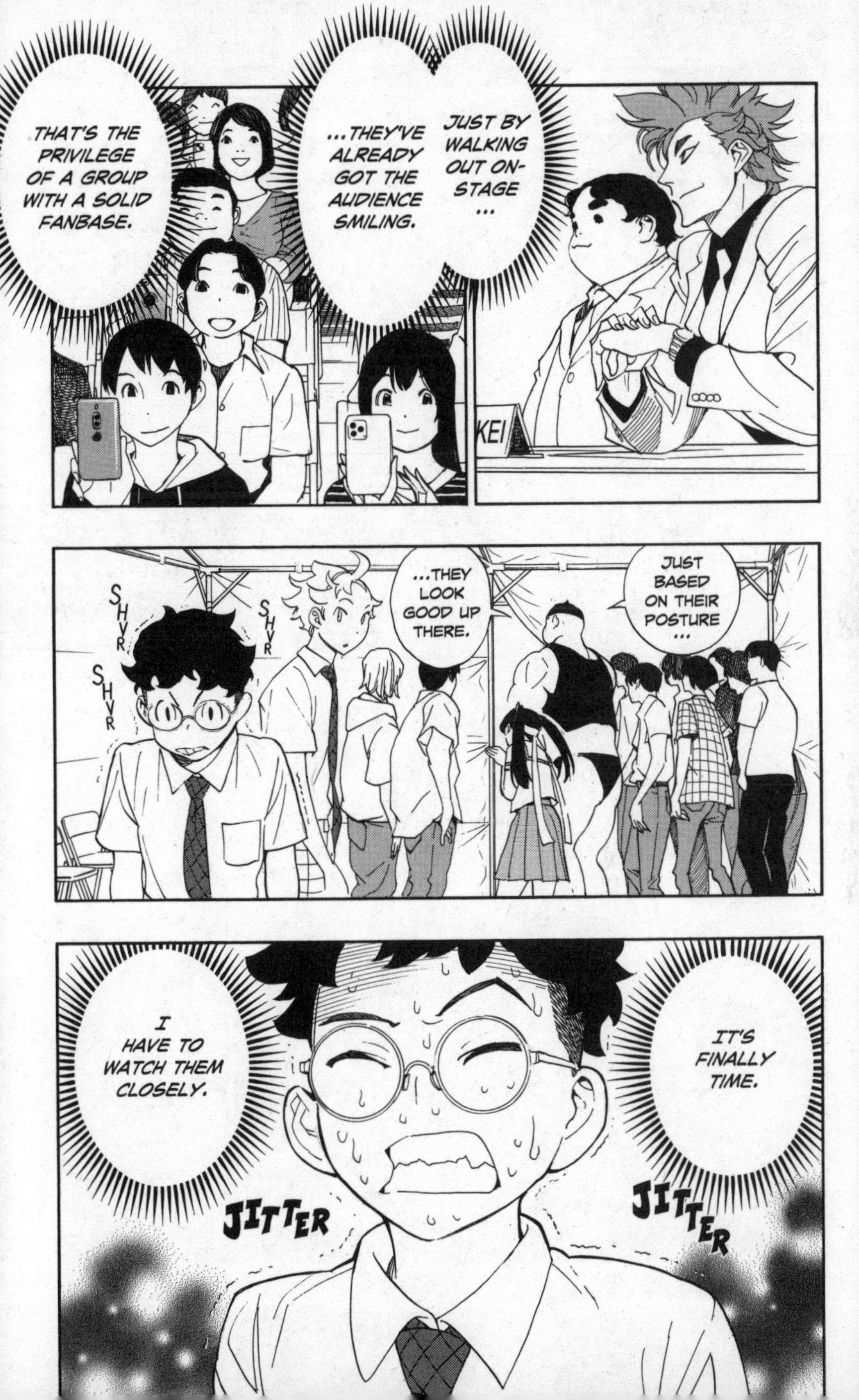
JUST BY WALKING OUT ON-STAGE ...
KEI
...THEY'VE ALREADY GOT THE AUDIENCE SMILING.
THAT'S THE PRIVILEGE OF A GROUP WITH A SOLID FANBASE.
JUST BASED ON THEIR POSTURE ...
...THEY LOOK GOOD UP THERE.
SHVR
SHVR
SHVR
IT'S FINALLY TIME.
I HAVE TO WATCH THEM CLOSELY.
JITTER
JITTER

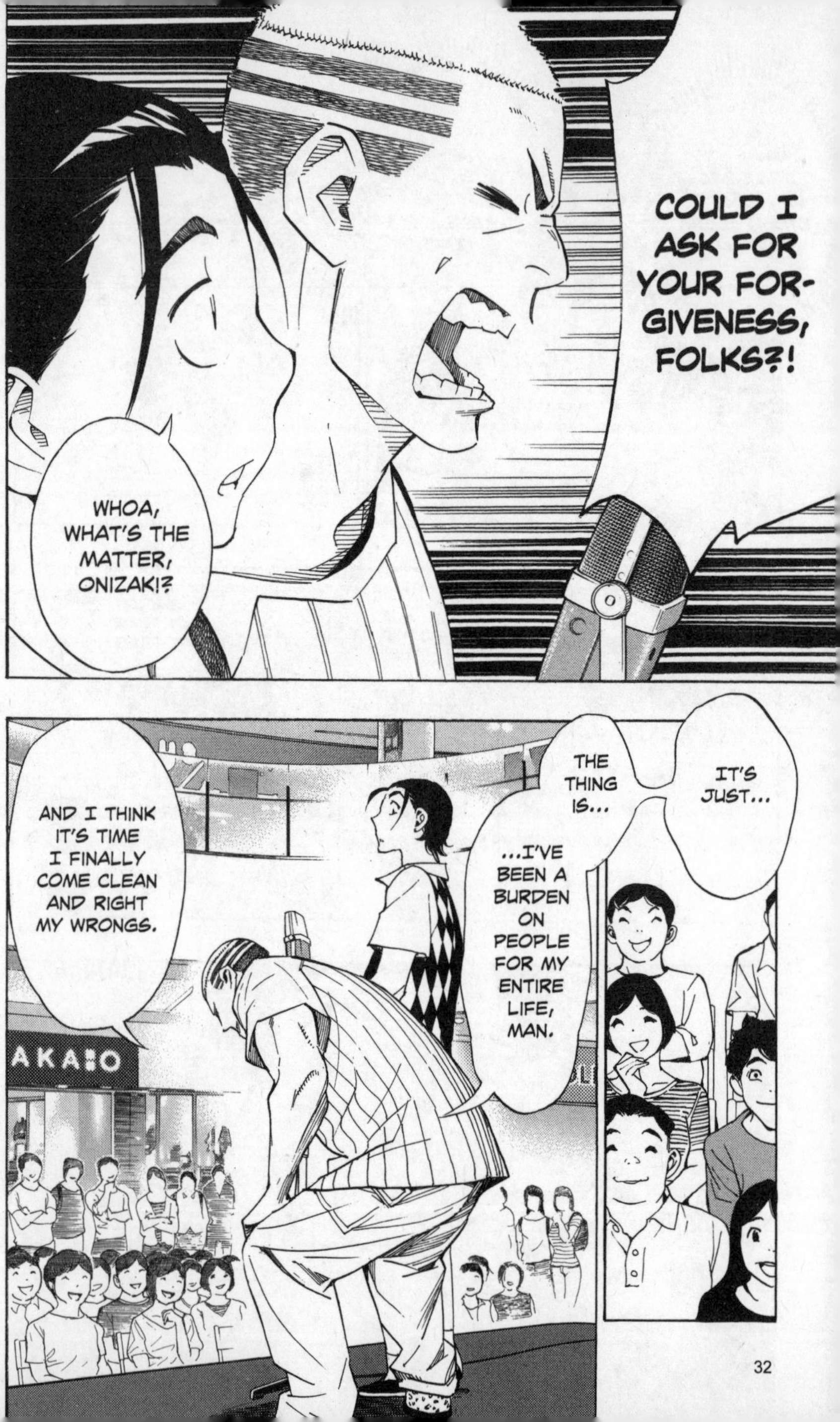
COULD I ASK FOR YOUR FOR-GIVENESS, FOLKS?!
WHOA, WHAT'S THE MATTER, ONIZAKI!?
IT'S JUST...
THE THING IS...
...I'VE BEEN A BURDEN ON PEOPLE FOR MY ENTIRE LIFE, MAN.
AND I THINK IT'S TIME I FINALLY COME CLEAN AND RIGHT MY WRONGS.
AKA O

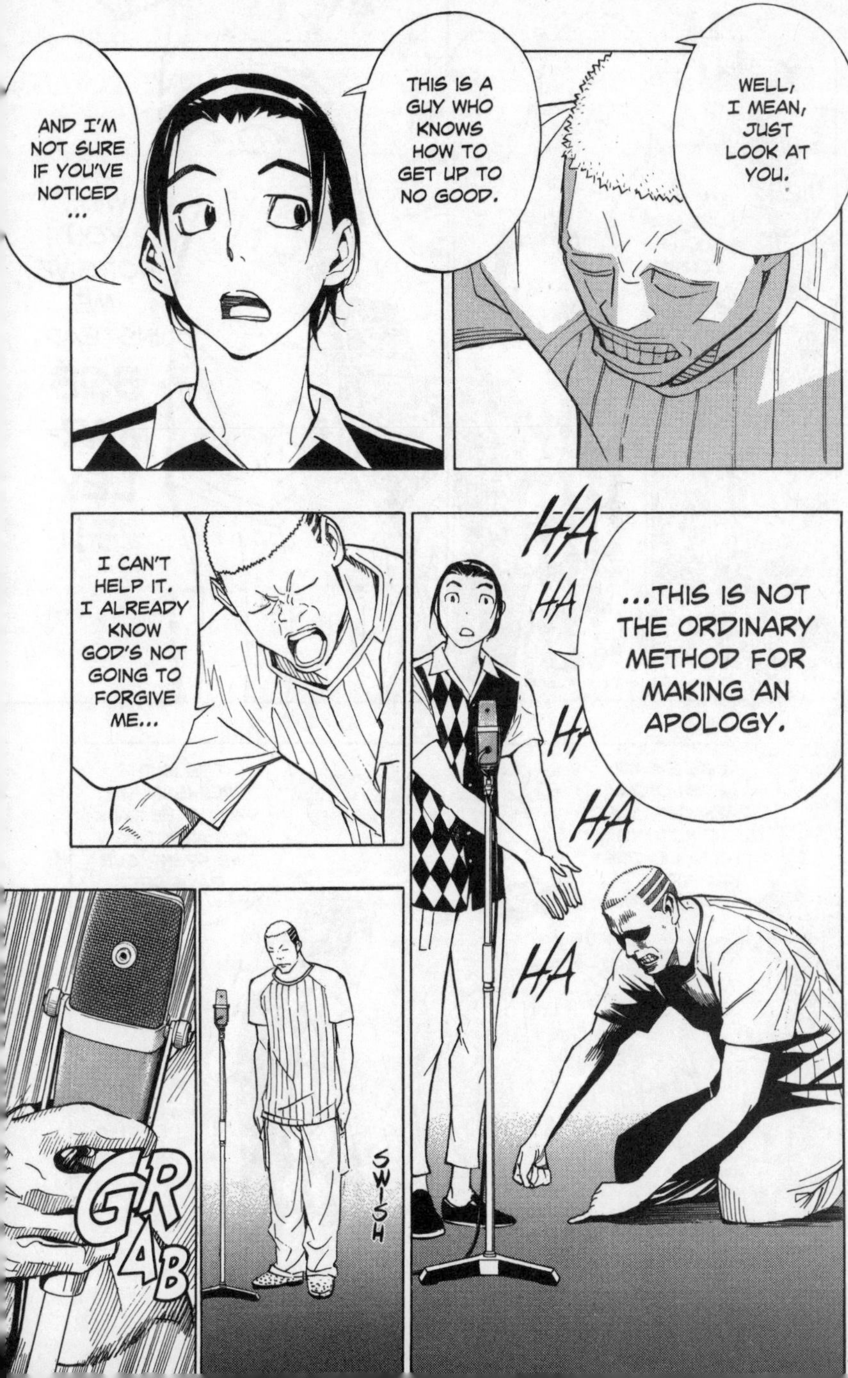
WELL, I MEAN, JUST LOOK AT YOU.
THIS IS A GUY WHO KNOWS HOW TO GET UP TO NO GOOD.
AND I'M NOT SURE IF YOU'VE NOTICED...
...THIS IS NOT THE ORDINARY METHOD FOR MAKING AN APOLOGY.
HA HA HA HA HA
I CAN'T HELP IT. I ALREADY KNOW GOD'S NOT GOING TO FORGIVE ME...
SWISH
GRAB

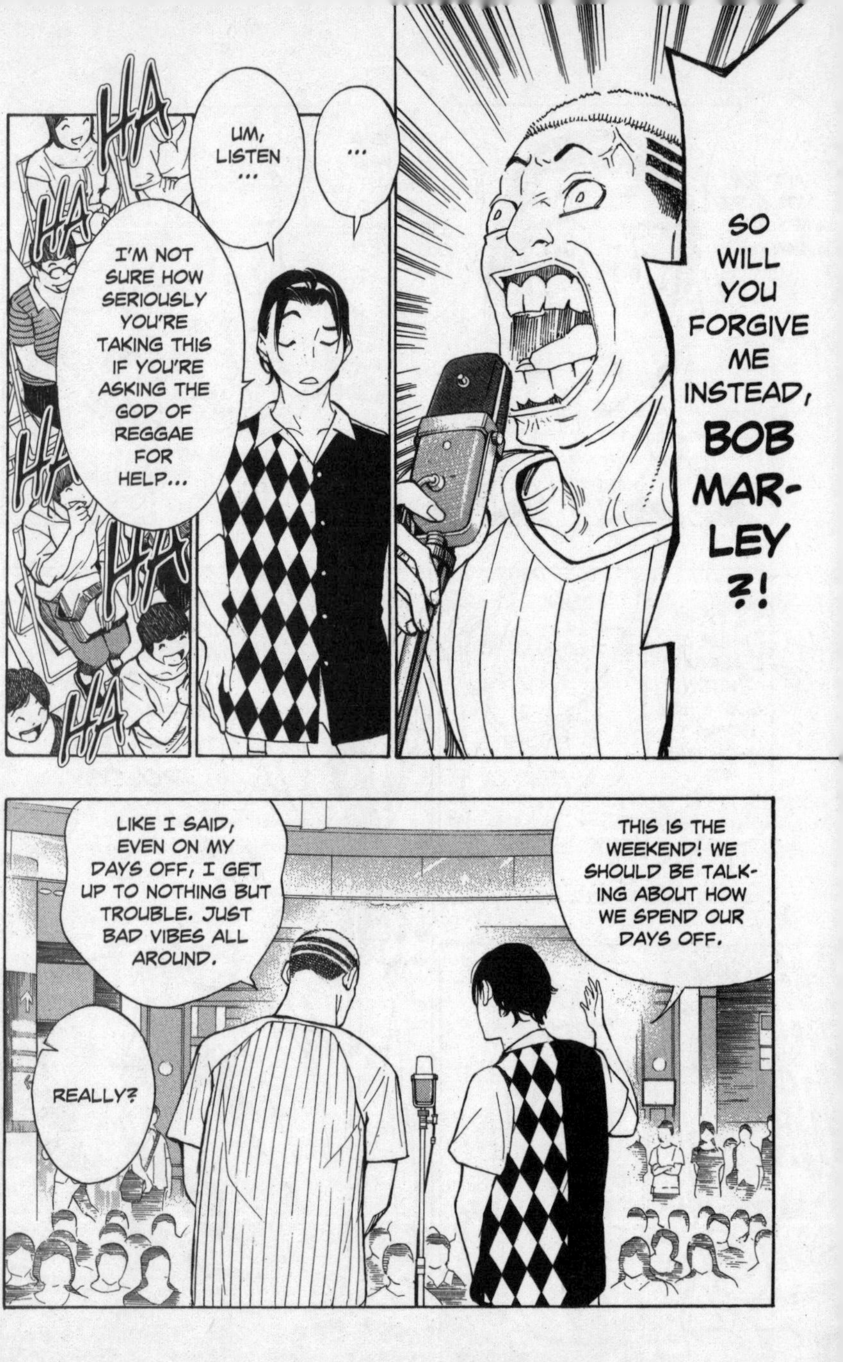
SO WILL YOU FORGIVE ME INSTEAD, BOB MAR-LEY ?!
...
UM, LISTEN ...
I'M NOT SURE HOW SERIOUSLY YOU'RE TAKING THIS IF YOU'RE ASKING THE GOD OF REGGAE FOR HELP...
HA HA HA HA HA HA
THIS IS THE WEEKEND! WE SHOULD BE TALK-ING ABOUT HOW WE SPEND OUR DAYS OFF.
LIKE I SAID, EVEN ON MY DAYS OFF, I GET UP TO NOTHING BUT TROUBLE. JUST BAD VIBES ALL AROUND.
REALLY?

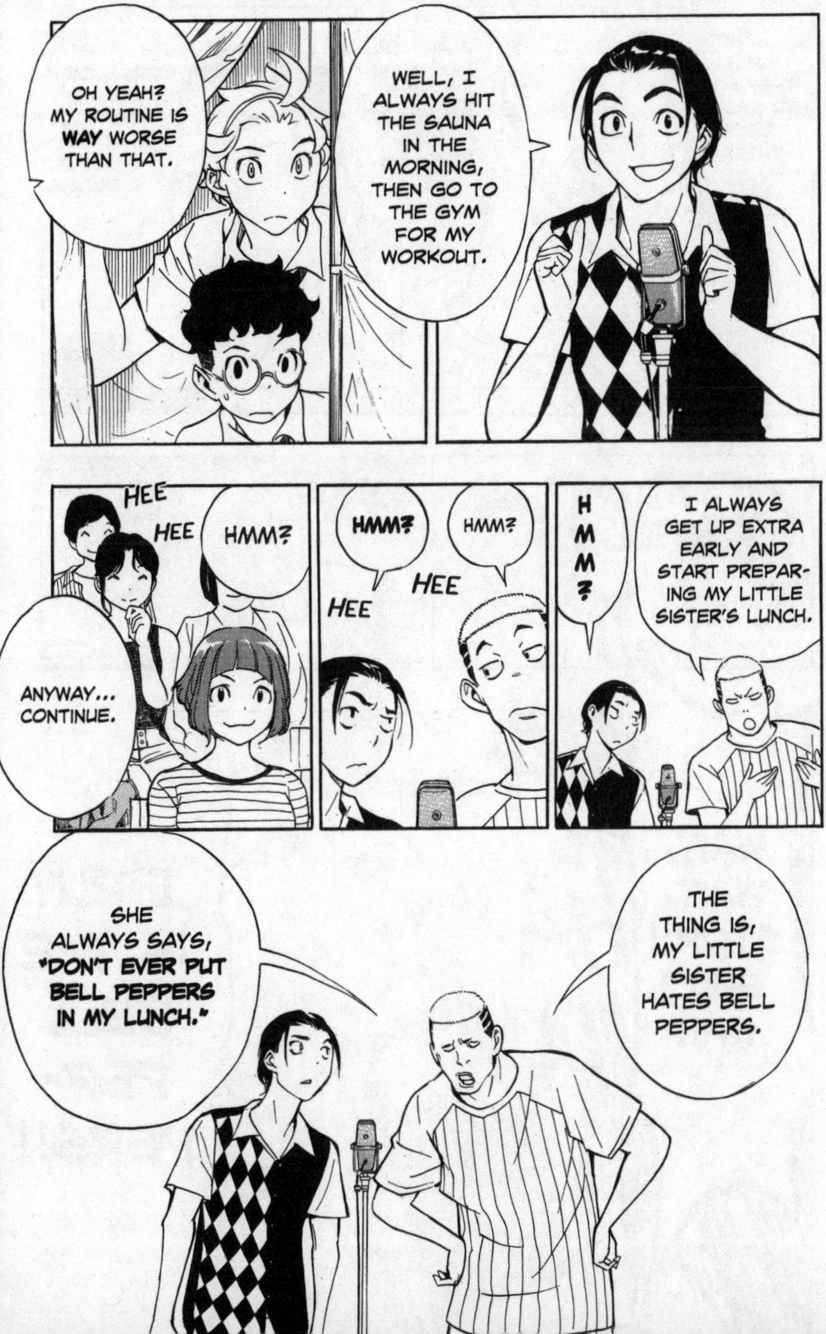
WELL, I ALWAYS HIT THE SAUNA IN THE MORNING, THEN GO TO THE GYM FOR MY WORKOUT.
OH YEAH? MY ROUTINE IS WAY WORSE THAN THAT.
I ALWAYS GET UP EXTRA EARLY AND START PREPARING MY LITTLE SISTER'S LUNCH.
HMM?
HMM?
HEE
HMM?
HEE
HMM?
HEE
HEE
ANYWAY... CONTINUE.
THE THING IS, MY LITTLE SISTER HATES BELL PEPPERS.
SHE ALWAYS SAYS, "DON'T EVER PUT BELL PEPPERS IN MY LUNCH."

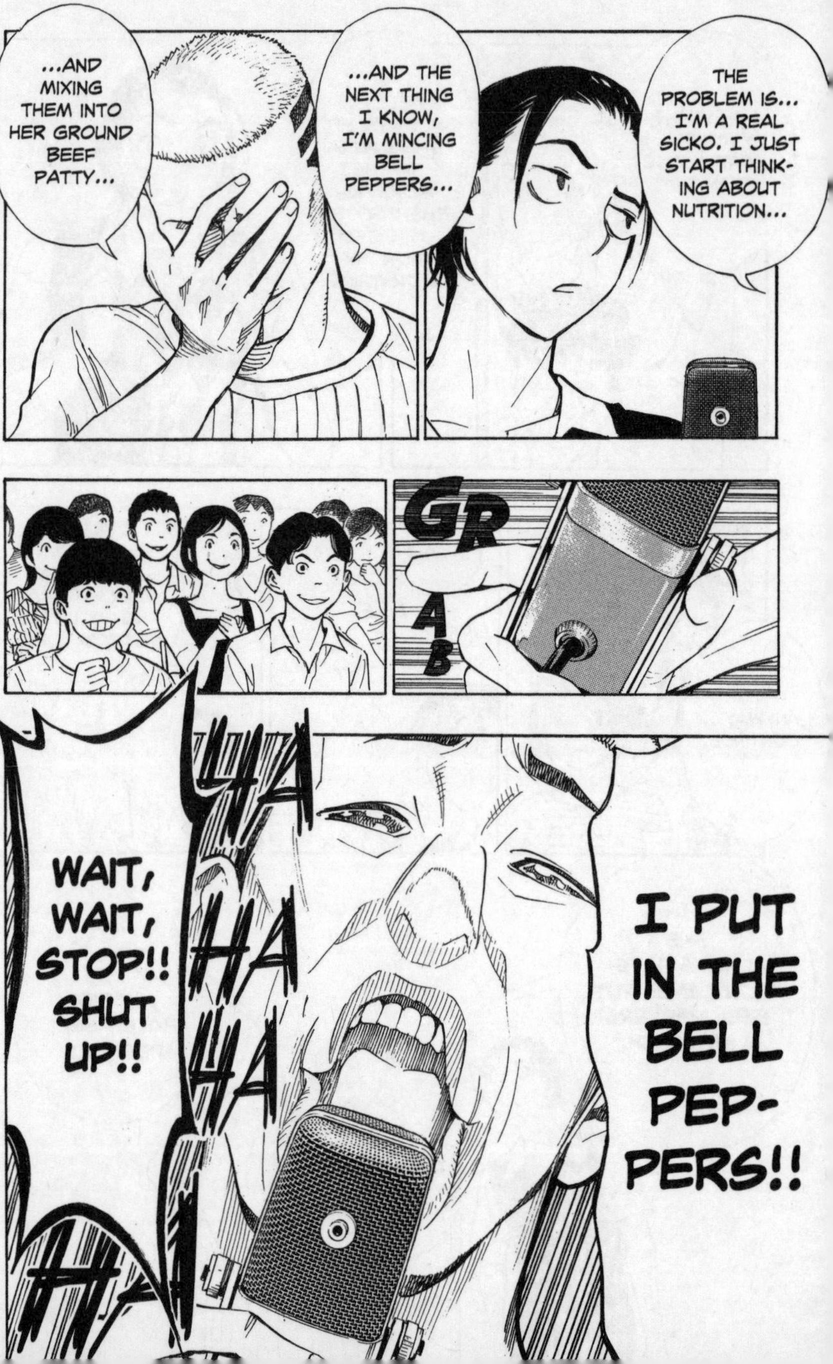
THE PROBLEM IS... I'M A REAL SICKO. I JUST START THINKING ABOUT NUTRITION...
...AND THE NEXT THING I KNOW, I'M MINCING BELL PEPPERS...
...AND MIXING THEM INTO HER GROUND BEEF PATTY...
GRAB
I PUT IN THE BELL PEPPERS!!
HA HA HA HA
WAIT, WAIT, STOP!! SHUT UP!!

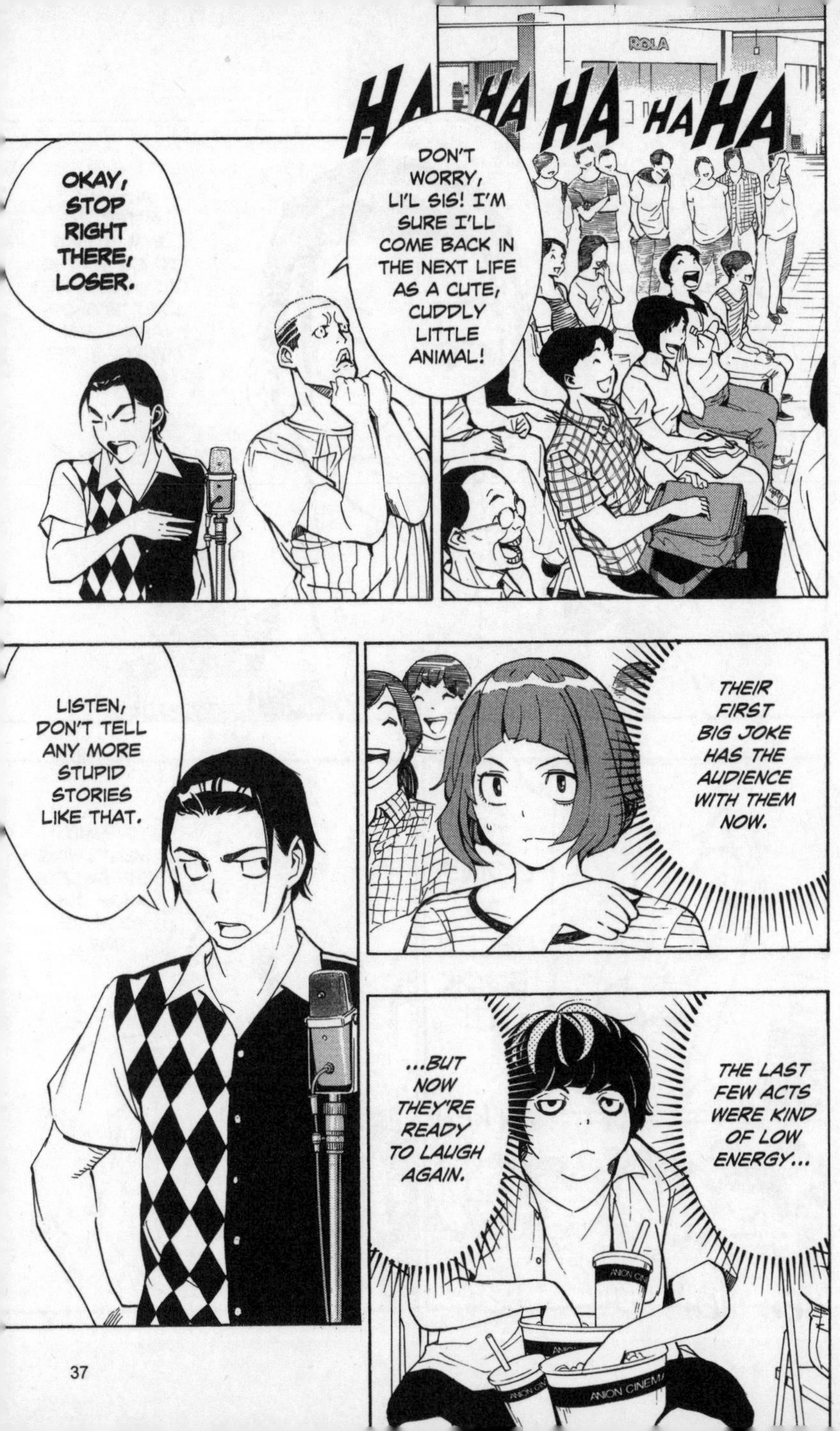
ROLA
HA HA HA HA HA
DON'T WORRY, LI'L SIS! I'M SURE I'LL COME BACK IN THE NEXT LIFE AS A CUTE, CUDDLY LITTLE ANIMAL!
OKAY, STOP RIGHT THERE, LOSER.
THEIR FIRST BIG JOKE HAS THE AUDIENCE WITH THEM NOW.
THE LAST FEW ACTS WERE KIND OF LOW ENERGY...
...BUT NOW THEY'RE READY TO LAUGH AGAIN.
ANION CINEMA
LISTEN, DON'T TELL ANY MORE STUPID STORIES LIKE THAT.

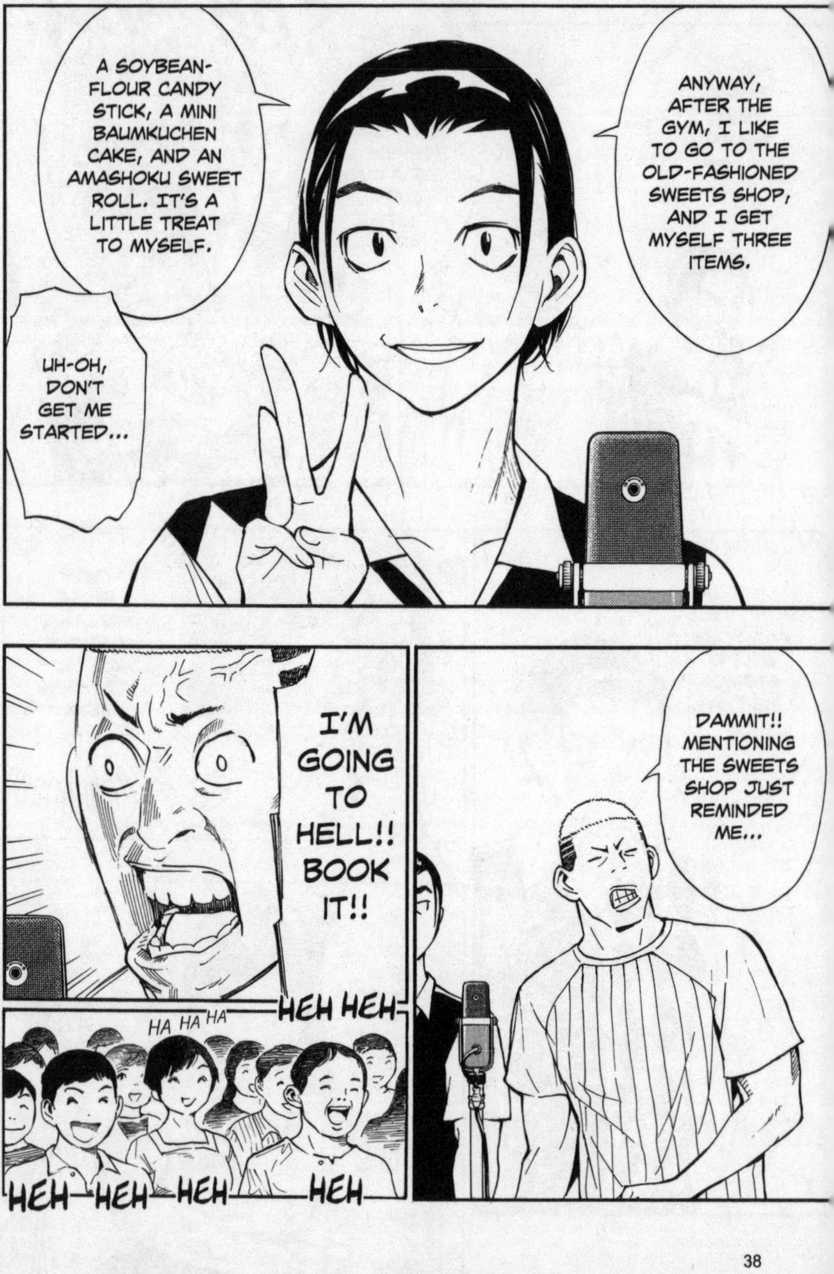
ANYWAY, AFTER THE GYM, I LIKE TO GO TO THE OLD-FASHIONED SWEETS SHOP, AND I GET MYSELF THREE ITEMS.
A SOYBEAN-FLOUR CANDY STICK, A MINI BAUMKUCHEN CAKE, AND AN AMASHOKU SWEET ROLL. IT'S A LITTLE TREAT TO MYSELF.
UH-OH, DON'T GET ME STARTED...
DAMMIT!! MENTIONING THE SWEETS SHOP JUST REMINDED ME...
I'M GOING TO HELL!! BOOK IT!!
HEH HEH
HA HA HA
HEH HEH HEH HEH

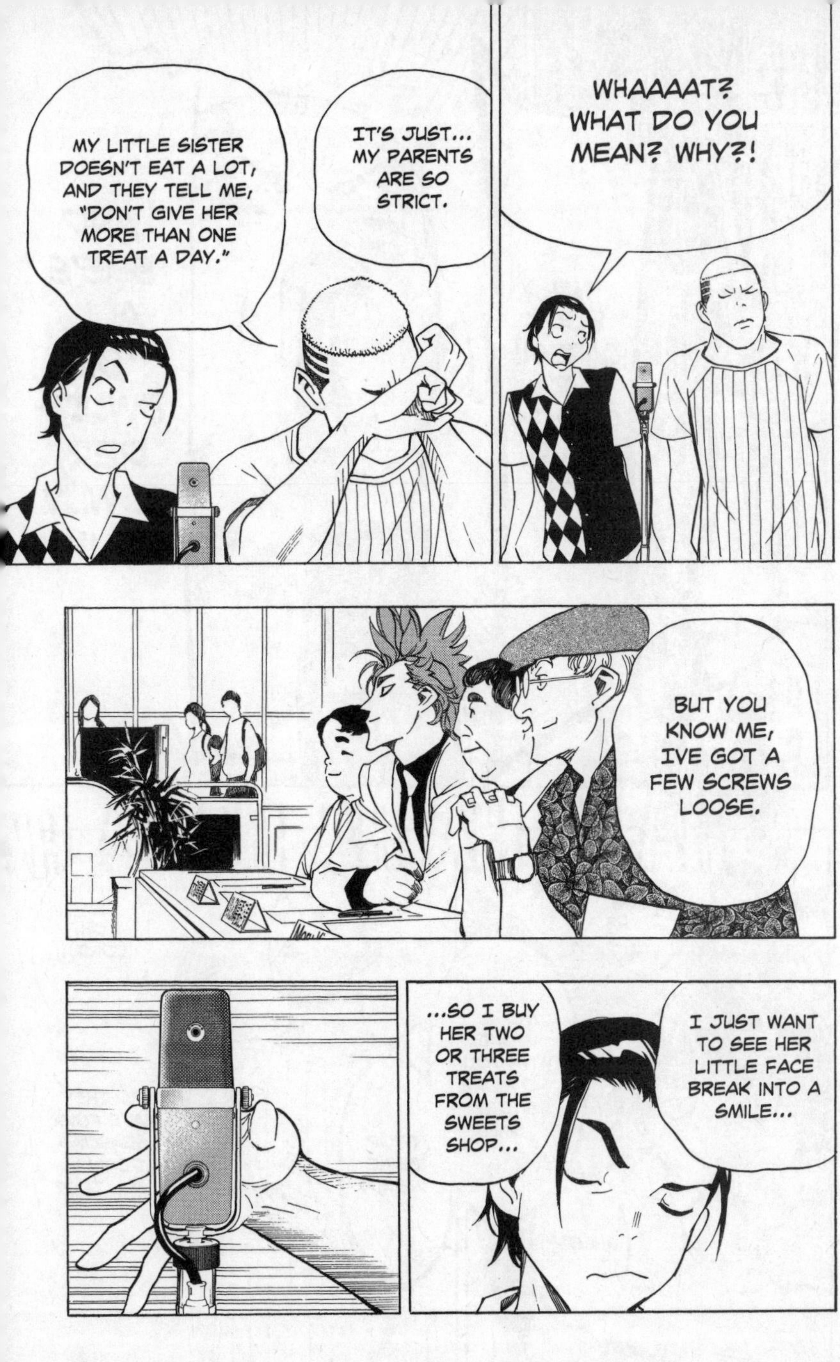

WHAAAAT? WHAT DO YOU MEAN? WHY?!
IT'S JUST... MY PARENTS ARE SO STRICT.
MY LITTLE SISTER DOESN'T EAT A LOT, AND THEY TELL ME, "DON'T GIVE HER MORE THAN ONE TREAT A DAY."
BUT YOU KNOW ME, IVE GOT A FEW SCREWS LOOSE.
I JUST WANT TO SEE HER LITTLE FACE BREAK INTO A SMILE...
...SO I BUY HER TWO OR THREE TREATS FROM THE SWEETS SHOP...

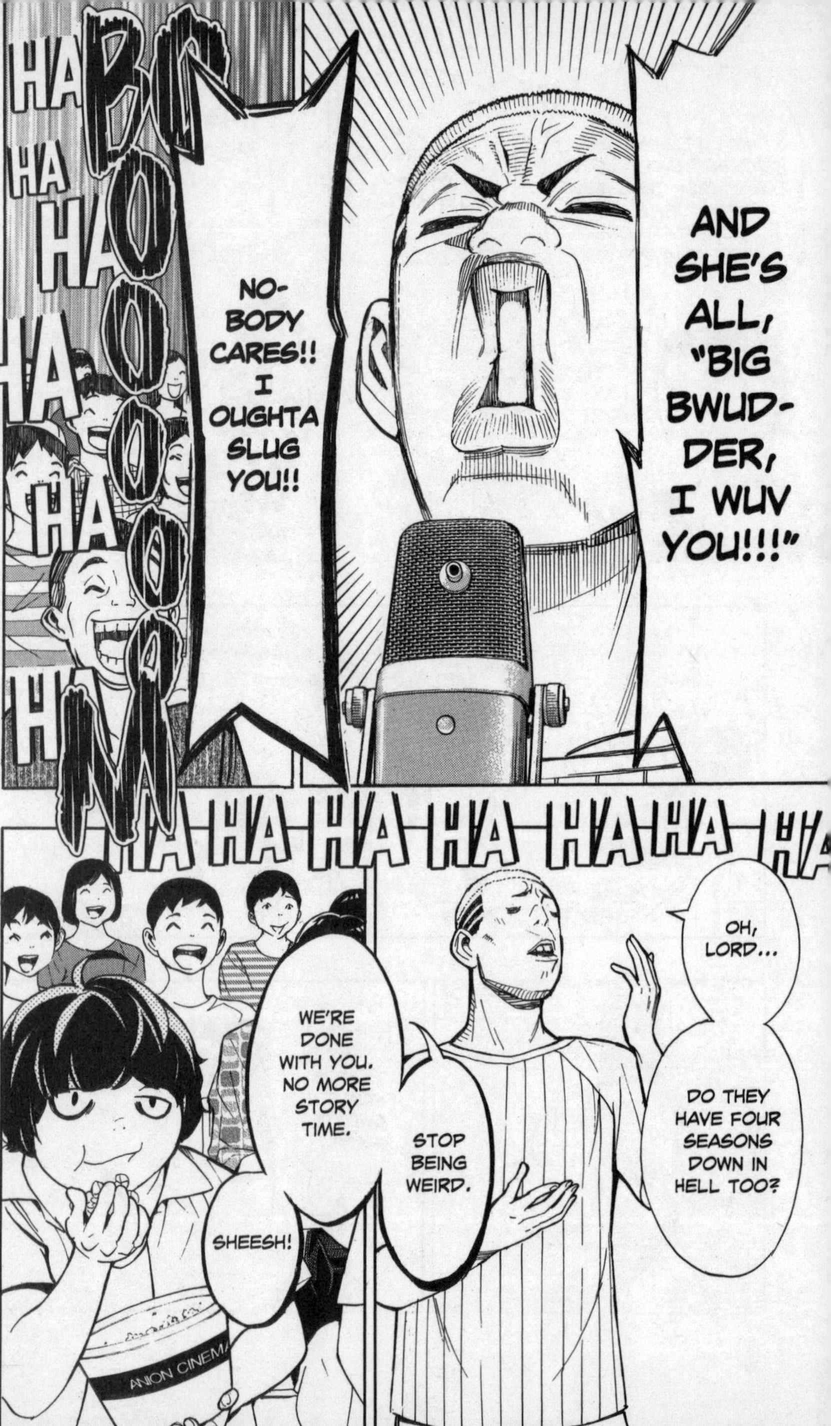
AND SHE'S ALL, "BIG BWUDDER, I WUV YOU!!!"
NO-BODY CARES!! I OUGHTA SLUG YOU!!
HA HA HA HA HA HA
HA HA HA HA HAHA HA
OH, LORD...
DO THEY HAVE FOUR SEASONS DOWN IN HELL TOO?
STOP BEING WEIRD.
WE'RE DONE WITH YOU. NO MORE STORY TIME.
SHEESH!
ANION CINEMA

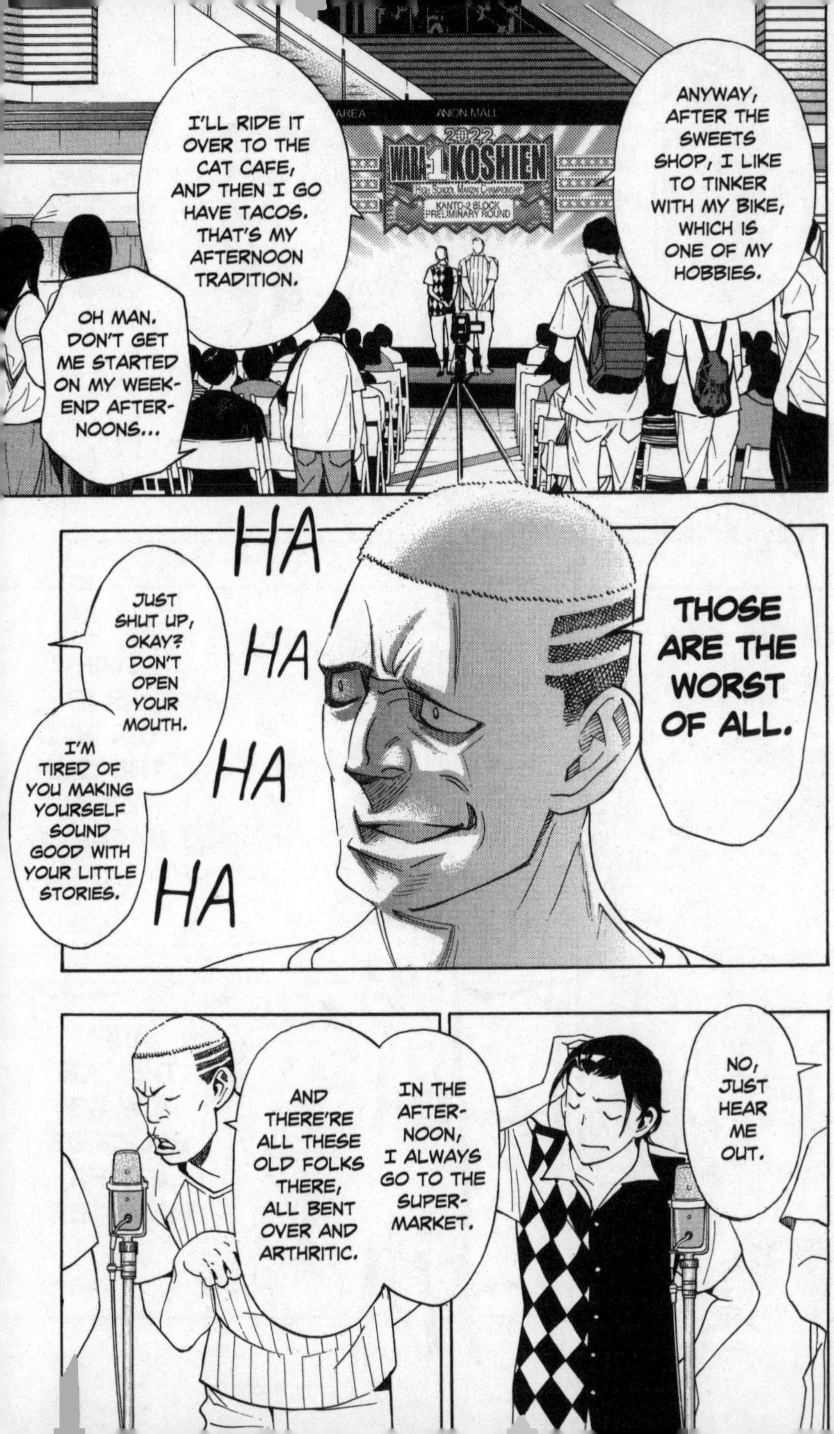
AREA
ANION MALL
2022 WARA-1 KOSHIEN
KANTO-2 BLOCK PRELIMINARY ROUND
ANYWAY, AFTER THE SWEETS SHOP, I LIKE TO TINKER WITH MY BIKE, WHICH IS ONE OF MY HOBBIES.
I'LL RIDE IT OVER TO THE CAT CAFE, AND THEN I GO HAVE TACOS. THAT'S MY AFTERNOON TRADITION.
OH MAN. DON'T GET ME STARTED ON MY WEEK-END AFTER-NOONS...
THOSE ARE THE WORST OF ALL.
HA HA HA HA
JUST SHUT UP, OKAY? DON'T OPEN YOUR MOUTH.
I'M TIRED OF YOU MAKING YOURSELF SOUND GOOD WITH YOUR LITTLE STORIES.
NO, JUST HEAR ME OUT.
IN THE AFTER-NOON, I ALWAYS GO TO THE SUPER-MARKET.
AND THERE'RE ALL THESE OLD FOLKS THERE, ALL BENT OVER AND ARTHRITIC.

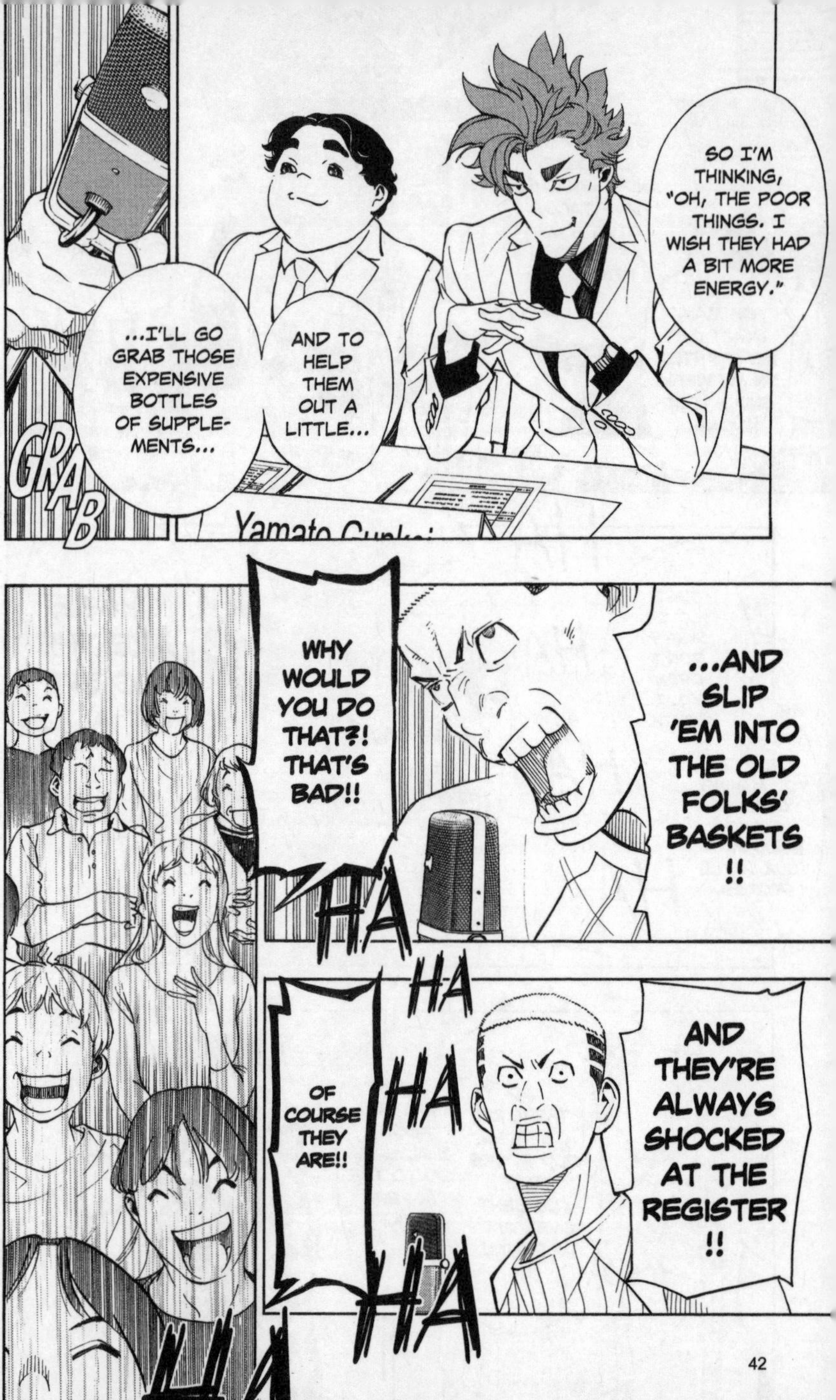
SO I'M THINKING, "OH, THE POOR THINGS. I WISH THEY HAD A BIT MORE ENERGY."
AND TO HELP THEM OUT A LITTLE...
...I'LL GO GRAB THOSE EXPENSIVE BOTTLES OF SUPPLE-MENTS...
GRAB
...AND SLIP 'EM INTO THE OLD FOLKS' BASKETS !!
WHY WOULD YOU DO THAT?! THAT'S BAD!!
HA
HA
AND THEY'RE ALWAYS SHOCKED AT THE REGISTER !!
OF COURSE THEY ARE!!
HA
HA
HA

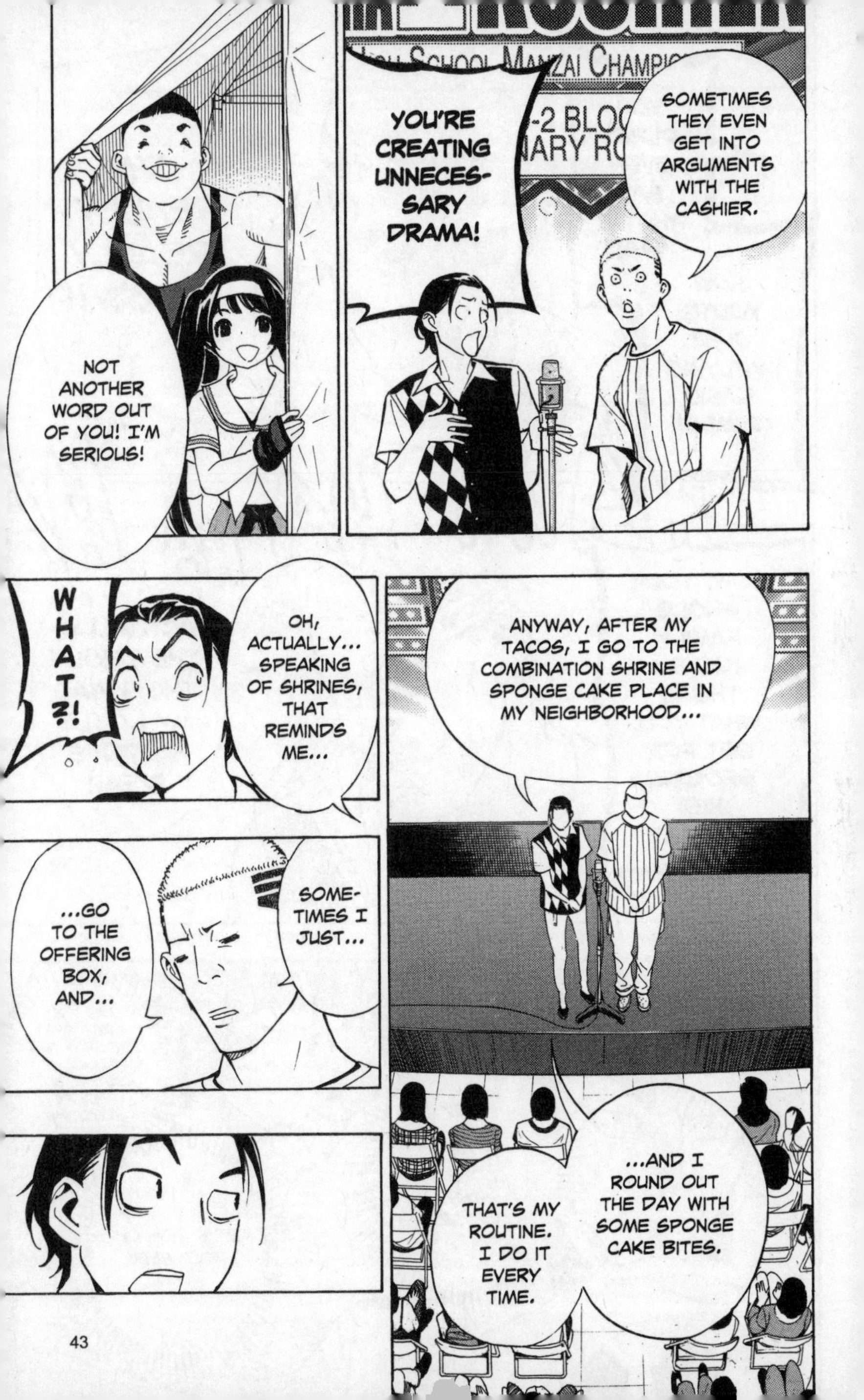
SOMETIMES THEY EVEN GET INTO ARGUMENTS WITH THE CASHIER.
YOU'RE CREATING UNNECES-SARY DRAMA!
NOT ANOTHER WORD OUT OF YOU! I'M SERIOUS!
ANYWAY, AFTER MY TACOS, I GO TO THE COMBINATION SHRINE AND SPONGE CAKE PLACE IN MY NEIGHBORHOOD...
OH, ACTUALLY... SPEAKING OF SHRINES, THAT REMINDS ME...
WHAT?!
SOME-TIMES I JUST...
...GO TO THE OFFERING BOX, AND...
...AND I ROUND OUT THE DAY WITH SOME SPONGE CAKE BITES.
THAT'S MY ROUTINE. I DO IT EVERY TIME.

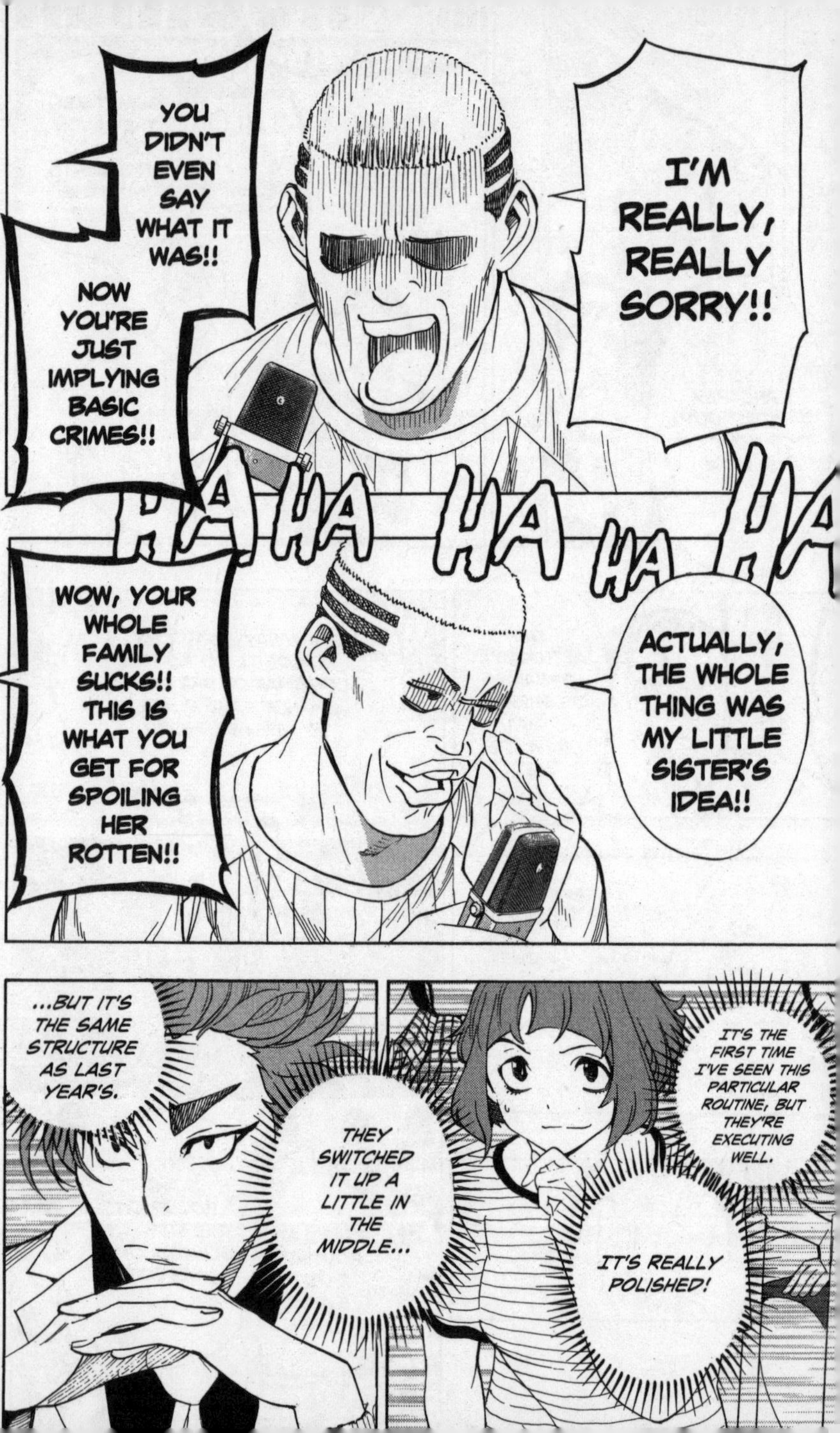
I'M REALLY, REALLY SORRY!!
YOU DIDN'T EVEN SAY WHAT IT WAS!!
NOW YOU'RE JUST IMPLYING BASIC CRIMES!!
HA HA HA HA HA
ACTUALLY, THE WHOLE THING WAS MY LITTLE SISTER'S IDEA!!
WOW, YOUR WHOLE FAMILY SUCKS!! THIS IS WHAT YOU GET FOR SPOILING HER ROTTEN!!
IT'S THE FIRST TIME I'VE SEEN THIS PARTICULAR ROUTINE, BUT THEY'RE EXECUTING WELL.
IT'S REALLY POLISHED!
...BUT IT'S THE SAME STRUCTURE AS LAST YEAR'S.
THEY SWITCHED IT UP A LITTLE IN THE MIDDLE...

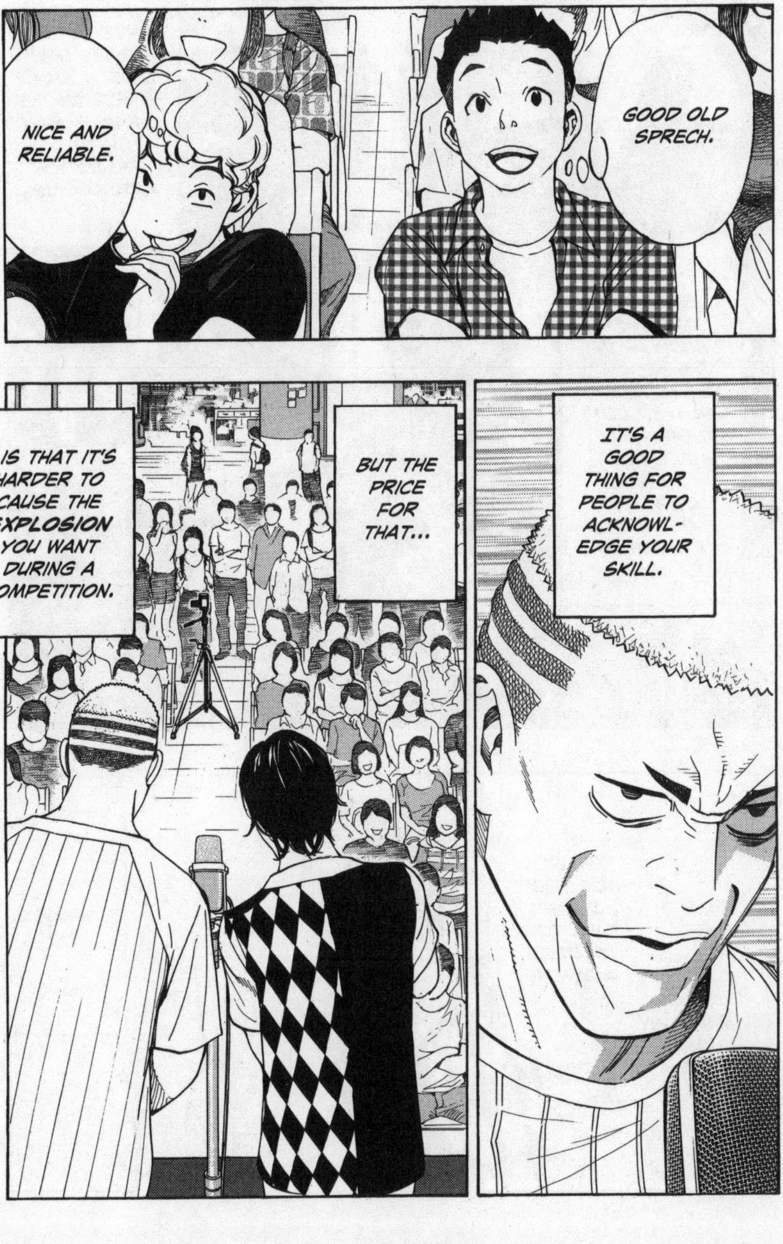
GOOD OLD SPRECH.
NICE AND RELIABLE.
IT'S A GOOD THING FOR PEOPLE TO ACKNOWLEDGE YOUR SKILL.
BUT THE PRICE FOR THAT...
...IS THAT IT'S HARDER TO CAUSE THE EXPLOSION YOU WANT DURING A COMPETITION.

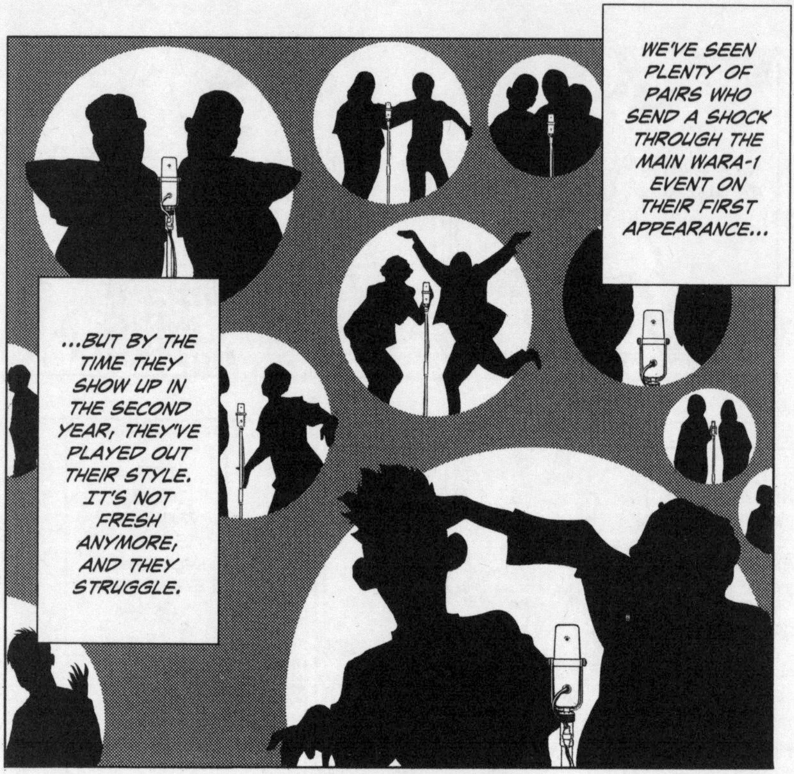
WE'VE SEEN PLENTY OF PAIRS WHO SEND A SHOCK THROUGH THE MAIN WARA-1 EVENT ON THEIR FIRST APPEARANCE...
...BUT BY THE TIME THEY SHOW UP IN THE SECOND YEAR, THEY'VE PLAYED OUT THEIR STYLE. IT'S NOT FRESH ANYMORE, AND THEY STRUGGLE.
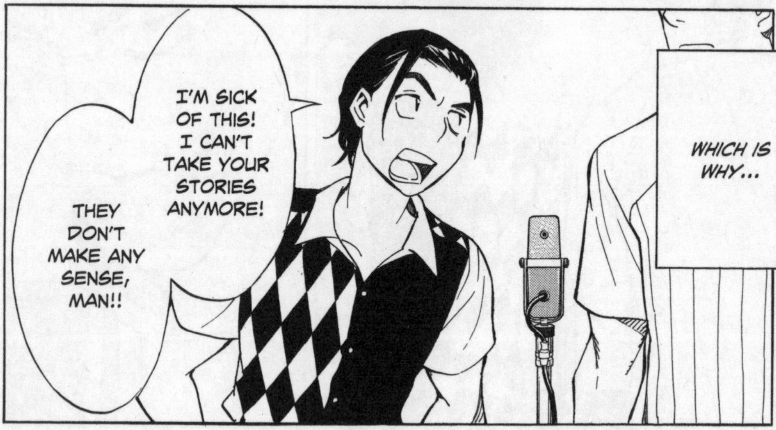
WHICH IS WHY...
I'M SICK OF THIS! I CAN'T TAKE YOUR STORIES ANYMORE!
THEY DON'T MAKE ANY SENSE, MAN!!

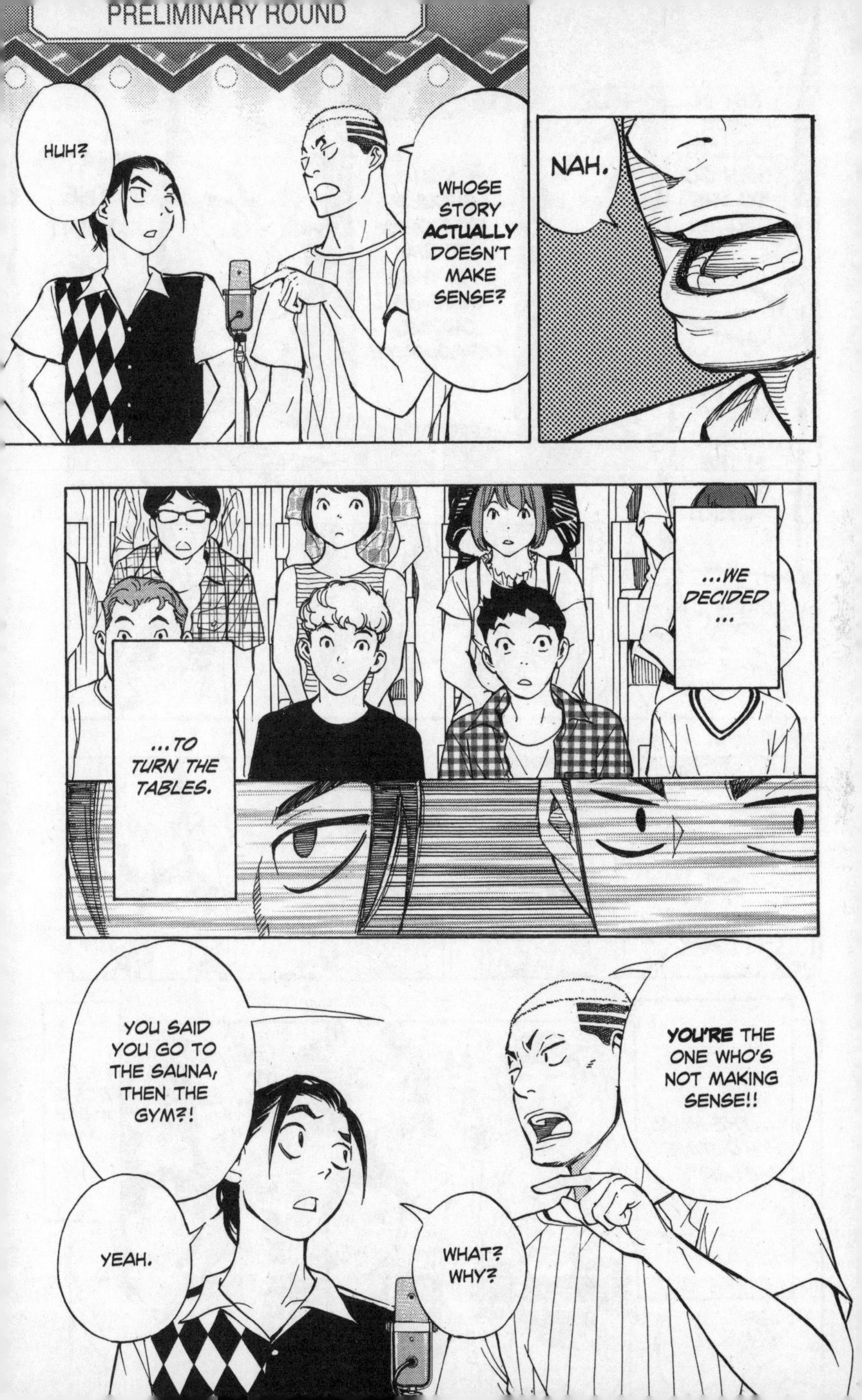
NAH.
PRELIMINARY ROUND
WHOSE STORY ACTUALLY DOESN'T MAKE SENSE?
HUH?
...WE DECIDED ...
...TO TURN THE TABLES.
YOU'RE THE ONE WHO'S NOT MAKING SENSE!!
YOU SAID YOU GO TO THE SAUNA, THEN THE GYM?!
WHAT? WHY?
YEAH.

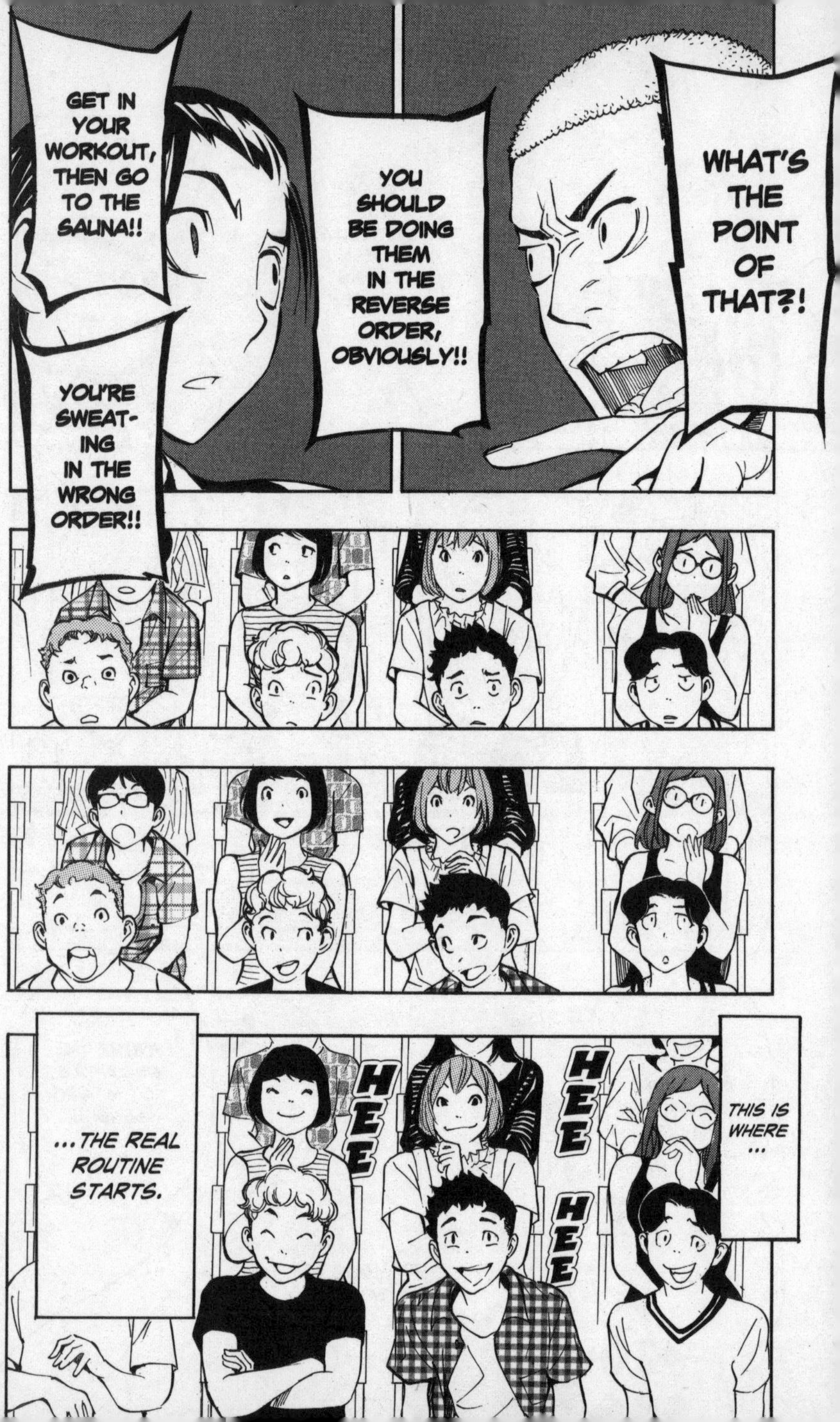
WHAT'S THE POINT OF THAT?!
YOU SHOULD BE DOING THEM IN THE REVERSE ORDER, OBVIOUSLY!!
GET IN YOUR WORKOUT, THEN GO TO THE SAUNA!!
YOU'RE SWEAT-ING IN THE WRONG ORDER!!
THIS IS WHERE...
HEE HEE
HEE HEE
HEE HEE
...THE REAL ROUTINE STARTS.

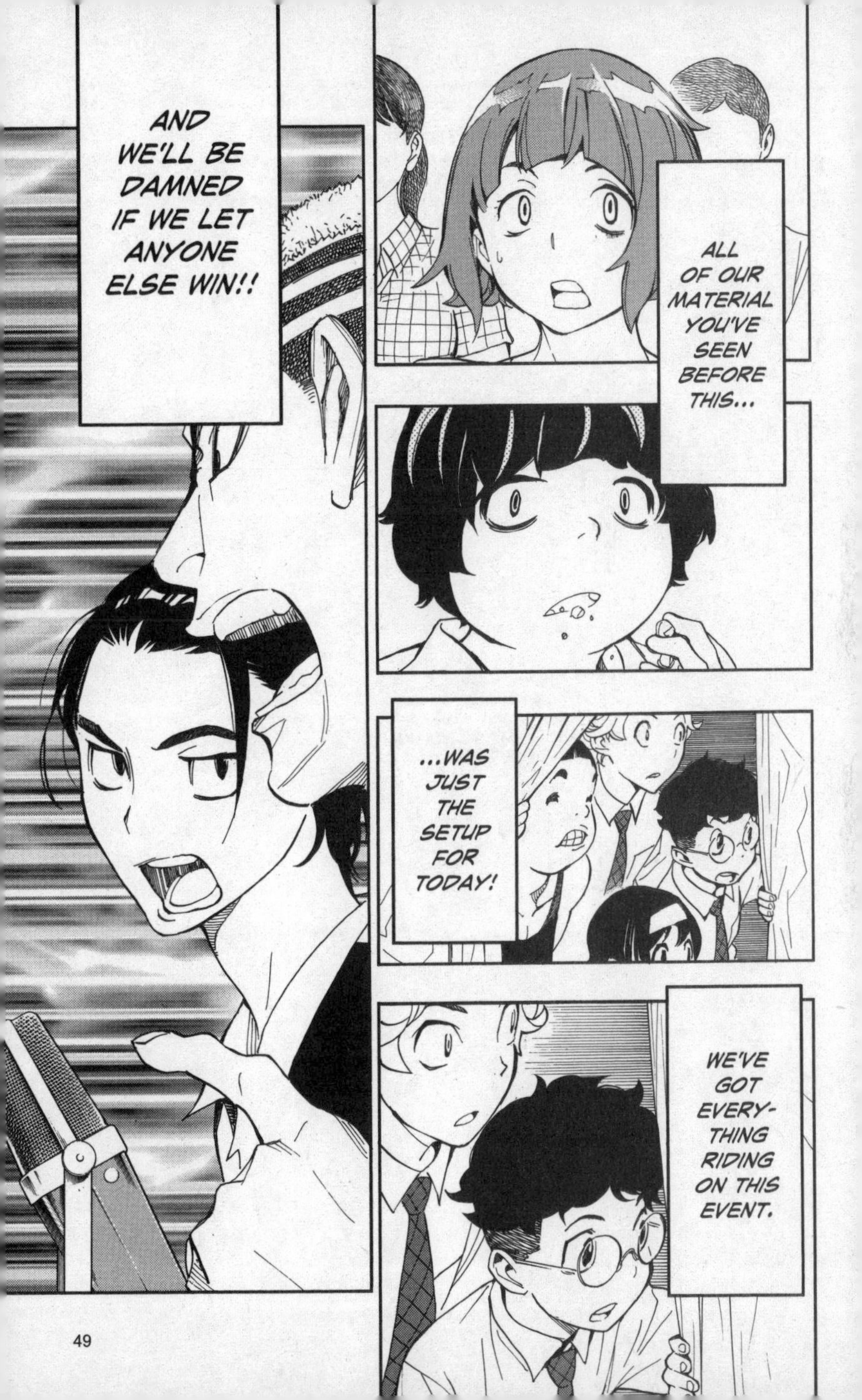
ALL OF OUR MATERIAL YOU'VE SEEN BEFORE THIS...
...WAS JUST THE SETUP FOR TODAY!
WE'VE GOT EVERY-THING RIDING ON THIS EVENT.
AND WE'LL BE DAMNED IF WE LET ANYONE ELSE WIN!!

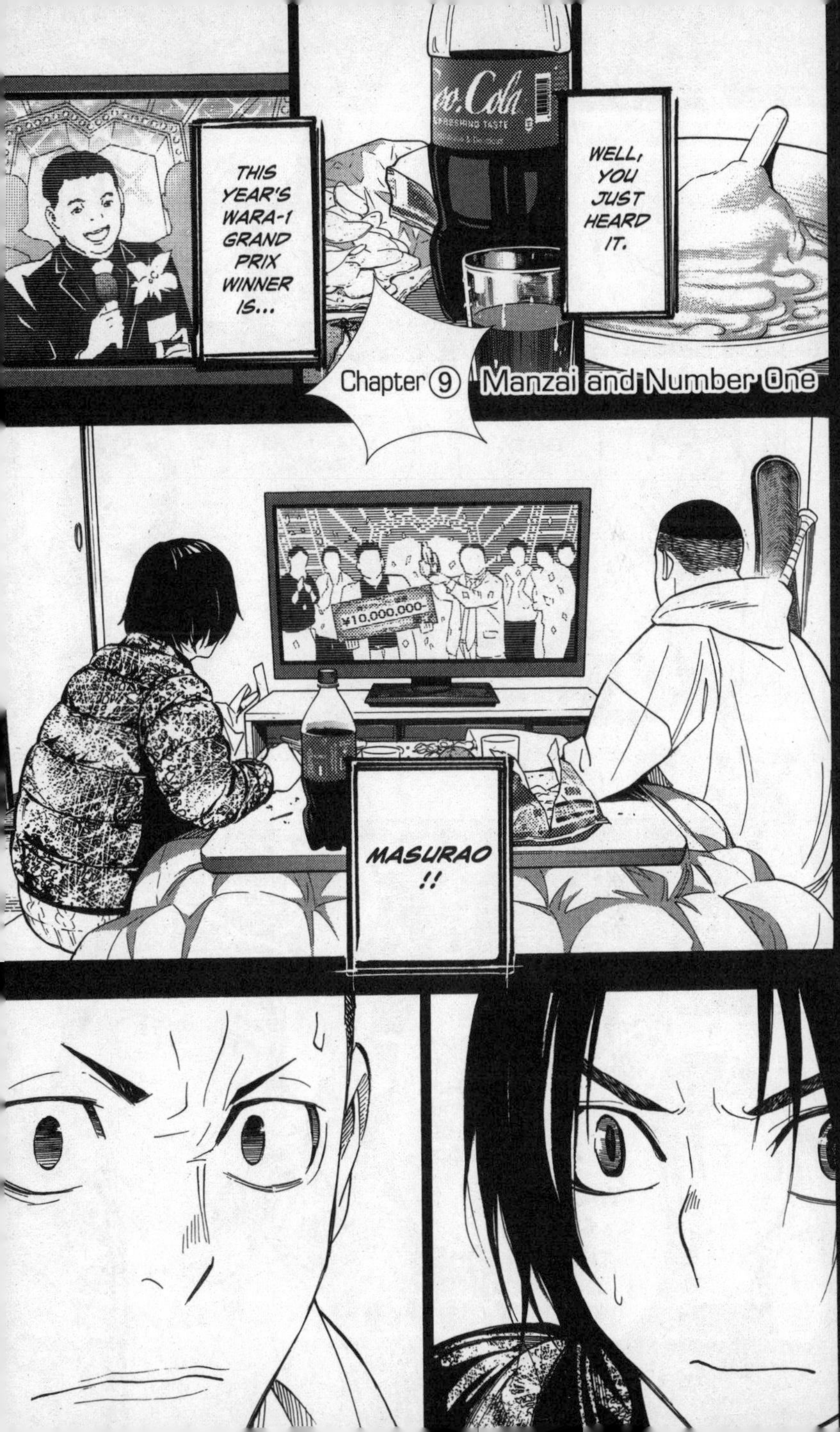
WELL, YOU JUST HEARD IT.
THIS YEAR'S WARA-1 GRAND PRIX WINNER IS...
Chapter 9 Manzai and Number One
¥10,000,000-
MASURAO !!

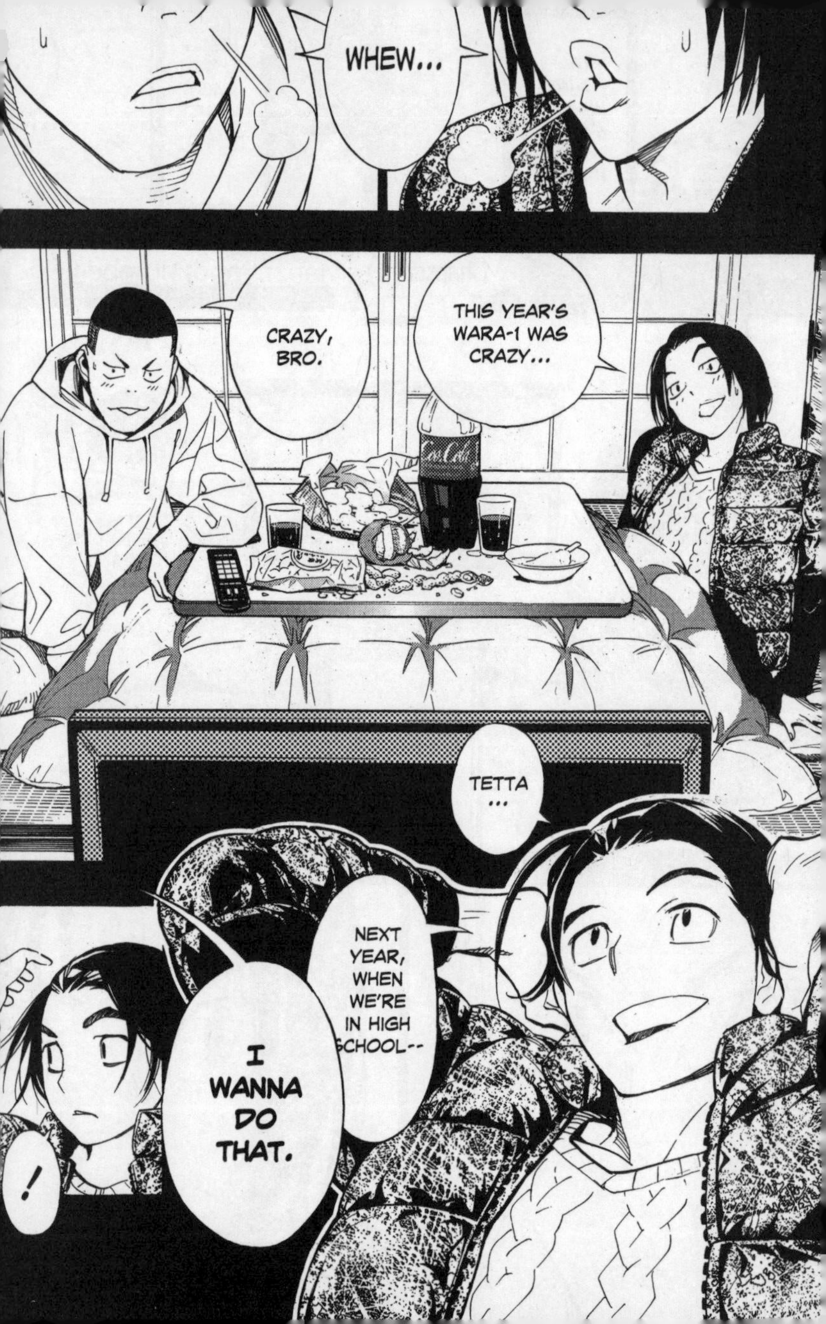
WHEW...
THIS YEAR'S WARA-1 WAS CRAZY...
CRAZY, BRO.
TETTA...
NEXT YEAR, WHEN WE'RE IN HIGH SCHOOL--
I WANNA DO THAT.
!

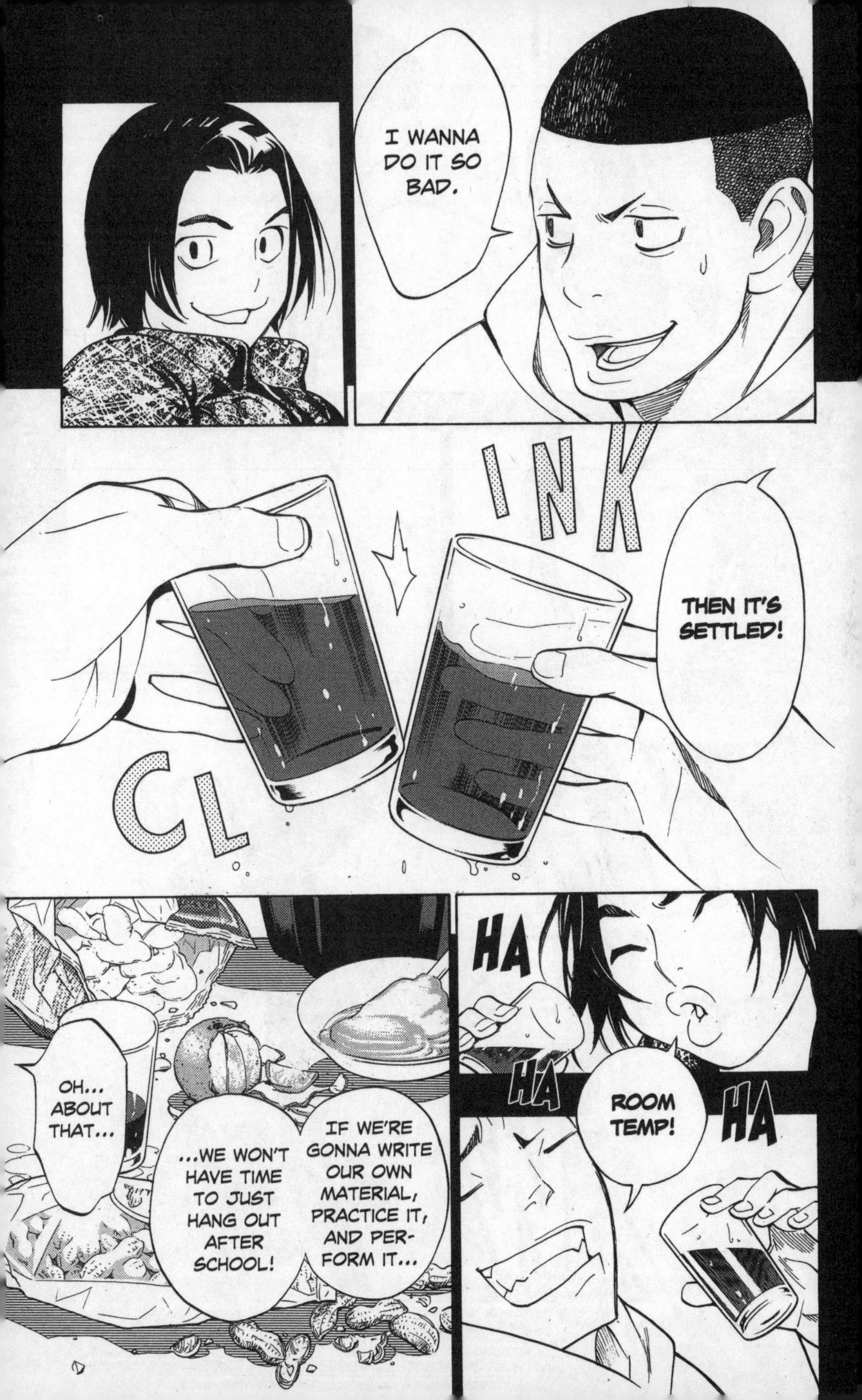
I WANNA DO IT SO BAD.
THEN IT'S SETTLED!
CLINK
HA
ROOM TEMP!
HA
HA
IF WE'RE GONNA WRITE OUR OWN MATERIAL, PRACTICE IT, AND PER-FORM IT...
...WE WON'T HAVE TIME TO JUST HANG OUT AFTER SCHOOL!
OH... ABOUT THAT...

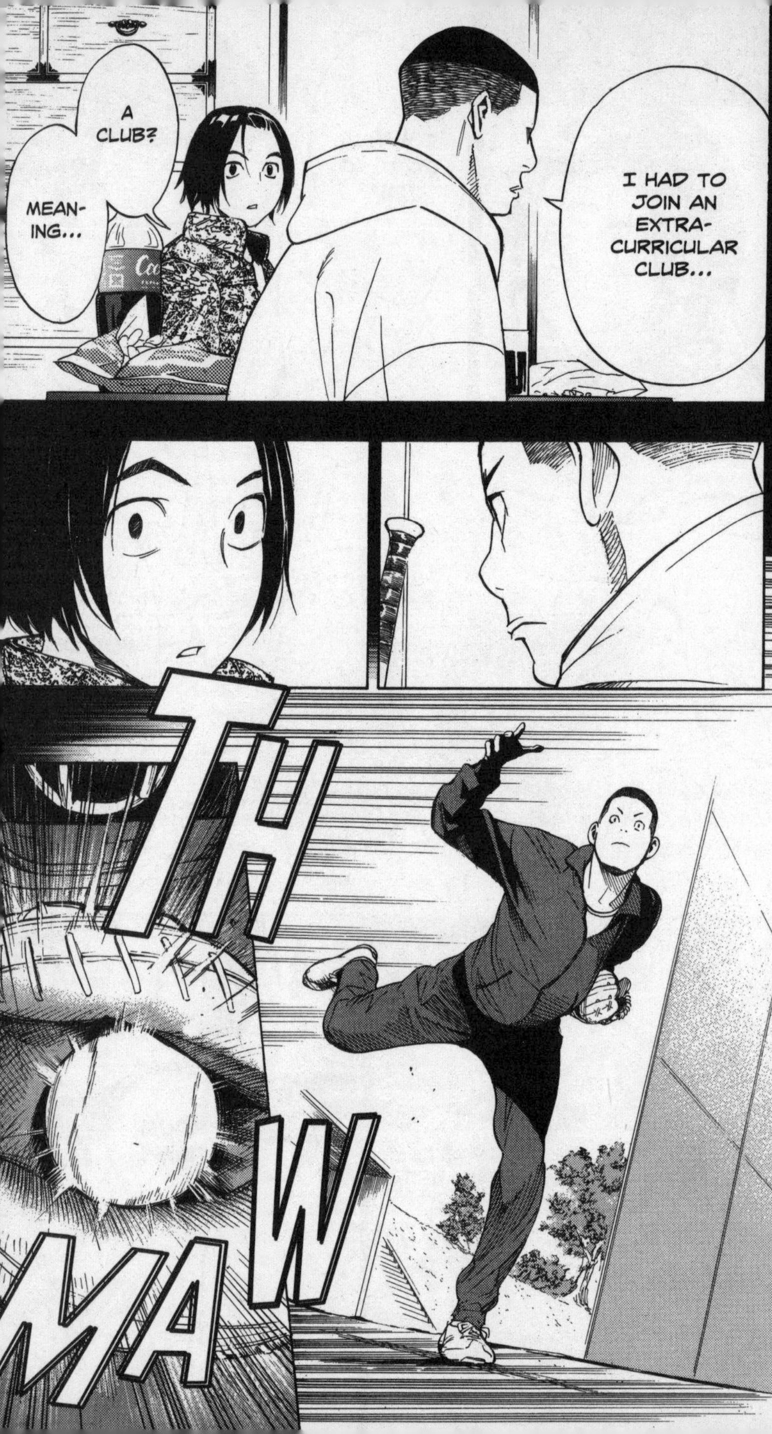
I HAD TO JOIN AN EXTRA-CURRICULAR CLUB...
A CLUB?
MEANING...
TH
W
MA

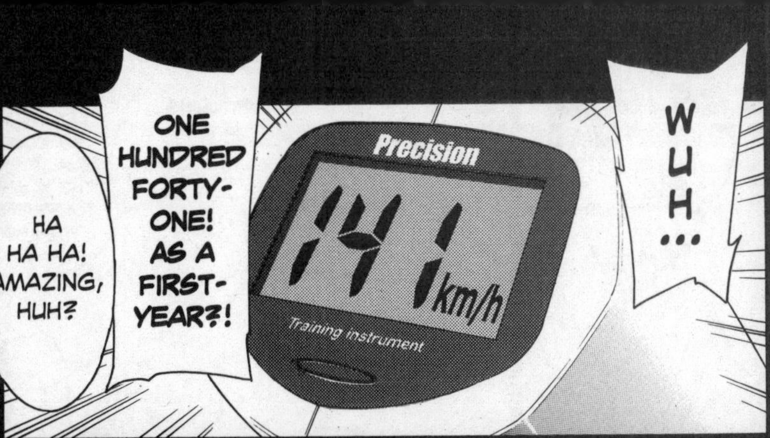
WUH...
ONE HUNDRED FORTY-ONE! AS A FIRST-YEAR?!
HA HA HA! AMAZING, HUH?
Precision
141 km/h
Training instrument

*87.6 MPH

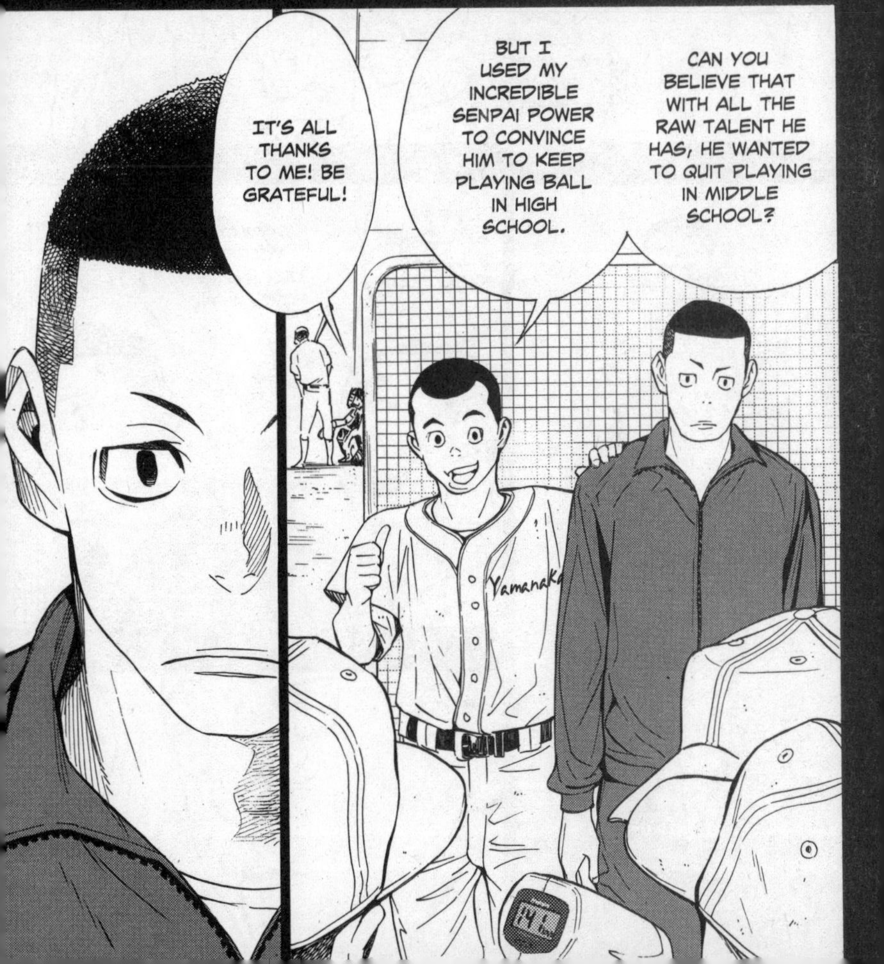
CAN YOU BELIEVE THAT WITH ALL THE RAW TALENT HE HAS, HE WANTED TO QUIT PLAYING IN MIDDLE SCHOOL?
BUT I USED MY INCREDIBLE SENPAI POWER TO CONVINCE HIM TO KEEP PLAYING BALL IN HIGH SCHOOL.
IT'S ALL THANKS TO ME! BE GRATEFUL!
Yamanaka

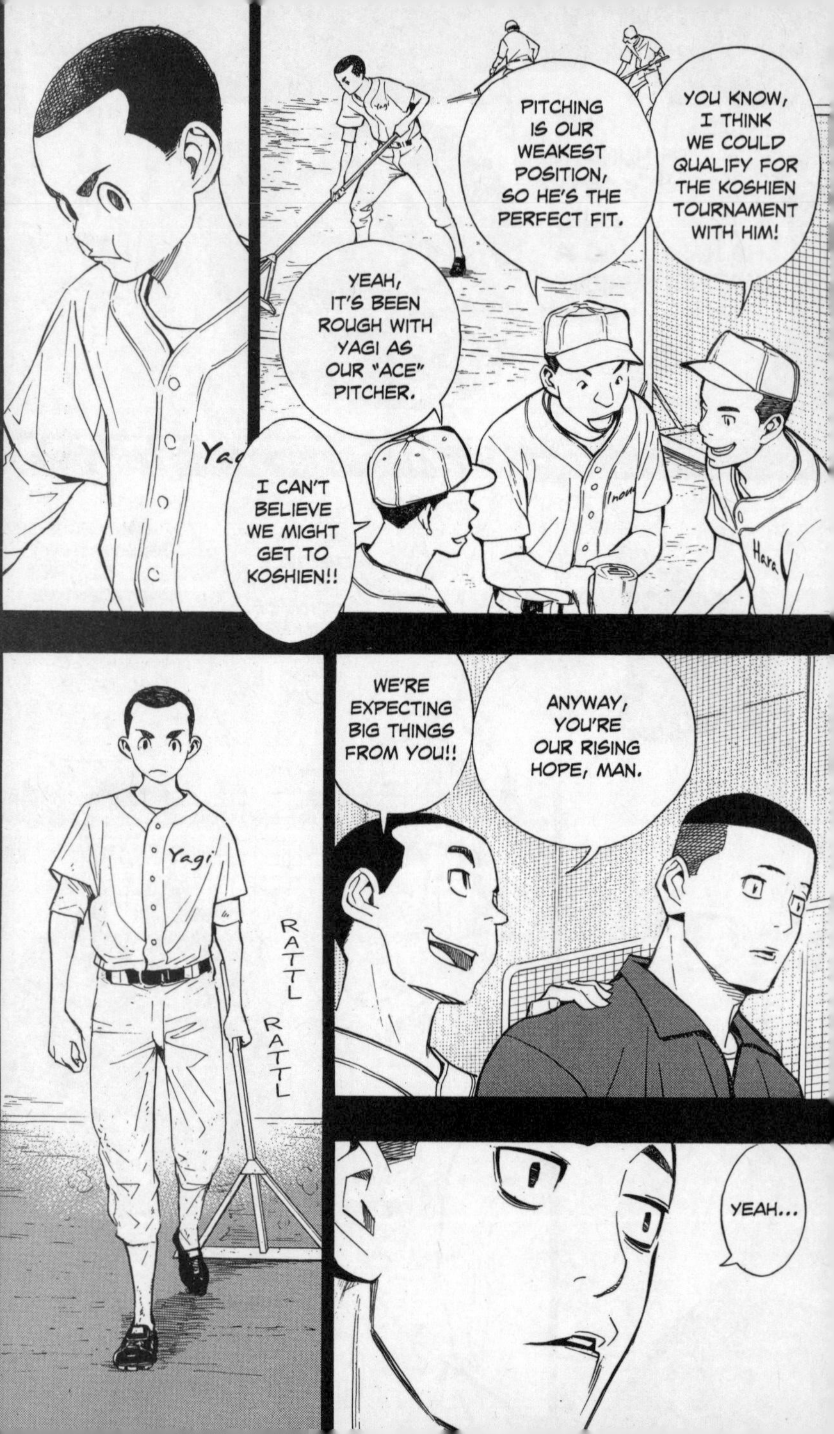
YOU KNOW, I THINK WE COULD QUALIFY FOR THE KOSHIEN TOURNAMENT WITH HIM!
PITCHING IS OUR WEAKEST POSITION, SO HE'S THE PERFECT FIT.
YEAH, IT'S BEEN ROUGH WITH YAGI AS OUR "ACE" PITCHER.
I CAN'T BELIEVE WE MIGHT GET TO KOSHIEN!!
ANYWAY, YOU'RE OUR RISING HOPE, MAN.
WE'RE EXPECTING BIG THINGS FROM YOU!!
YEAH...
RATTL
RATTL

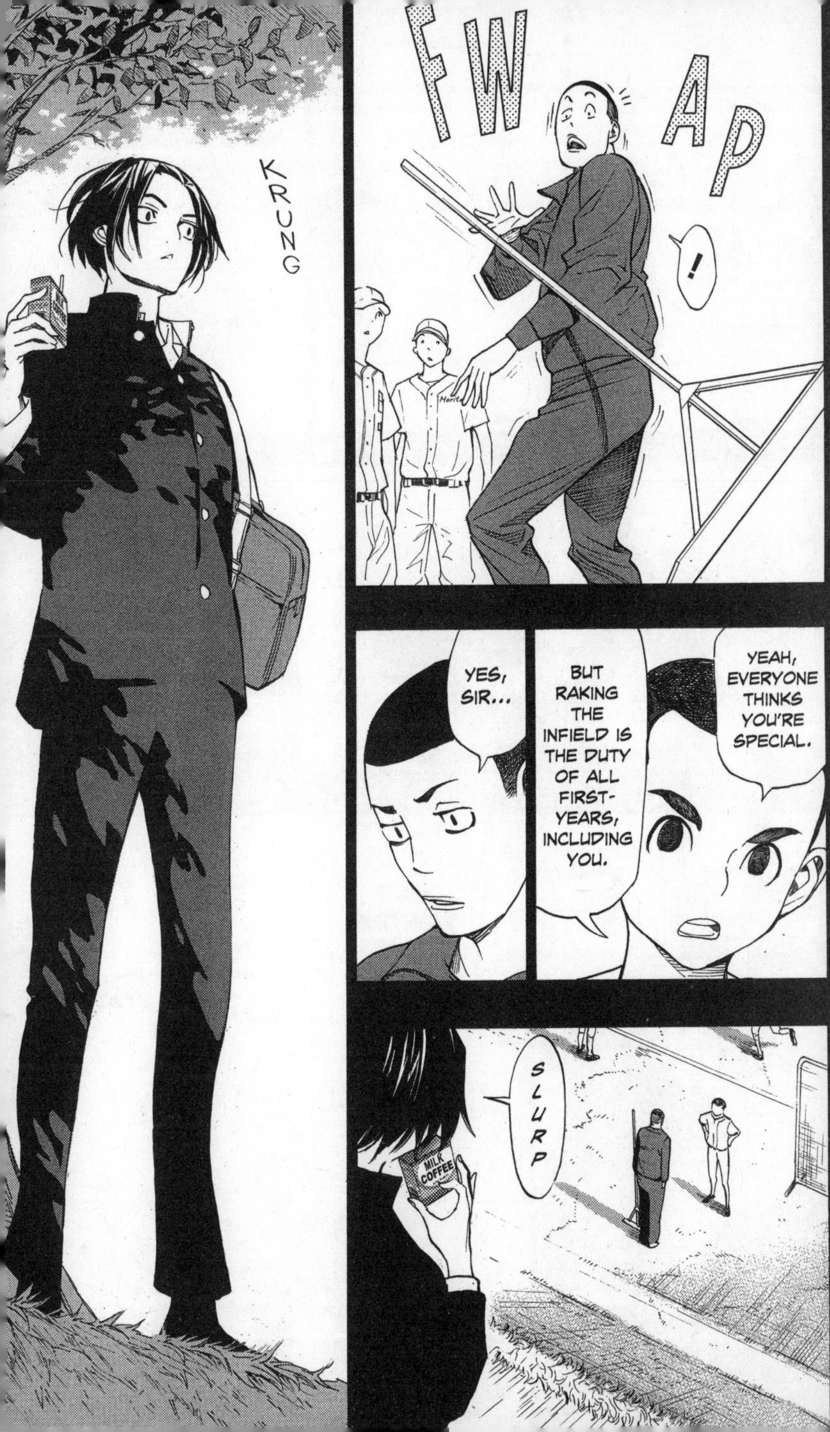
FWAP
!
YEAH, EVERYONE THINKS YOU'RE SPECIAL.
BUT RAKING THE INFIELD IS THE DUTY OF ALL FIRST-YEARS, INCLUDING YOU.
YES, SIR...
SLURP
MILK COFFEE
KRUNG

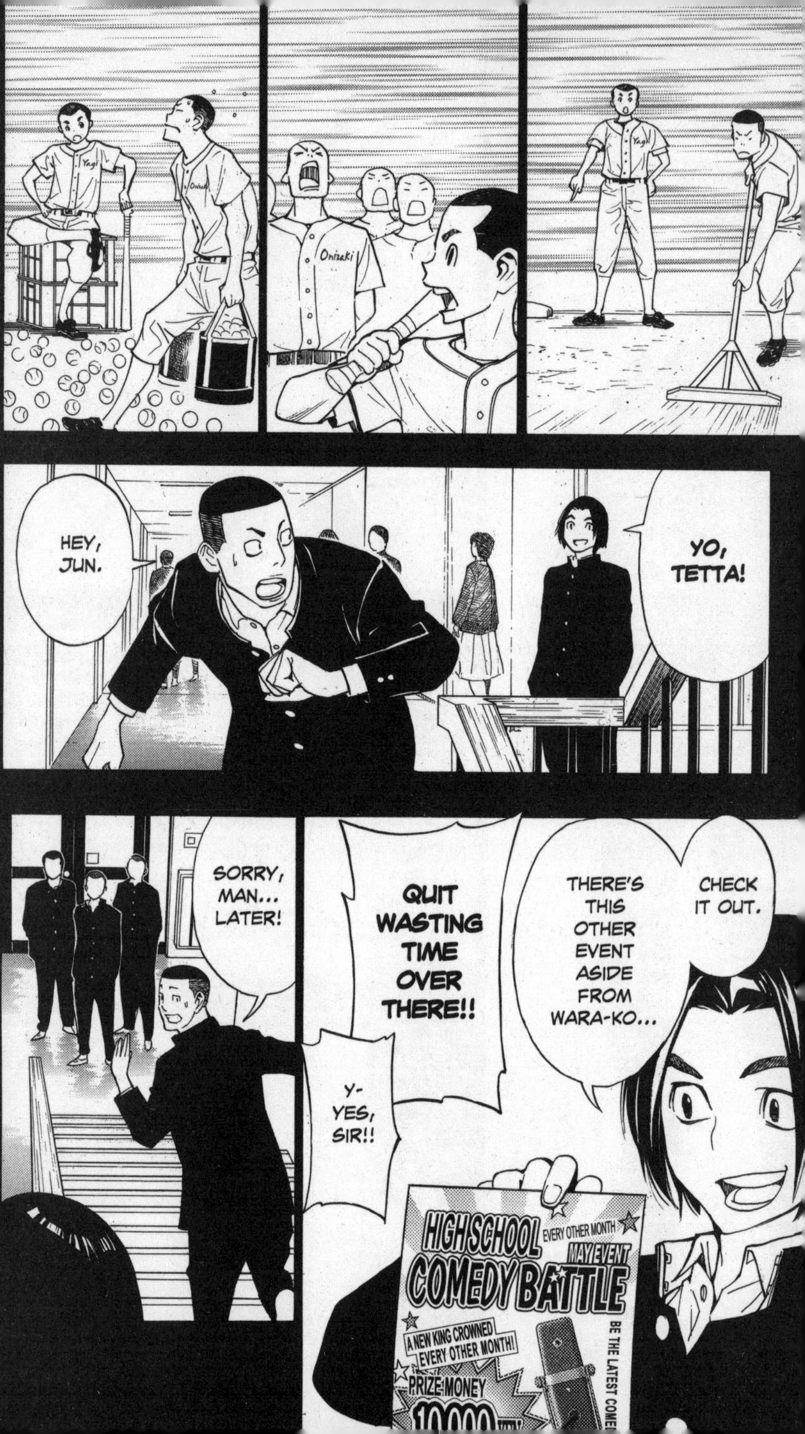

YO, TETTA!
HEY, JUN.
CHECK IT OUT.
THERE'S THIS OTHER EVENT ASIDE FROM WARA-KO...
QUIT WASTING TIME OVER THERE!!
Y-YES, SIR!!
HIGH SCHOOL COMEDY BATTLE
EVERY OTHER MONTH
MAY EVENT
A NEW KING CROWNED EVERY OTHER MONTH!
PRIZE MONEY
SORRY, MAN... LATER!

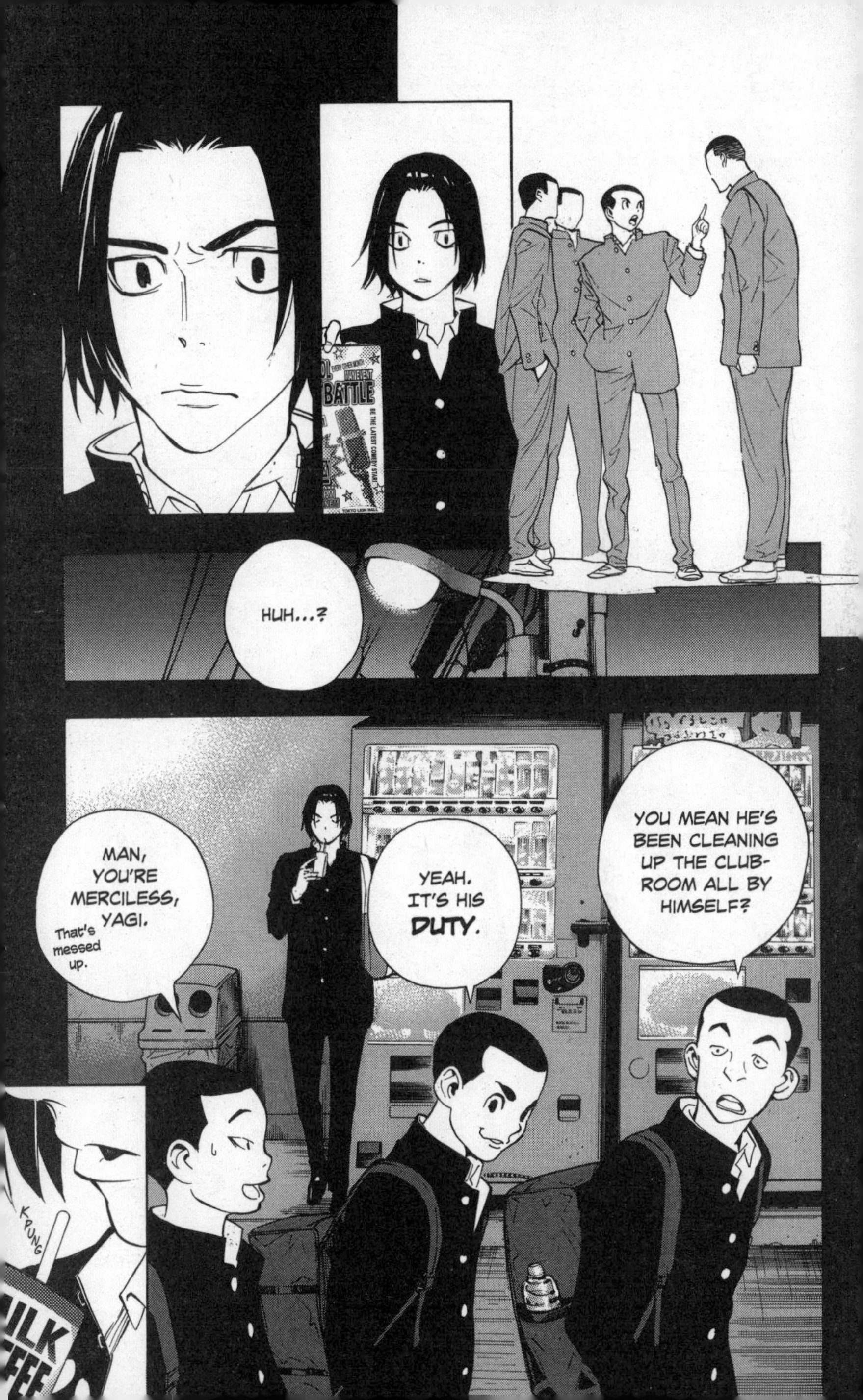
BATTLE
BE THE LATEST COMEDY STAR!
TOKYO LION HALL
HUH...?
YOU MEAN HE'S BEEN CLEANING UP THE CLUB-ROOM ALL BY HIMSELF?
YEAH. IT'S HIS DUTY.
MAN, YOU'RE MERCILESS, YAGI.
That's messed up.
KPUNG

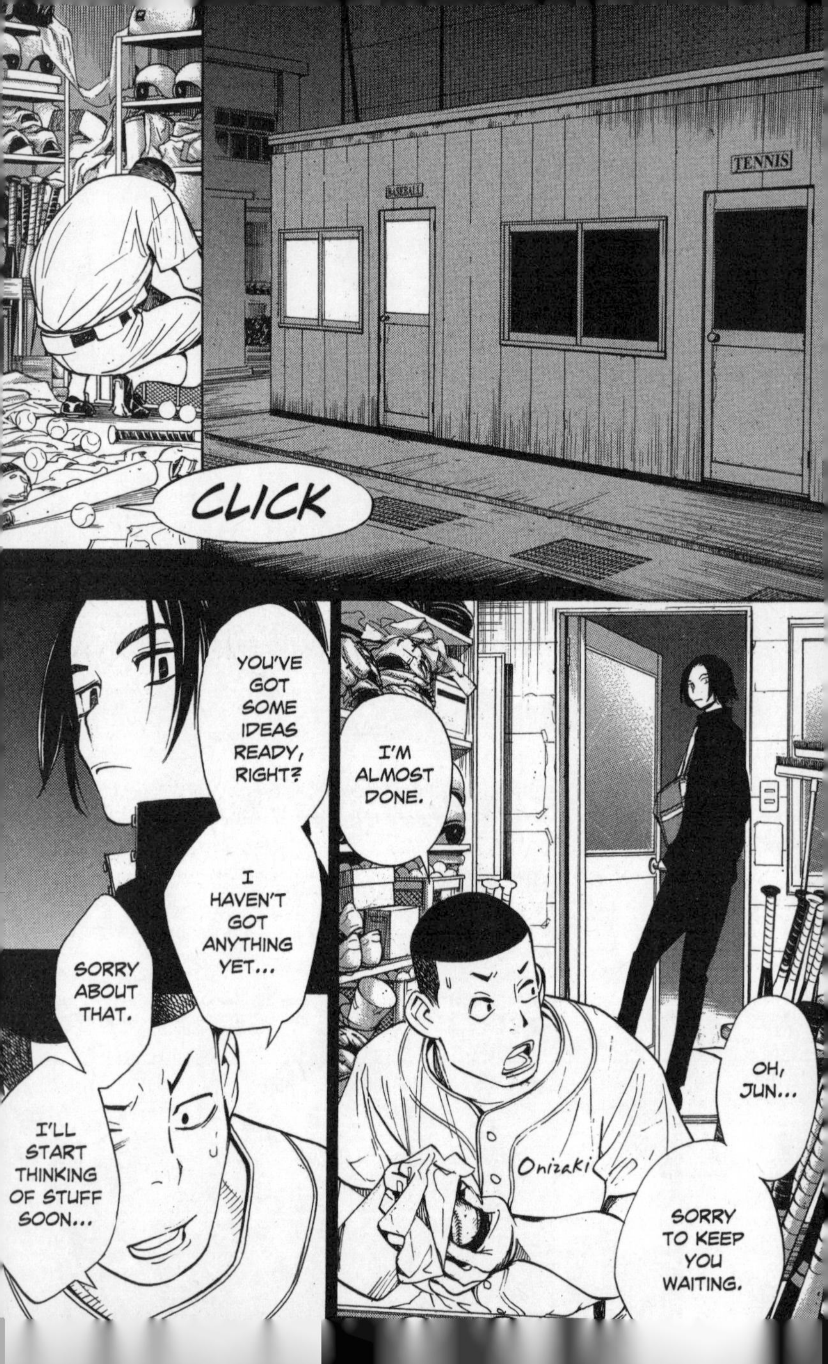
TENNIS
BASEBALL
CLICK
OH, JUN...
SORRY TO KEEP YOU WAITING.
Onizaki
I'M ALMOST DONE.
YOU'VE GOT SOME IDEAS READY, RIGHT?
I HAVEN'T GOT ANYTHING YET...
SORRY ABOUT THAT.
I'LL START THINKING OF STUFF SOON...

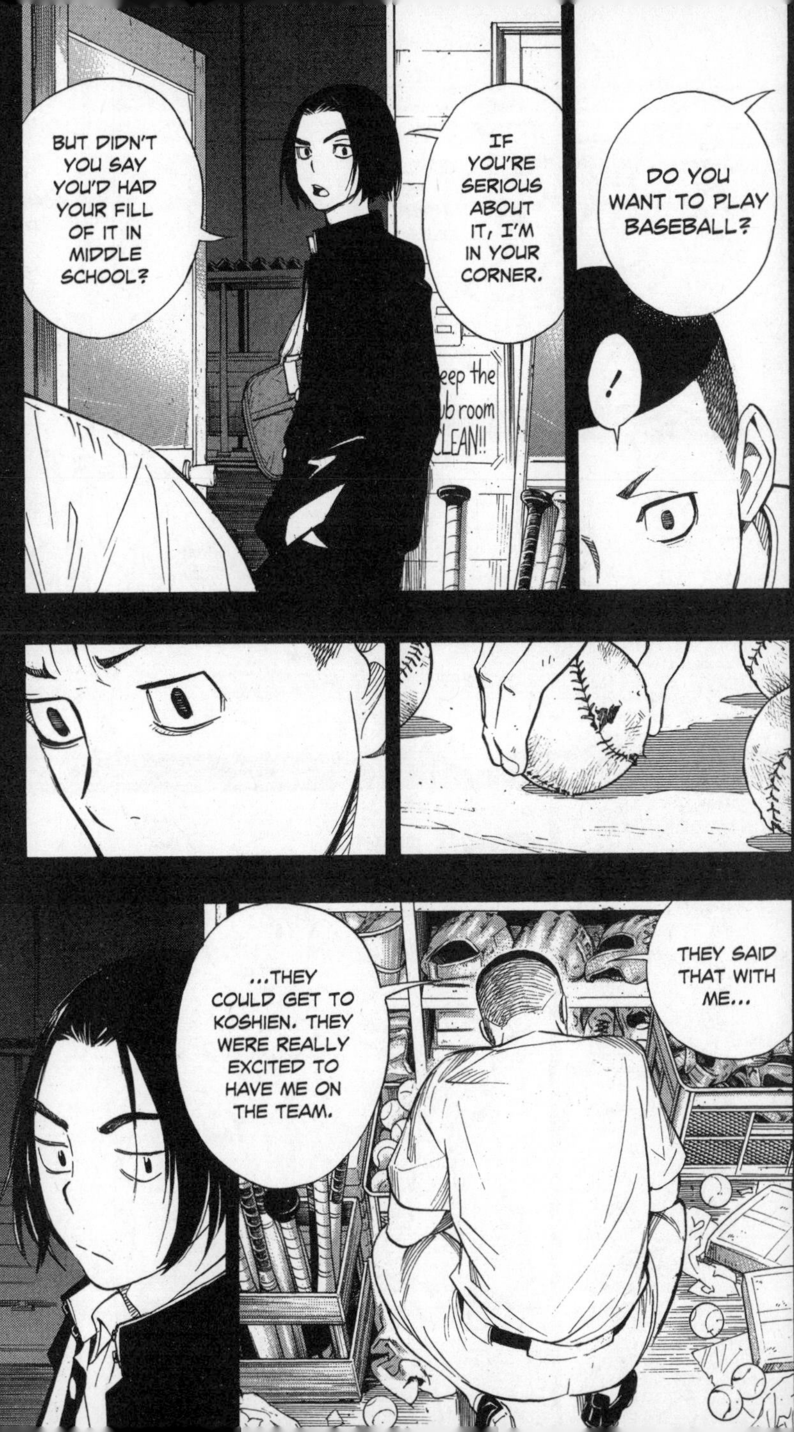
DO YOU WANT TO PLAY BASEBALL?
!
IF YOU'RE SERIOUS ABOUT IT, I'M IN YOUR CORNER.
BUT DIDN'T YOU SAY YOU'D HAD YOUR FILL OF IT IN MIDDLE SCHOOL?
THEY SAID THAT WITH ME...
...THEY COULD GET TO KOSHIEN. THEY WERE REALLY EXCITED TO HAVE ME ON THE TEAM.

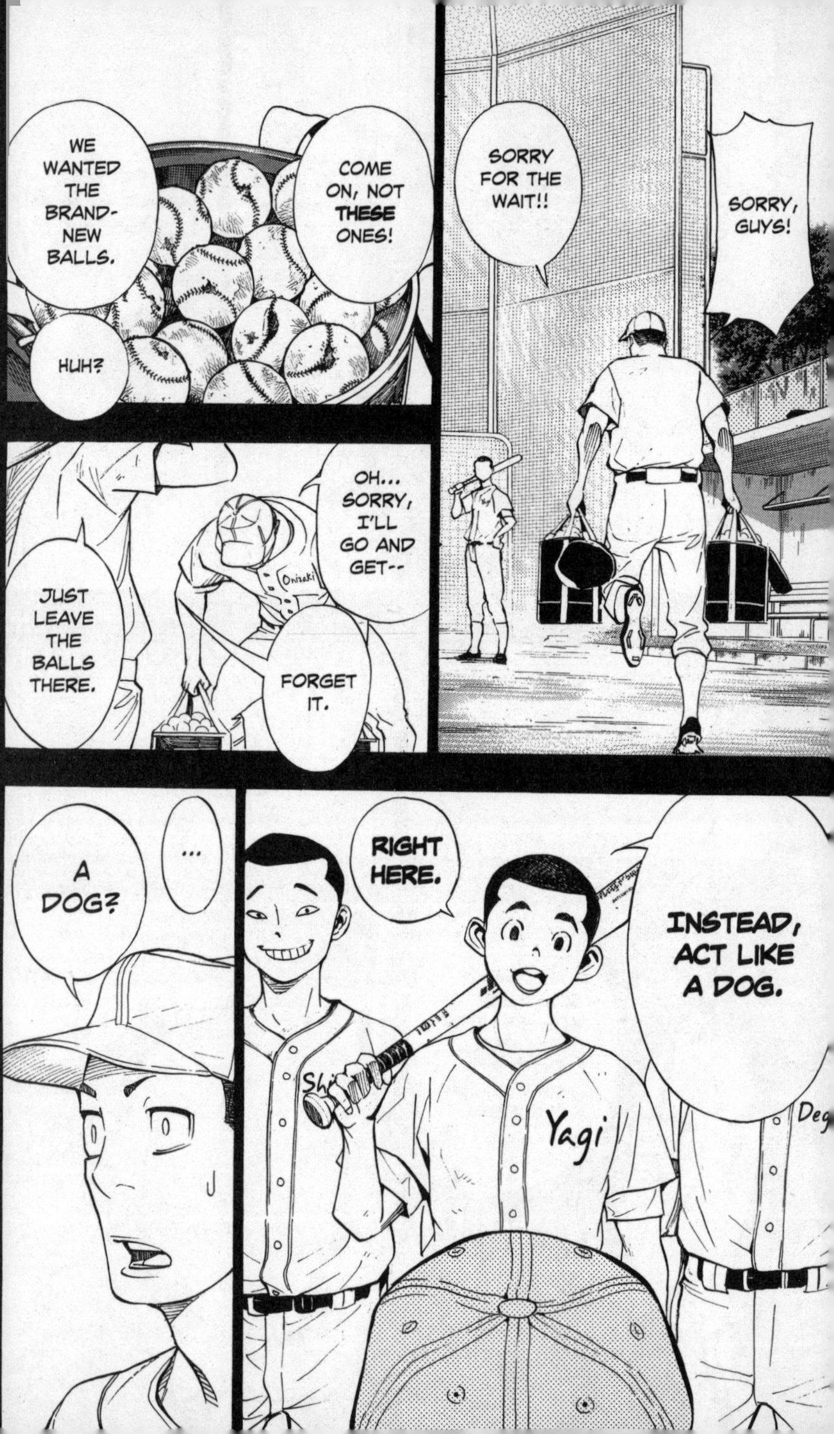
SORRY, GUYS!
SORRY FOR THE WAIT!!
COME ON, NOT THESE ONES!
WE WANTED THE BRAND-NEW BALLS.
HUH?
OH... SORRY, I'LL GO AND GET--
Onizaki
FORGET IT.
JUST LEAVE THE BALLS THERE.
INSTEAD, ACT LIKE A DOG.
Yagi
RIGHT HERE.
...
A DOG?

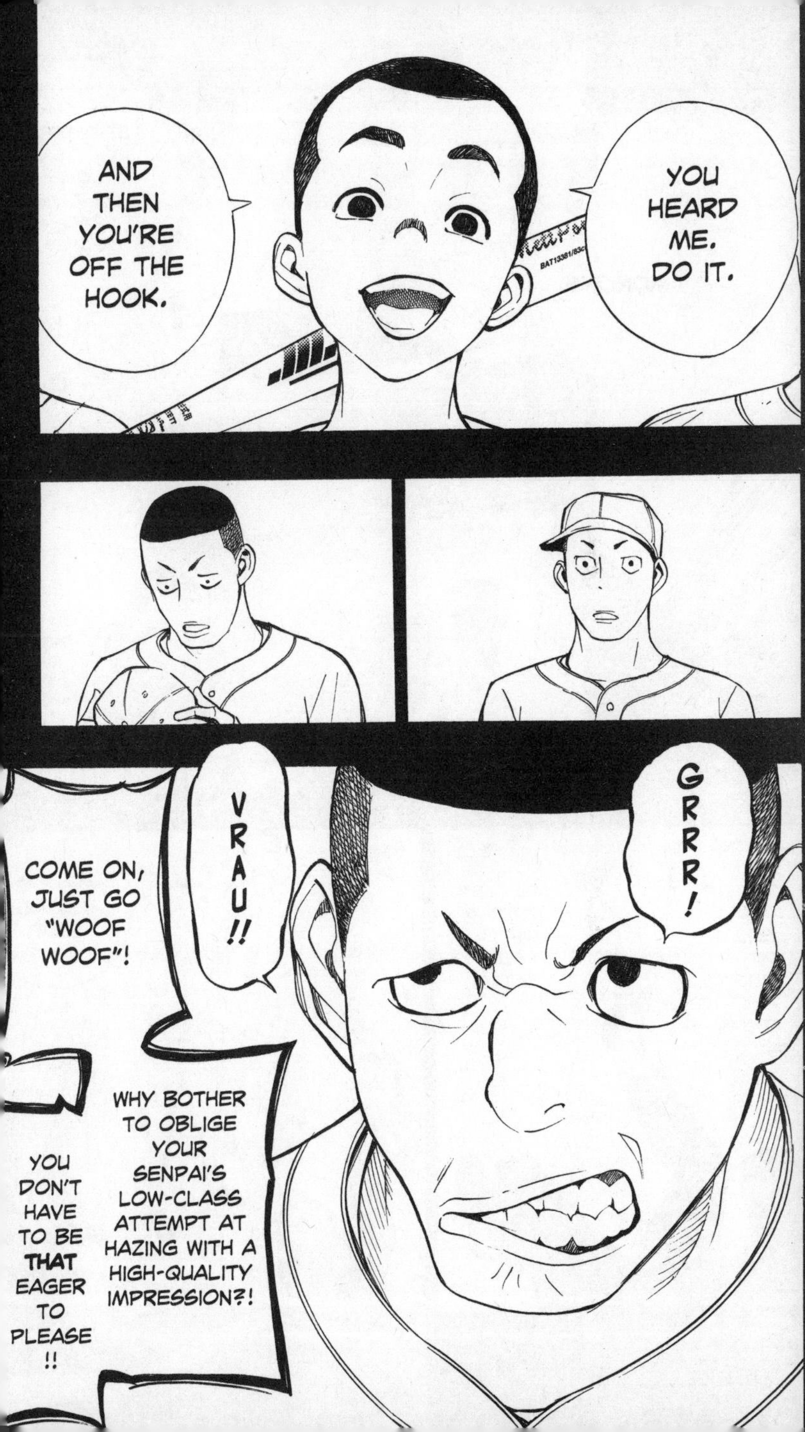
YOU HEARD ME. DO IT.
AND THEN YOU'RE OFF THE HOOK.
GRRR!
VRAU!!
COME ON, JUST GO "WOOF WOOF"!
WHY BOTHER TO OBLIGE YOUR SENPAI'S LOW-CLASS ATTEMPT AT HAZING WITH A HIGH-QUALITY IMPRESSION?!
YOU DON'T HAVE TO BE **THAT** EAGER TO PLEASE!!

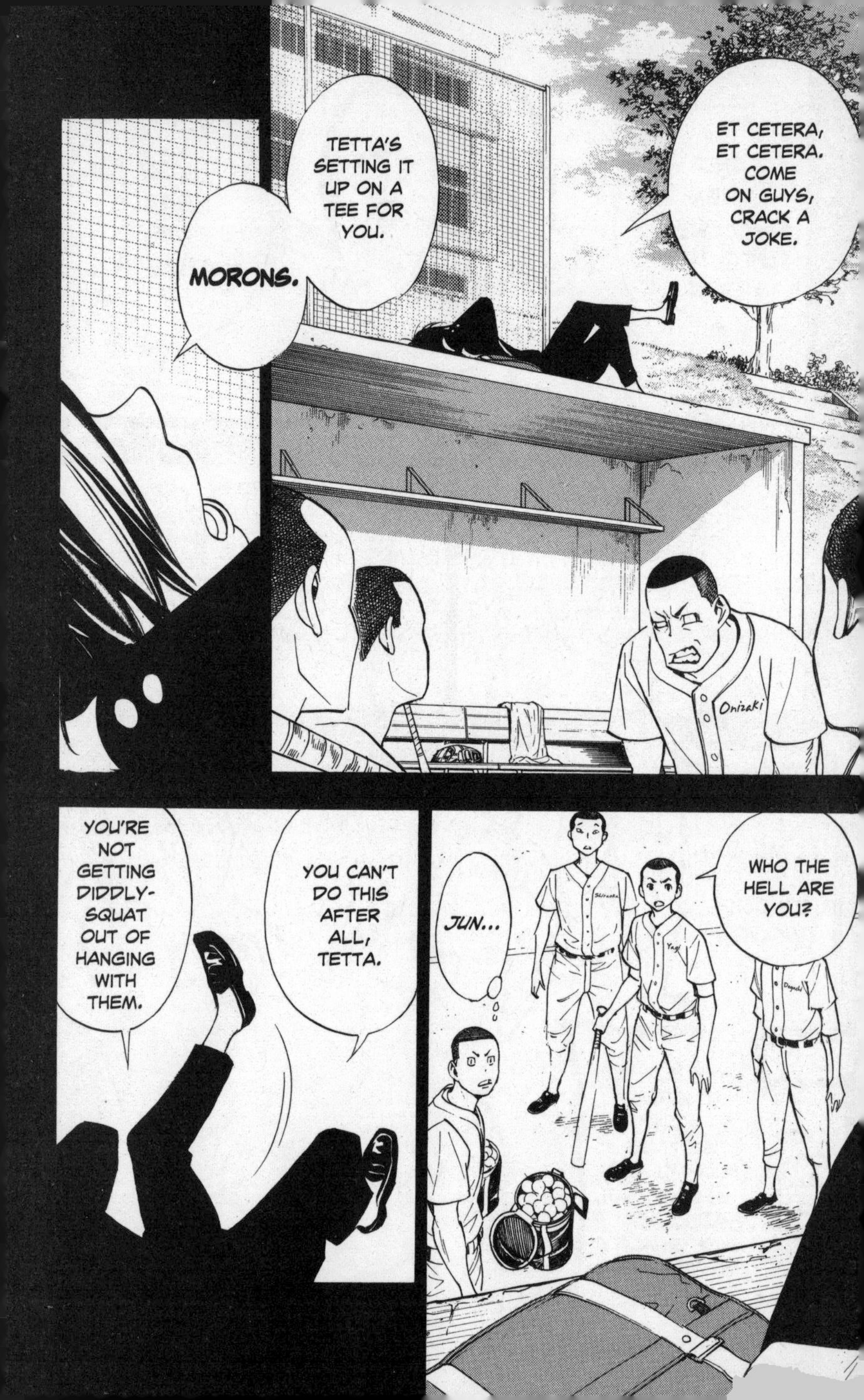
ET CETERA, ET CETERA. COME ON GUYS, CRACK A JOKE.
TETTA'S SETTING IT UP ON A TEE FOR YOU.
MORONS.
WHO THE HELL ARE YOU?
JUN...
YOU CAN'T DO THIS AFTER ALL, TETTA.
YOU'RE NOT GETTING DIDDLY-SQUAT OUT OF HANGING WITH THEM.

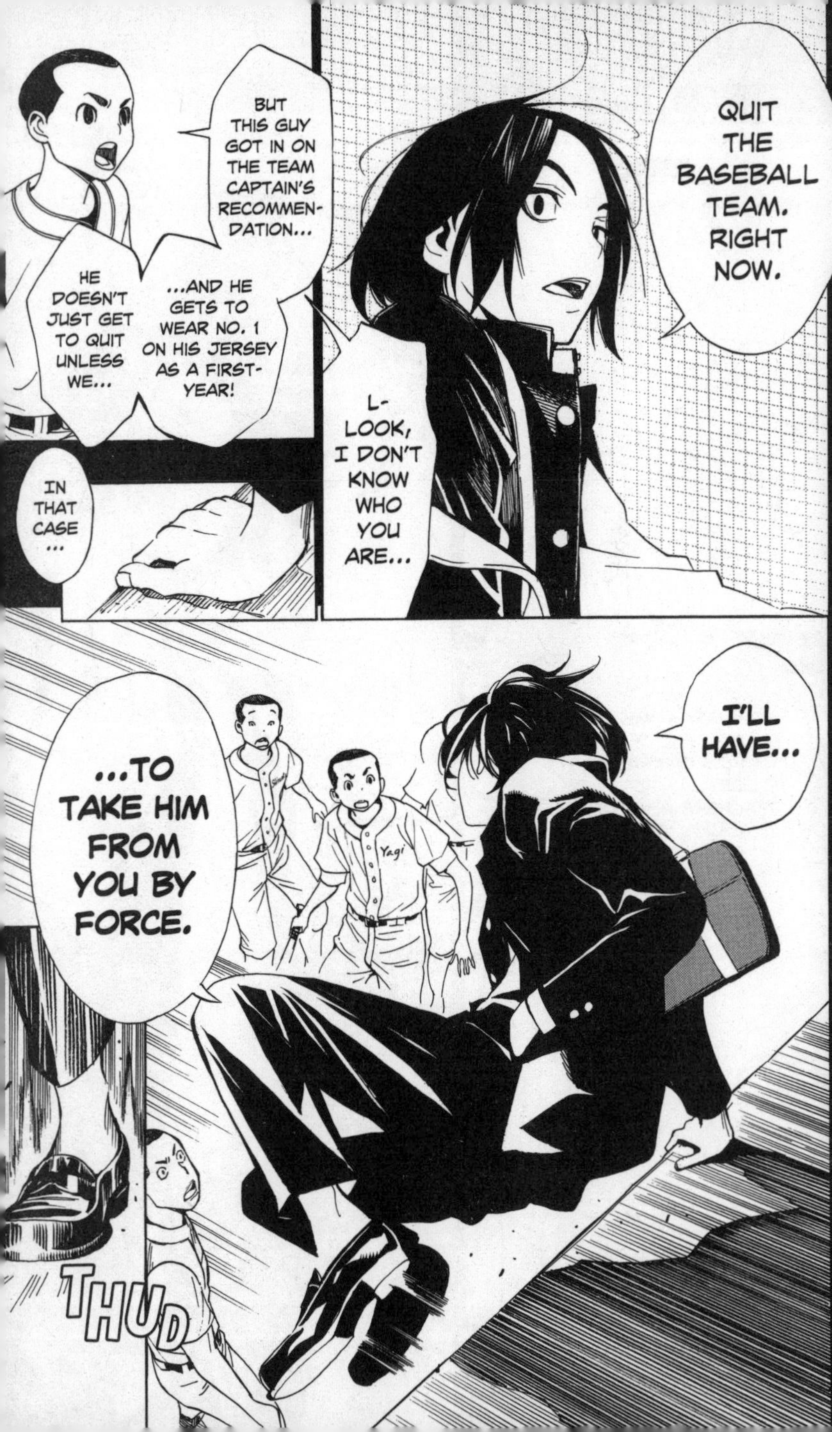
QUIT THE BASEBALL TEAM. RIGHT NOW.
L- LOOK, I DON'T KNOW WHO YOU ARE...
BUT THIS GUY GOT IN ON THE TEAM CAPTAIN'S RECOMMEN- DATION...
...AND HE GETS TO WEAR NO. 1 ON HIS JERSEY AS A FIRST- YEAR!
HE DOESN'T JUST GET TO QUIT UNLESS WE...
IN THAT CASE...
I'LL HAVE...
...TO TAKE HIM FROM YOU BY FORCE.
THUD

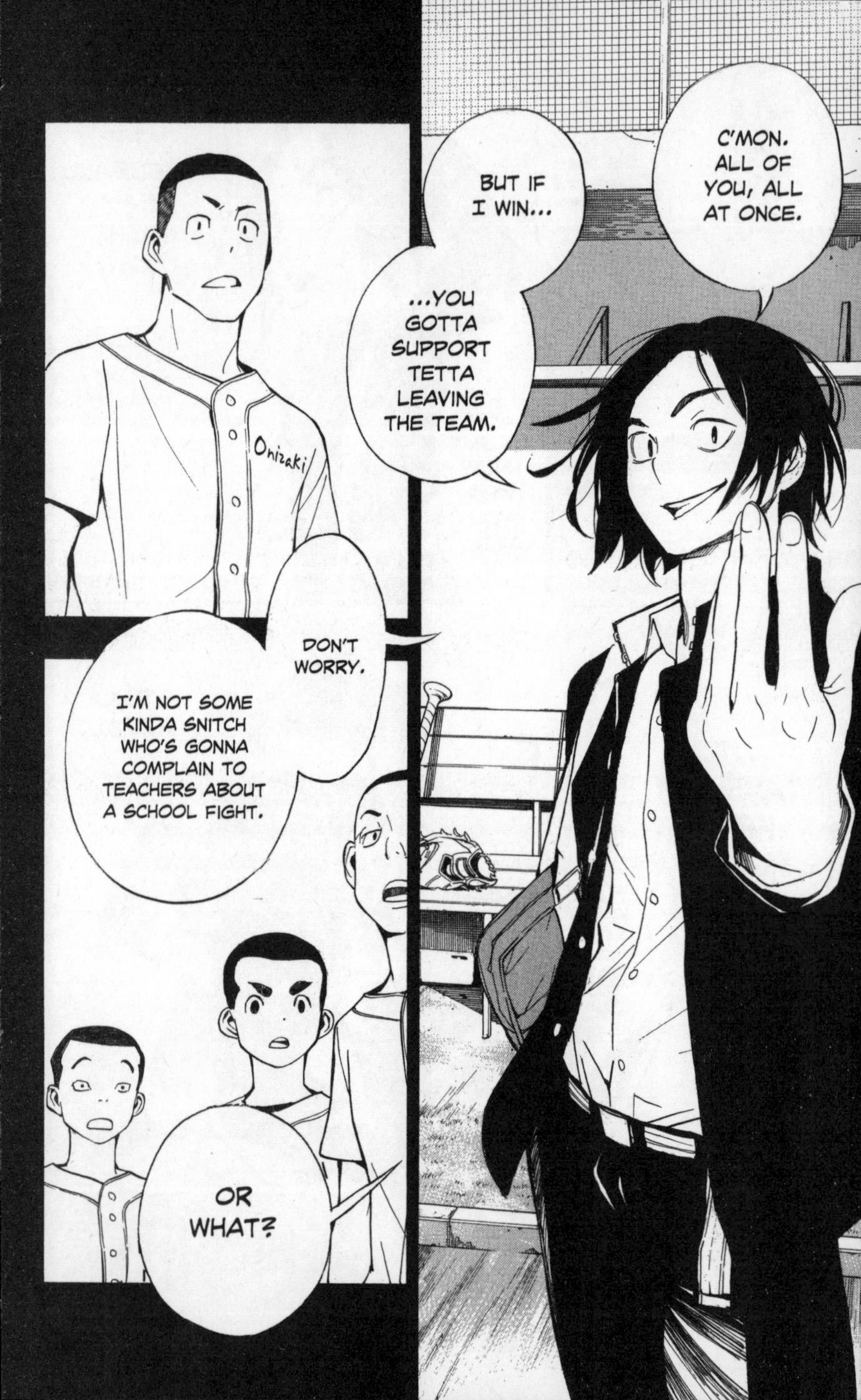
C'MON. ALL OF YOU, ALL AT ONCE.
BUT IF I WIN...
...YOU GOTTA SUPPORT TETTA LEAVING THE TEAM.
Onizaki
DON'T WORRY.
I'M NOT SOME KINDA SNITCH WHO'S GONNA COMPLAIN TO TEACHERS ABOUT A SCHOOL FIGHT.
OR WHAT?

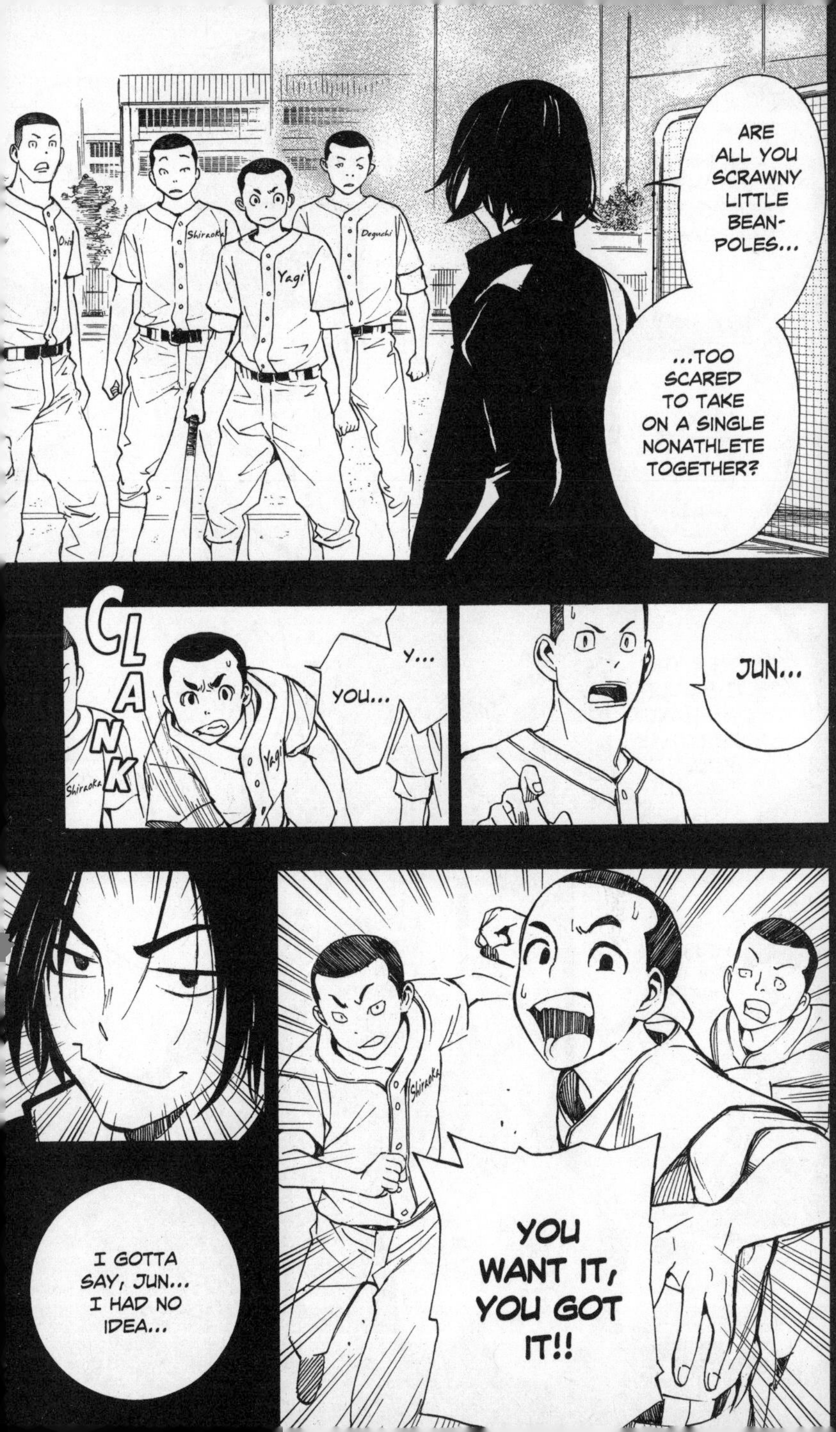
ARE ALL YOU SCRAWNY LITTLE BEAN-POLES...
...TOO SCARED TO TAKE ON A SINGLE NONATHLETE TOGETHER?
JUN...
Y... YOU...
CLANK
YOU WANT IT, YOU GOT IT!!
I GOTTA SAY, JUN... I HAD NO IDEA...

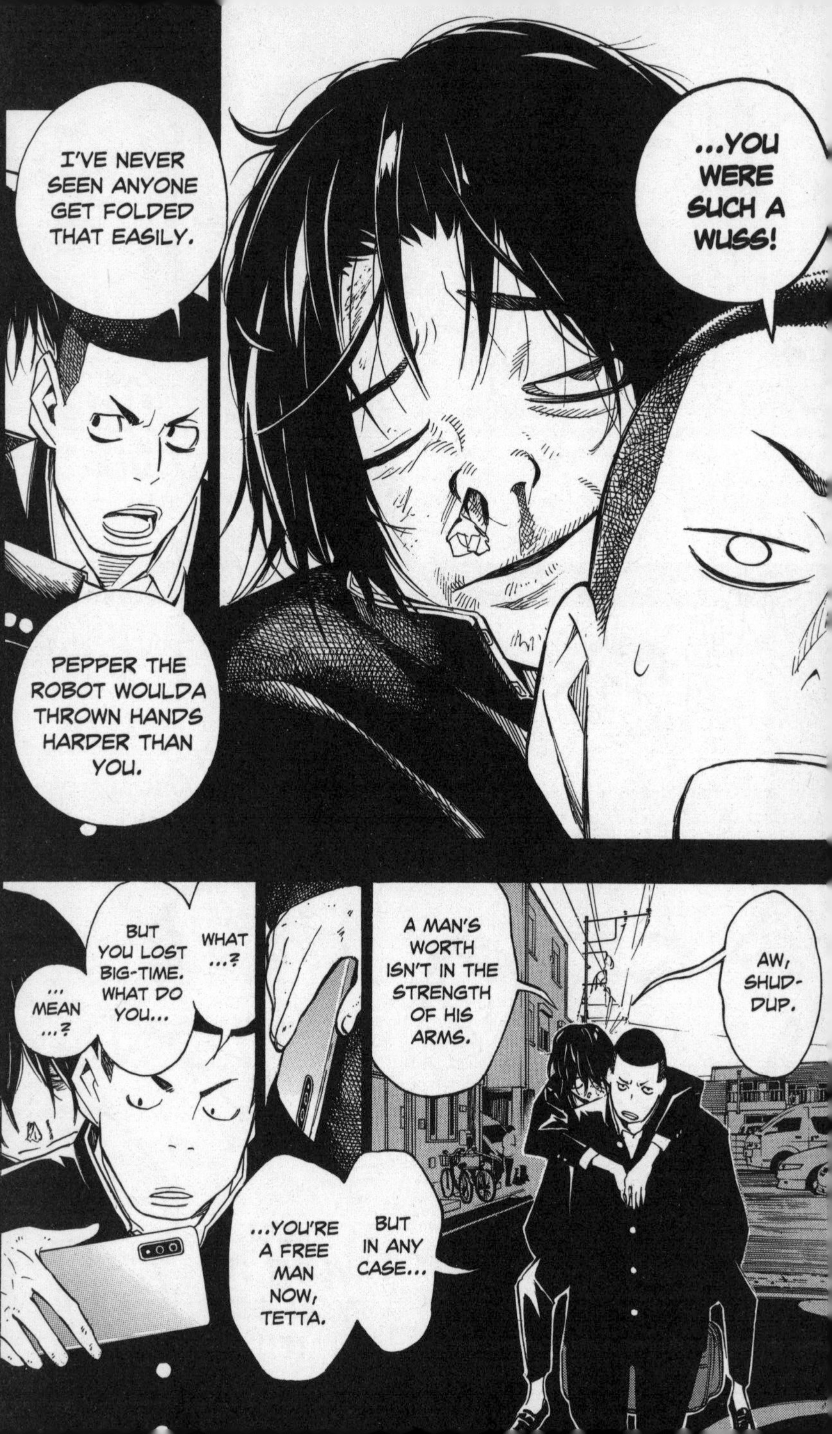
...YOU WERE SUCH A WUSS!
I'VE NEVER SEEN ANYONE GET FOLDED THAT EASILY.
PEPPER THE ROBOT WOULDA THROWN HANDS HARDER THAN YOU.
AW, SHUDDUP.
A MAN'S WORTH ISN'T IN THE STRENGTH OF HIS ARMS.
BUT IN ANY CASE...
...YOU'RE A FREE MAN NOW, TETTA.
BUT YOU LOST BIG-TIME. WHAT DO YOU...
... MEAN ...?
WHAT ...?

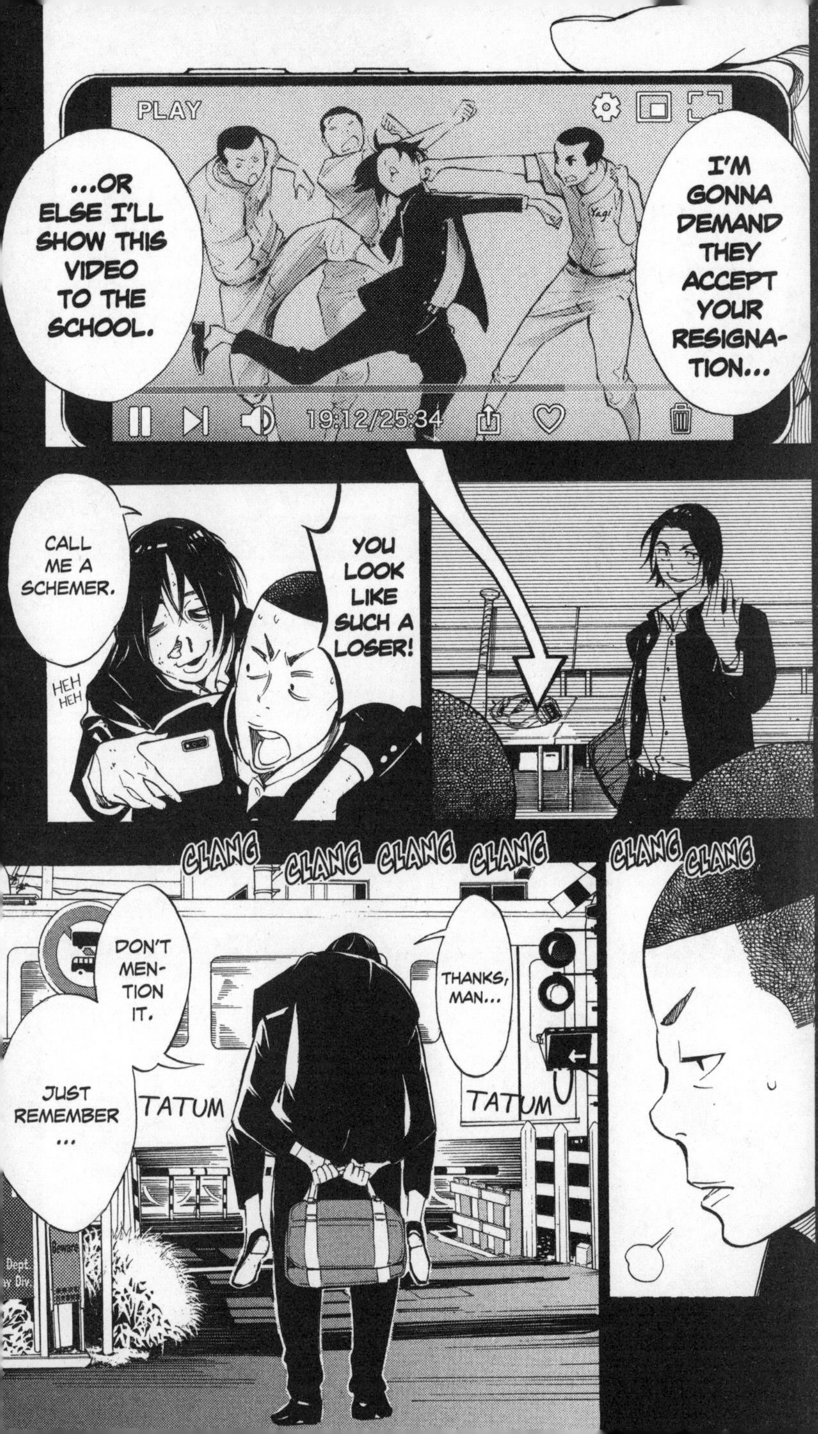
I'M GONNA DEMAND THEY ACCEPT YOUR RESIGNATION...
PLAY
19:12/25:34
...OR ELSE I'LL SHOW THIS VIDEO TO THE SCHOOL.
YOU LOOK LIKE SUCH A LOSER!
CALL ME A SCHEMER.
HEH HEH
CLANG CLANG
CLANG CLANG CLANG CLANG
THANKS, MAN...
TATUM
DON'T MENTION IT.
JUST REMEMBER...
TATUM

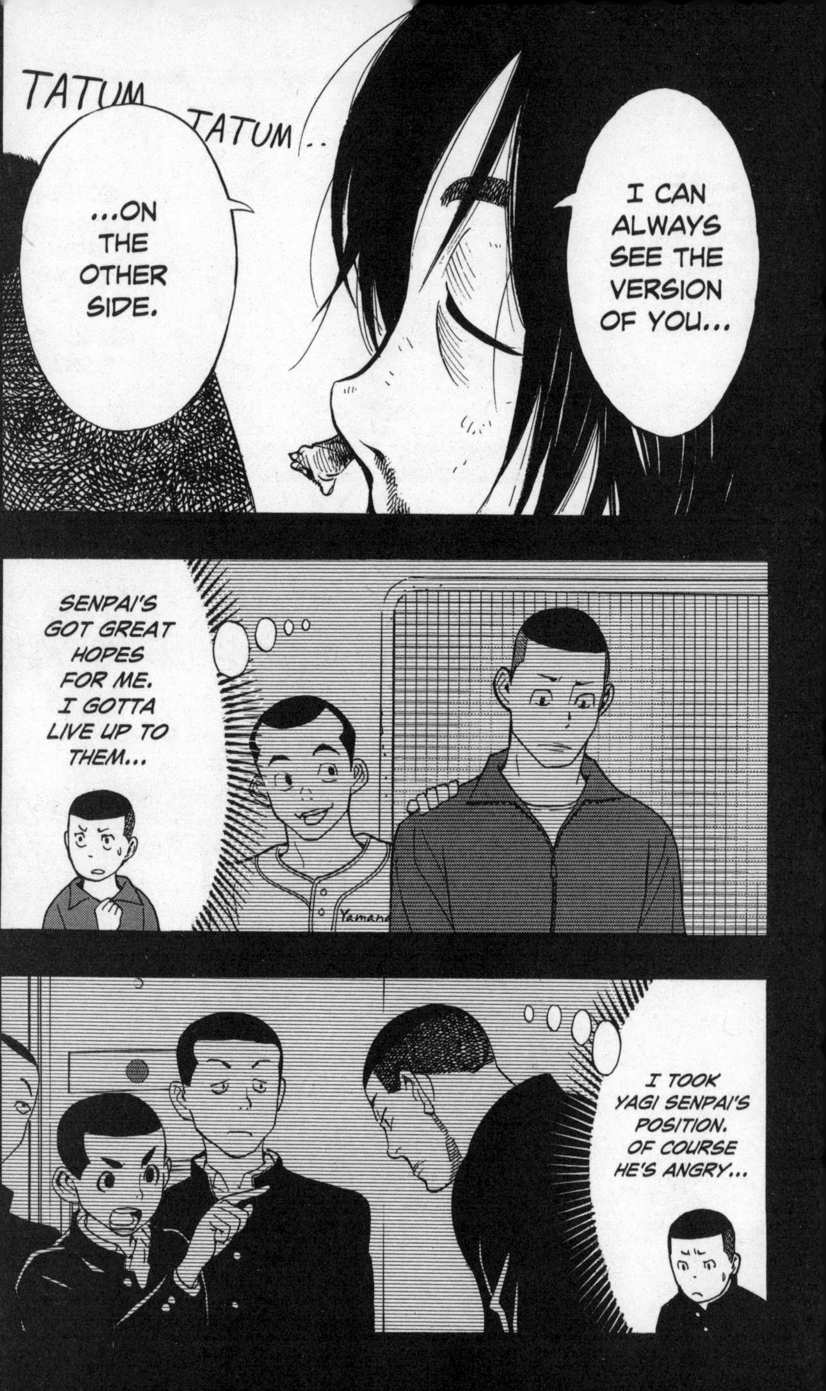
I CAN ALWAYS SEE THE VERSION OF YOU...
TATUM TATUM...
...ON THE OTHER SIDE.
SENPAI'S GOT GREAT HOPES FOR ME. I GOTTA LIVE UP TO THEM...
Yamana
I TOOK YAGI SENPAI'S POSITION. OF COURSE HE'S ANGRY...

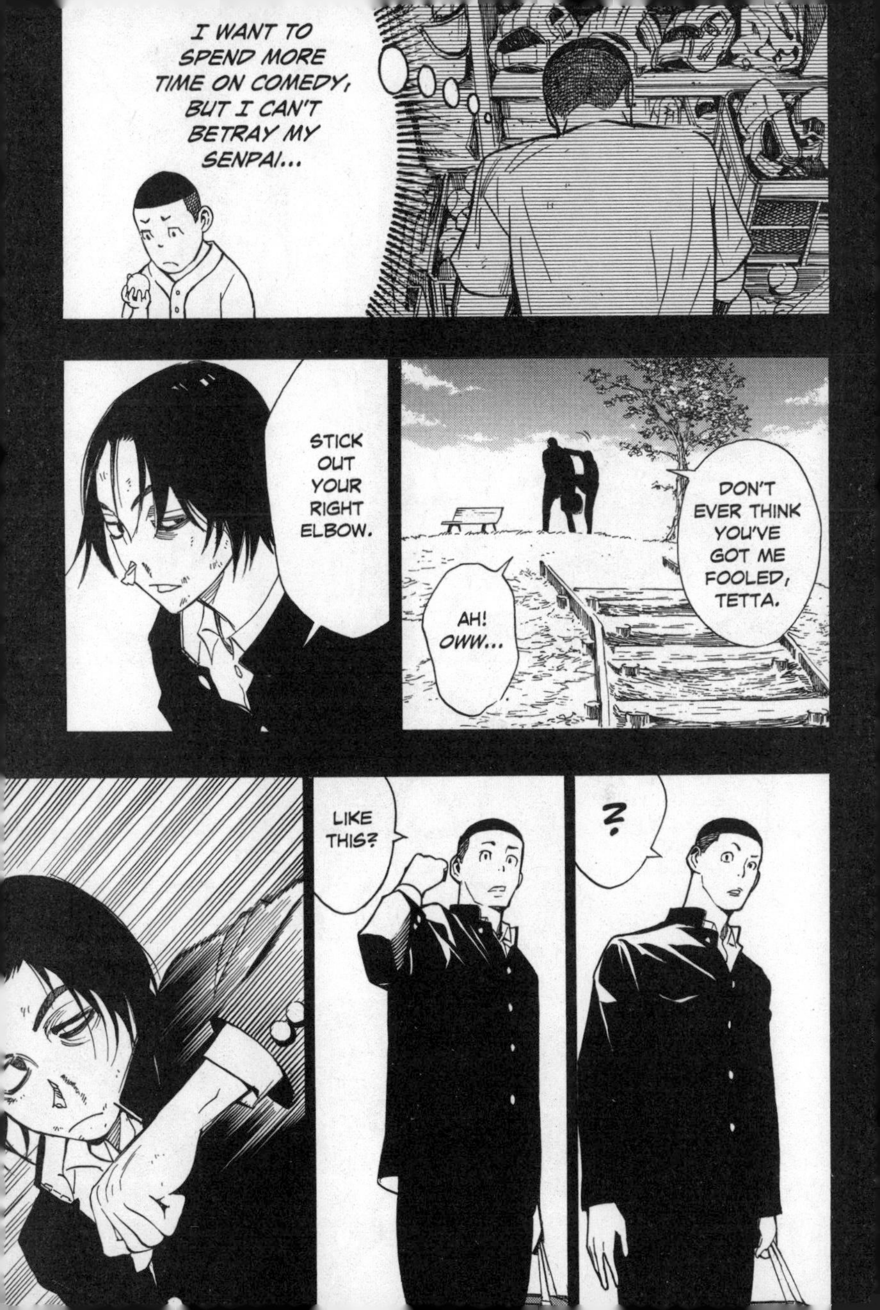
I WANT TO SPEND MORE TIME ON COMEDY, BUT I CAN'T BETRAY MY SENPAI...
DON'T EVER THINK YOU'VE GOT ME FOOLED, TETTA.
AH! OWW...
STICK OUT YOUR RIGHT ELBOW.
?
LIKE THIS?

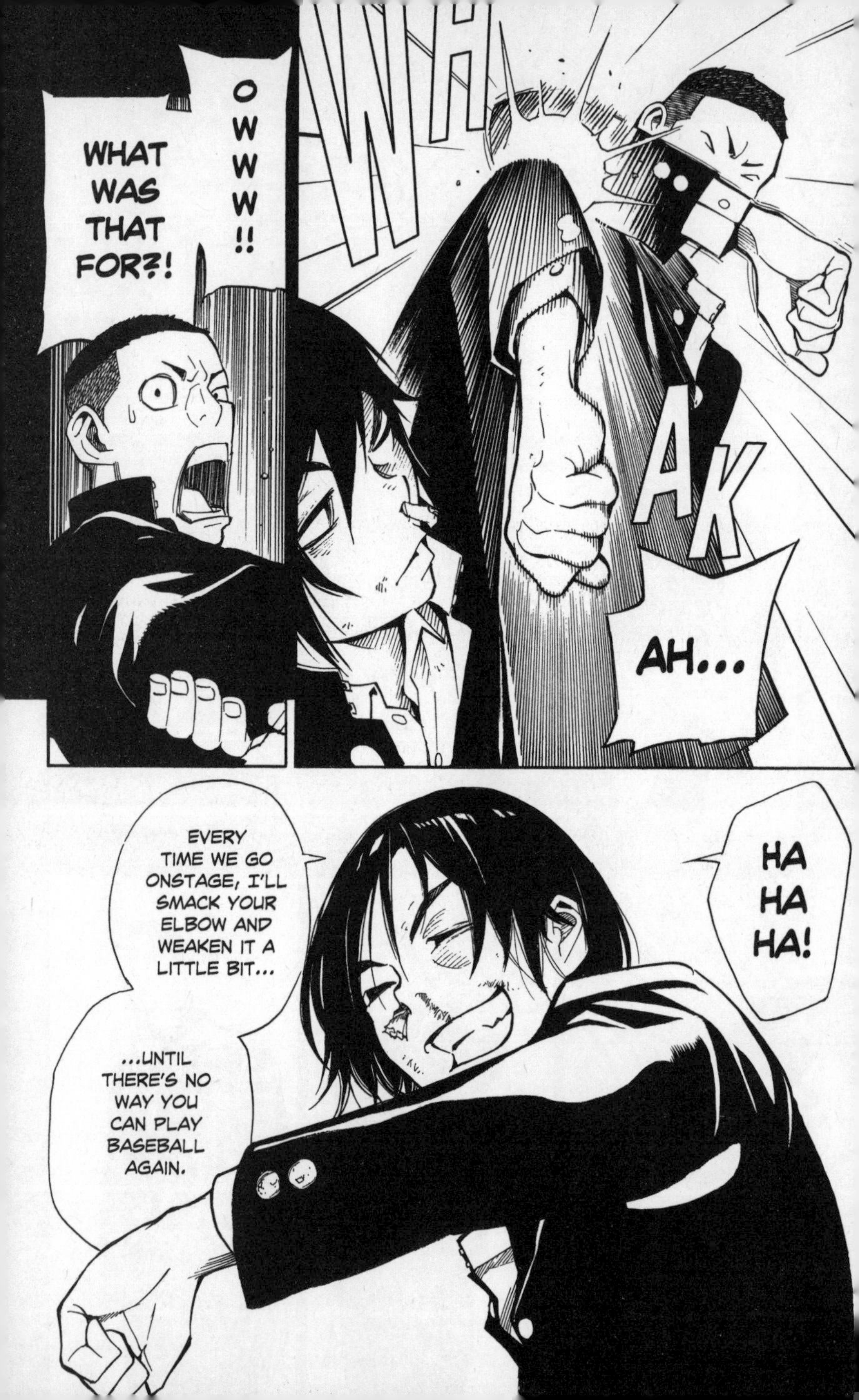
WHA
AK
AH...
OWWW!!
WHAT WAS THAT FOR?!
HA HA HA!
EVERY TIME WE GO ONSTAGE, I'LL SMACK YOUR ELBOW AND WEAKEN IT A LITTLE BIT...
...UNTIL THERE'S NO WAY YOU CAN PLAY BASEBALL AGAIN.

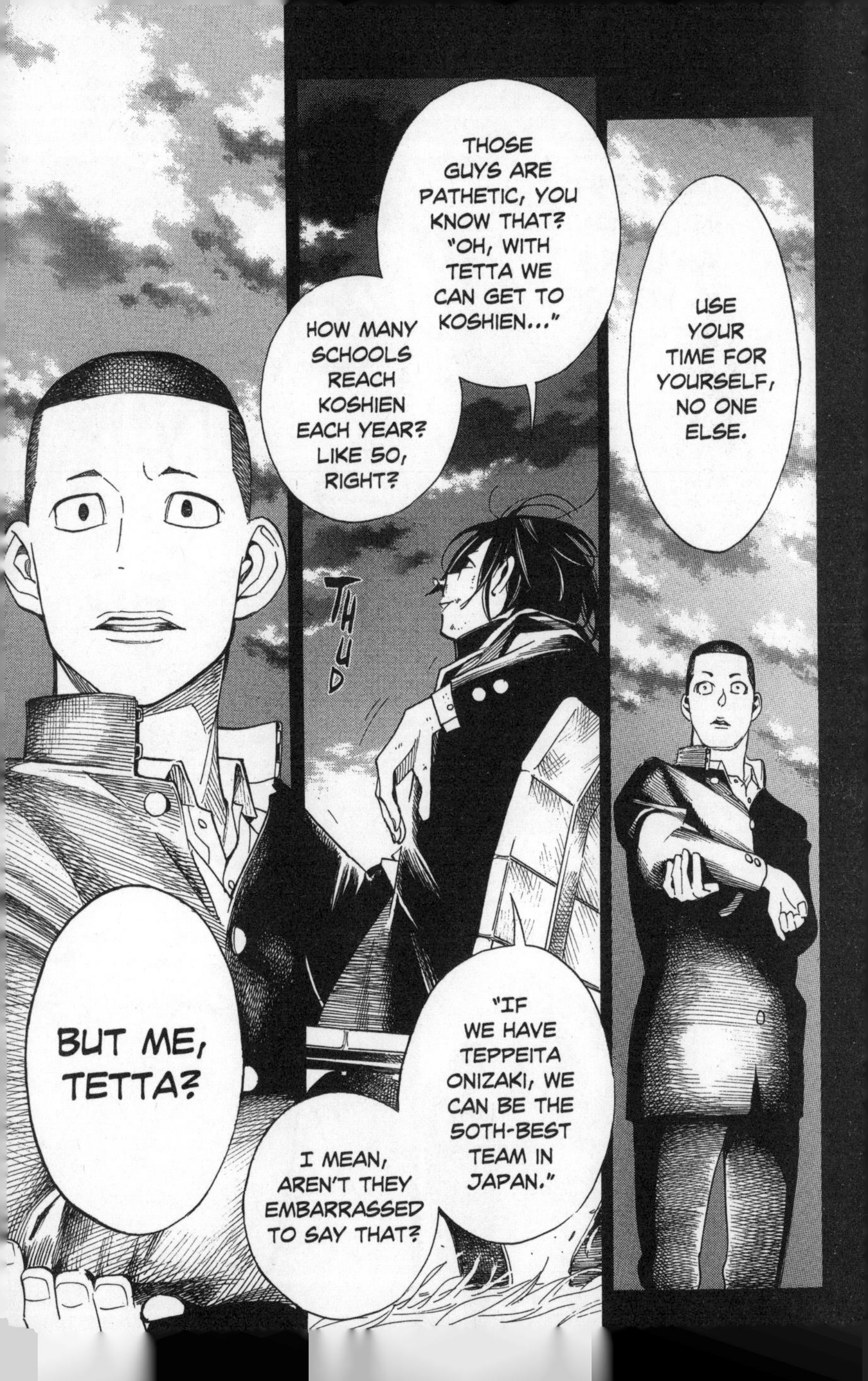
USE YOUR TIME FOR YOURSELF, NO ONE ELSE.
THOSE GUYS ARE PATHETIC, YOU KNOW THAT? "OH, WITH TETTA WE CAN GET TO KOSHIEN..."
HOW MANY SCHOOLS REACH KOSHIEN EACH YEAR? LIKE 50, RIGHT?
THUD
"IF WE HAVE TEPPEITA ONIZAKI, WE CAN BE THE 50TH-BEST TEAM IN JAPAN."
I MEAN, AREN'T THEY EMBARRASSED TO SAY THAT?
BUT ME, TETTA?

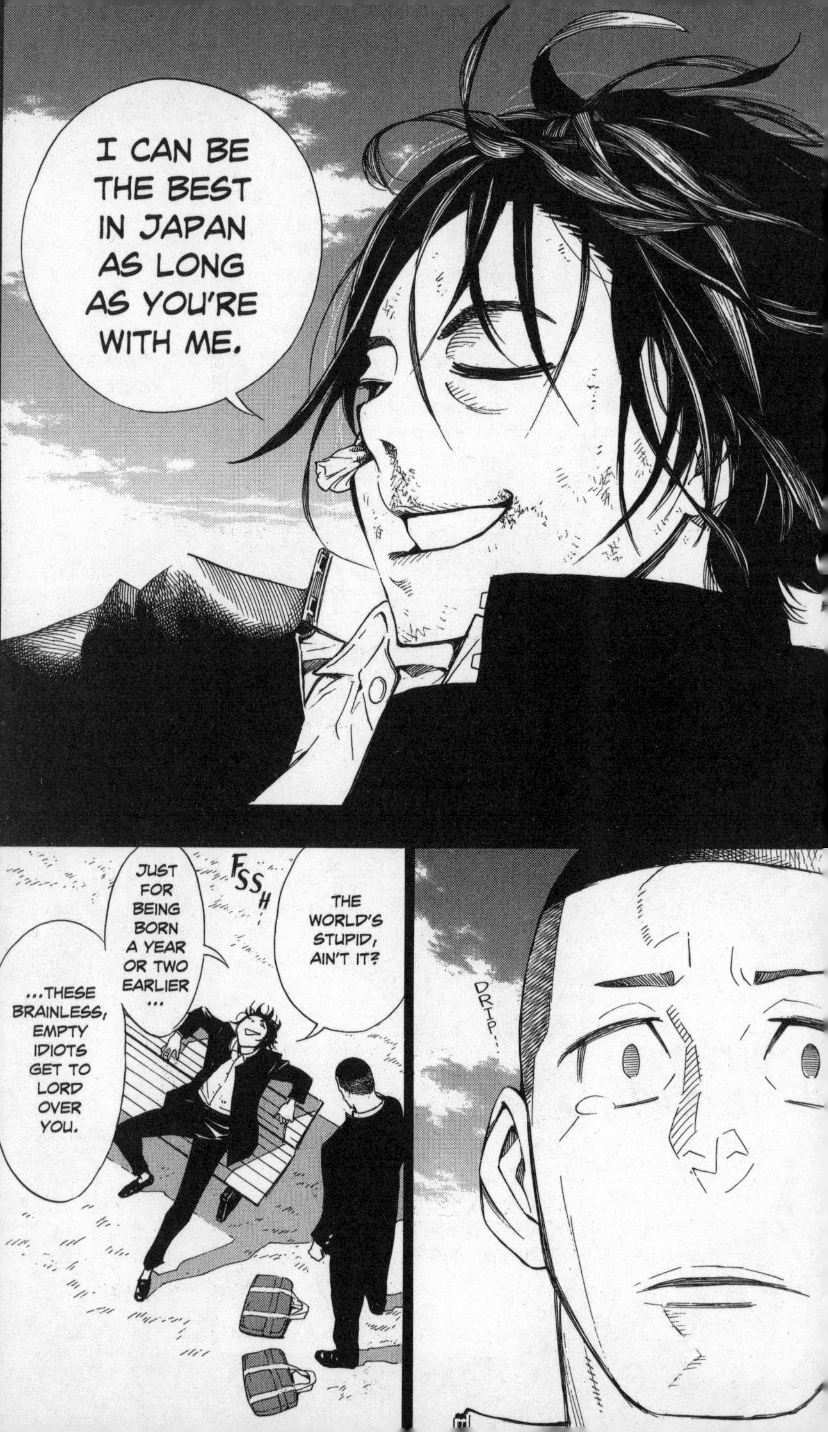
I CAN BE THE BEST IN JAPAN AS LONG AS YOU'RE WITH ME.
DRIP...
THE WORLD'S STUPID, AIN'T IT?
FSSH
JUST FOR BEING BORN A YEAR OR TWO EARLIER...
...THESE BRAINLESS, EMPTY IDIOTS GET TO LORD OVER YOU.

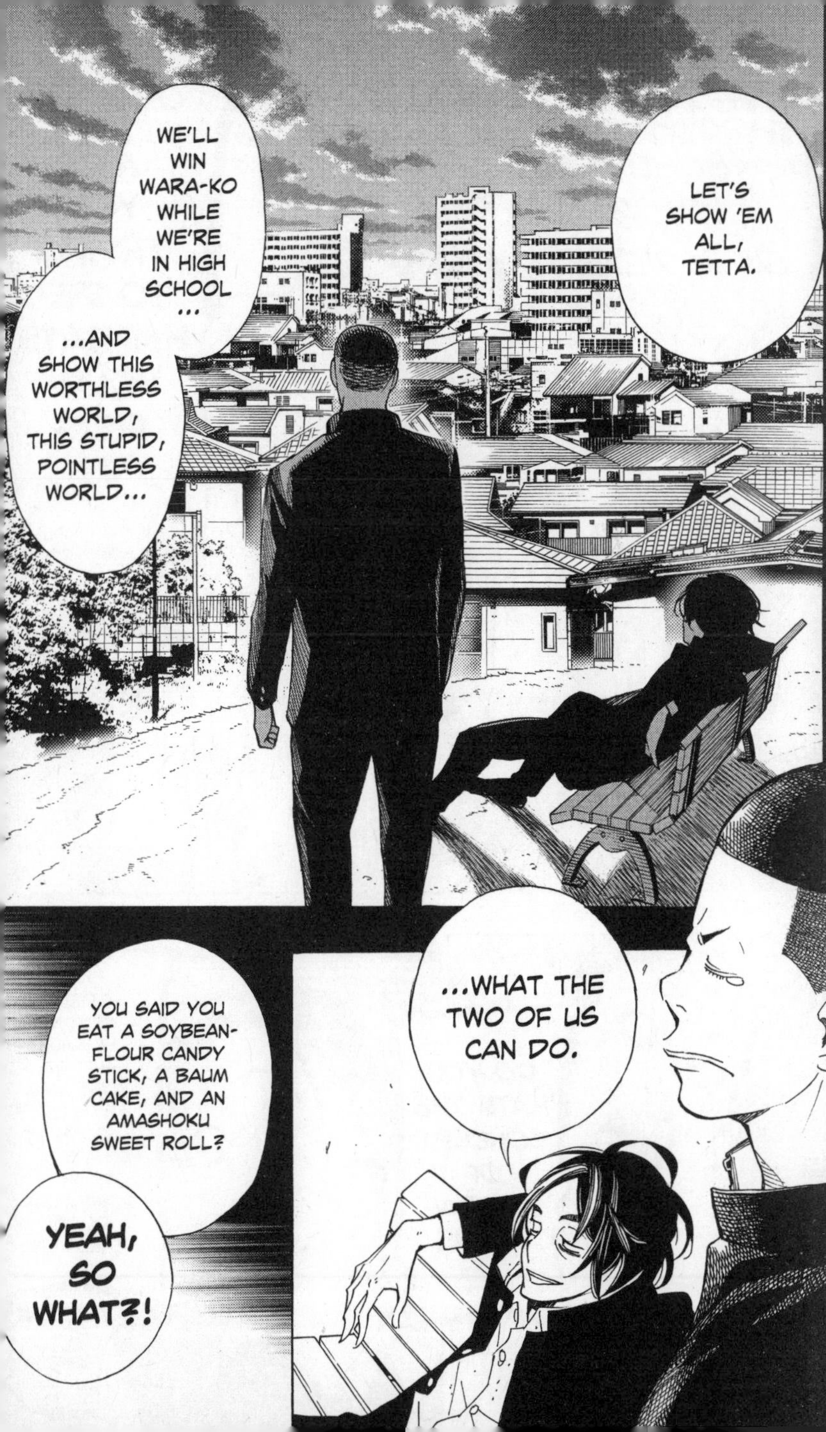
LET'S SHOW 'EM ALL, TETTA.
WE'LL WIN WARA-KO WHILE WE'RE IN HIGH SCHOOL...
...AND SHOW THIS WORTHLESS WORLD, THIS STUPID, POINTLESS WORLD...
...WHAT THE TWO OF US CAN DO.
YOU SAID YOU EAT A SOYBEAN-FLOUR CANDY STICK, A BAUM CAKE, AND AN AMASHOKU SWEET ROLL?
YEAH, SO WHAT?!

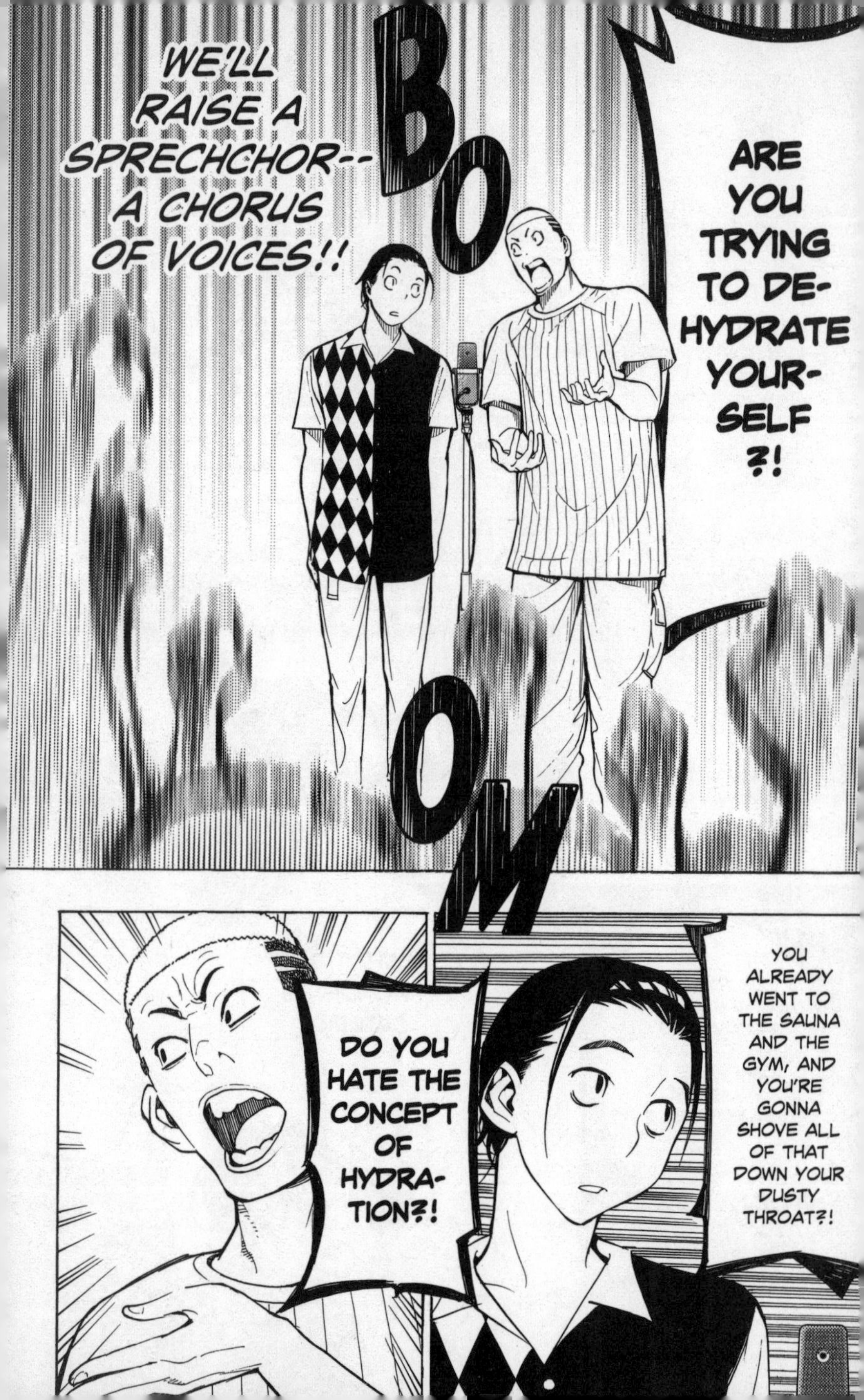
WE'LL RAISE A SPRECHCHOR-- A CHORUS OF VOICES!!
BOOM
ARE YOU TRYING TO DE-HYDRATE YOUR-SELF?!
YOU ALREADY WENT TO THE SAUNA AND THE GYM, AND YOU'RE GONNA SHOVE ALL OF THAT DOWN YOUR DUSTY THROAT?!
DO YOU HATE THE CONCEPT OF HYDRA-TION?!

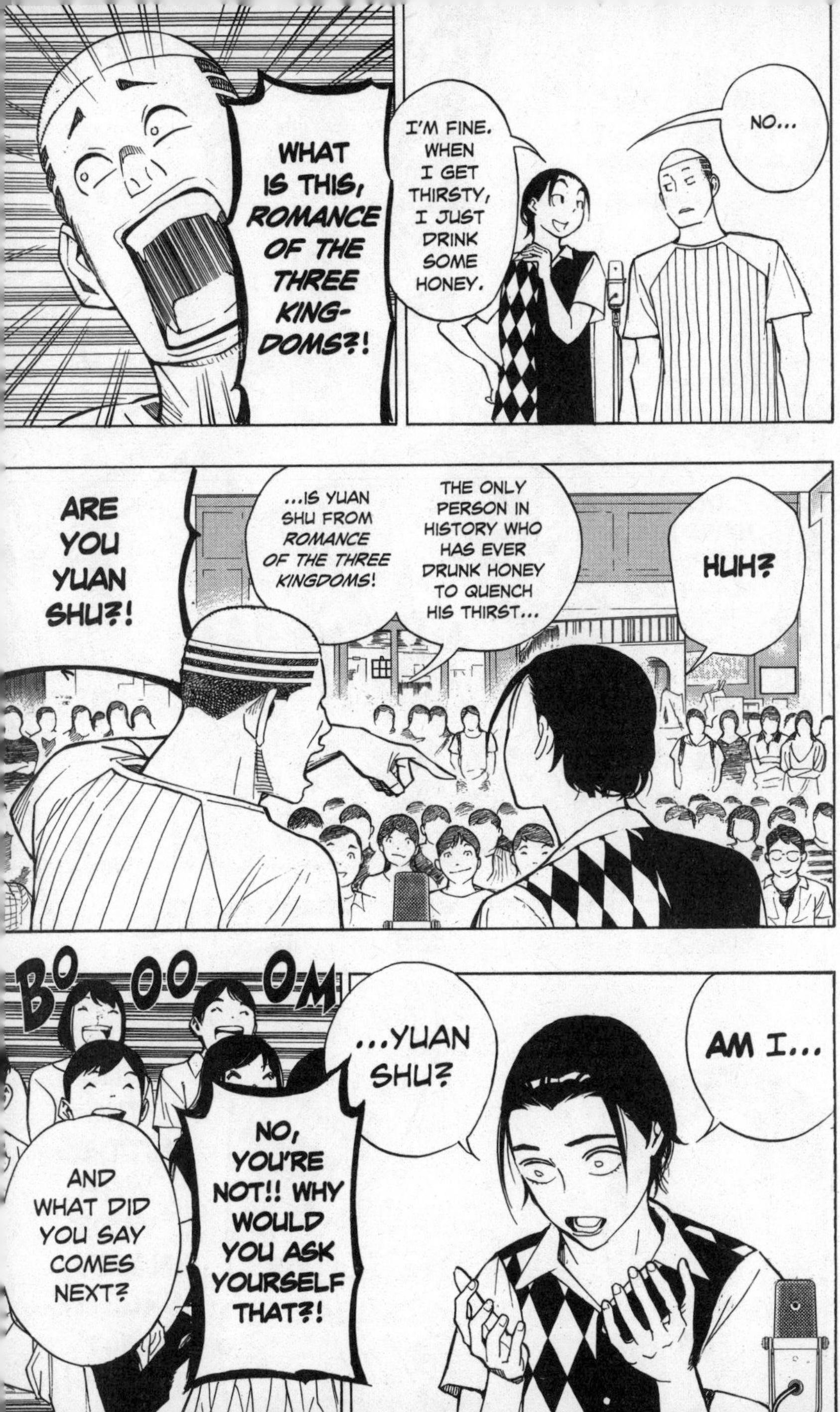
NO...
I'M FINE. WHEN I GET THIRSTY, I JUST DRINK SOME HONEY.
WHAT IS THIS, ROMANCE OF THE THREE KINGDOMS?!
HUH?
THE ONLY PERSON IN HISTORY WHO HAS EVER DRUNK HONEY TO QUENCH HIS THIRST...
...IS YUAN SHU FROM ROMANCE OF THE THREE KINGDOMS!
ARE YOU YUAN SHU?!
AM I...
...YUAN SHU?
BOOOOM
NO, YOU'RE NOT!! WHY WOULD YOU ASK YOURSELF THAT?!
AND WHAT DID YOU SAY COMES NEXT?

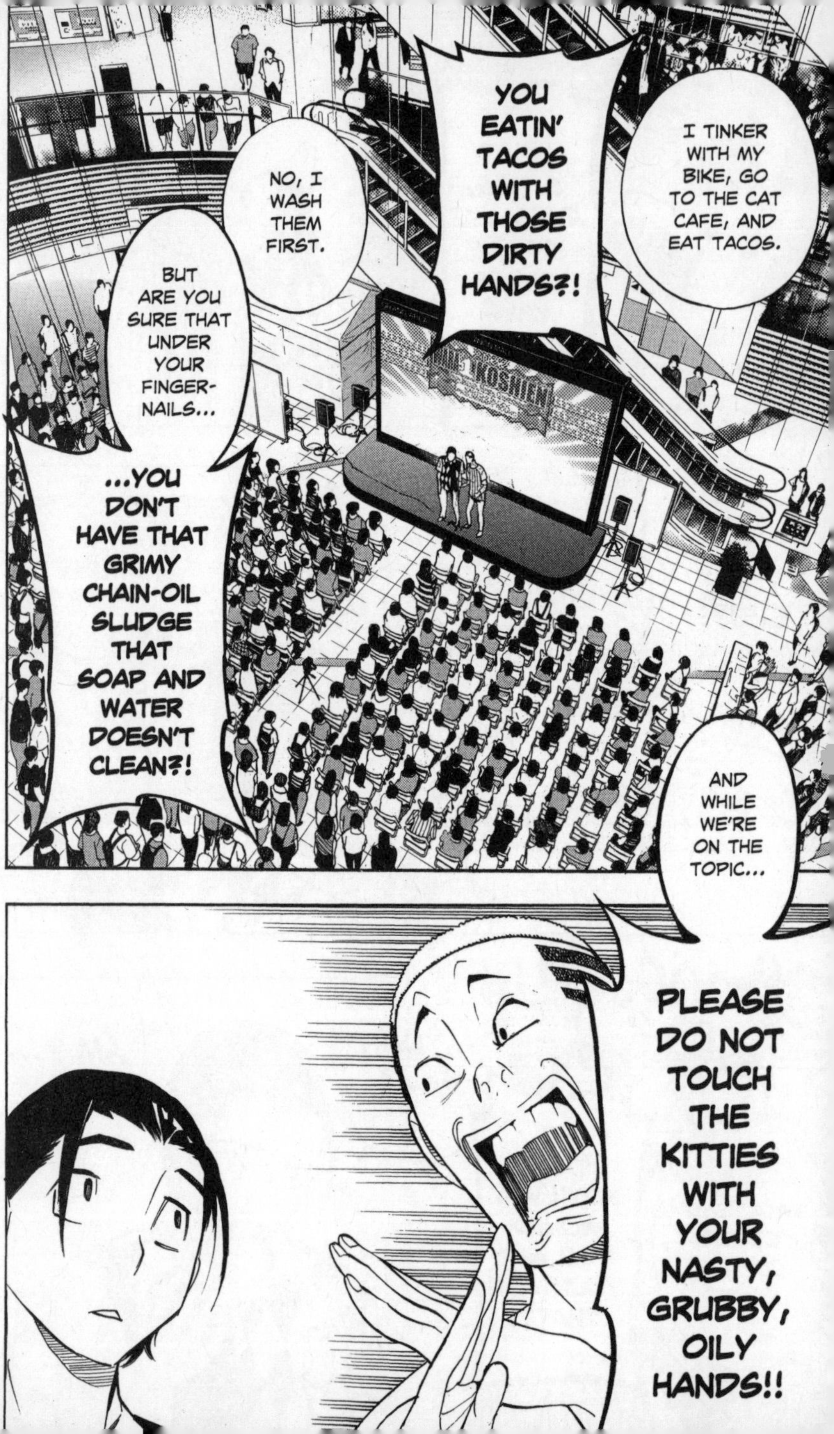
I TINKER WITH MY BIKE, GO TO THE CAT CAFE, AND EAT TACOS.
YOU EATIN' TACOS WITH THOSE DIRTY HANDS?!
NO, I WASH THEM FIRST.
BUT ARE YOU SURE THAT UNDER YOUR FINGER-NAILS...
...YOU DON'T HAVE THAT GRIMY CHAIN-OIL SLUDGE THAT SOAP AND WATER DOESN'T CLEAN?!
AND WHILE WE'RE ON THE TOPIC...
PLEASE DO NOT TOUCH THE KITTIES WITH YOUR NASTY, GRUBBY, OILY HANDS!!

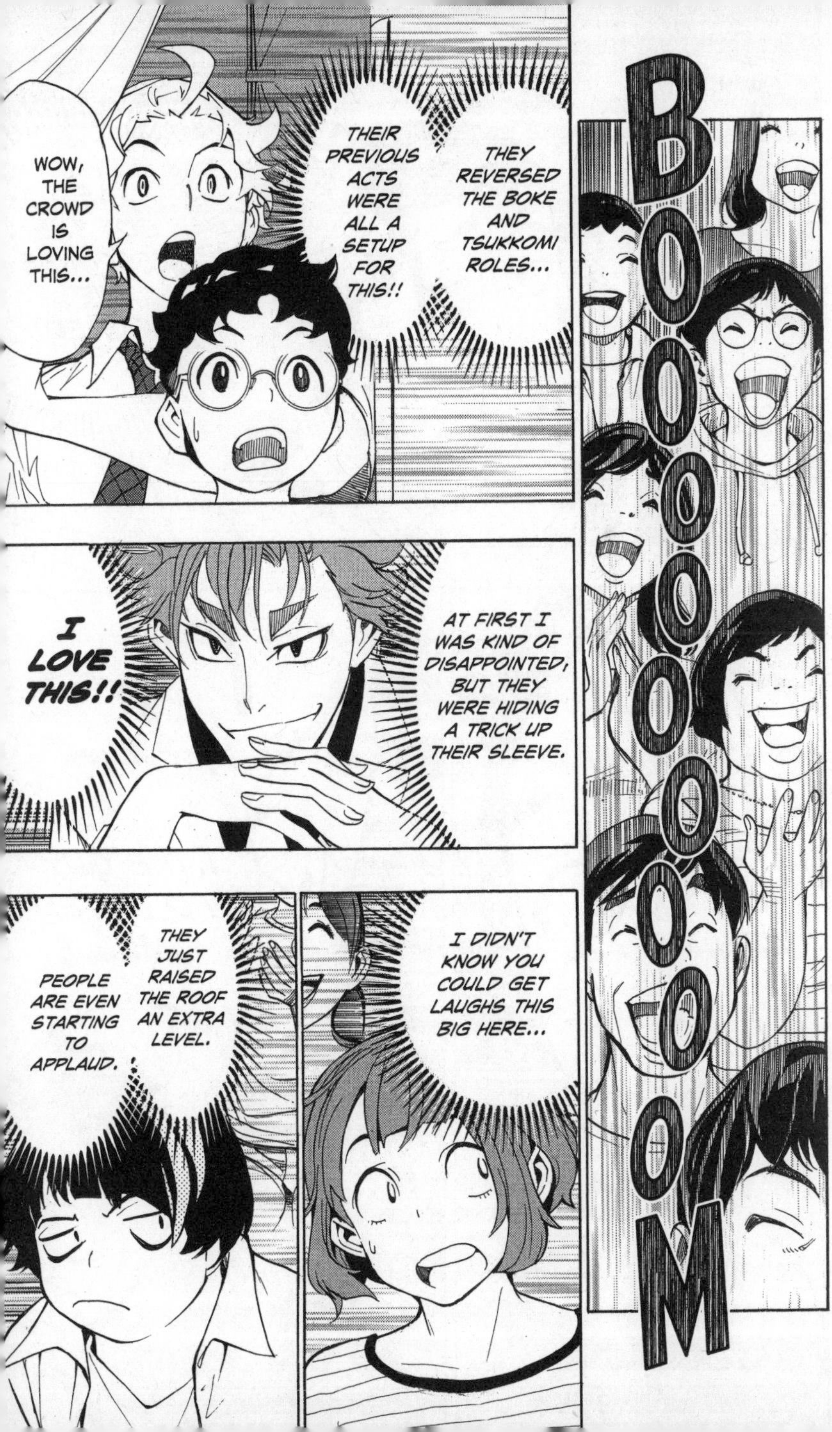
BOOOOOOOOOM
THEY REVERSED THE BOKE AND TSUKKOMI ROLES...
THEIR PREVIOUS ACTS WERE ALL A SETUP FOR THIS!!
WOW, THE CROWD IS LOVING THIS...
AT FIRST I WAS KIND OF DISAPPOINTED, BUT THEY WERE HIDING A TRICK UP THEIR SLEEVE.
I LOVE THIS!!
I DIDN'T KNOW YOU COULD GET LAUGHS THIS BIG HERE...
THEY JUST RAISED THE ROOF AN EXTRA LEVEL.
PEOPLE ARE EVEN STARTING TO APPLAUD.

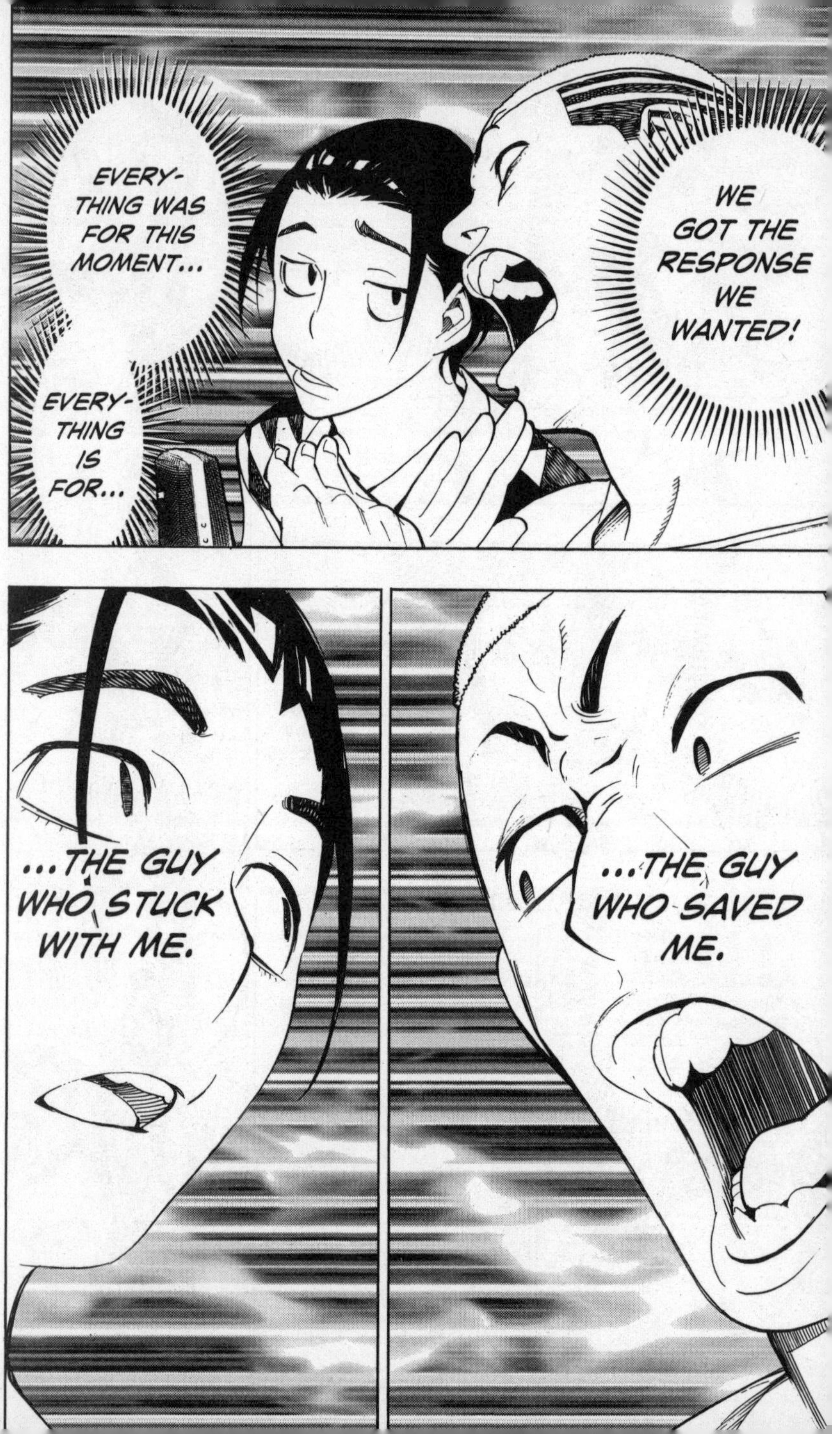

WE GOT THE RESPONSE WE WANTED!
EVERYTHING WAS FOR THIS MOMENT...
EVERYTHING IS FOR...
...THE GUY WHO SAVED ME.
...THE GUY WHO STUCK WITH ME.

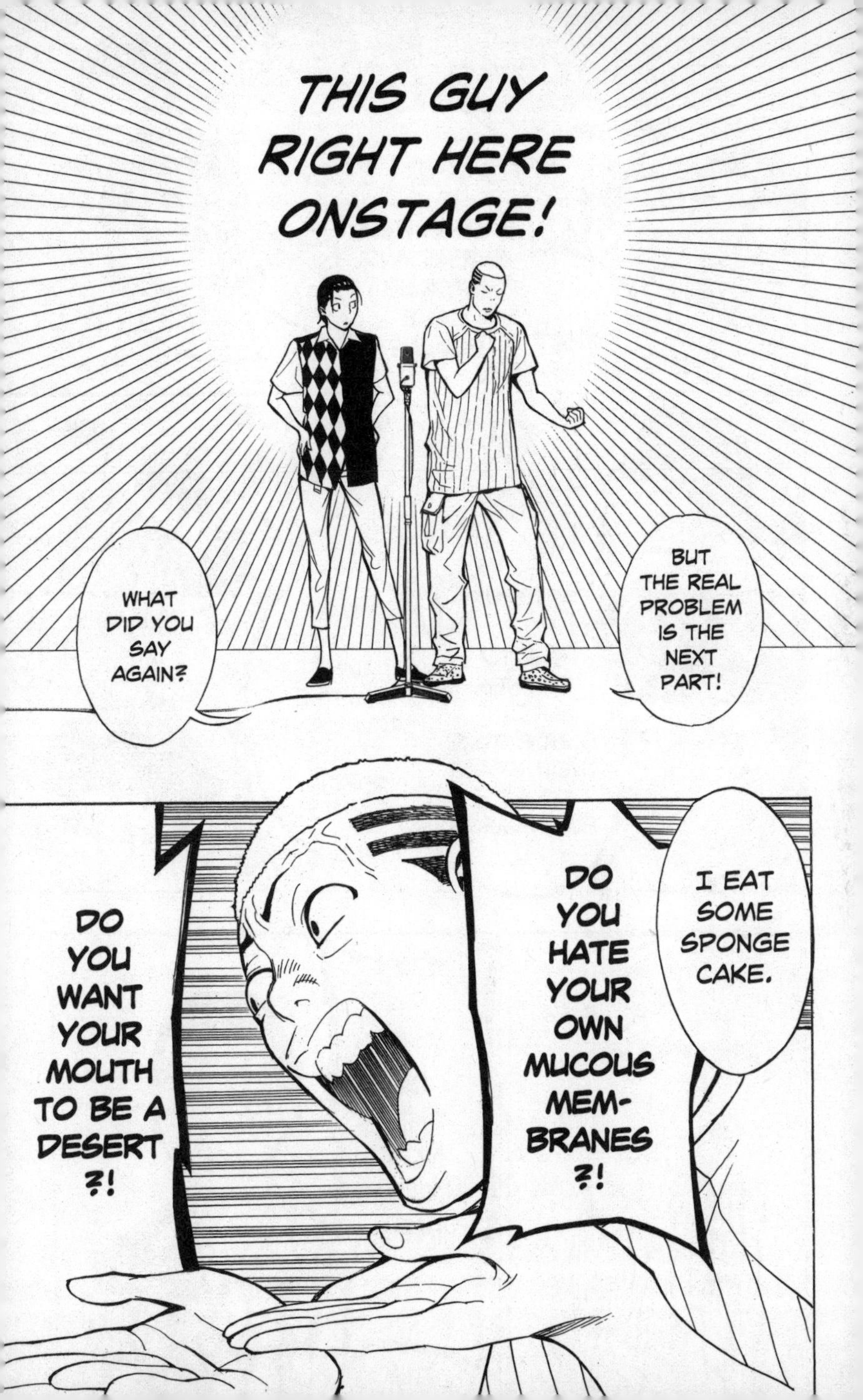
THIS GUY RIGHT HERE ONSTAGE!
BUT THE REAL PROBLEM IS THE NEXT PART!
WHAT DID YOU SAY AGAIN?
I EAT SOME SPONGE CAKE.
DO YOU HATE YOUR OWN MUCOUS MEM-BRANES?!
DO YOU WANT YOUR MOUTH TO BE A DESERT?!

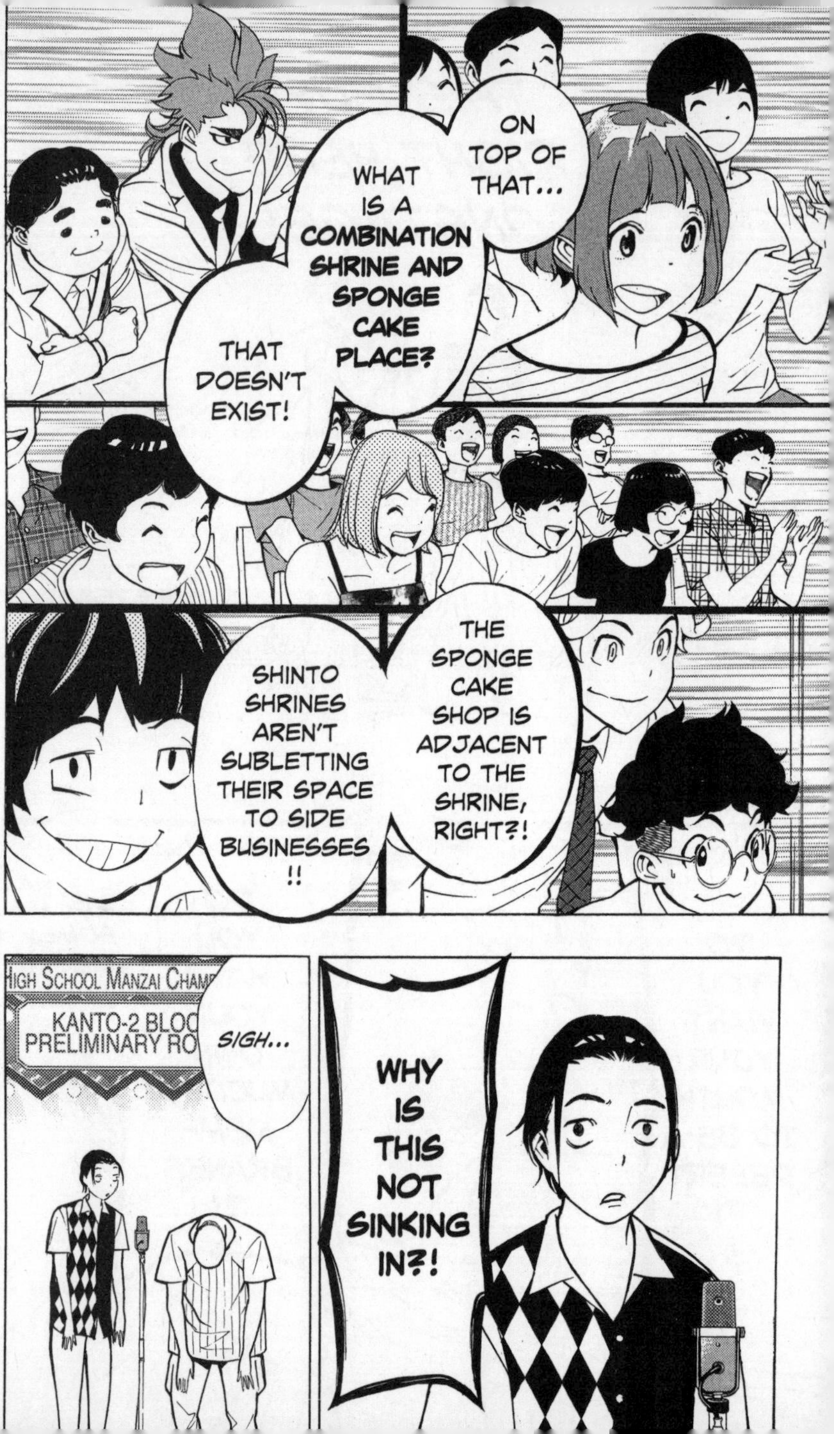
ON TOP OF THAT...
WHAT IS A COMBINATION SHRINE AND SPONGE CAKE PLACE?
THAT DOESN'T EXIST!
THE SPONGE CAKE SHOP IS ADJACENT TO THE SHRINE, RIGHT?!
SHINTO SHRINES AREN'T SUBLETTING THEIR SPACE TO SIDE BUSINESSES!!
WHY IS THIS NOT SINKING IN?!
HIGH SCHOOL MANZAI
KANTO-2
PRELIMINARY
SIGH...

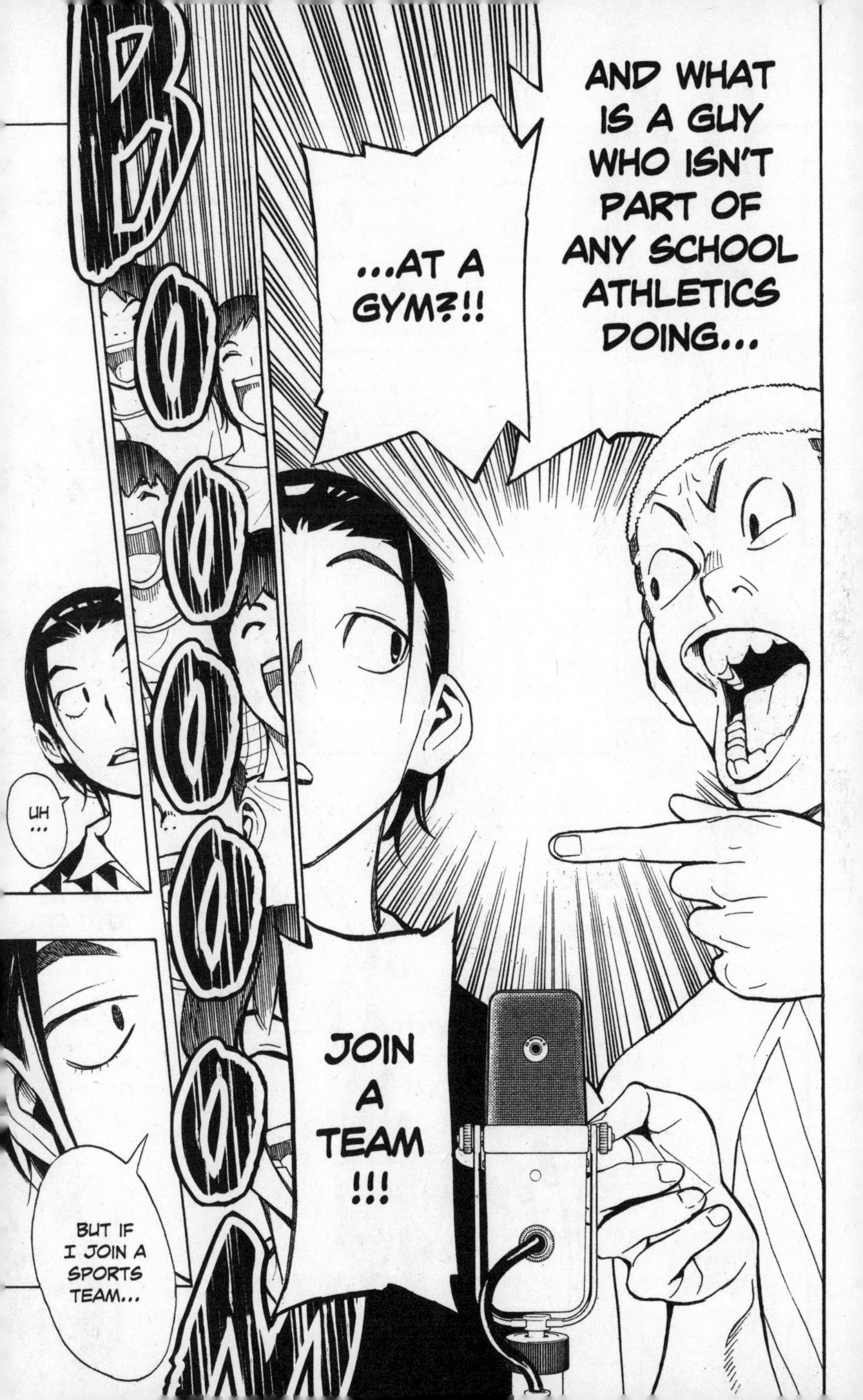
AND WHAT IS A GUY WHO ISN'T PART OF ANY SCHOOL ATHLETICS DOING...
...AT A GYM?!!
JOIN A TEAM !!!
UH ...
BUT IF I JOIN A SPORTS TEAM...

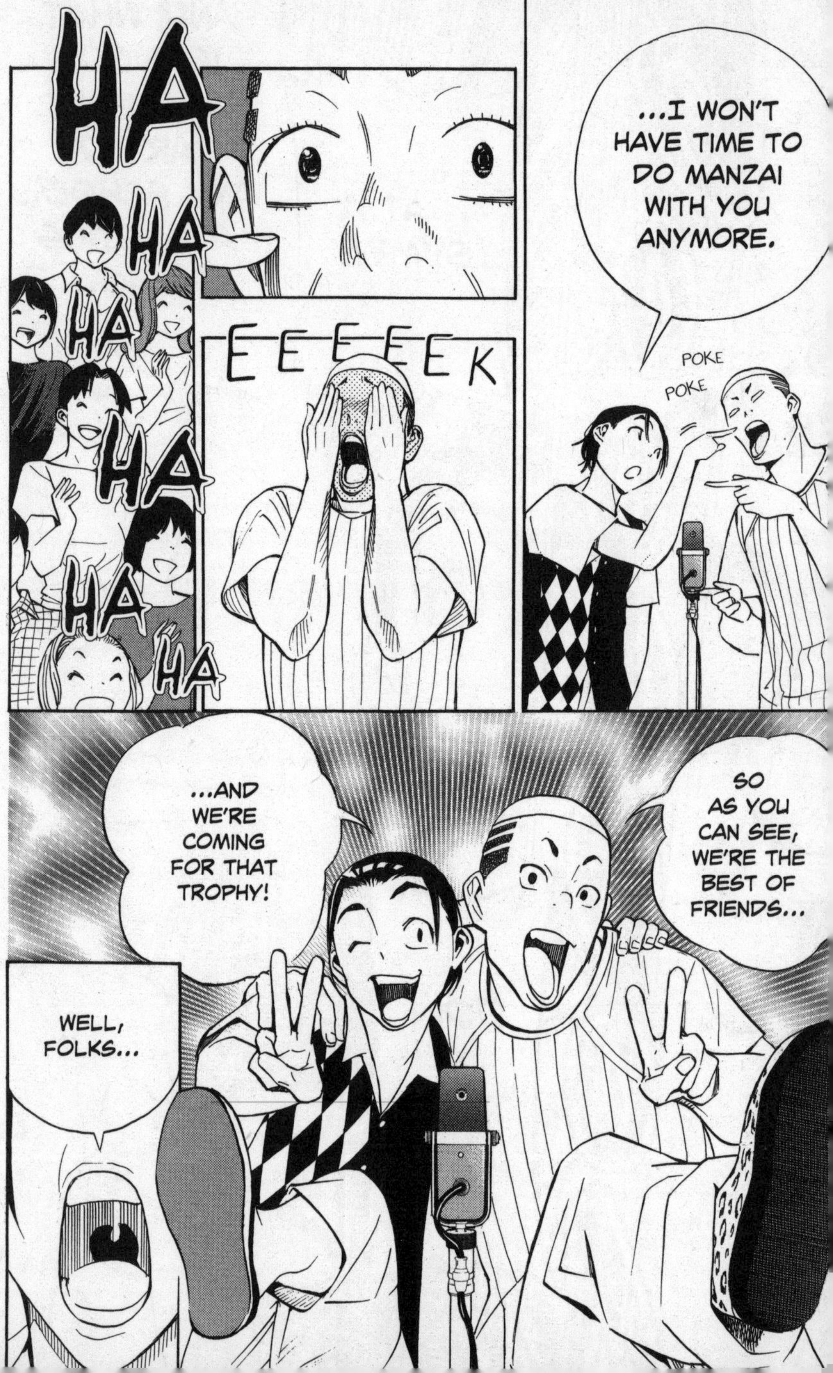
...I WON'T HAVE TIME TO DO MANZAI WITH YOU ANYMORE.
POKE
POKE
EEEEEK
HA
HA
HA
HA
HA
HA
SO AS YOU CAN SEE, WE'RE THE BEST OF FRIENDS...
...AND WE'RE COMING FOR THAT TROPHY!
WELL, FOLKS...

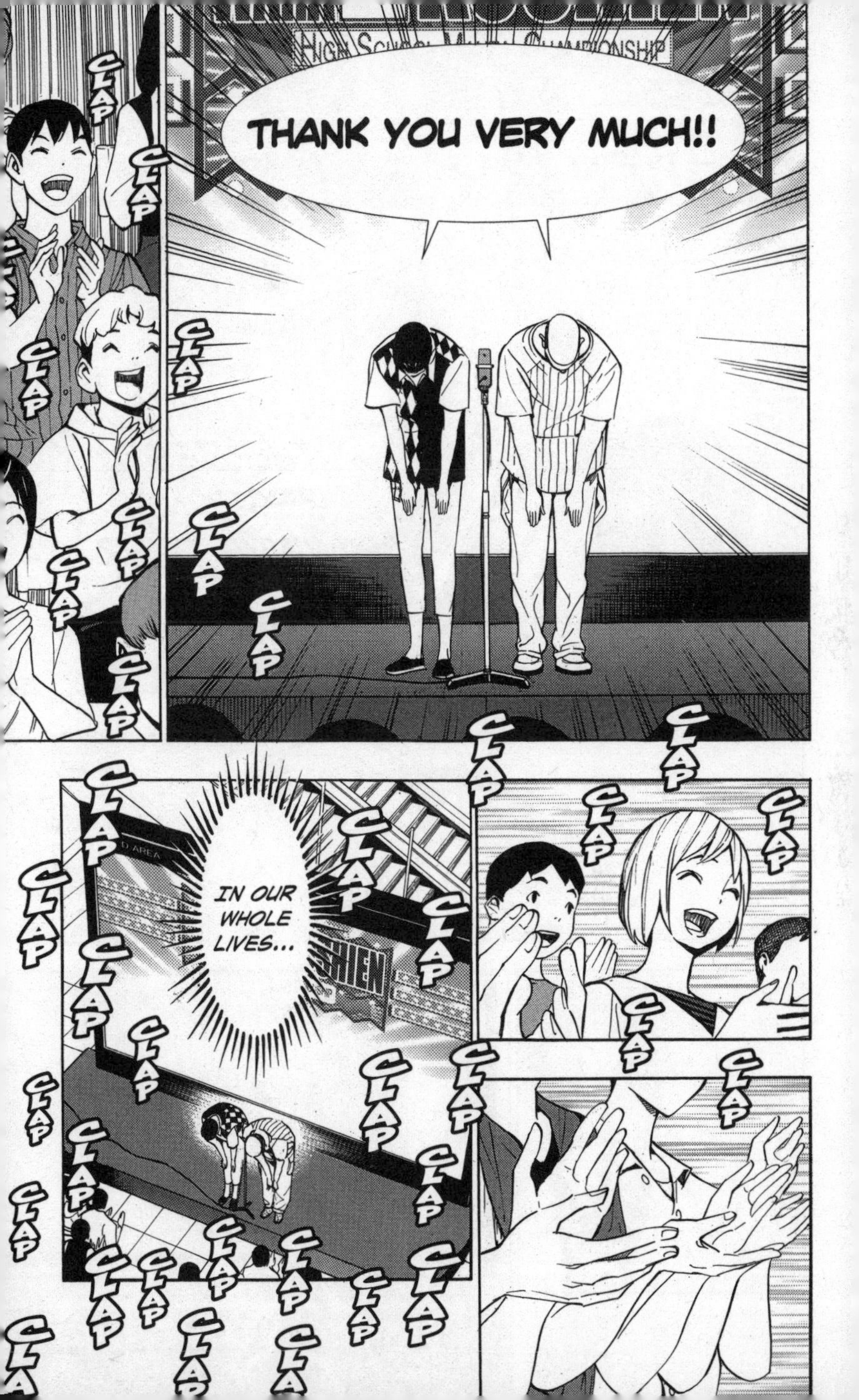
THANK YOU VERY MUCH!!
CLAP
CLAP
CLAP
IN OUR WHOLE LIVES...
CLAP

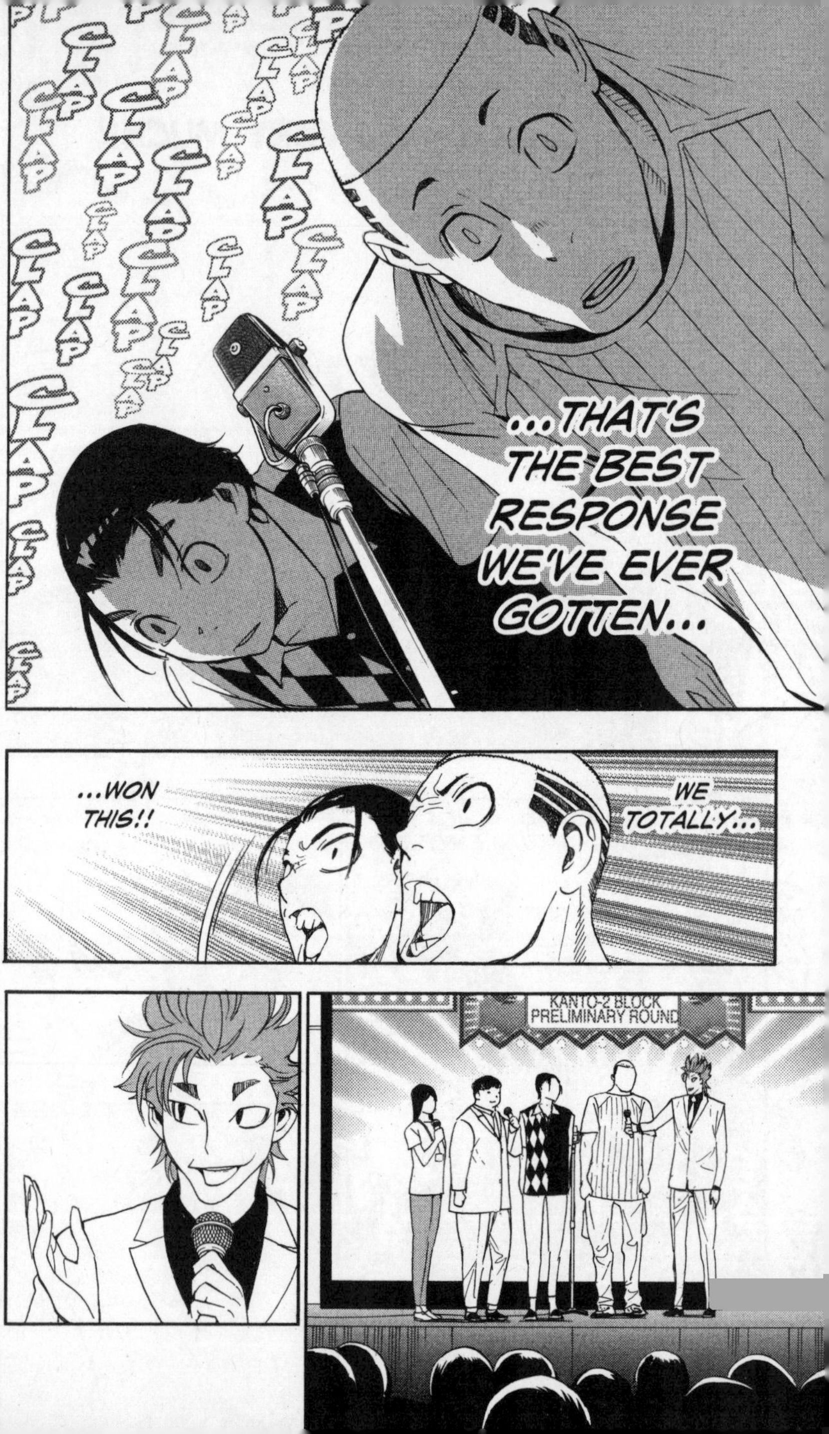
CLAP CLAP CLAP CLAP CLAP CLAP CLAP CLAP
...THAT'S THE BEST RESPONSE WE'VE EVER GOTTEN...
WE TOTALLY...
...WON THIS!!
KANTO-2 BLOCK PRELIMINARY ROUND

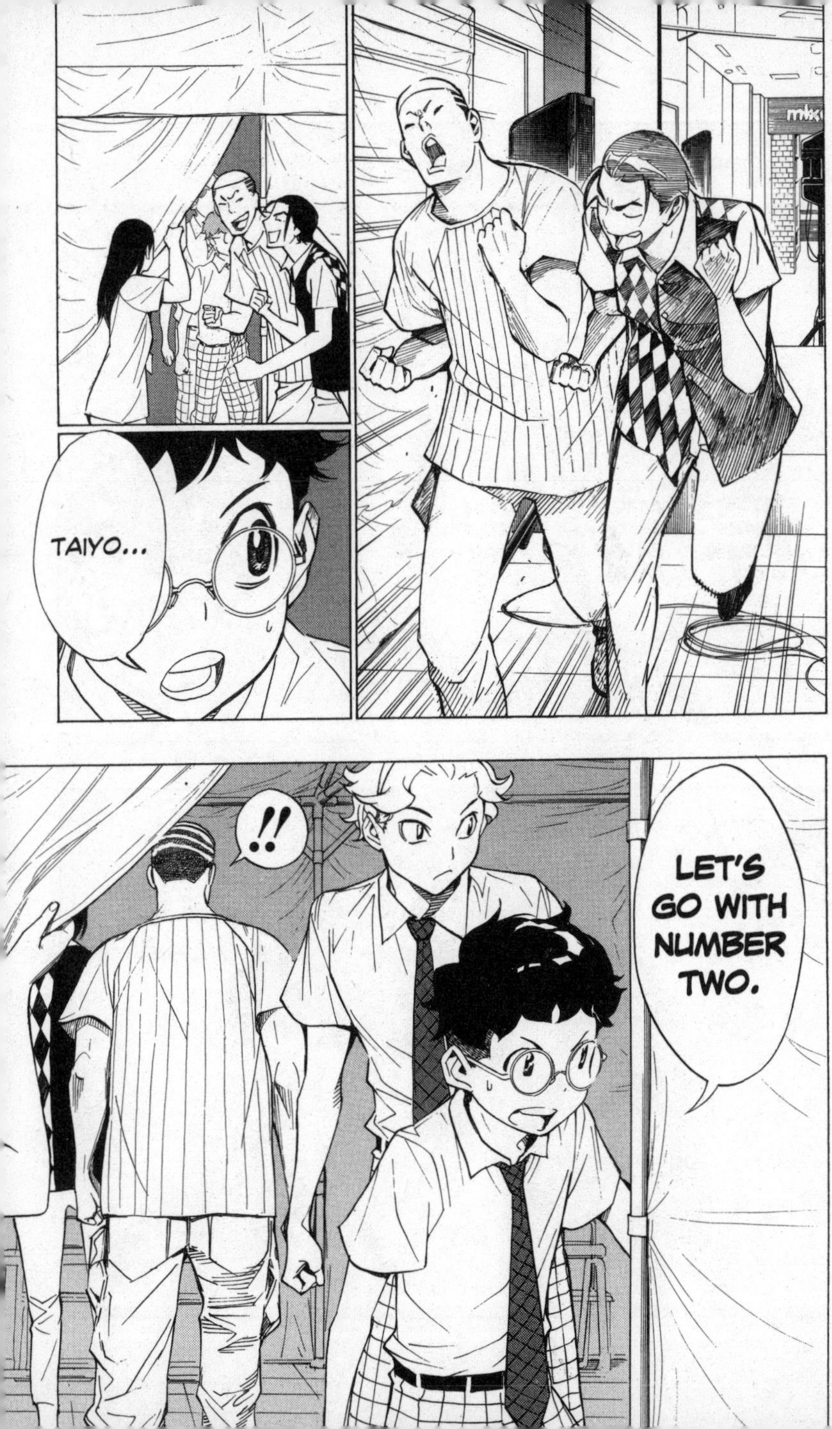
TAIYO...
LET'S GO WITH NUMBER TWO.
!!

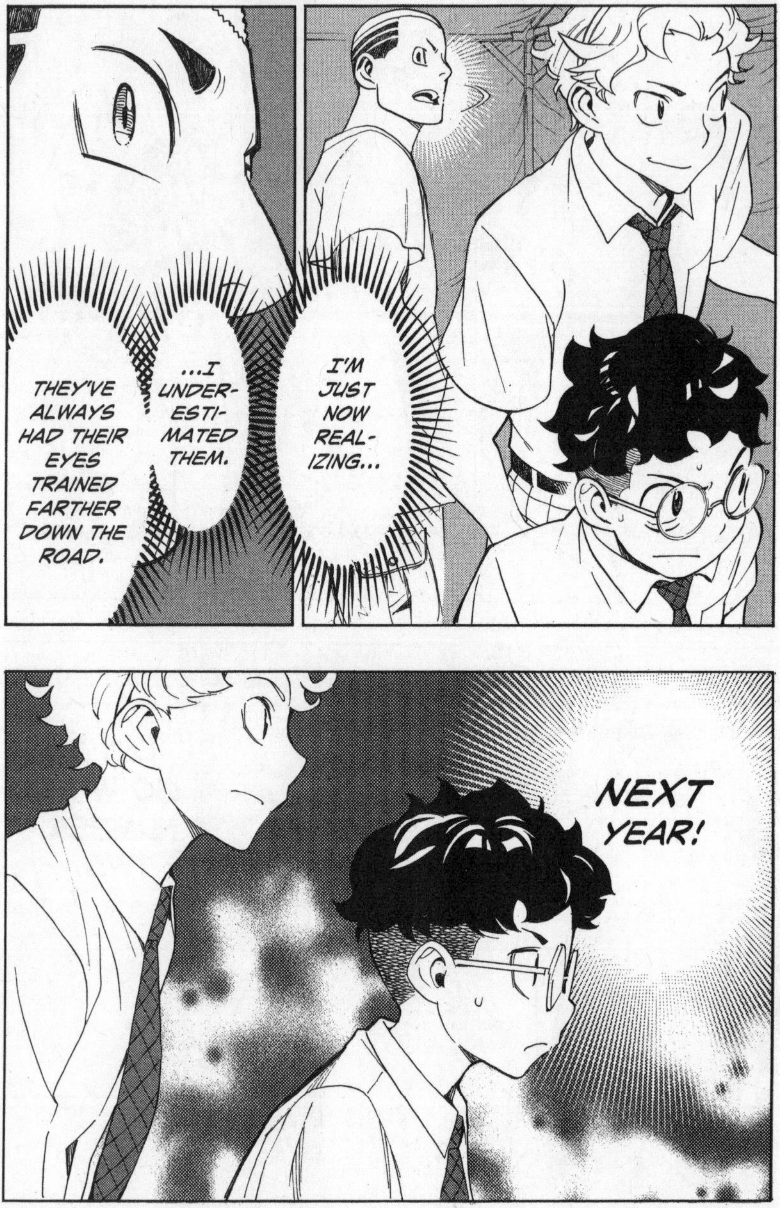
I'M JUST NOW REAL-IZING...
...I UNDER-ESTI-MATED THEM.
THEY'VE ALWAYS HAD THEIR EYES TRAINED FARTHER DOWN THE ROAD.
NEXT YEAR!

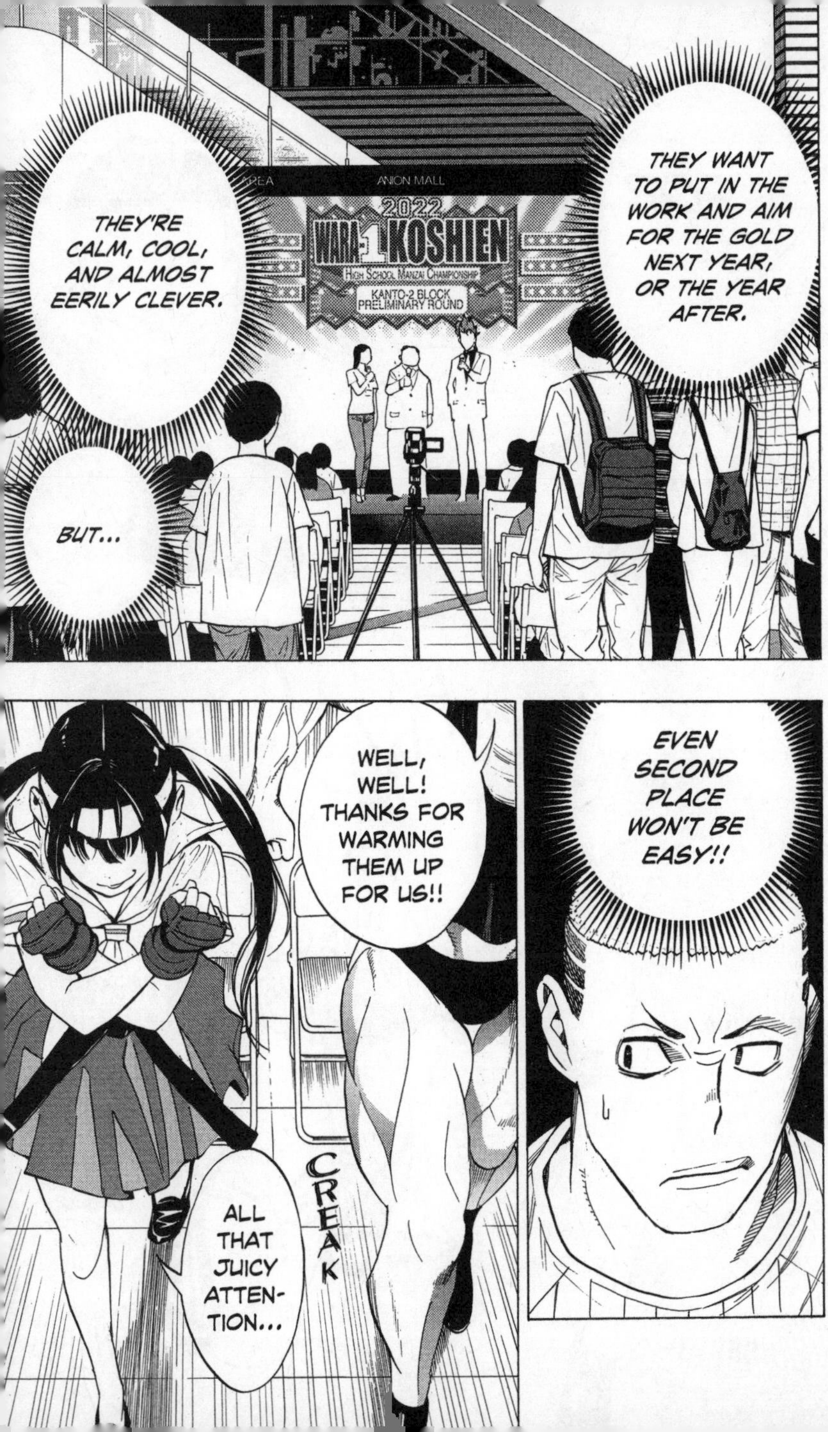
THEY WANT TO PUT IN THE WORK AND AIM FOR THE GOLD NEXT YEAR, OR THE YEAR AFTER.
ANION MALL
2022 WARA-1 KOSHIEN
HIGH SCHOOL MANZAI CHAMPIONSHIP
KANTO-2 BLOCK PRELIMINARY ROUND
THEY'RE CALM, COOL, AND ALMOST EERILY CLEVER.
BUT...
EVEN SECOND PLACE WON'T BE EASY!!
WELL, WELL! THANKS FOR WARMING THEM UP FOR US!!
CREAK
ALL THAT JUICY ATTEN-TION...

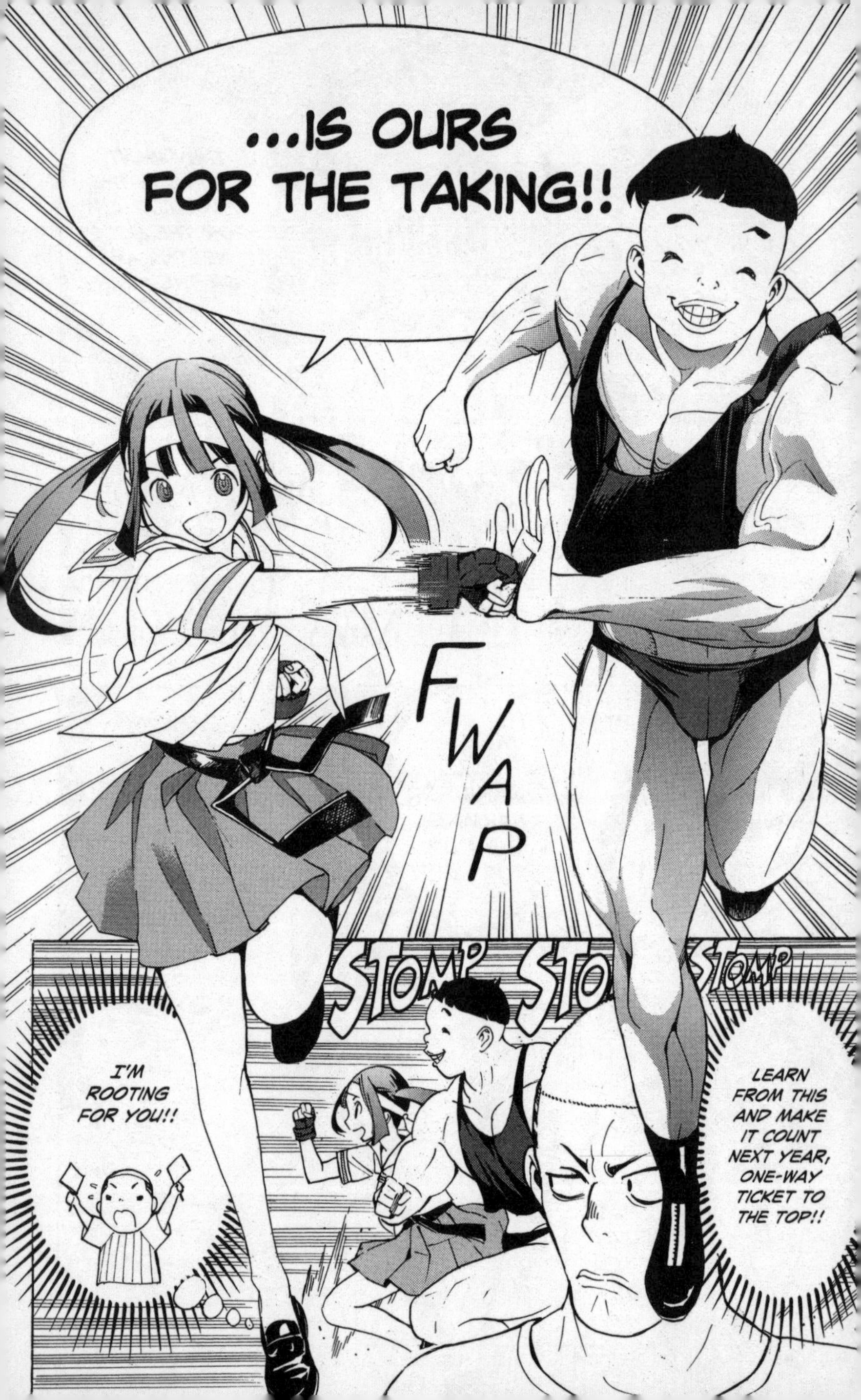
...IS OURS FOR THE TAKING!!
FWAP
STOMP STOMP STOMP
LEARN FROM THIS AND MAKE IT COUNT NEXT YEAR, ONE-WAY TICKET TO THE TOP!!
I'M ROOTING FOR YOU!!

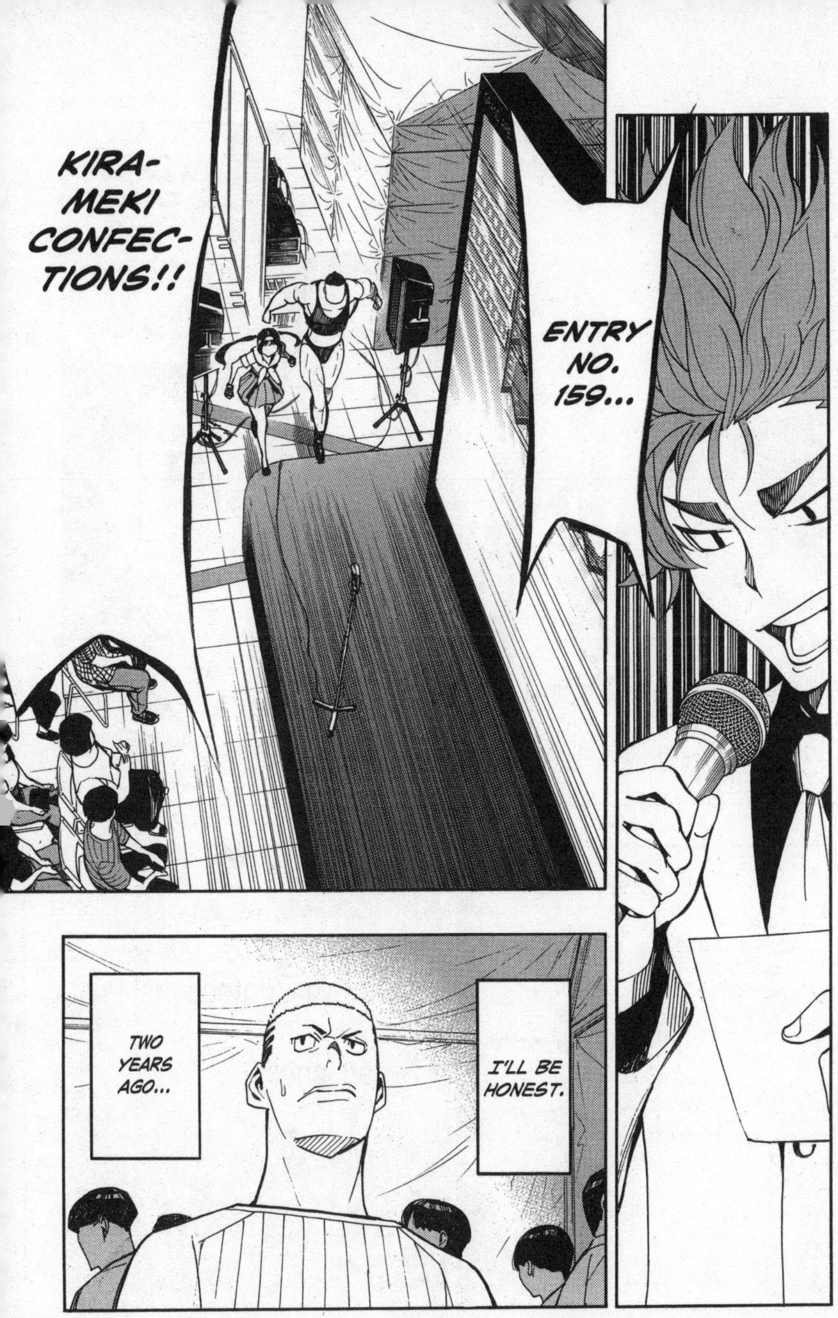
ENTRY NO. 159...
KIRA-MEKI CONFEC-TIONS!!
I'LL BE HONEST.
TWO YEARS AGO...

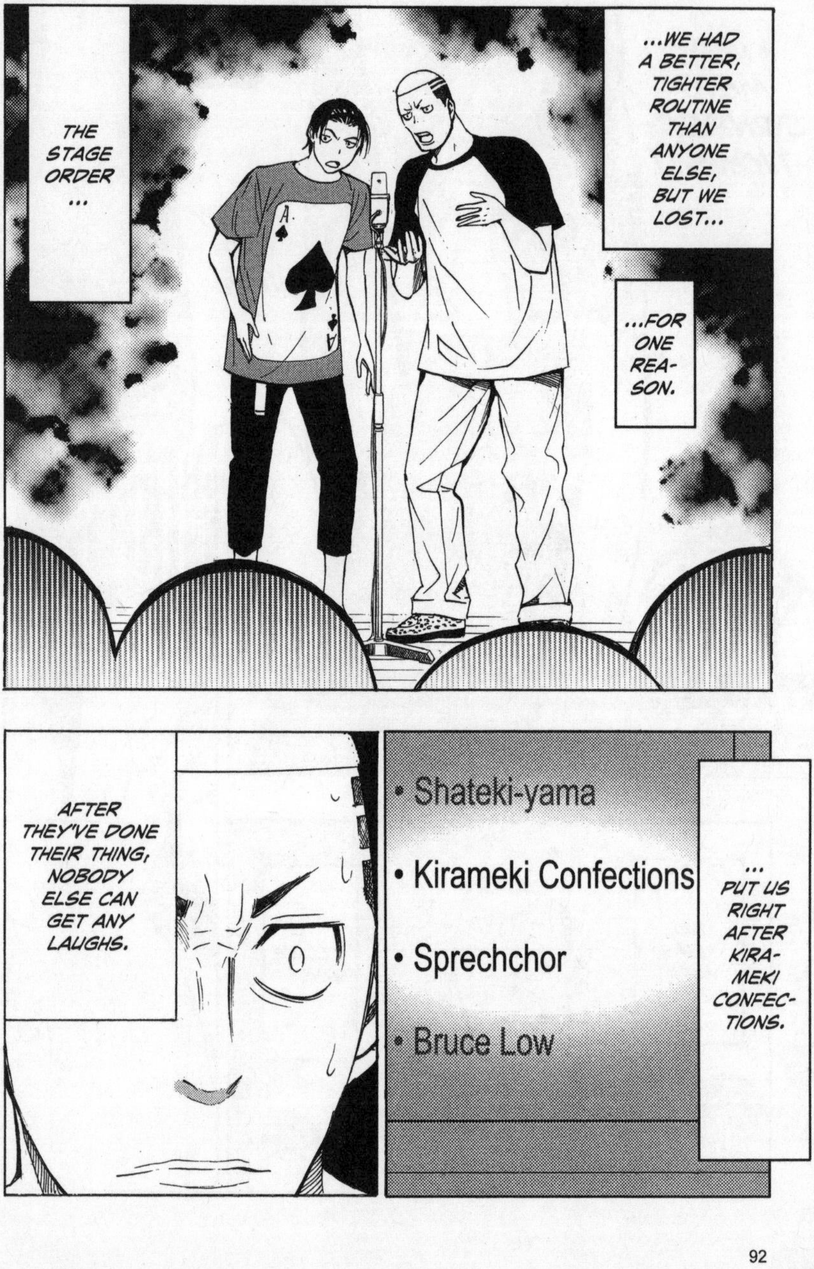
...WE HAD A BETTER, TIGHTER ROUTINE THAN ANYONE ELSE, BUT WE LOST...
...FOR ONE REA-SON.
THE STAGE ORDER ...
... PUT US RIGHT AFTER KIRA-MEKI CONFEC-TIONS.
• Shateki-yama
• Kirameki Confections
• Sprechchor
• Bruce Low
AFTER THEY'VE DONE THEIR THING, NOBODY ELSE CAN GET ANY LAUGHS.

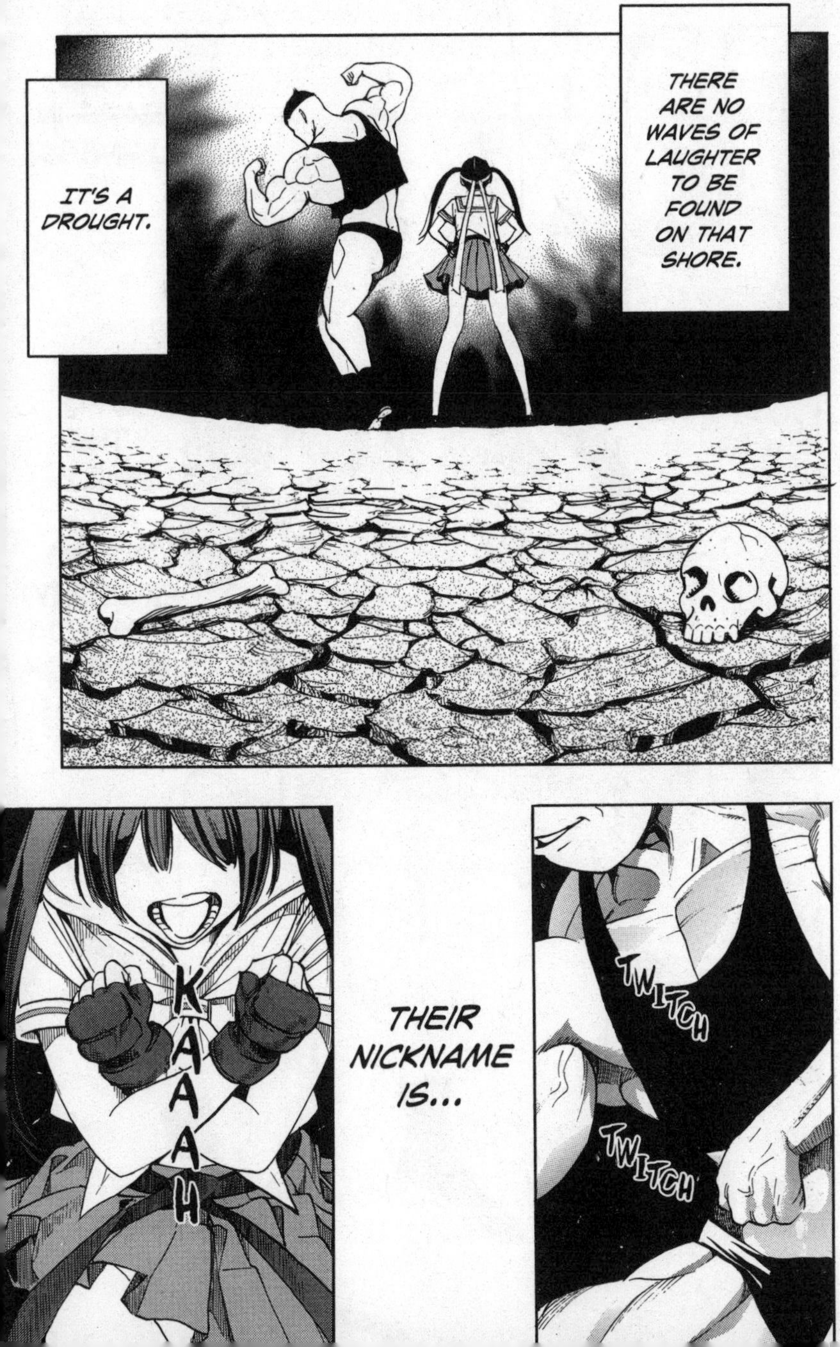
THERE ARE NO WAVES OF LAUGHTER TO BE FOUND ON THAT SHORE.
IT'S A DROUGHT.
TWITCH
TWITCH
THEIR NICKNAME IS...
KAAAAH

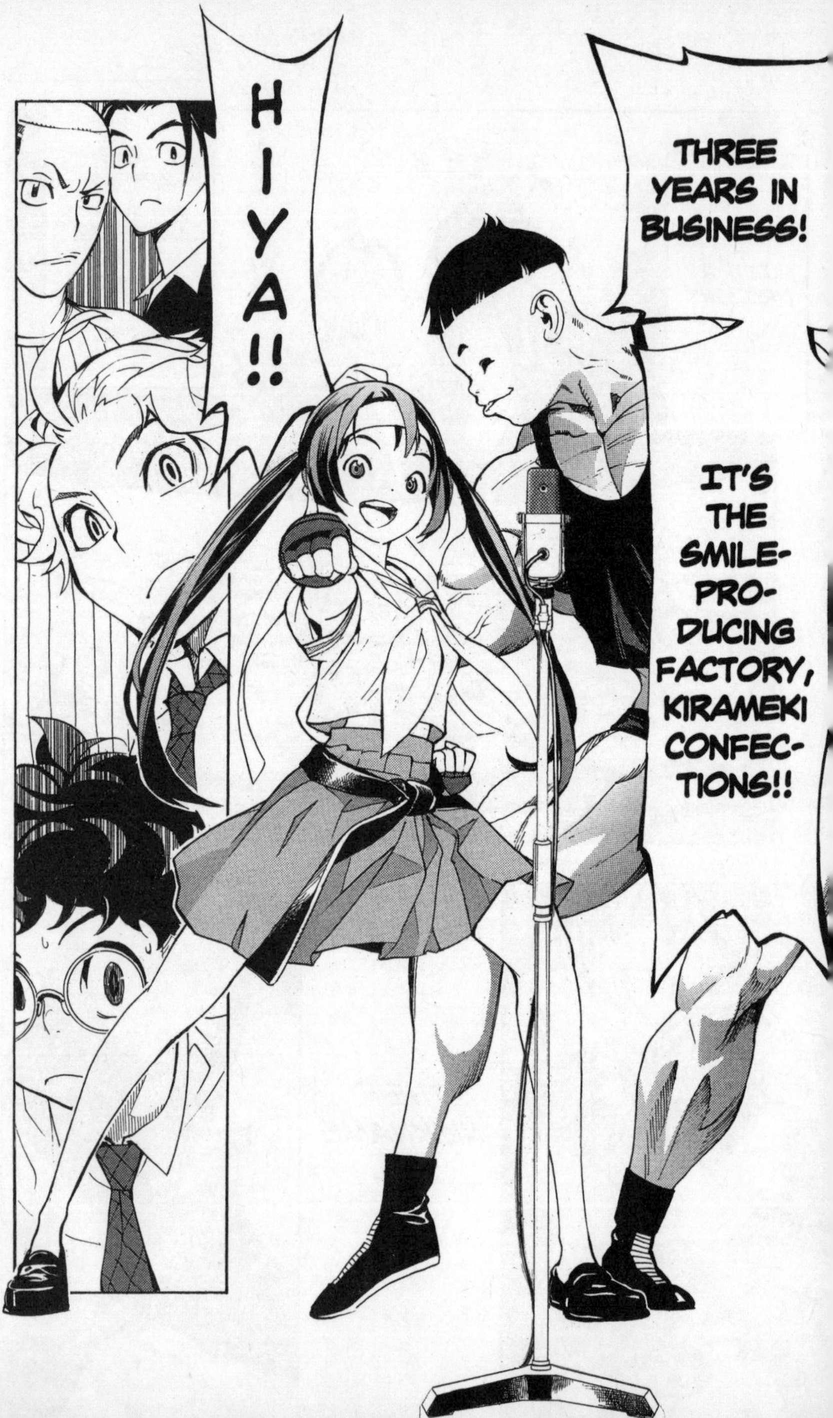
THREE YEARS IN BUSINESS!
IT'S THE SMILE-PRODUCING FACTORY, KIRAMEKI CONFECTIONS!!
HIYA!!

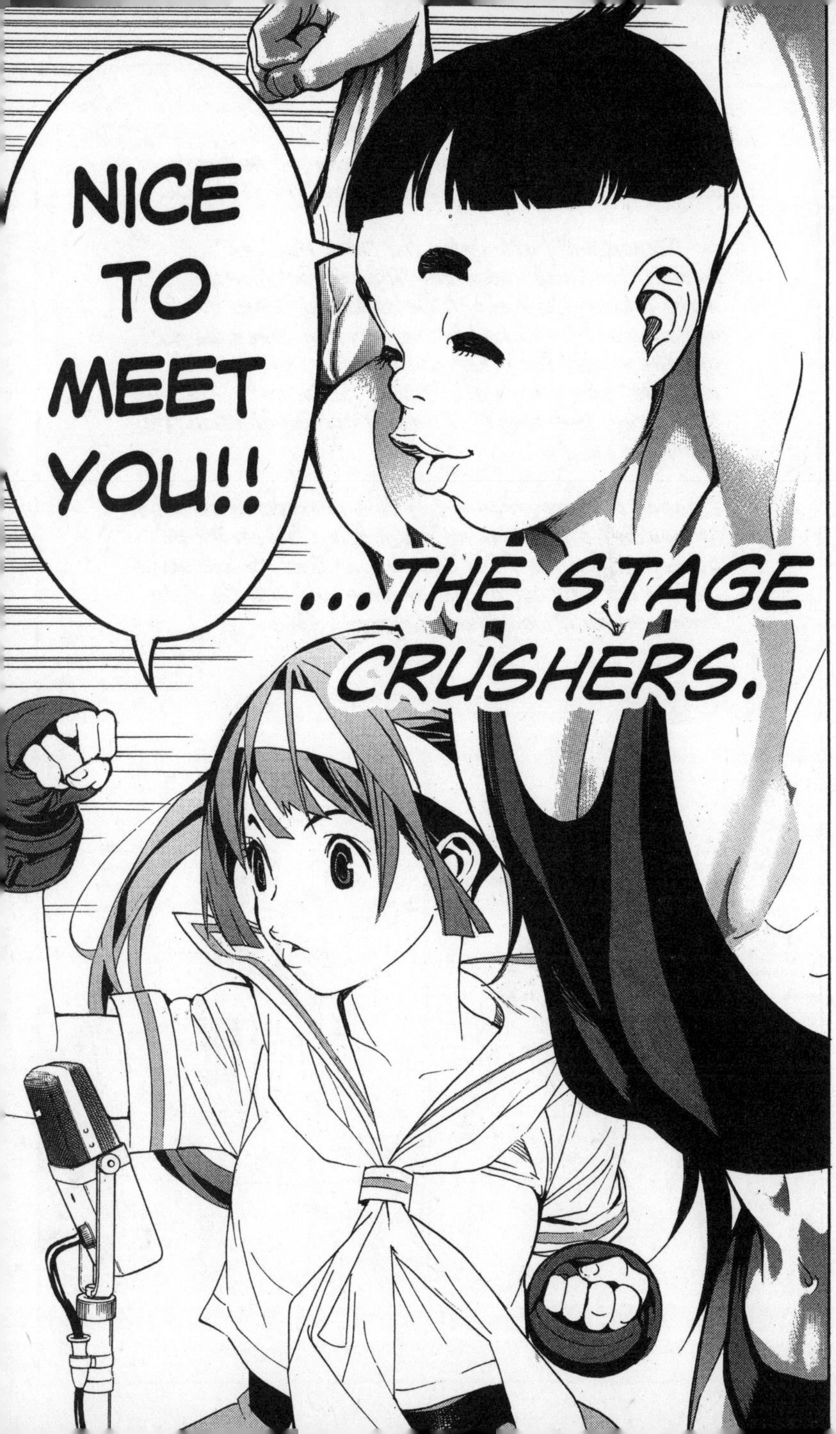
NICE TO MEET YOU!!
...THE STAGE CRUSHERS.

Column

Hello. I'm Akinari Asakura, the writer of this manga. Thank you very much for checking out the third volume.

So Jicchan and I attempted the "M-1 Koshien" competition (now known as "High School Manzai"). To make a long story short, we absolutely killed it. We were honestly shocked by the reaction. When we got off the stage, the other contestants came over to us. "That was amazing!" "You're geniuses!" "Have you been doing this long?" It wasn't our imagination. We really did kill it...

Pleased but embarrassed by this unexpected success, we couldn't stop grinning from being the center of adoration for the first time in our lives. So we were well on our way out of the prelims and into the final event...or so it would have seemed... (LOL)

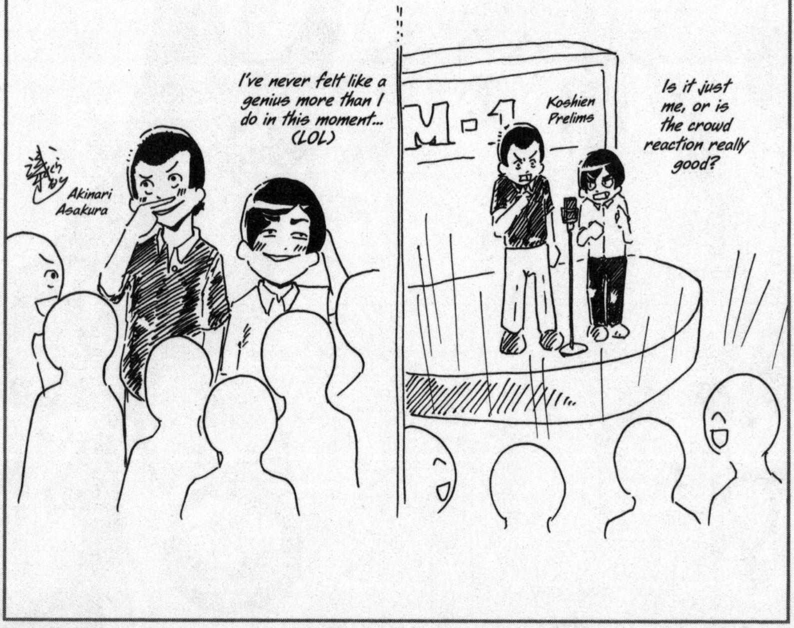
M-1
Koshien Prelims
Is it just me, or is the crowd reaction really good?
I've never felt like a genius more than I do in this moment... (LOL)
Akinari Asakura

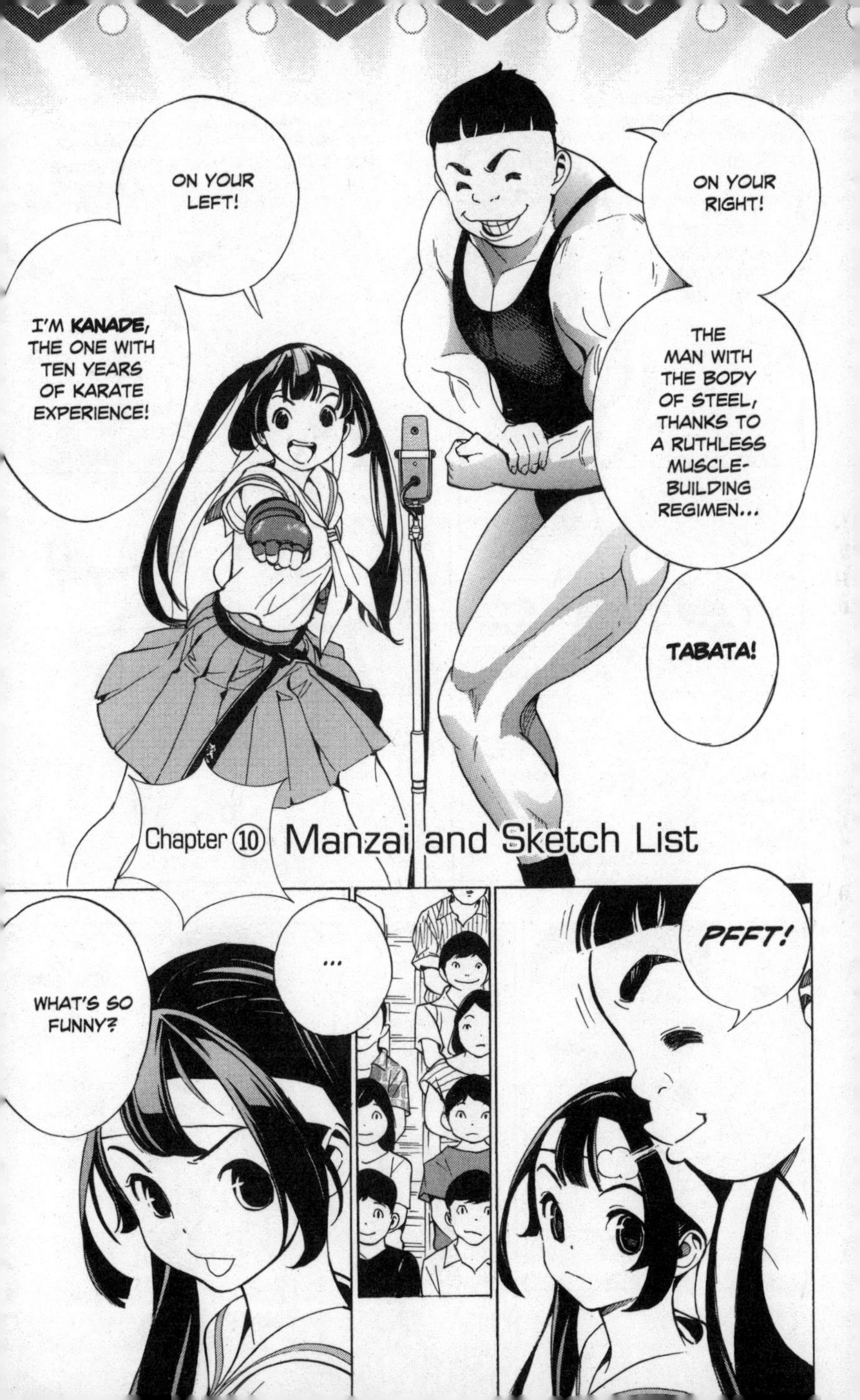
ON YOUR RIGHT!
THE MAN WITH THE BODY OF STEEL, THANKS TO A RUTHLESS MUSCLE-BUILDING REGIMEN...
TABATA!
ON YOUR LEFT!
I'M **KANADE**, THE ONE WITH TEN YEARS OF KARATE EXPERIENCE!
Chapter 10 Manzai and Sketch List
PFFT!
...
WHAT'S SO FUNNY?

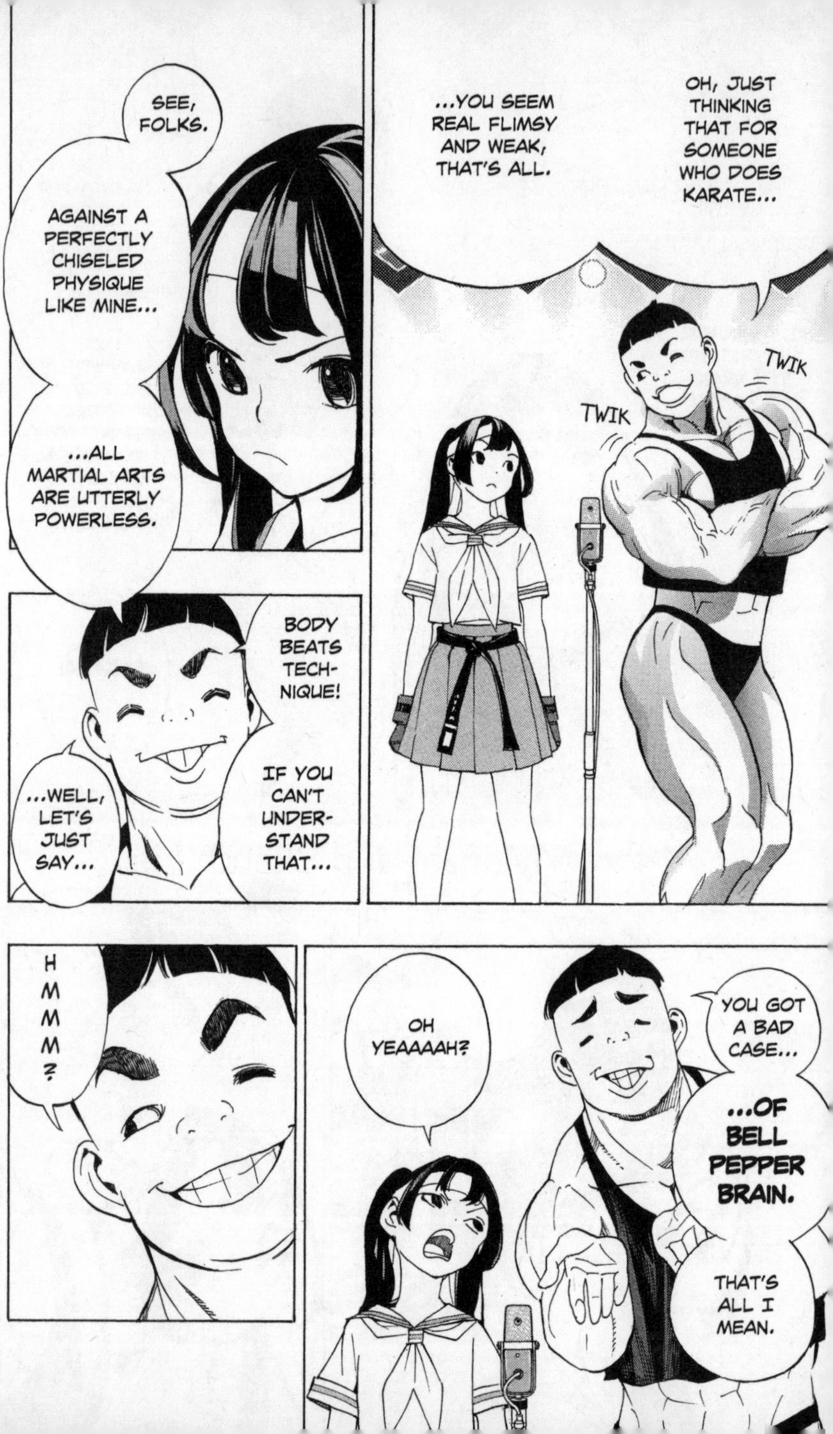
OH, JUST THINKING THAT FOR SOMEONE WHO DOES KARATE...
...YOU SEEM REAL FLIMSY AND WEAK, THAT'S ALL.
TWIK
TWIK
SEE, FOLKS.
AGAINST A PERFECTLY CHISELED PHYSIQUE LIKE MINE...
...ALL MARTIAL ARTS ARE UTTERLY POWERLESS.
BODY BEATS TECHNIQUE!
IF YOU CAN'T UNDERSTAND THAT...
...WELL, LET'S JUST SAY...
YOU GOT A BAD CASE...
...OF BELL PEPPER BRAIN.
THAT'S ALL I MEAN.
OH YEAAAAH?
HMMM?

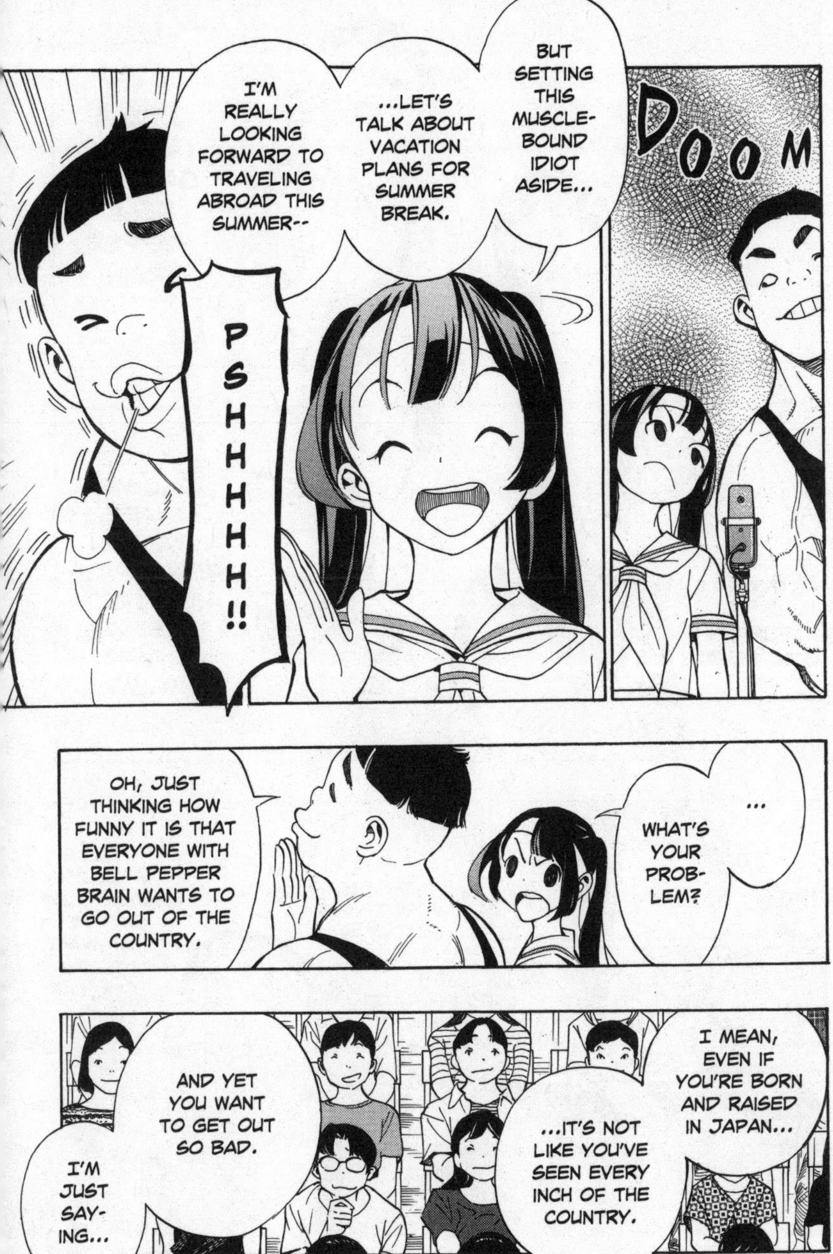
DOOM
BUT SETTING THIS MUSCLE-BOUND IDIOT ASIDE...
...LET'S TALK ABOUT VACATION PLANS FOR SUMMER BREAK.
I'M REALLY LOOKING FORWARD TO TRAVELING ABROAD THIS SUMMER--
PSHHHHHH!!
...
WHAT'S YOUR PROB-LEM?
OH, JUST THINKING HOW FUNNY IT IS THAT EVERYONE WITH BELL PEPPER BRAIN WANTS TO GO OUT OF THE COUNTRY.
I MEAN, EVEN IF YOU'RE BORN AND RAISED IN JAPAN...
...IT'S NOT LIKE YOU'VE SEEN EVERY INCH OF THE COUNTRY.
AND YET YOU WANT TO GET OUT SO BAD.
I'M JUST SAY-ING...

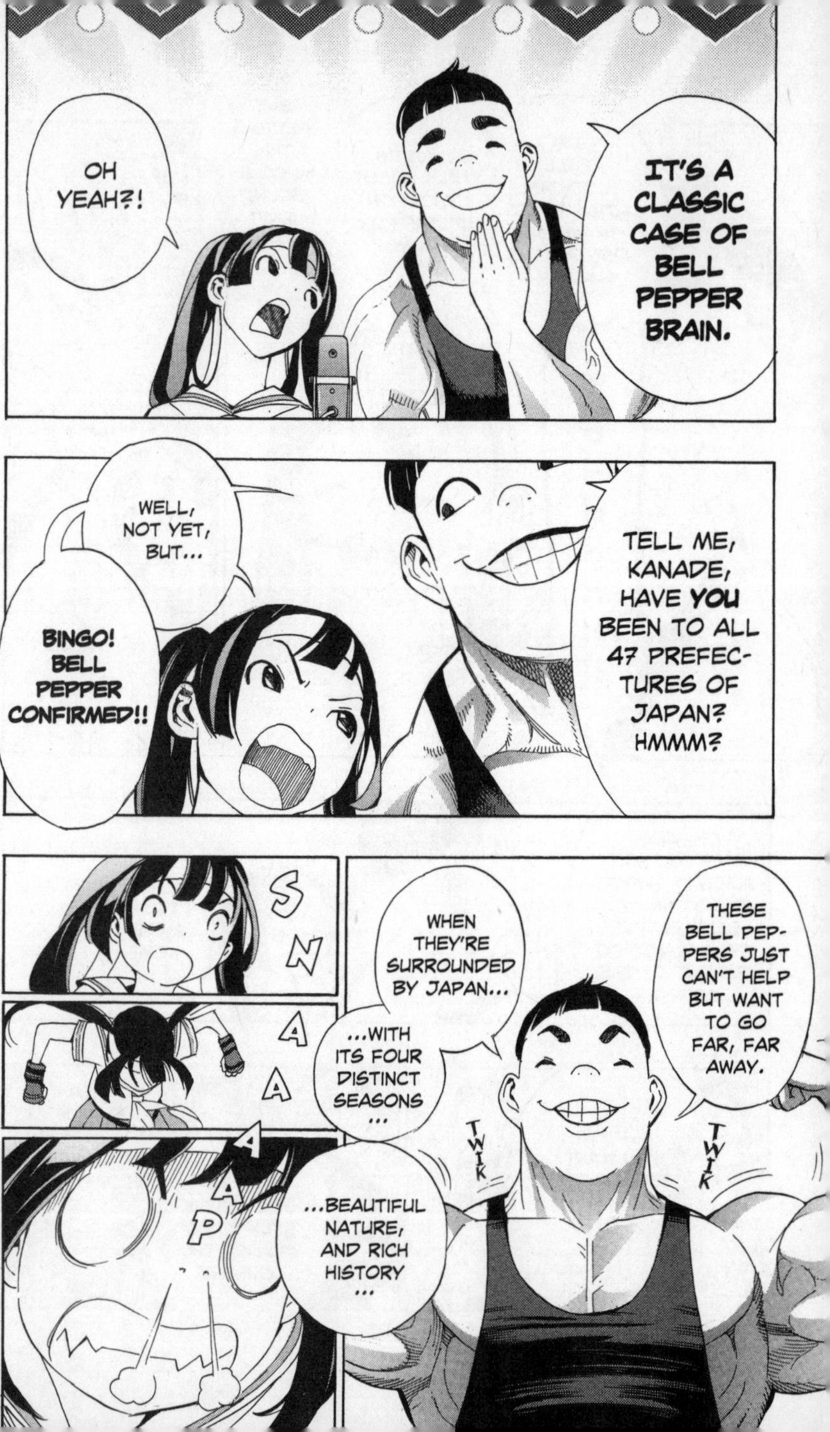
IT'S A CLASSIC CASE OF BELL PEPPER BRAIN.
OH YEAH?!
TELL ME, KANADE, HAVE YOU BEEN TO ALL 47 PREFECTURES OF JAPAN? HMMM?
WELL, NOT YET, BUT...
BINGO! BELL PEPPER CONFIRMED!!
THESE BELL PEPPERS JUST CAN'T HELP BUT WANT TO GO FAR, FAR AWAY.
WHEN THEY'RE SURROUNDED BY JAPAN...
...WITH ITS FOUR DISTINCT SEASONS...
...BEAUTIFUL NATURE, AND RICH HISTORY...
TWIK
TWIK
SNAAAAP

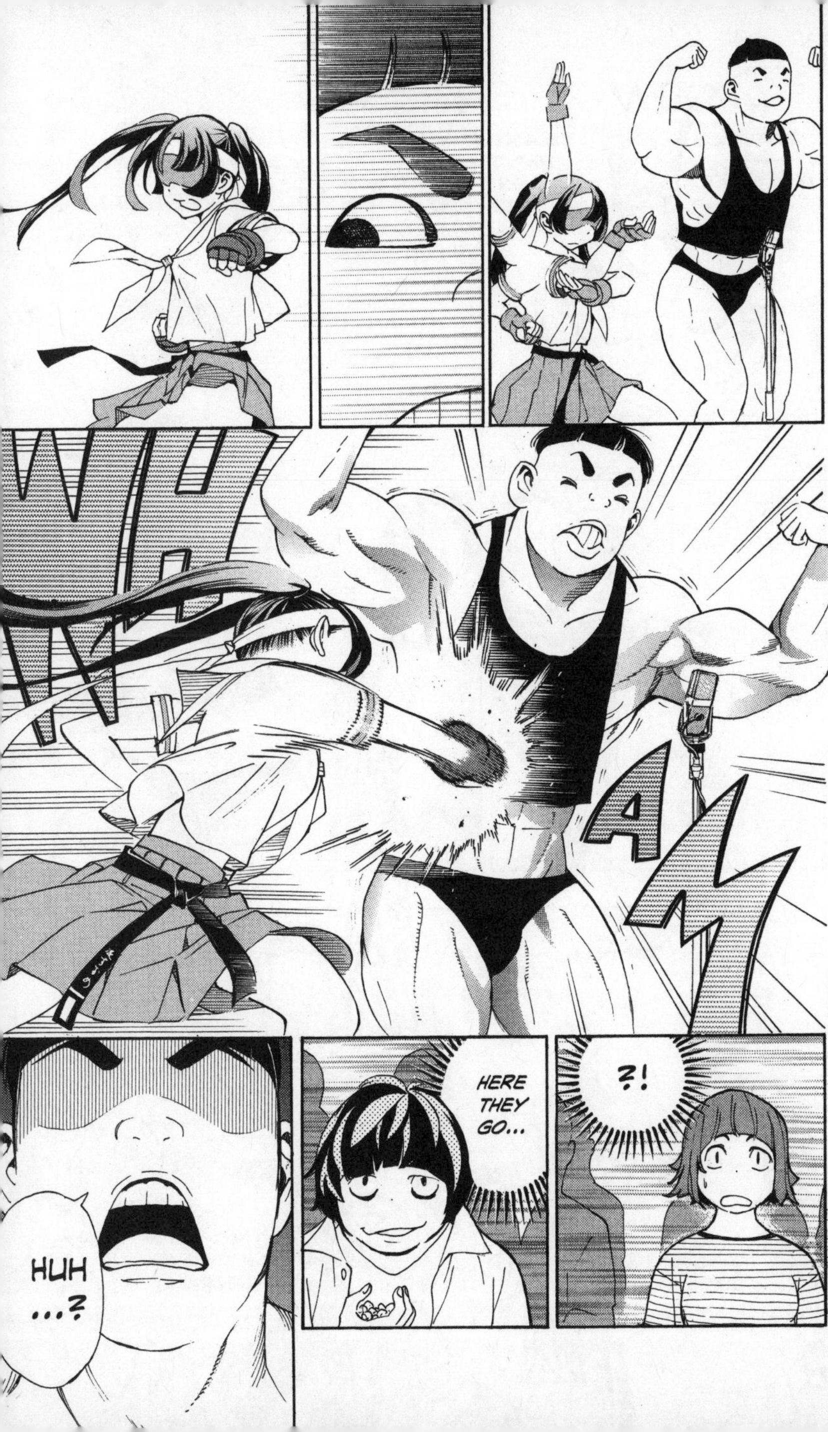
WHAM
?!
HERE THEY GO...
HUH ...?

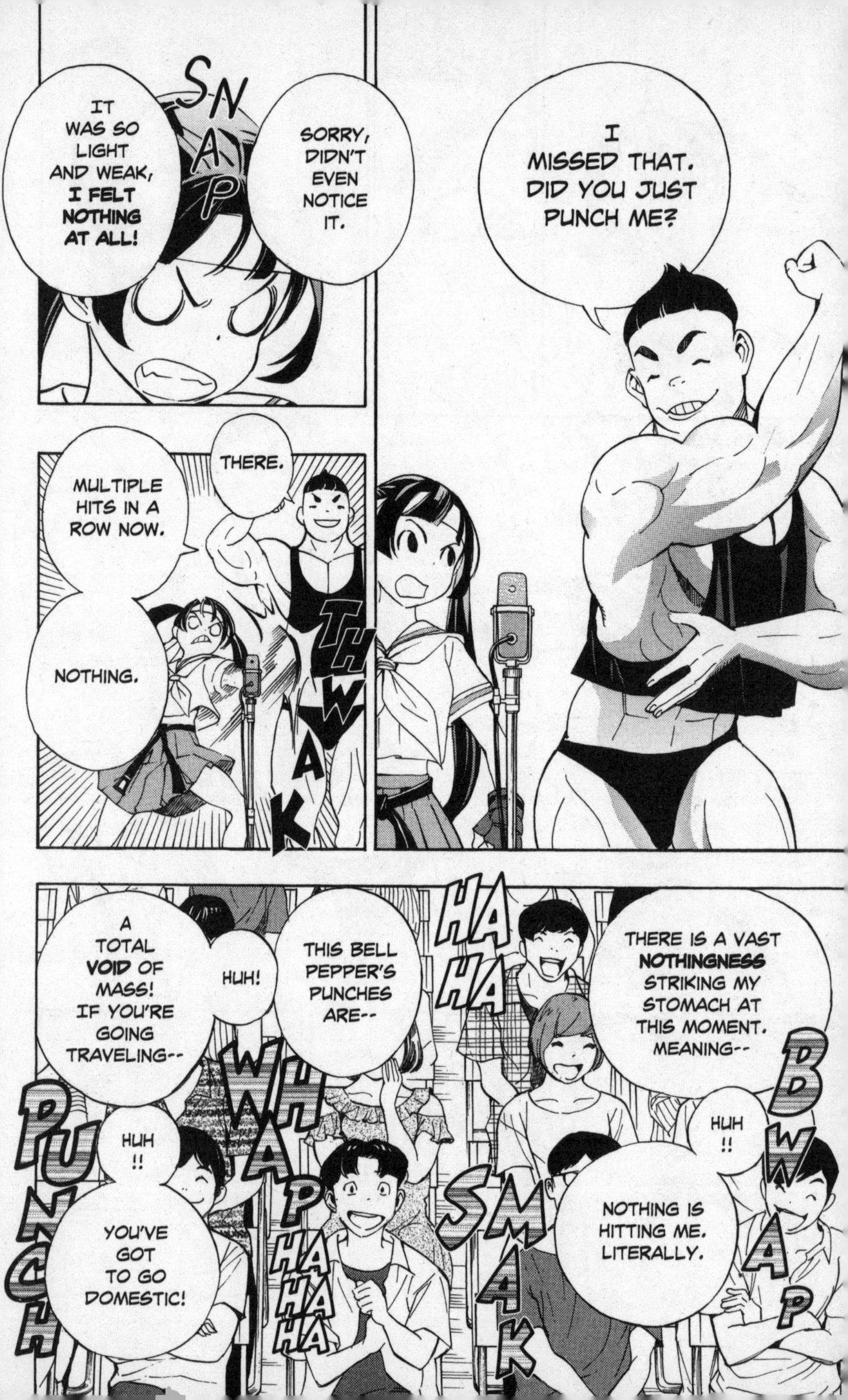
I MISSED THAT. DID YOU JUST PUNCH ME?
SNAP
SORRY, DIDN'T EVEN NOTICE IT.
IT WAS SO LIGHT AND WEAK, I FELT NOTHING AT ALL!
THERE.
MULTIPLE HITS IN A ROW NOW.
THWAK
NOTHING.
THERE IS A VAST NOTHINGNESS STRIKING MY STOMACH AT THIS MOMENT. MEANING--
HA HA
THIS BELL PEPPER'S PUNCHES ARE--
HUH!
A TOTAL VOID OF MASS! IF YOU'RE GOING TRAVELING--
BWAP
HUH !!
NOTHING IS HITTING ME. LITERALLY.
SMAK
WHAP
HA HA HA
HUH !!
YOU'VE GOT TO GO DOMESTIC!
PUNCH

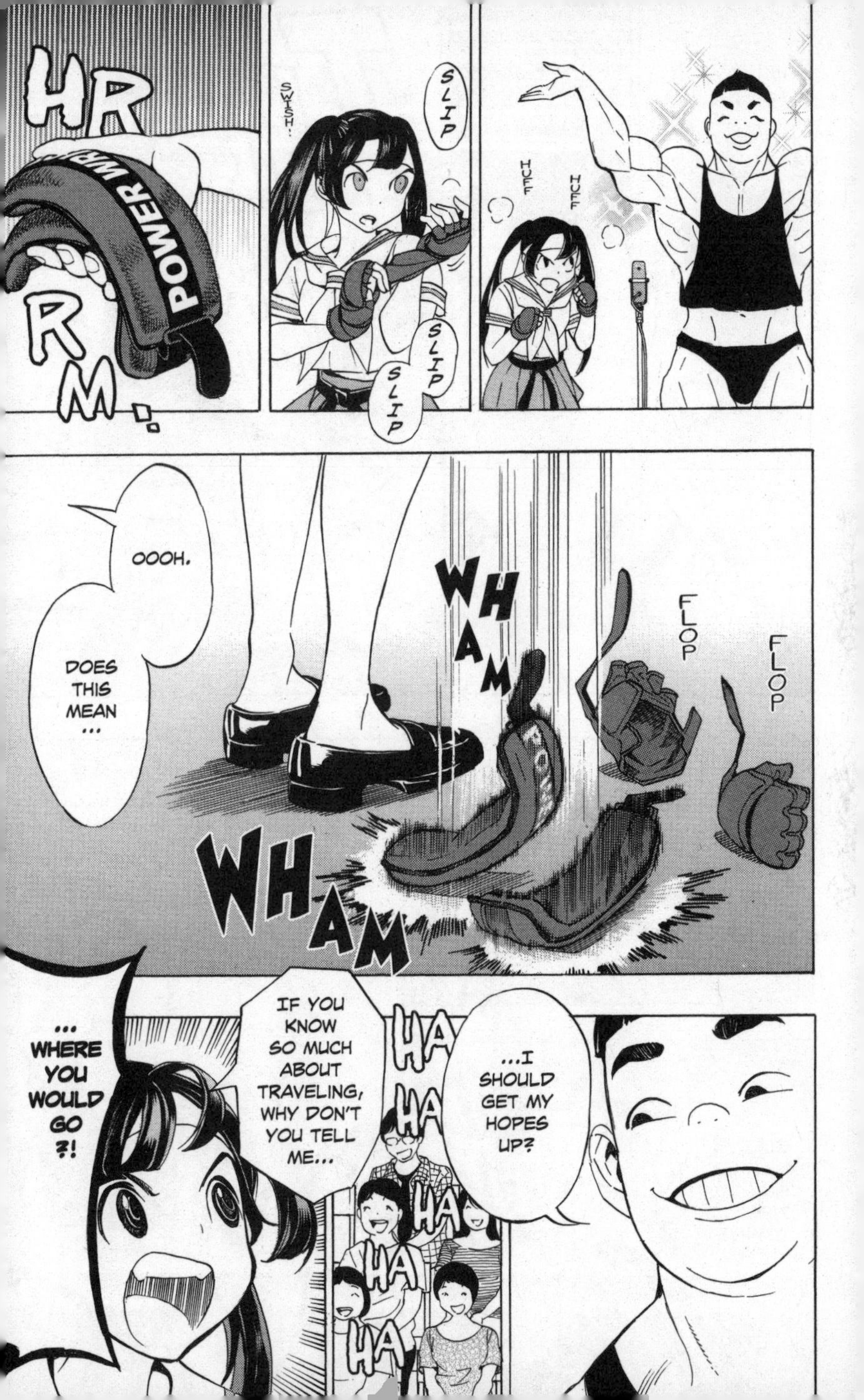
HUFF HUFF
SWISH!
SLIP
SLIP SLIP SLIP
HRRM.
FLOP FLOP
WHAM
WHAM
OOOH.
DOES THIS MEAN ...
...I SHOULD GET MY HOPES UP?
HA HA HA HA HA HA
IF YOU KNOW SO MUCH ABOUT TRAVELING, WHY DON'T YOU TELL ME...
... WHERE YOU WOULD GO ?!

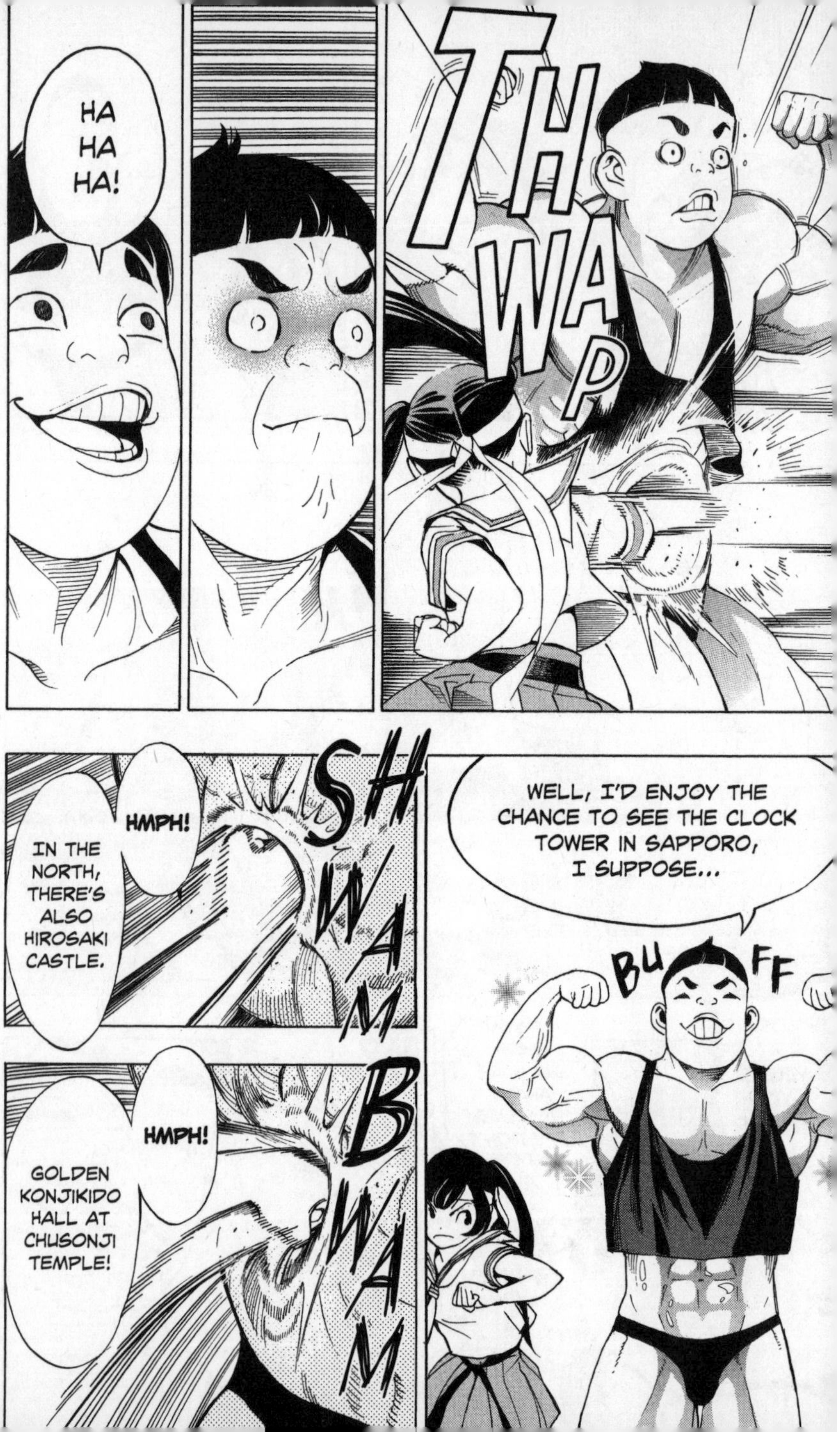
THWAP
HA HA HA!
WELL, I'D ENJOY THE CHANCE TO SEE THE CLOCK TOWER IN SAPPORO, I SUPPOSE...
BUFF
SHWAM
HMPH!
IN THE NORTH, THERE'S ALSO HIROSAKI CASTLE.
BWAM
HMPH!
GOLDEN KONJIKIDO HALL AT CHUSONJI TEMPLE!

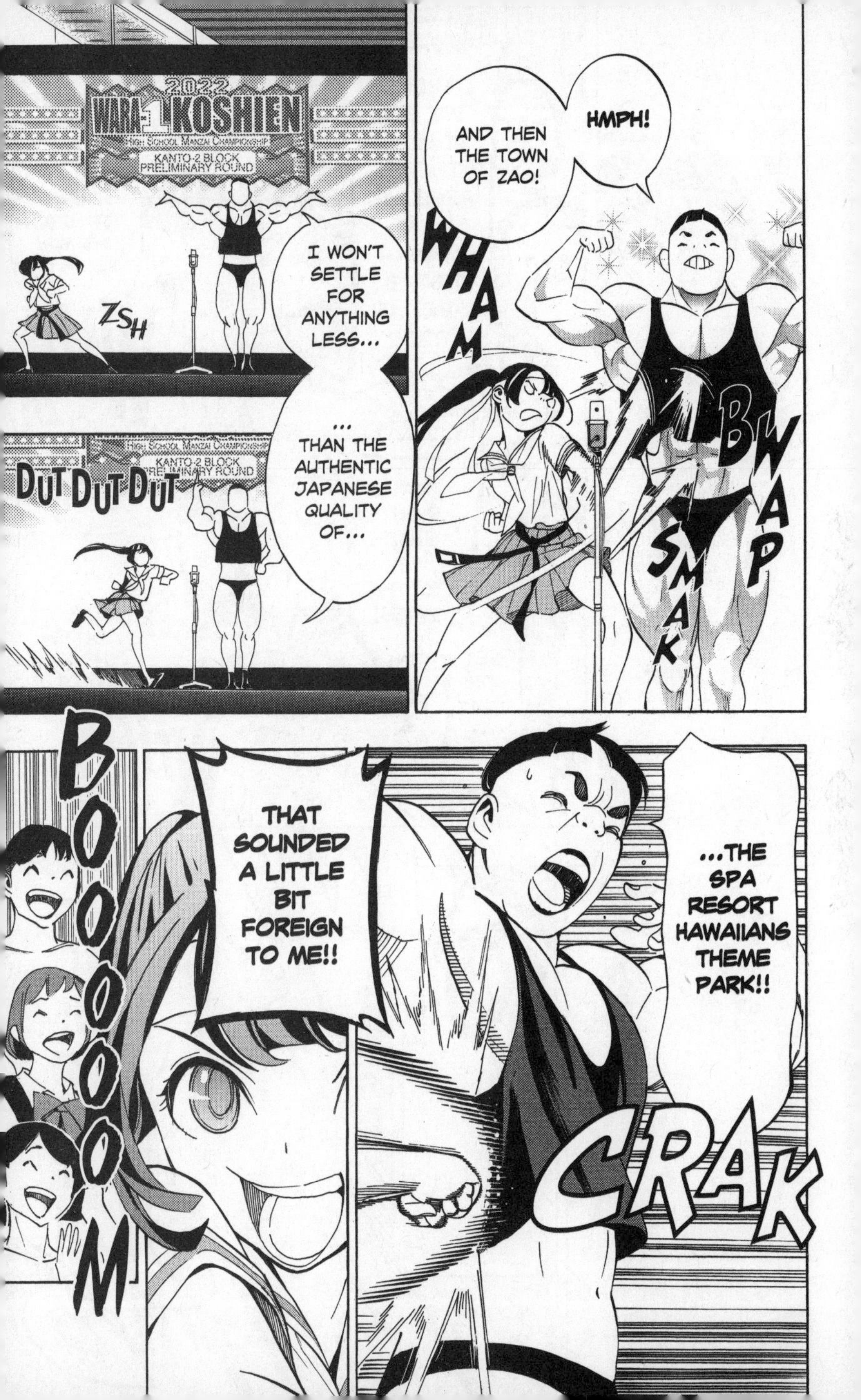
HMPH!
AND THEN THE TOWN OF ZAO!
WHAM
BWAP
SMAK
2022 WARA-1 KOSHIEN
HIGH SCHOOL MANZAI CHAMPIONSHIP
KANTO-2 BLOCK PRELIMINARY ROUND
I WON'T SETTLE FOR ANYTHING LESS...
ZSH
... THAN THE AUTHENTIC JAPANESE QUALITY OF...
HIGH SCHOOL MANZAI CHAMPIONSHIP
KANTO-2 BLOCK PRELIMINARY ROUND
DUT DUT DUT
...THE SPA RESORT HAWAIIANS THEME PARK!!
CRAK
THAT SOUNDED A LITTLE BIT FOREIGN TO ME!!
BOOOOOOOM

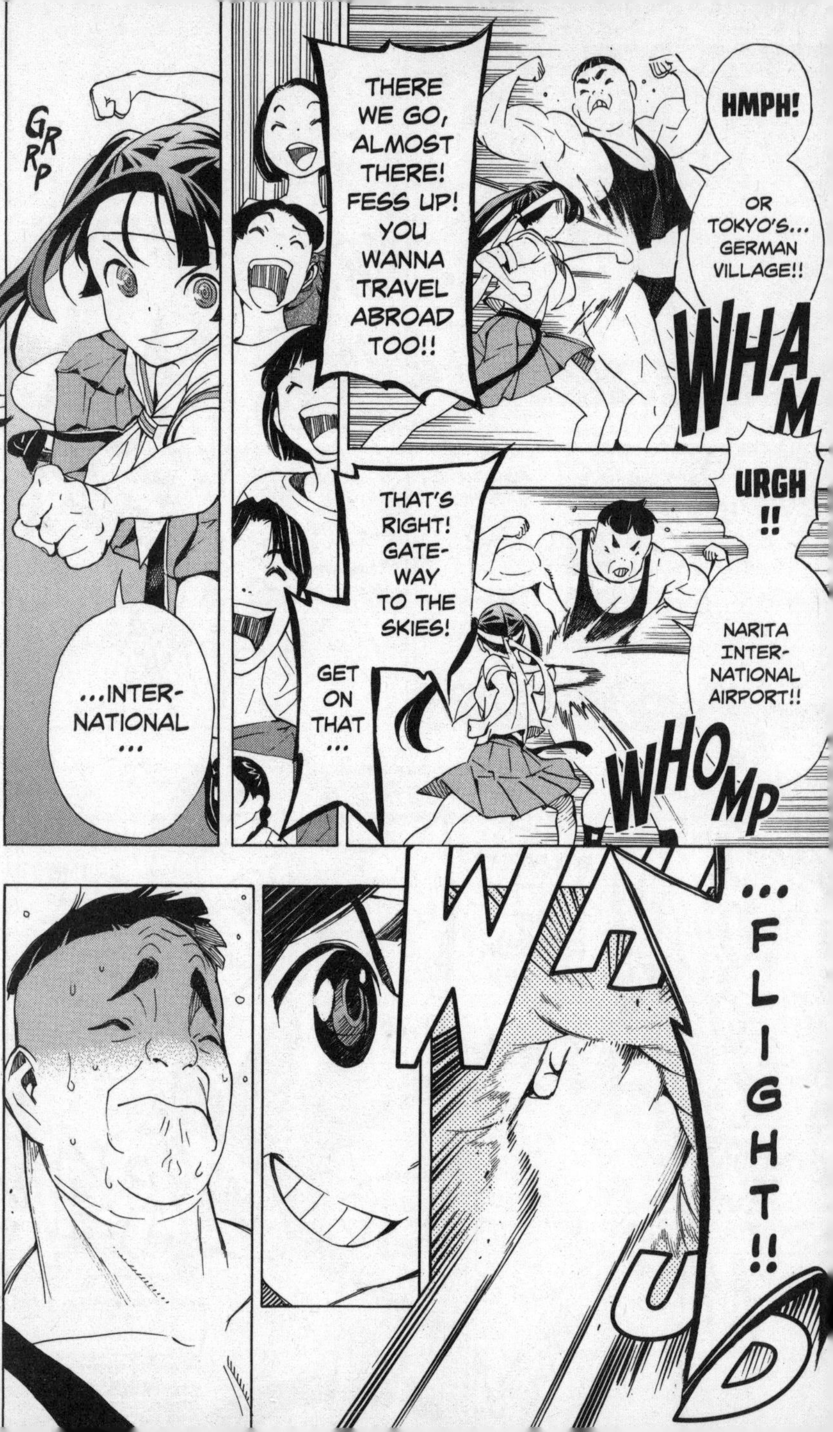
HMPH!
OR TOKYO'S... GERMAN VILLAGE!!
WHAM
URGH!!
NARITA INTERNATIONAL AIRPORT!!
WHOMP
THERE WE GO, ALMOST THERE! FESS UP! YOU WANNA TRAVEL ABROAD TOO!!
THAT'S RIGHT! GATEWAY TO THE SKIES!
GET ON THAT...
GRRP
...INTERNATIONAL...
...FLIGHT!!
WHUD

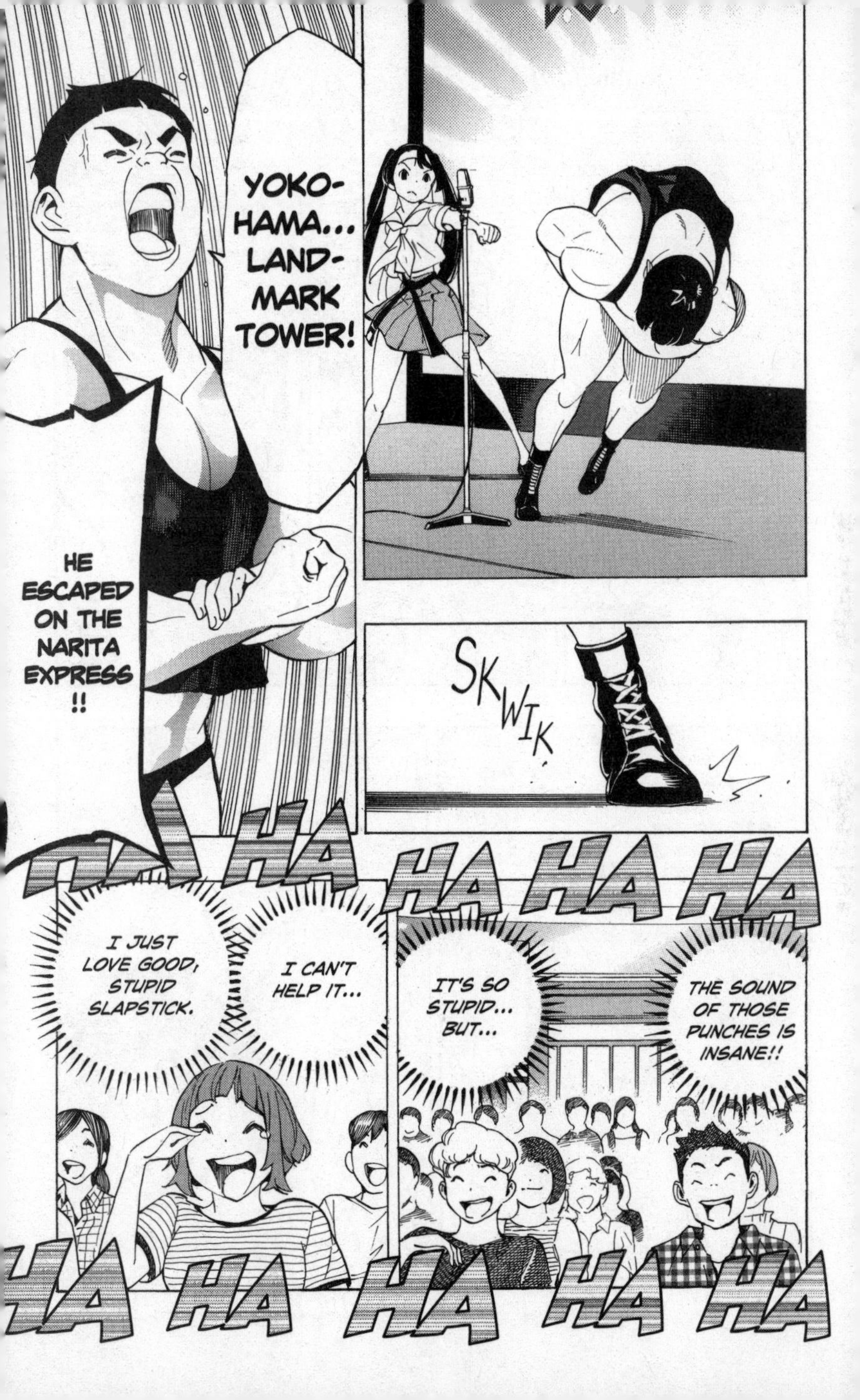
SKWIK
YOKOHAMA... LANDMARK TOWER!
HE ESCAPED ON THE NARITA EXPRESS!!
HA HA HA HA HA
THE SOUND OF THOSE PUNCHES IS INSANE!!
IT'S SO STUPID... BUT...
I CAN'T HELP IT...
I JUST LOVE GOOD, STUPID SLAPSTICK.
HA HA HA HA HA

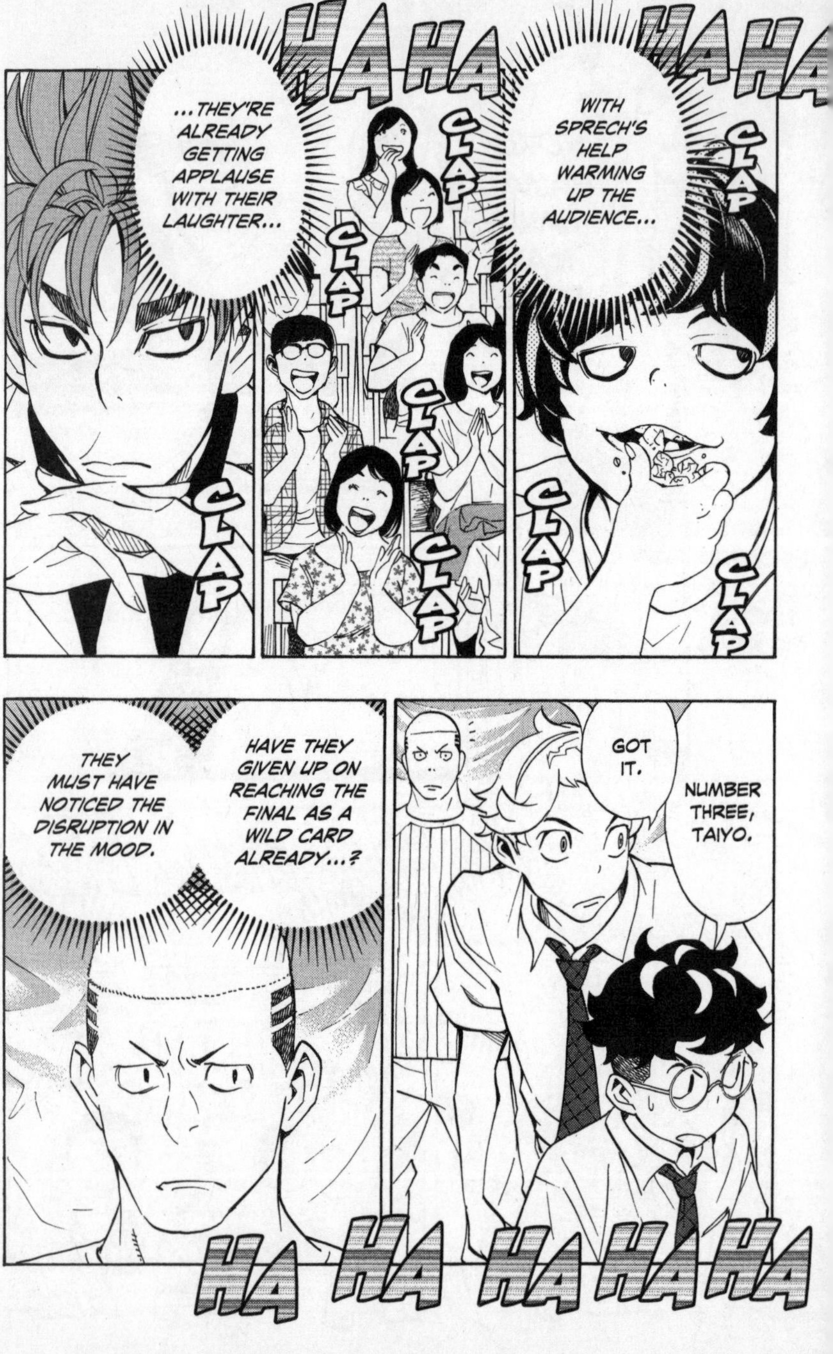
HAHA
HAHA
WITH SPRECH'S HELP WARMING UP THE AUDIENCE...
CLAP
CLAP
CLAP
CLAP
CLAP
CLAP
CLAP
CLAP
...THEY'RE ALREADY GETTING APPLAUSE WITH THEIR LAUGHTER...
CLAP
NUMBER THREE, TAIYO.
GOT IT.
HAVE THEY GIVEN UP ON REACHING THE FINAL AS A WILD CARD ALREADY...?
THEY MUST HAVE NOTICED THE DISRUPTION IN THE MOOD.
HA HA HA HA HA HA

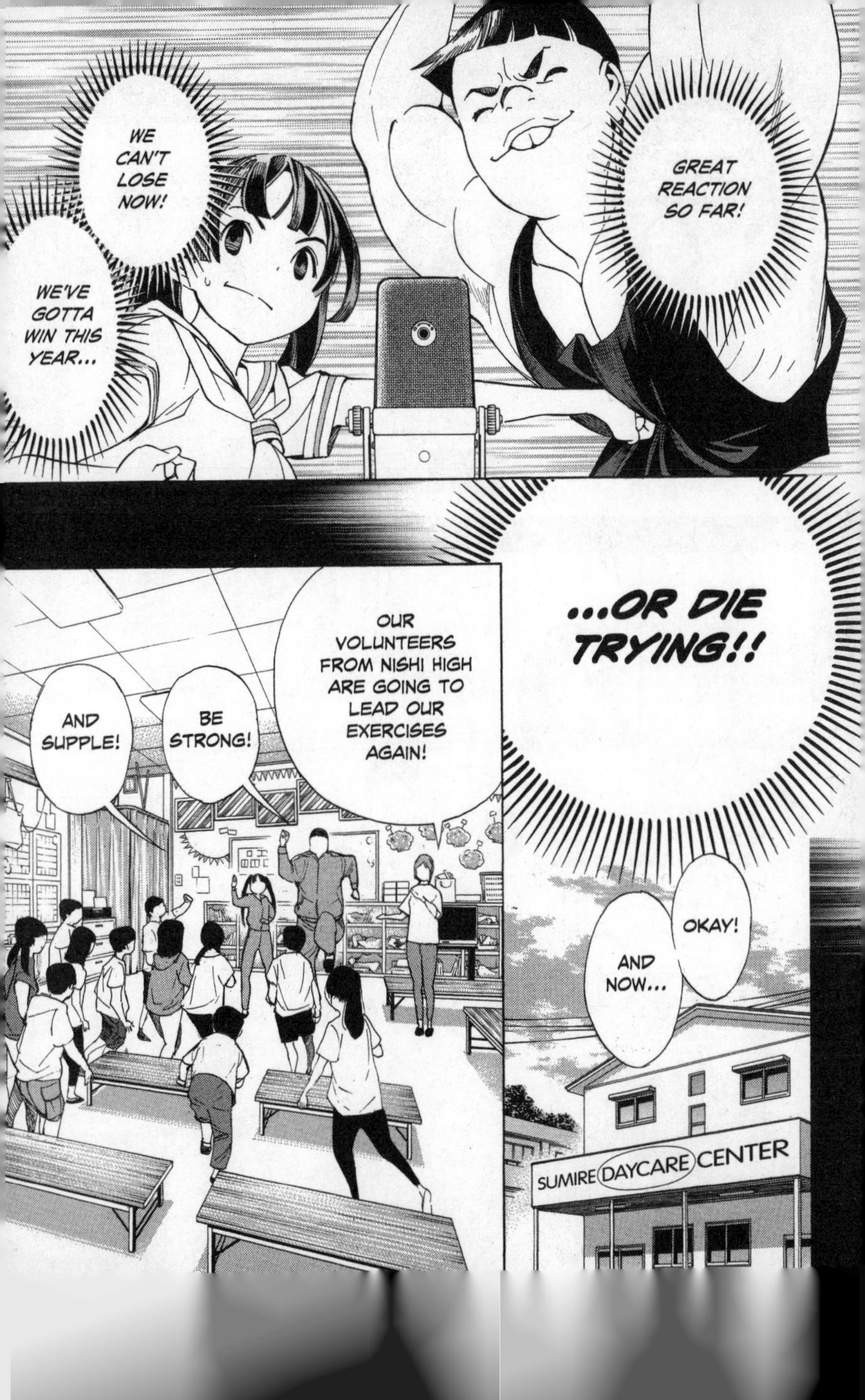
GREAT REACTION SO FAR!
WE CAN'T LOSE NOW!
WE'VE GOTTA WIN THIS YEAR...
...OR DIE TRYING!!
OKAY!
AND NOW...
SUMIRE DAYCARE CENTER
OUR VOLUNTEERS FROM NISHI HIGH ARE GOING TO LEAD OUR EXERCISES AGAIN!
BE STRONG!
AND SUPPLE!

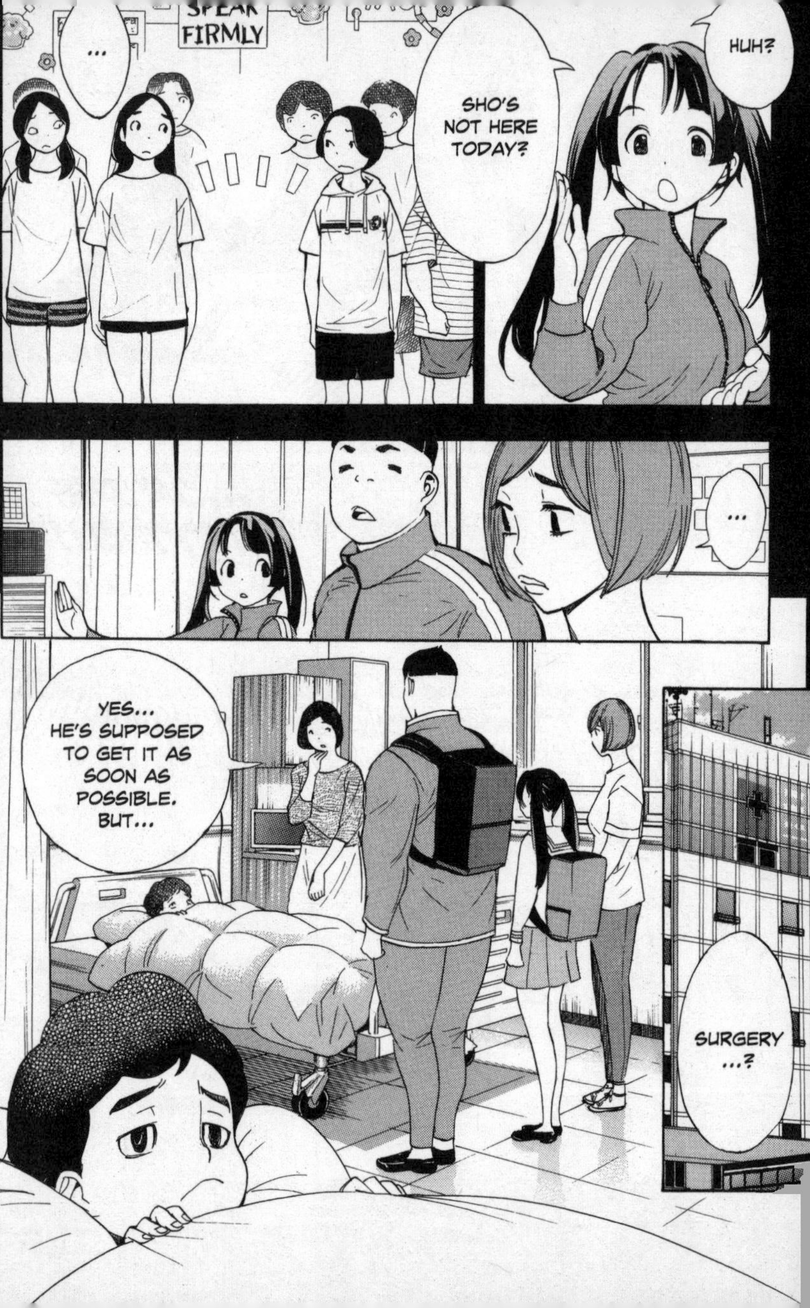
HUH?
SHO'S NOT HERE TODAY?
FIRMLY
...
...
SURGERY ...?
YES... HE'S SUPPOSED TO GET IT AS SOON AS POSSIBLE. BUT...

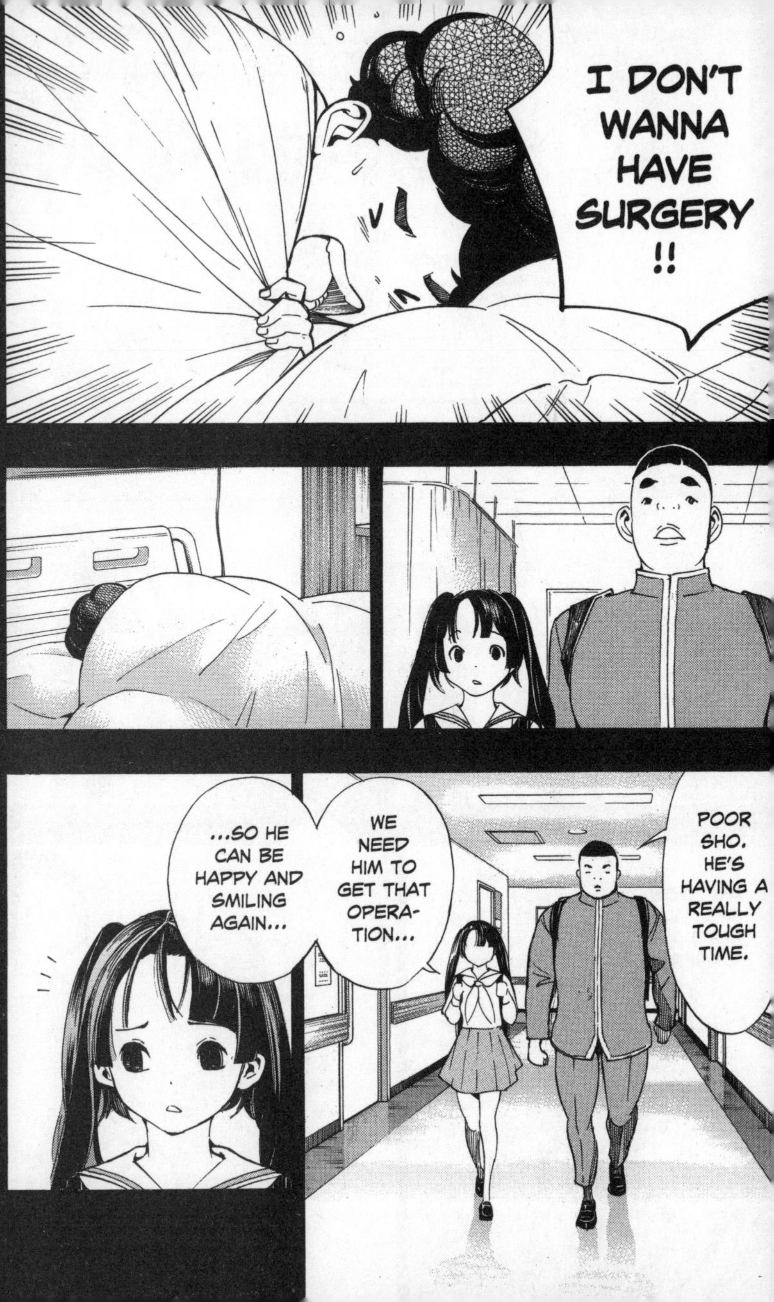
I DON'T WANNA HAVE SURGERY !!
POOR SHO. HE'S HAVING A REALLY TOUGH TIME.
WE NEED HIM TO GET THAT OPERATION...
...SO HE CAN BE HAPPY AND SMILING AGAIN...

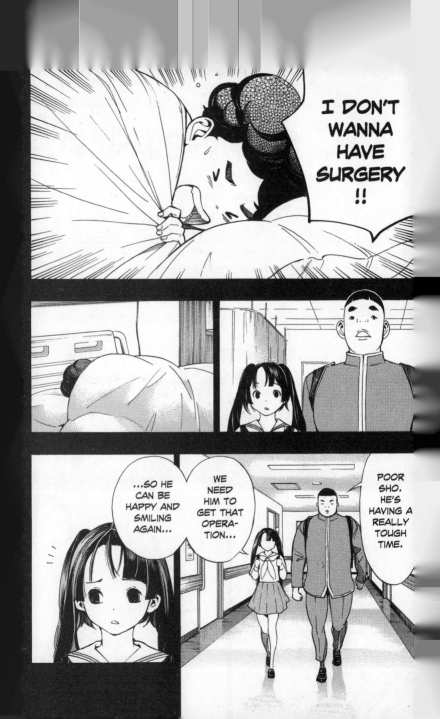

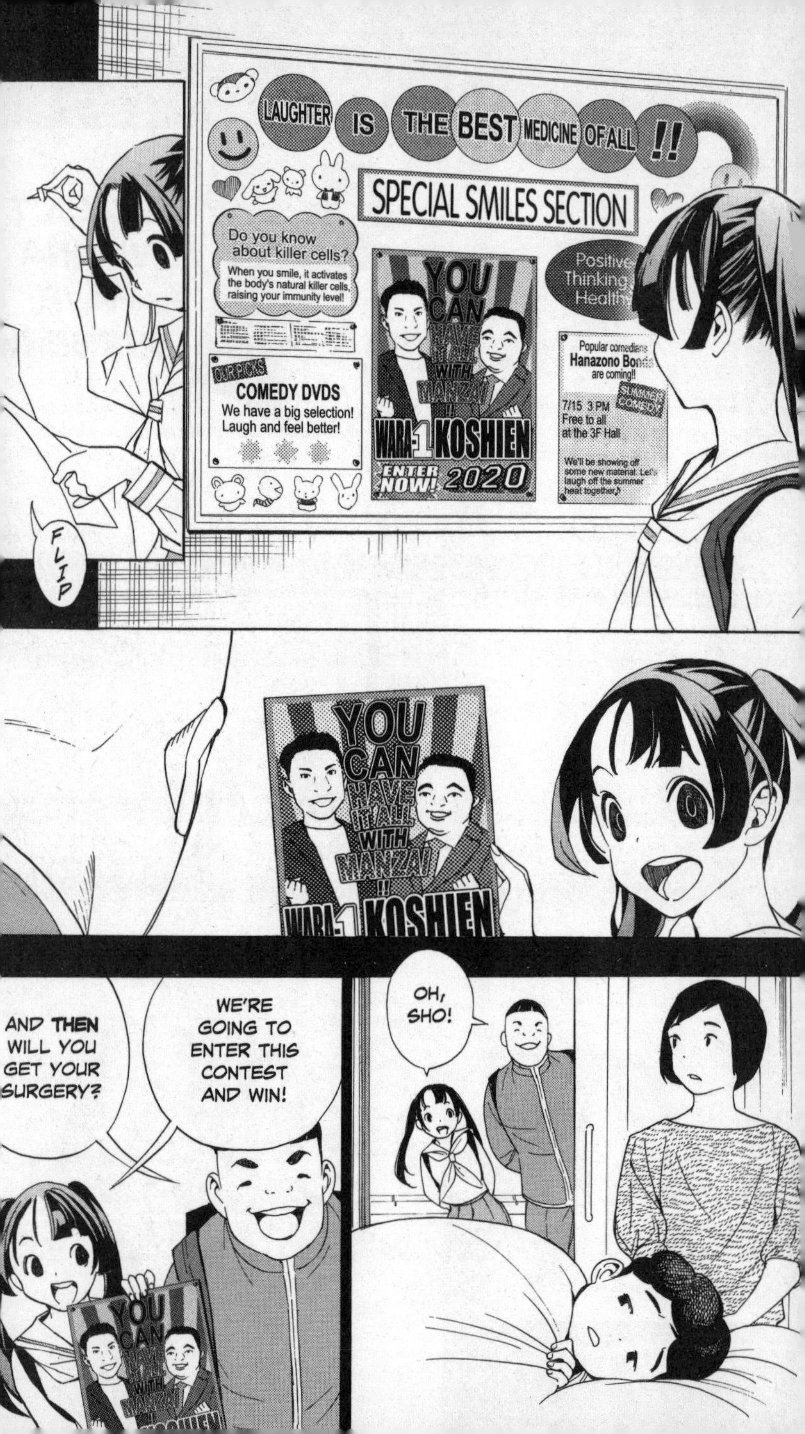
LAUGHTER IS THE BEST MEDICINE OF ALL !!
SPECIAL SMILES SECTION
Do you know about killer cells?
When you smile, it activates the body's natural killer cells, raising your immunity level!
OUR PICKS
COMEDY DVDS
We have a big selection! Laugh and feel better!
YOU CAN HAVE IT ALL WITH MANZAI!! WARA-1 KOSHIEN 2020
ENTER NOW!
Popular comedians
are coming!!
7/15 3 PM
Free to all
at the 3F Hall
We'll be showing off some new material. Let's laugh off the summer heat together♪
FLIP
YOU CAN HAVE IT ALL WITH MANZAI!! WARA-1 KOSHIEN
OH, SHO!
WE'RE GOING TO ENTER THIS CONTEST AND WIN!
AND THEN WILL YOU GET YOUR SURGERY?

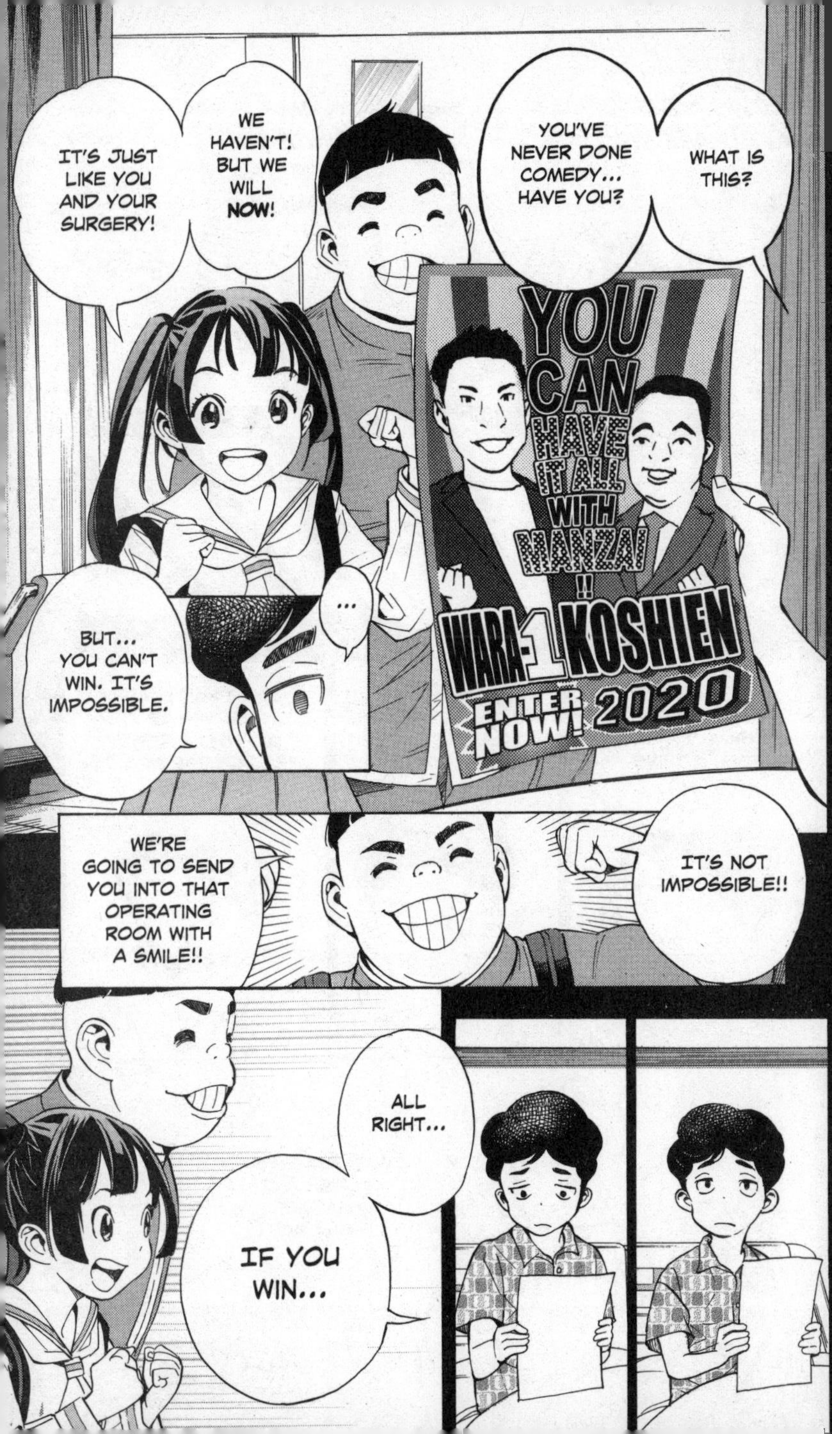
WHAT IS THIS?
YOU'VE NEVER DONE COMEDY... HAVE YOU?
WE HAVEN'T! BUT WE WILL NOW!
IT'S JUST LIKE YOU AND YOUR SURGERY!
YOU CAN HAVE IT ALL WITH MANZAI!!
WARA-1 KOSHIEN 2020
ENTER NOW!
...
BUT... YOU CAN'T WIN. IT'S IMPOSSIBLE.
IT'S NOT IMPOSSIBLE!!
WE'RE GOING TO SEND YOU INTO THAT OPERATING ROOM WITH A SMILE!!
ALL RIGHT...
IF YOU WIN...

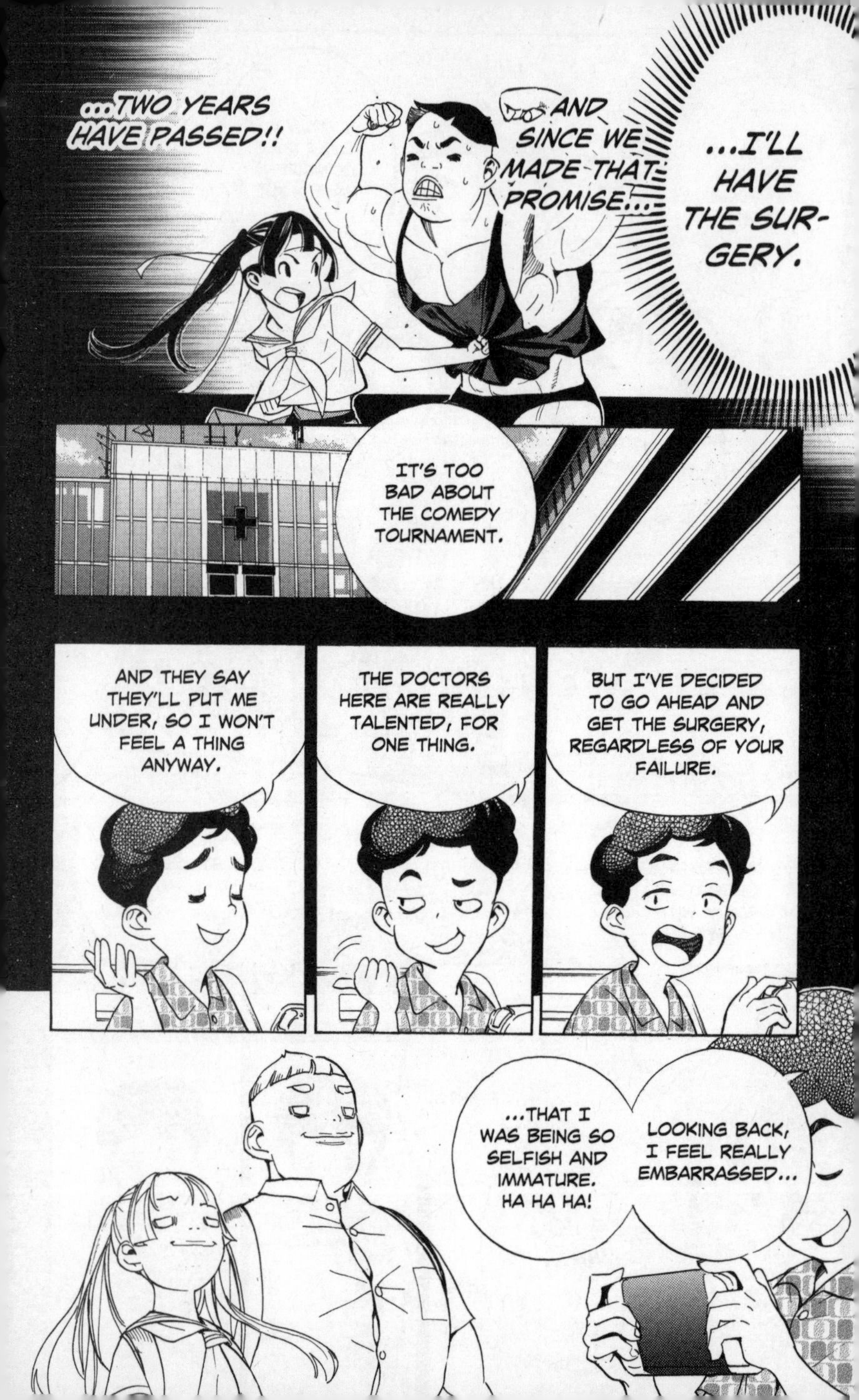
...I'LL HAVE THE SURGERY.
AND SINCE WE MADE THAT PROMISE...
...TWO YEARS HAVE PASSED!!
IT'S TOO BAD ABOUT THE COMEDY TOURNAMENT.
BUT I'VE DECIDED TO GO AHEAD AND GET THE SURGERY, REGARDLESS OF YOUR FAILURE.
THE DOCTORS HERE ARE REALLY TALENTED, FOR ONE THING.
AND THEY SAY THEY'LL PUT ME UNDER, SO I WON'T FEEL A THING ANYWAY.
LOOKING BACK, I FEEL REALLY EMBARRASSED...
...THAT I WAS BEING SO SELFISH AND IMMATURE. HA HA HA!

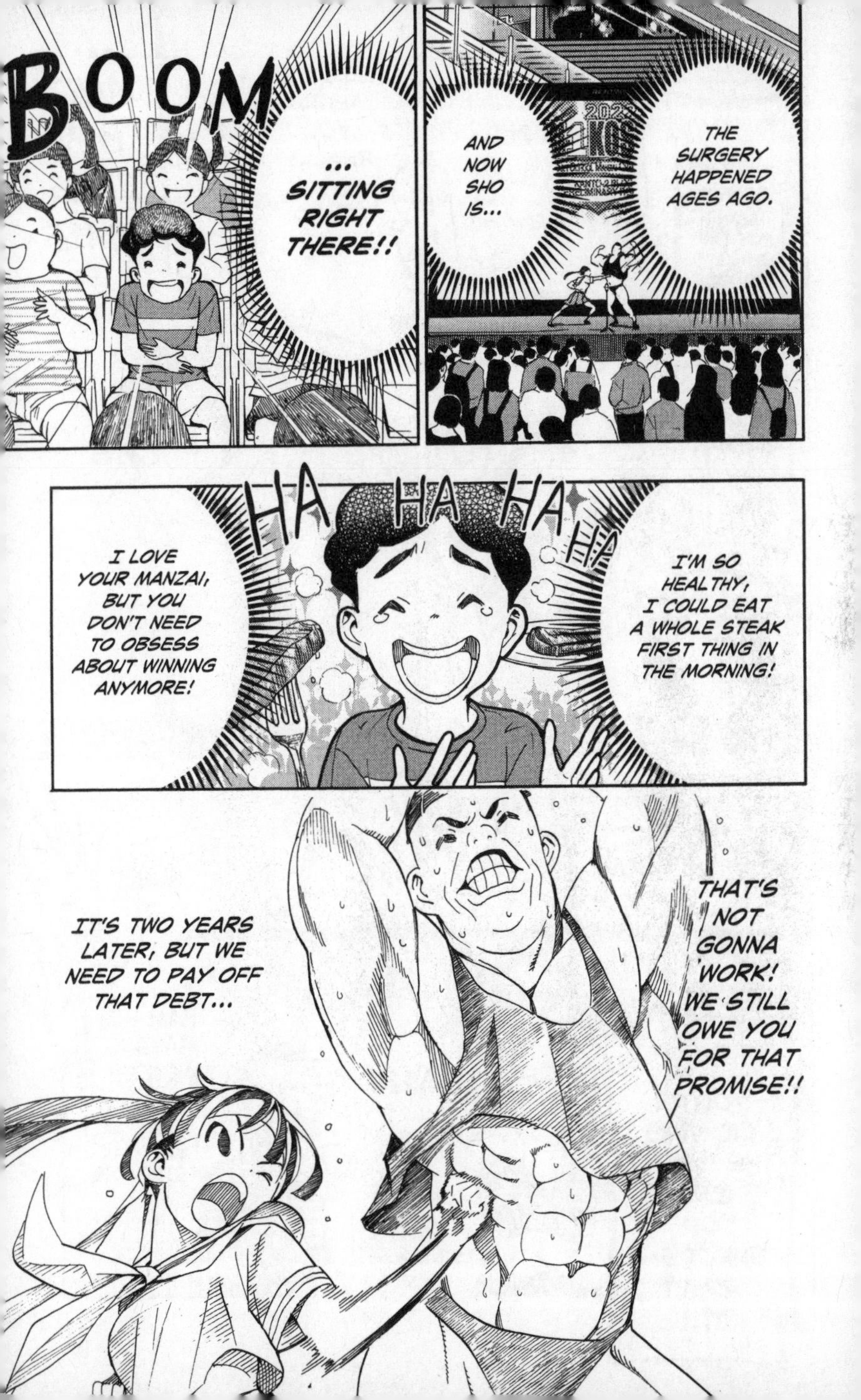
THE SURGERY HAPPENED AGES AGO.
AND NOW SHO IS...
... SITTING RIGHT THERE!!
BOOM
I'M SO HEALTHY, I COULD EAT A WHOLE STEAK FIRST THING IN THE MORNING!
HA HA HA HA
I LOVE YOUR MANZAI, BUT YOU DON'T NEED TO OBSESS ABOUT WINNING ANYMORE!
THAT'S NOT GONNA WORK! WE STILL OWE YOU FOR THAT PROMISE!!
IT'S TWO YEARS LATER, BUT WE NEED TO PAY OFF THAT DEBT...

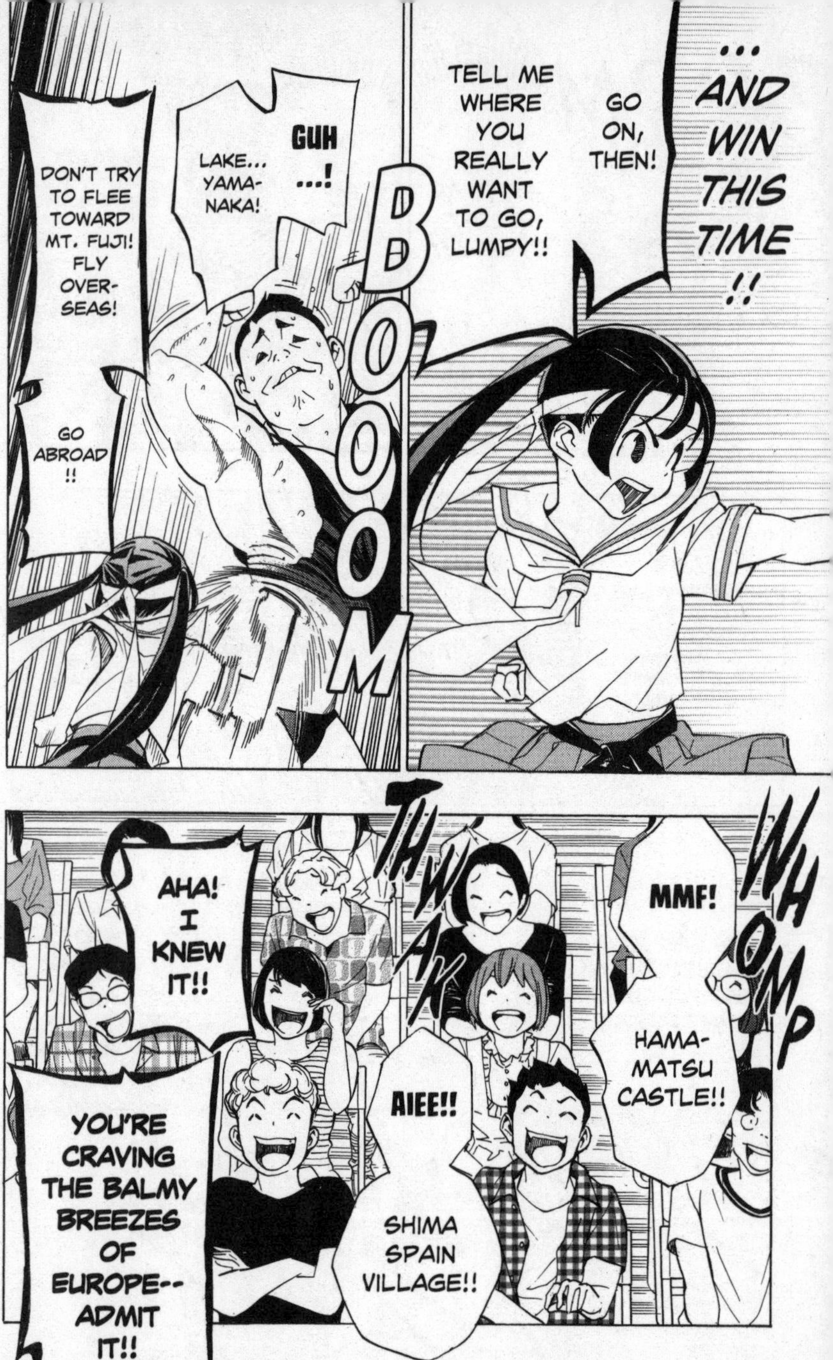
...AND WIN THIS TIME!!
GO ON, THEN!
TELL ME WHERE YOU REALLY WANT TO GO, LUMPY!!
BOOOOOM
GUH ...!
LAKE... YAMANAKA!
DON'T TRY TO FLEE TOWARD MT. FUJI! FLY OVERSEAS!
GO ABROAD!!
WHOMP
MMF!
HAMAMATSU CASTLE!!
THWAK
AIEE!!
SHIMA SPAIN VILLAGE!!
AHA! I KNEW IT!!
YOU'RE CRAVING THE BALMY BREEZES OF EUROPE--ADMIT IT!!

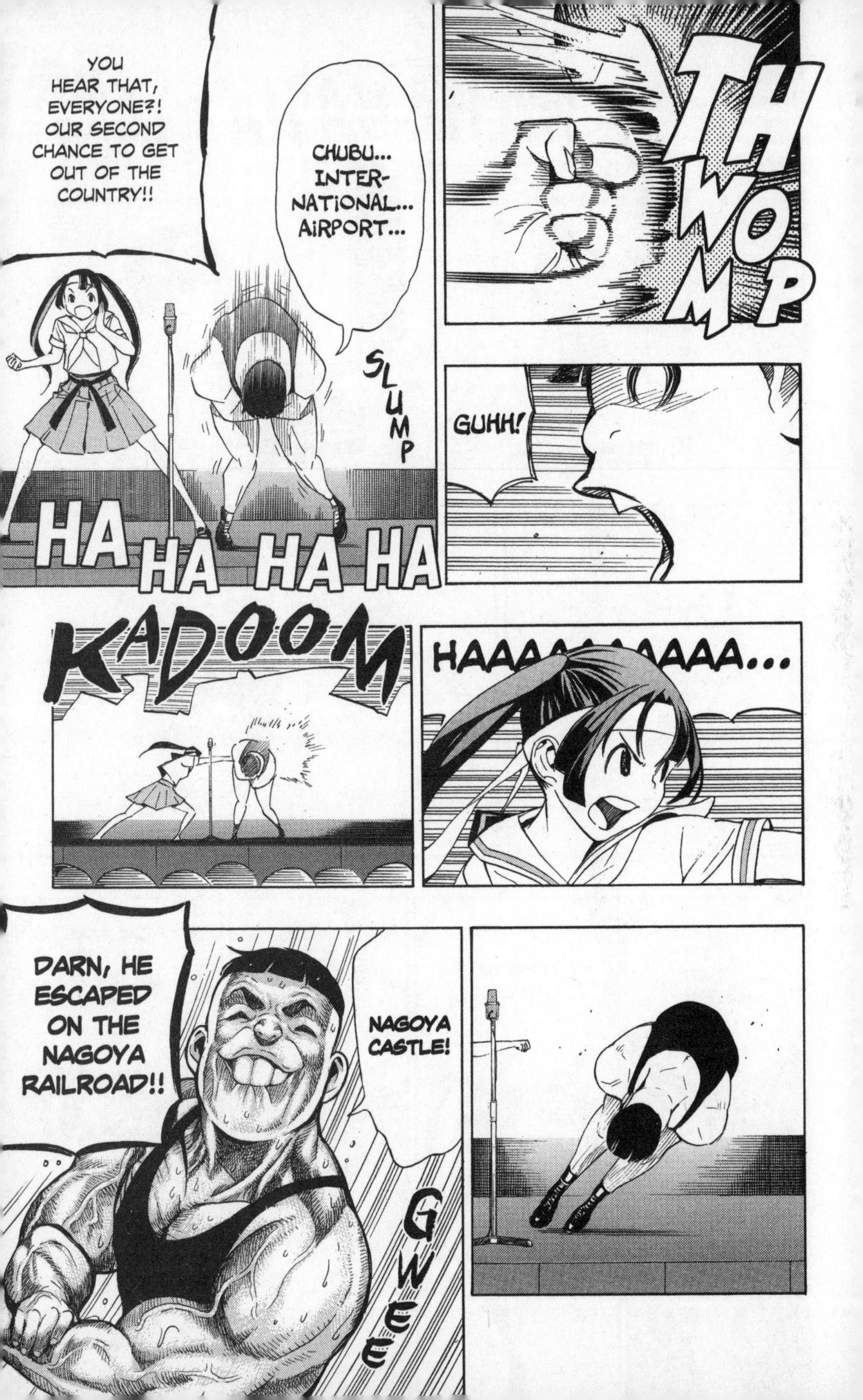
THWOMP
GUHH!
CHUBU... INTER-NATIONAL... AIRPORT...
YOU HEAR THAT, EVERYONE?! OUR SECOND CHANCE TO GET OUT OF THE COUNTRY!!
SLUMP
HA HA HA HA HA
HAAAAAAAAAA...
KADOOM
NAGOYA CASTLE!
DARN, HE ESCAPED ON THE NAGOYA RAILROAD!!
GWEE

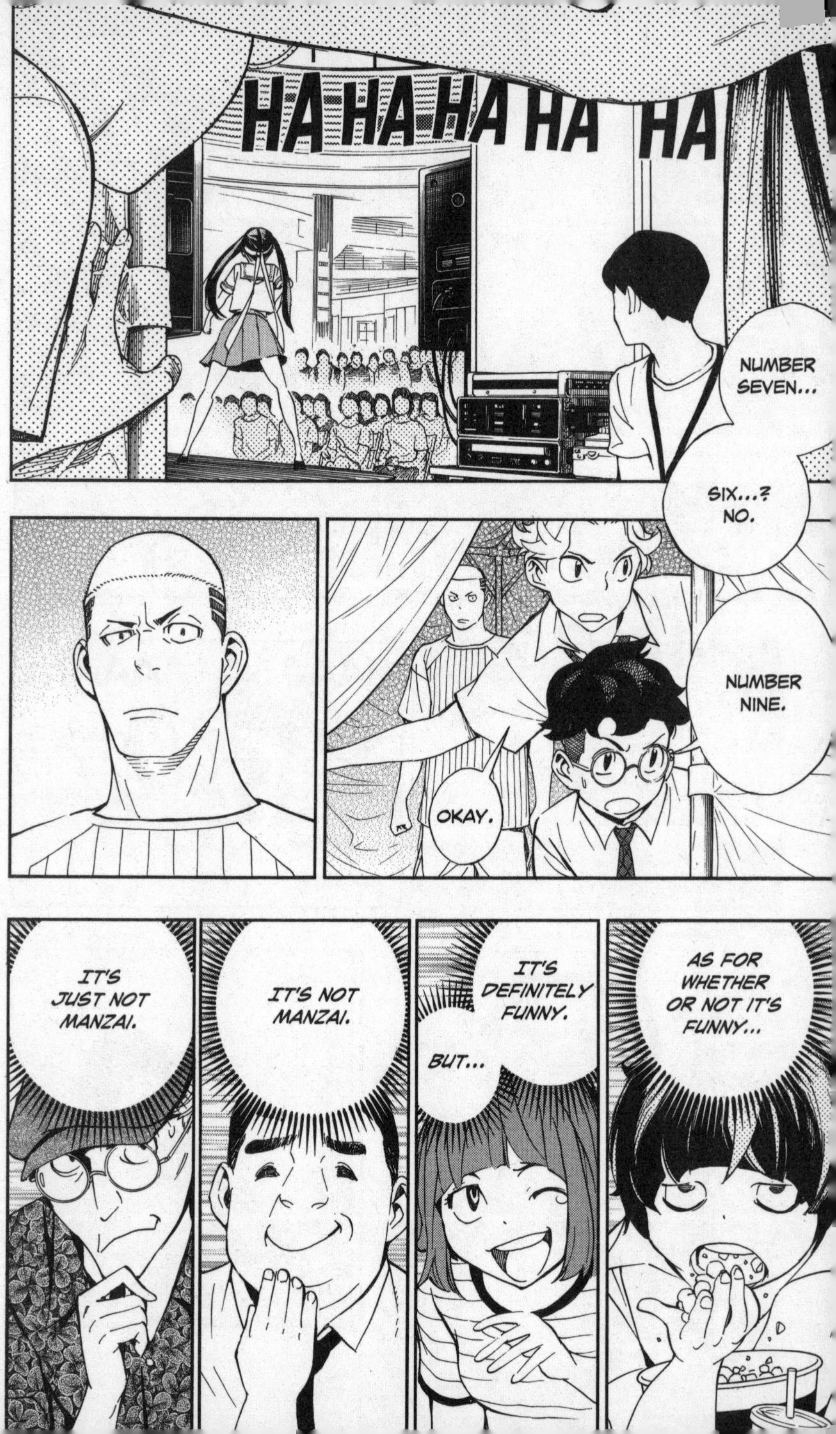
HA HA HA HA HA
NUMBER SEVEN...
SIX...? NO.
NUMBER NINE.
OKAY.
AS FOR WHETHER OR NOT IT'S FUNNY...
IT'S DEFINITELY FUNNY.
BUT...
IT'S NOT MANZAI.
IT'S JUST NOT MANZAI.

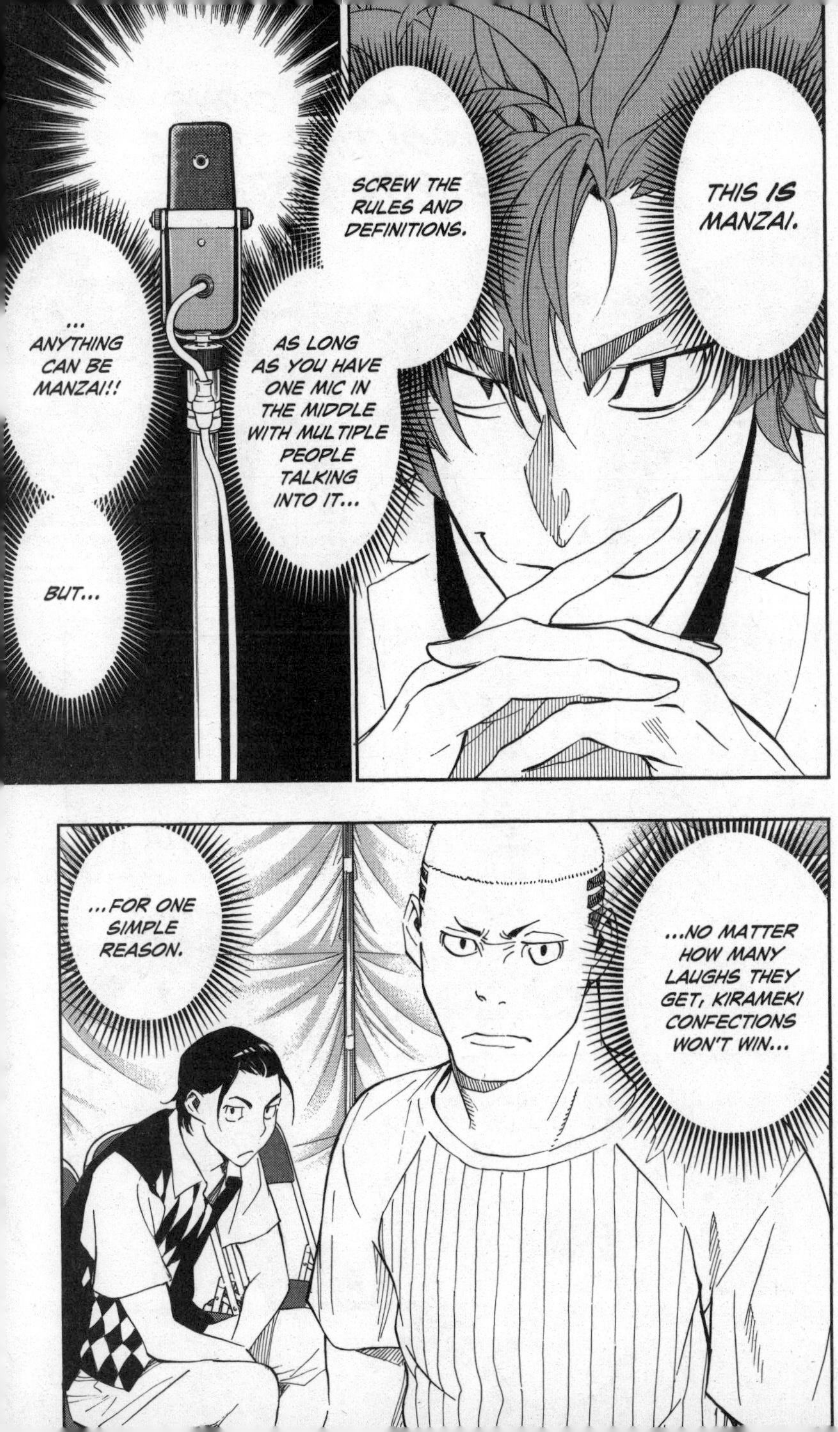
THIS IS MANZAI.
SCREW THE RULES AND DEFINITIONS.
AS LONG AS YOU HAVE ONE MIC IN THE MIDDLE WITH MULTIPLE PEOPLE TALKING INTO IT...
...ANYTHING CAN BE MANZAI!!
BUT...
...NO MATTER HOW MANY LAUGHS THEY GET, KIRAMEKI CONFECTIONS WON'T WIN...
...FOR ONE SIMPLE REASON.

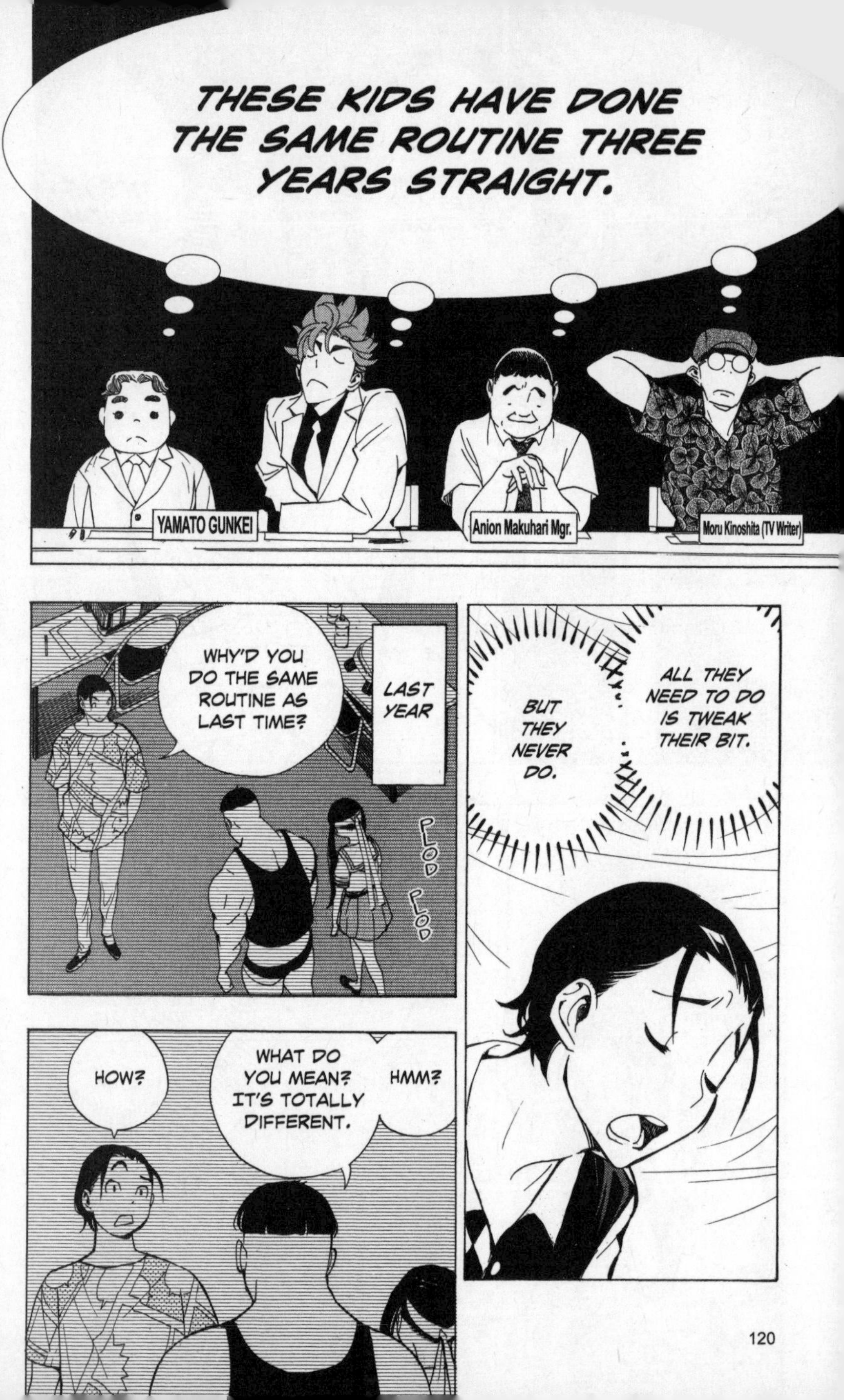
THESE KIDS HAVE DONE THE SAME ROUTINE THREE YEARS STRAIGHT.
Moru Kinoshita (TV Writer)
Anion Makuhari Mgr.
YAMATO GUNKEI
ALL THEY NEED TO DO IS TWEAK THEIR BIT.
BUT THEY NEVER DO.
LAST YEAR
WHY'D YOU DO THE SAME ROUTINE AS LAST TIME?
PLOD PLOD
HMM?
WHAT DO YOU MEAN? IT'S TOTALLY DIFFERENT.
HOW?

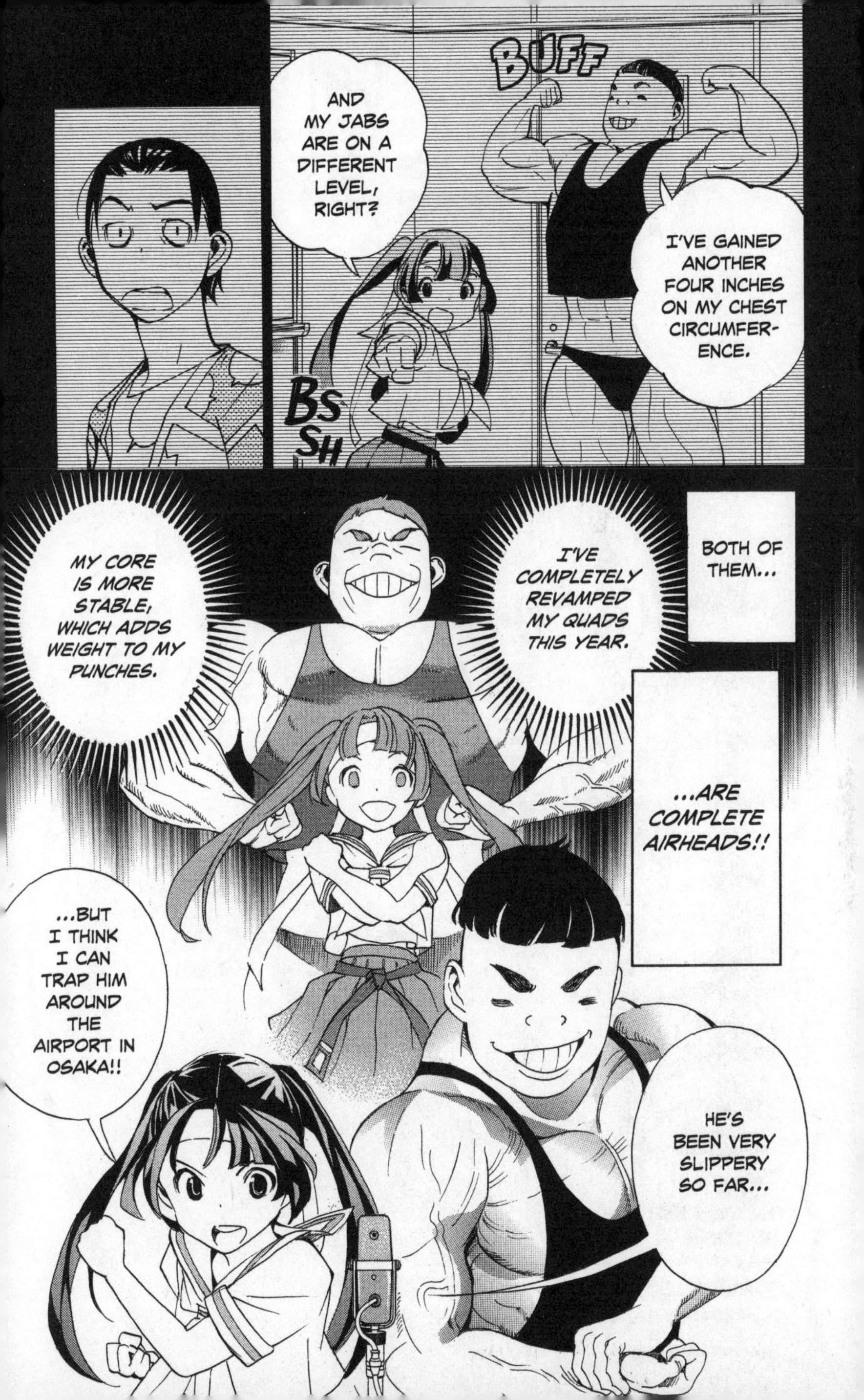
BUFF
I'VE GAINED ANOTHER FOUR INCHES ON MY CHEST CIRCUMFERENCE.
AND MY JABS ARE ON A DIFFERENT LEVEL, RIGHT?
BSSH
BOTH OF THEM...
I'VE COMPLETELY REVAMPED MY QUADS THIS YEAR.
MY CORE IS MORE STABLE, WHICH ADDS WEIGHT TO MY PUNCHES.
...ARE COMPLETE AIRHEADS!!
HE'S BEEN VERY SLIPPERY SO FAR...
...BUT I THINK I CAN TRAP HIM AROUND THE AIRPORT IN OSAKA!!

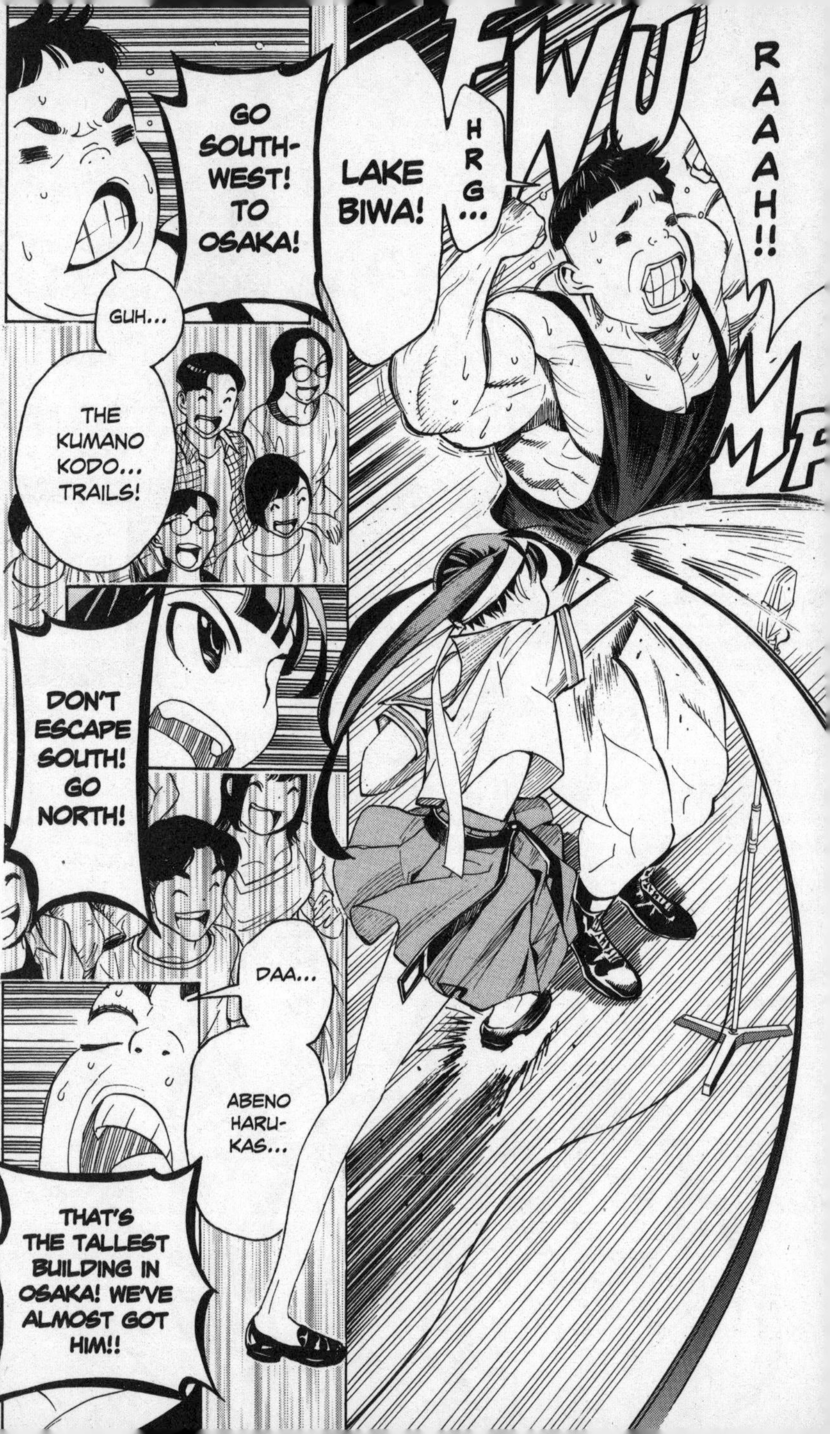
RAAAH!!
FWUMMP
HRG...
LAKE BIWA!
GO SOUTH-WEST! TO OSAKA!
GUH...
THE KUMANO KODO... TRAILS!
DON'T ESCAPE SOUTH! GO NORTH!
DAA...
ABENO HARU-KAS...
THAT'S THE TALLEST BUILDING IN OSAKA! WE'VE ALMOST GOT HIM!!

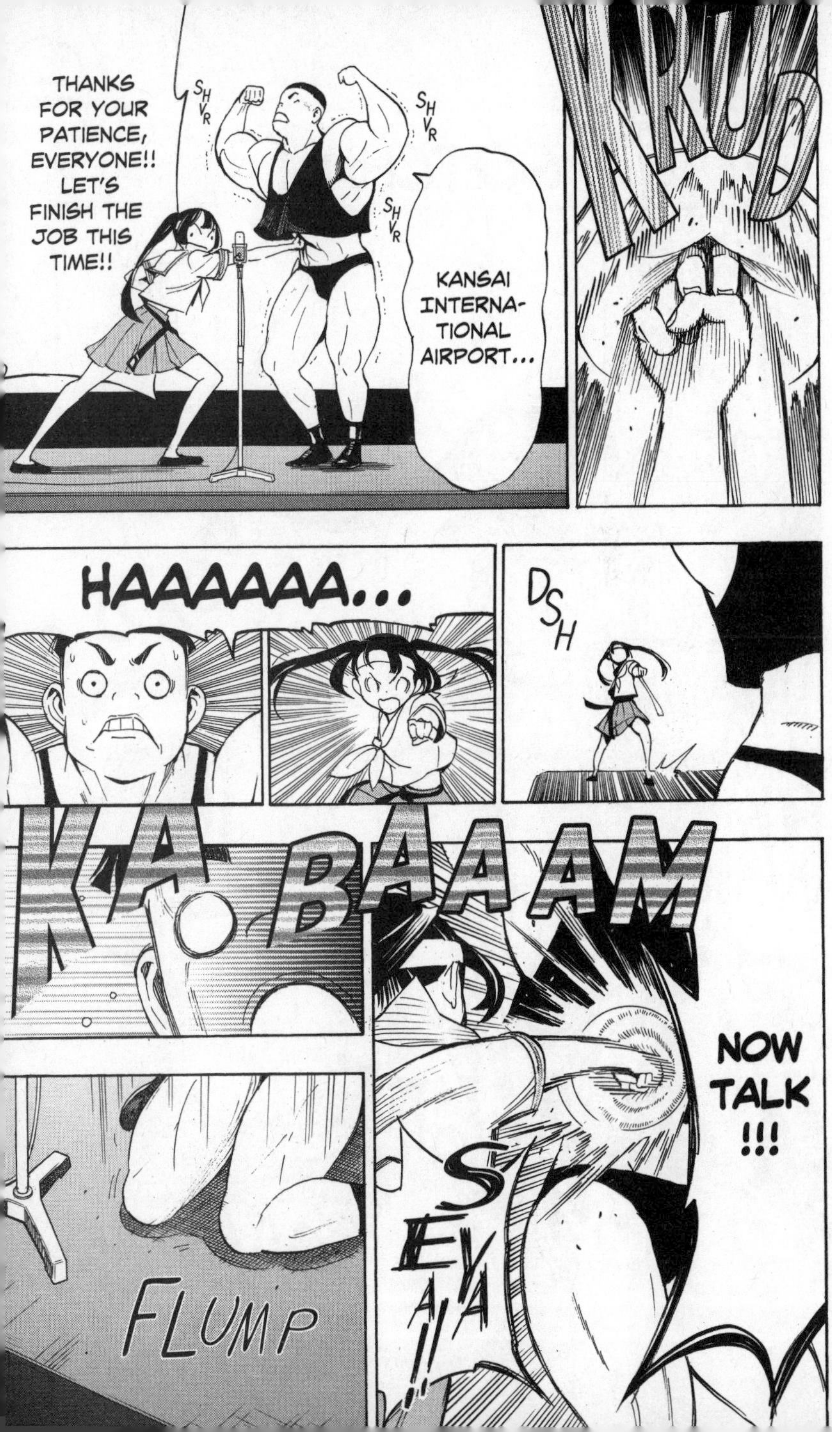
KRUD
SHVR
SHVR
SHVR
KANSAI INTERNATIONAL AIRPORT...
THANKS FOR YOUR PATIENCE, EVERYONE!! LET'S FINISH THE JOB THIS TIME!!
DSH
HAAAAAAA...
KA-BAAAM
NOW TALK!!!
SEEYAAA!!
FLUMP

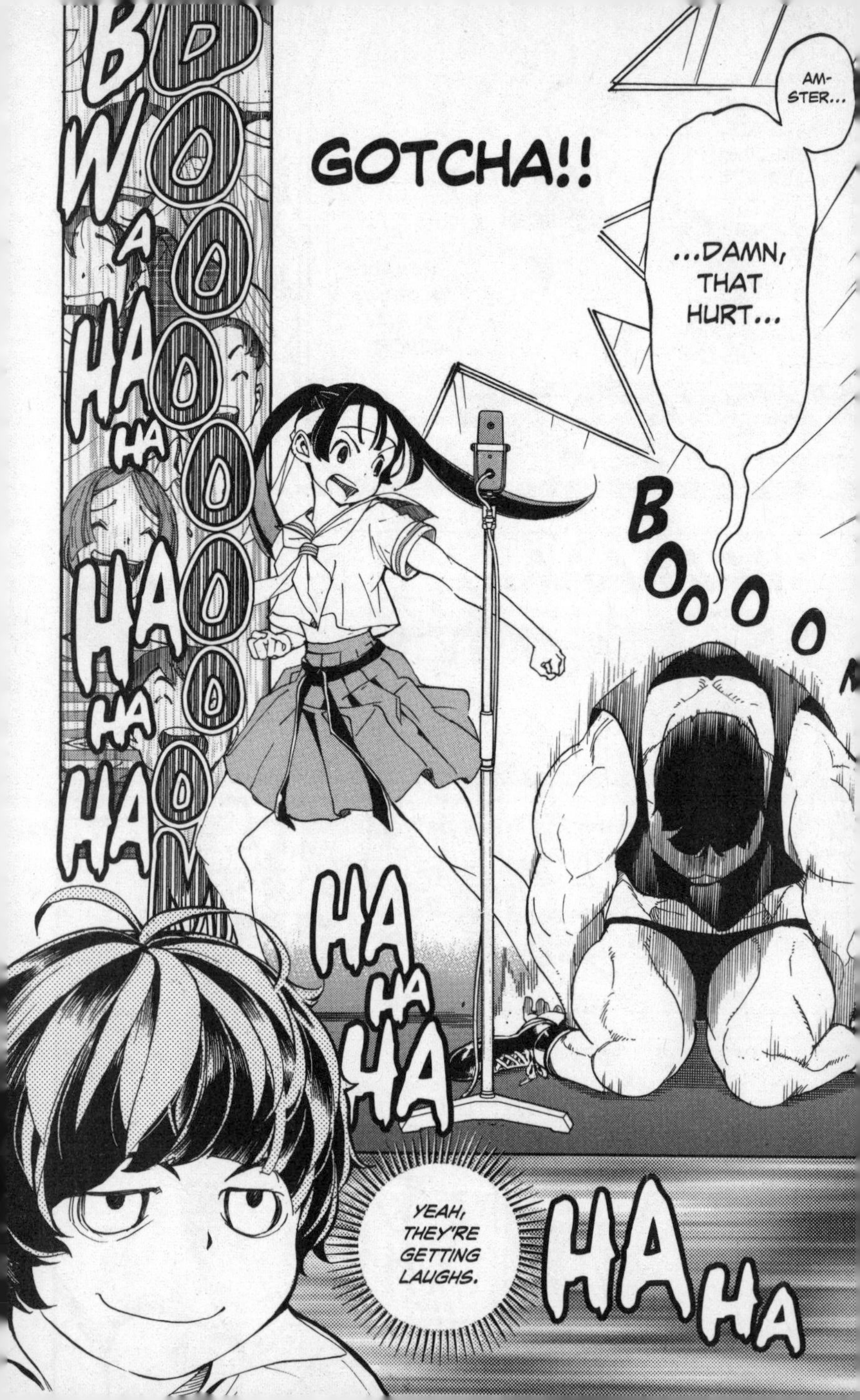

AM-STER...
...DAMN, THAT HURT...
BOOOO
GOTCHA!!
BWA HA HA HA HA HA HA
BOOOOOOOOO
HA HA HA
YEAH, THEY'RE GETTING LAUGHS.
HA HA HA

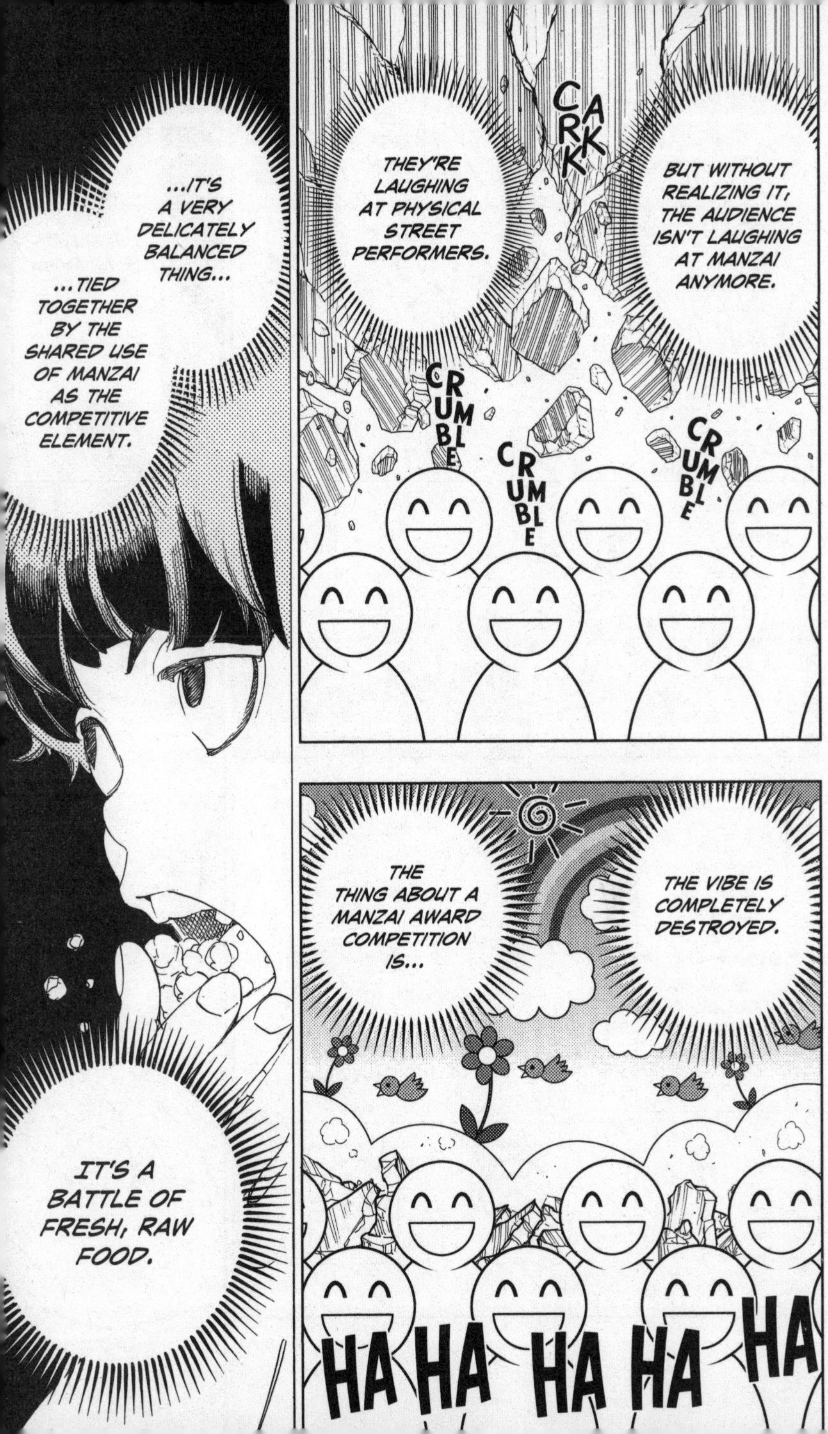
BUT WITHOUT REALIZING IT, THE AUDIENCE ISN'T LAUGHING AT MANZAI ANYMORE.
CARKK
THEY'RE LAUGHING AT PHYSICAL STREET PERFORMERS.
CRUMBLE
CRUMBLE
CRUMBLE
THE VIBE IS COMPLETELY DESTROYED.
THE THING ABOUT A MANZAI AWARD COMPETITION IS...
HA HA HA HA HA HA
...IT'S A VERY DELICATELY BALANCED THING...
...TIED TOGETHER BY THE SHARED USE OF MANZAI AS THE COMPETITIVE ELEMENT.
IT'S A BATTLE OF FRESH, RAW FOOD.

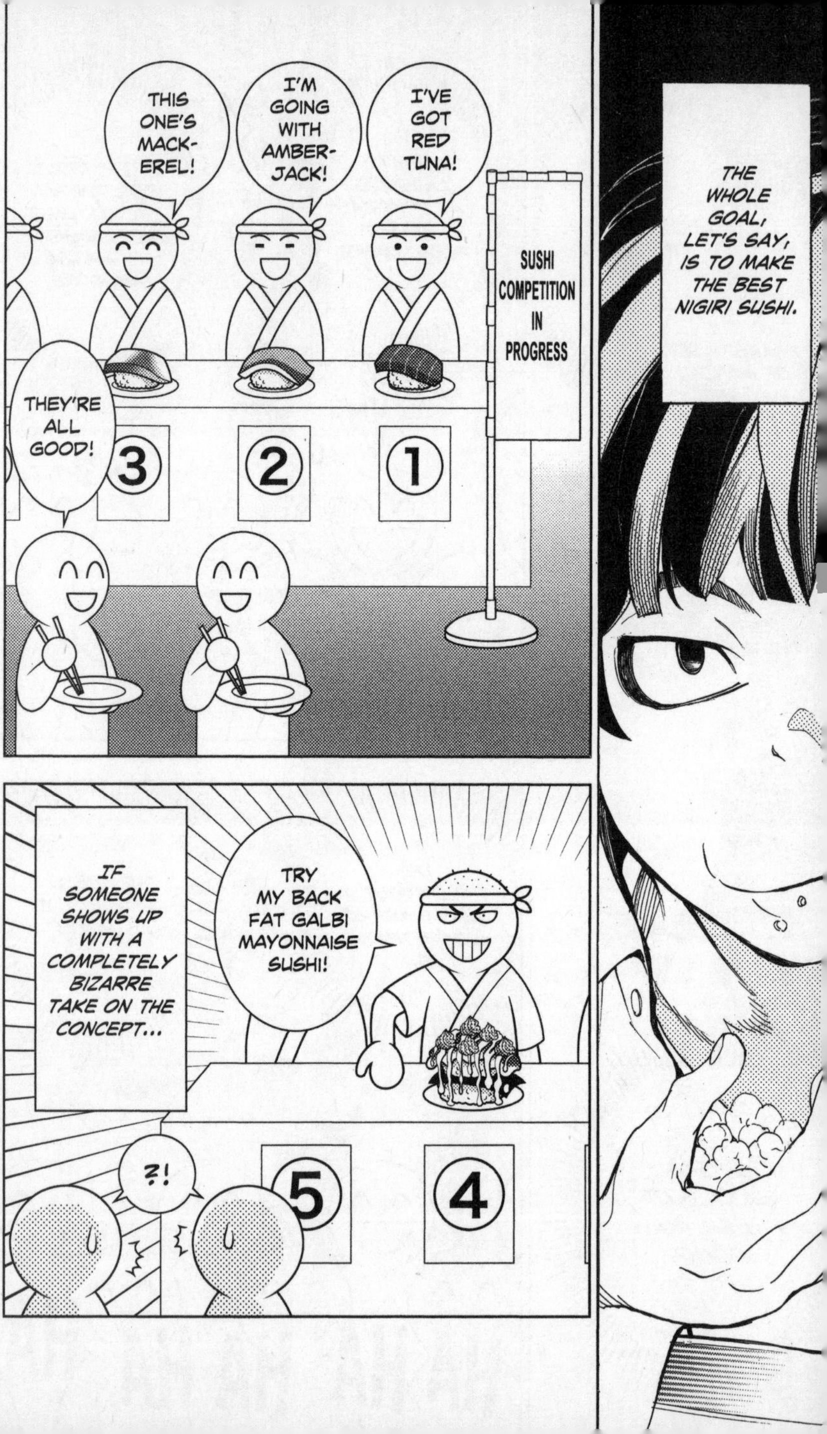

THE WHOLE GOAL, LET'S SAY, IS TO MAKE THE BEST NIGIRI SUSHI.
SUSHI COMPETITION IN PROGRESS
I'VE GOT RED TUNA!
I'M GOING WITH AMBER-JACK!
THIS ONE'S MACK-EREL!
THEY'RE ALL GOOD!
IF SOMEONE SHOWS UP WITH A COMPLETELY BIZARRE TAKE ON THE CONCEPT...
TRY MY BACK FAT GALBI MAYONNAISE SUSHI!
?!

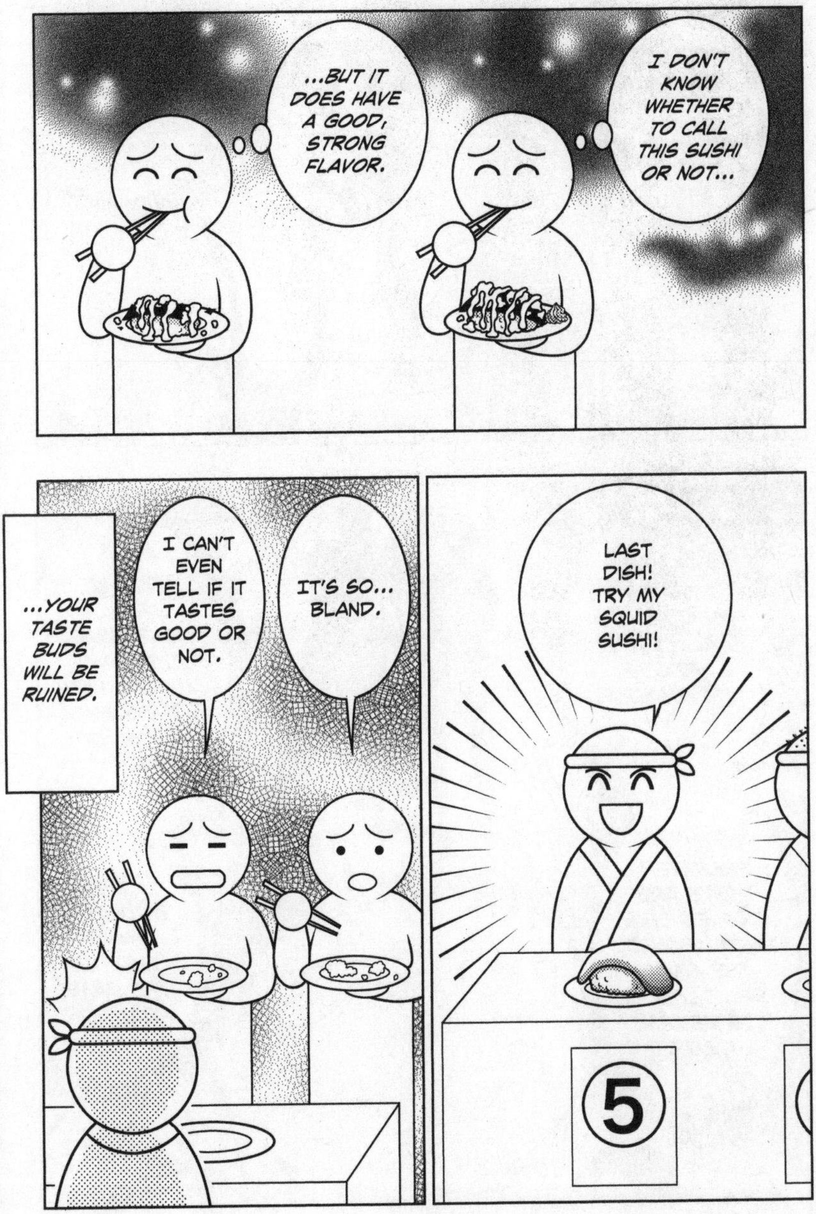
I DON'T KNOW WHETHER TO CALL THIS SUSHI OR NOT...
...BUT IT DOES HAVE A GOOD, STRONG FLAVOR.
LAST DISH! TRY MY SQUID SUSHI!
IT'S SO... BLAND.
I CAN'T EVEN TELL IF IT TASTES GOOD OR NOT.
...YOUR TASTE BUDS WILL BE RUINED.
5

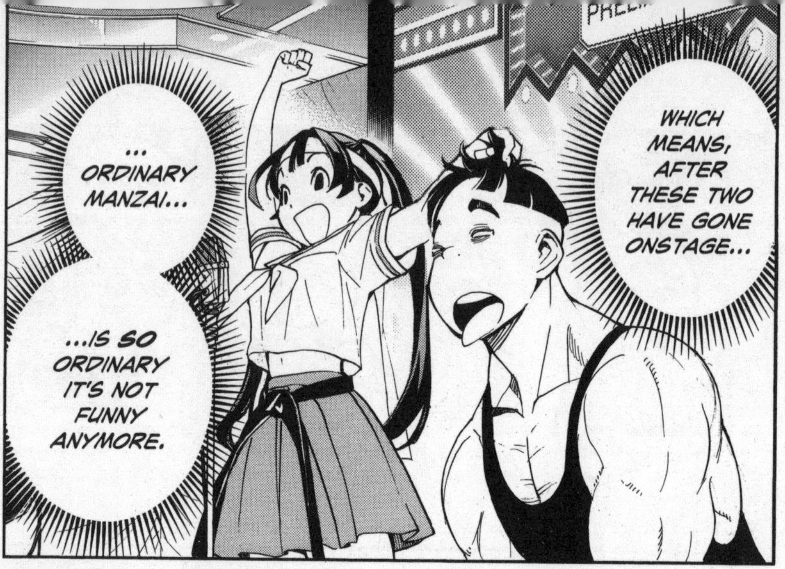
PRELI
WHICH MEANS, AFTER THESE TWO HAVE GONE ONSTAGE...
... ORDINARY MANZAI...
...IS SO ORDINARY IT'S NOT FUNNY ANYMORE.
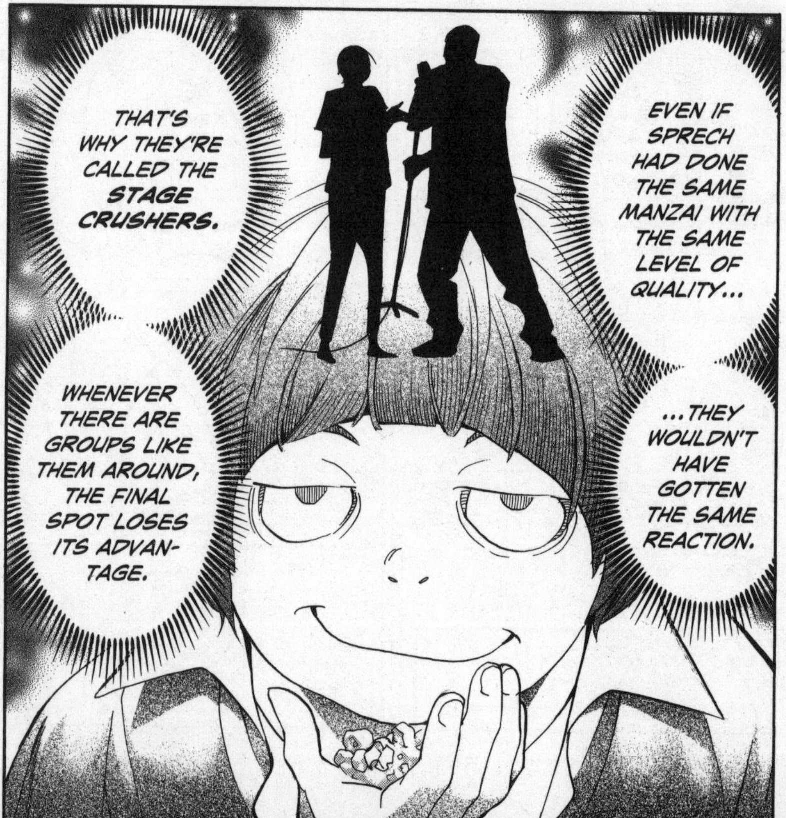
EVEN IF SPRECH HAD DONE THE SAME MANZAI WITH THE SAME LEVEL OF QUALITY...
...THEY WOULDN'T HAVE GOTTEN THE SAME REACTION.
THAT'S WHY THEY'RE CALLED THE STAGE CRUSHERS.
WHENEVER THERE ARE GROUPS LIKE THEM AROUND, THE FINAL SPOT LOSES ITS ADVAN-TAGE.

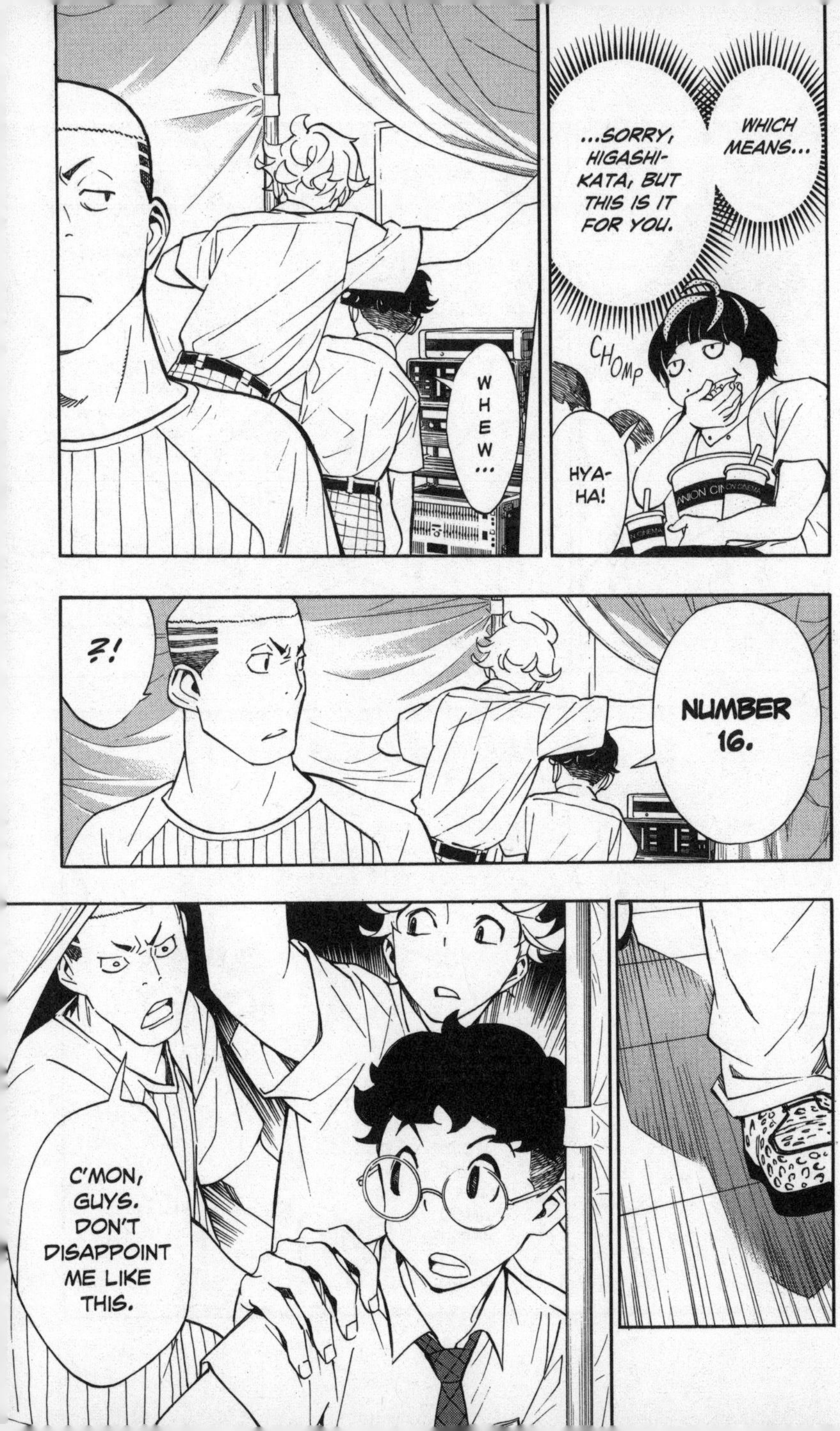
WHICH MEANS...
...SORRY, HIGASHI-KATA, BUT THIS IS IT FOR YOU.
CHOMP
HYA-HA!
WHEW...
NUMBER 16.
?!
C'MON, GUYS. DON'T DISAPPOINT ME LIKE THIS.

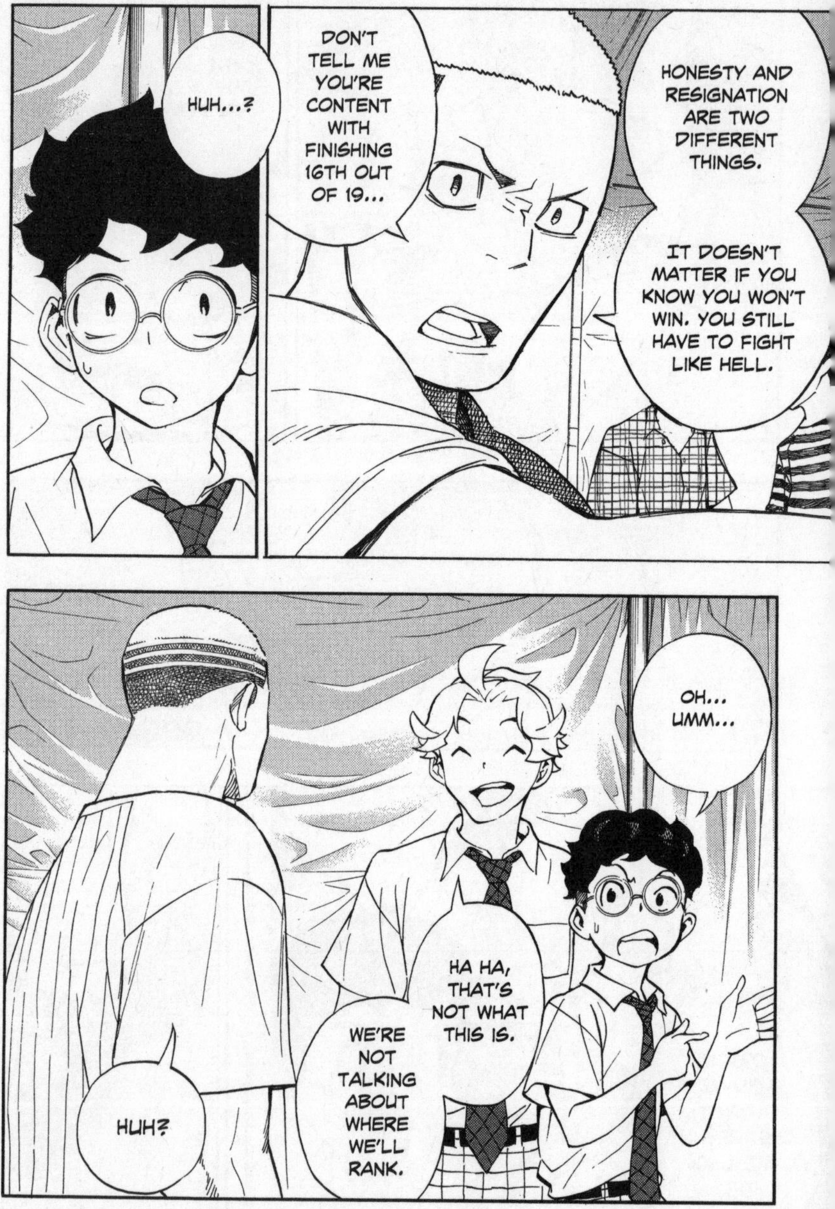
HONESTY AND RESIGNATION ARE TWO DIFFERENT THINGS.
IT DOESN'T MATTER IF YOU KNOW YOU WON'T WIN. YOU STILL HAVE TO FIGHT LIKE HELL.
DON'T TELL ME YOU'RE CONTENT WITH FINISHING 16TH OUT OF 19...
HUH...?
OH... UMM...
HA HA, THAT'S NOT WHAT THIS IS.
WE'RE NOT TALKING ABOUT WHERE WE'LL RANK.
HUH?

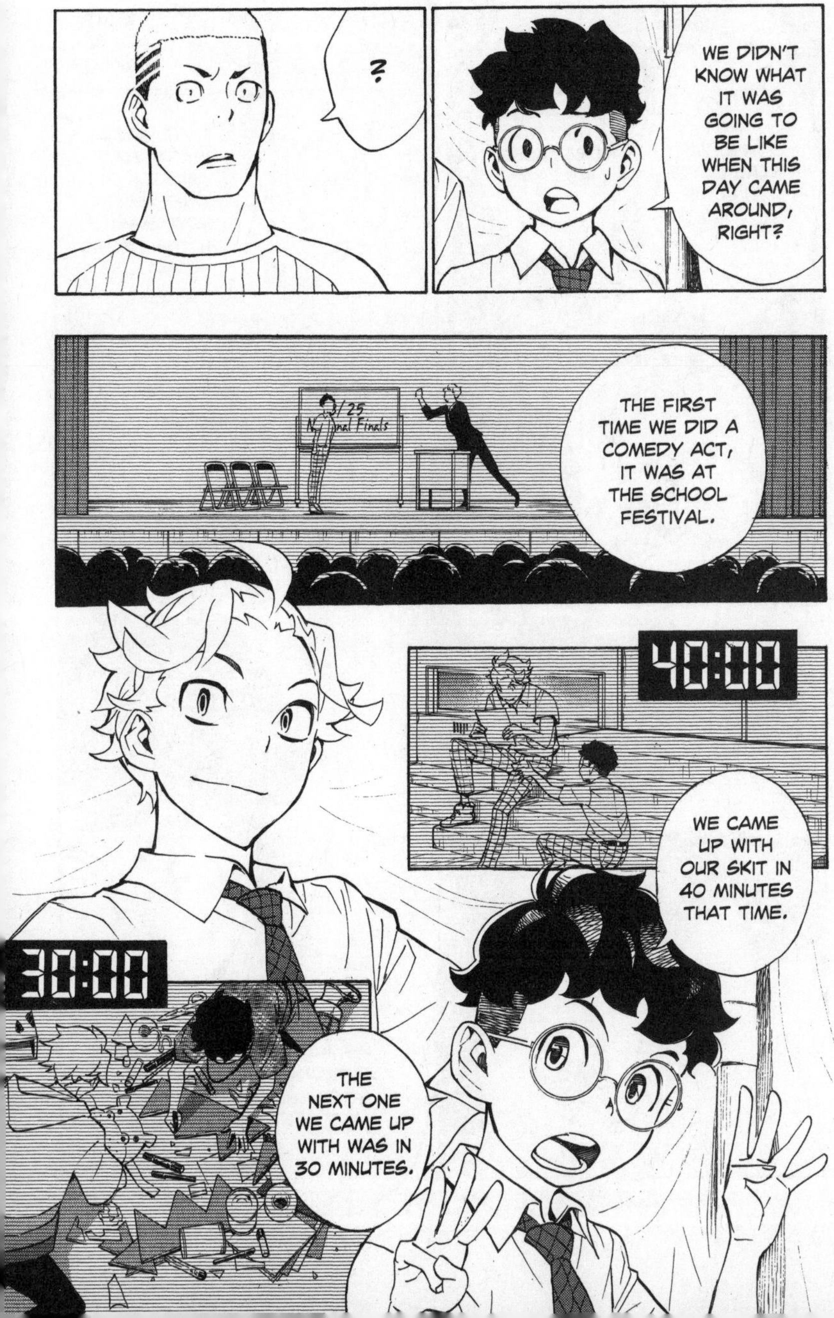
WE DIDN'T KNOW WHAT IT WAS GOING TO BE LIKE WHEN THIS DAY CAME AROUND, RIGHT?
?
THE FIRST TIME WE DID A COMEDY ACT, IT WAS AT THE SCHOOL FESTIVAL.
40:00
WE CAME UP WITH OUR SKIT IN 40 MINUTES THAT TIME.
30:00
THE NEXT ONE WE CAME UP WITH WAS IN 30 MINUTES.

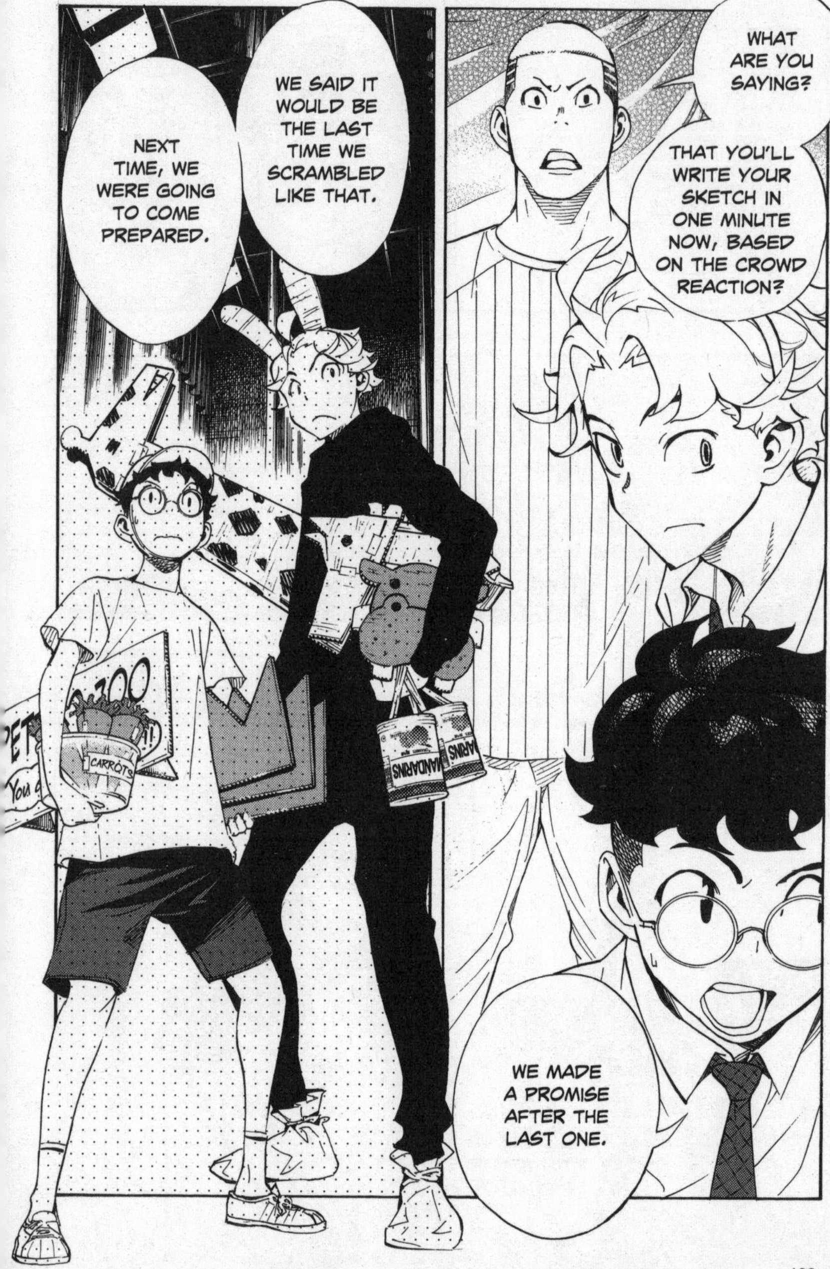
WHAT ARE YOU SAYING?
THAT YOU'LL WRITE YOUR SKETCH IN ONE MINUTE NOW, BASED ON THE CROWD REACTION?
WE MADE A PROMISE AFTER THE LAST ONE.
WE SAID IT WOULD BE THE LAST TIME WE SCRAMBLED LIKE THAT.
NEXT TIME, WE WERE GOING TO COME PREPARED.

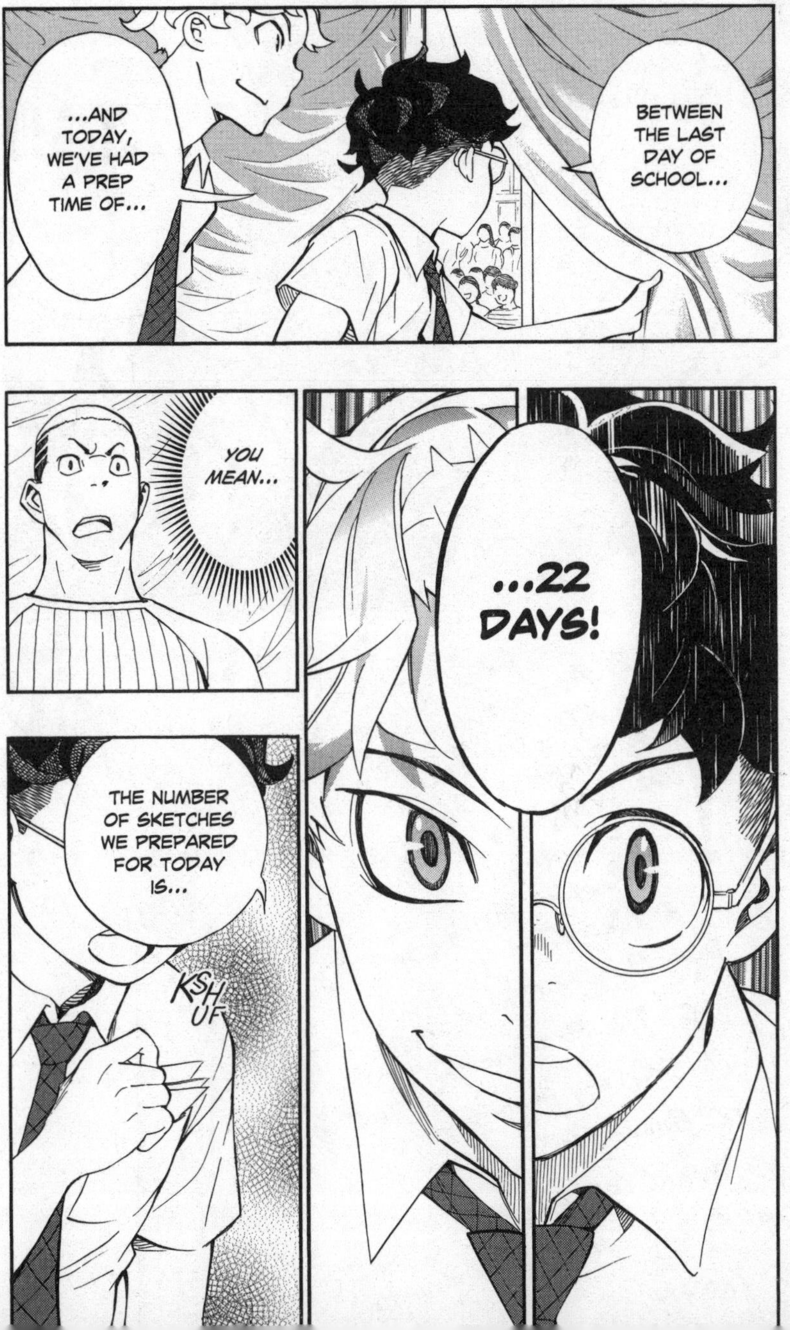
BETWEEN THE LAST DAY OF SCHOOL...
...AND TODAY, WE'VE HAD A PREP TIME OF...
...22 DAYS!
YOU MEAN...
THE NUMBER OF SKETCHES WE PREPARED FOR TODAY IS...
KSHUF

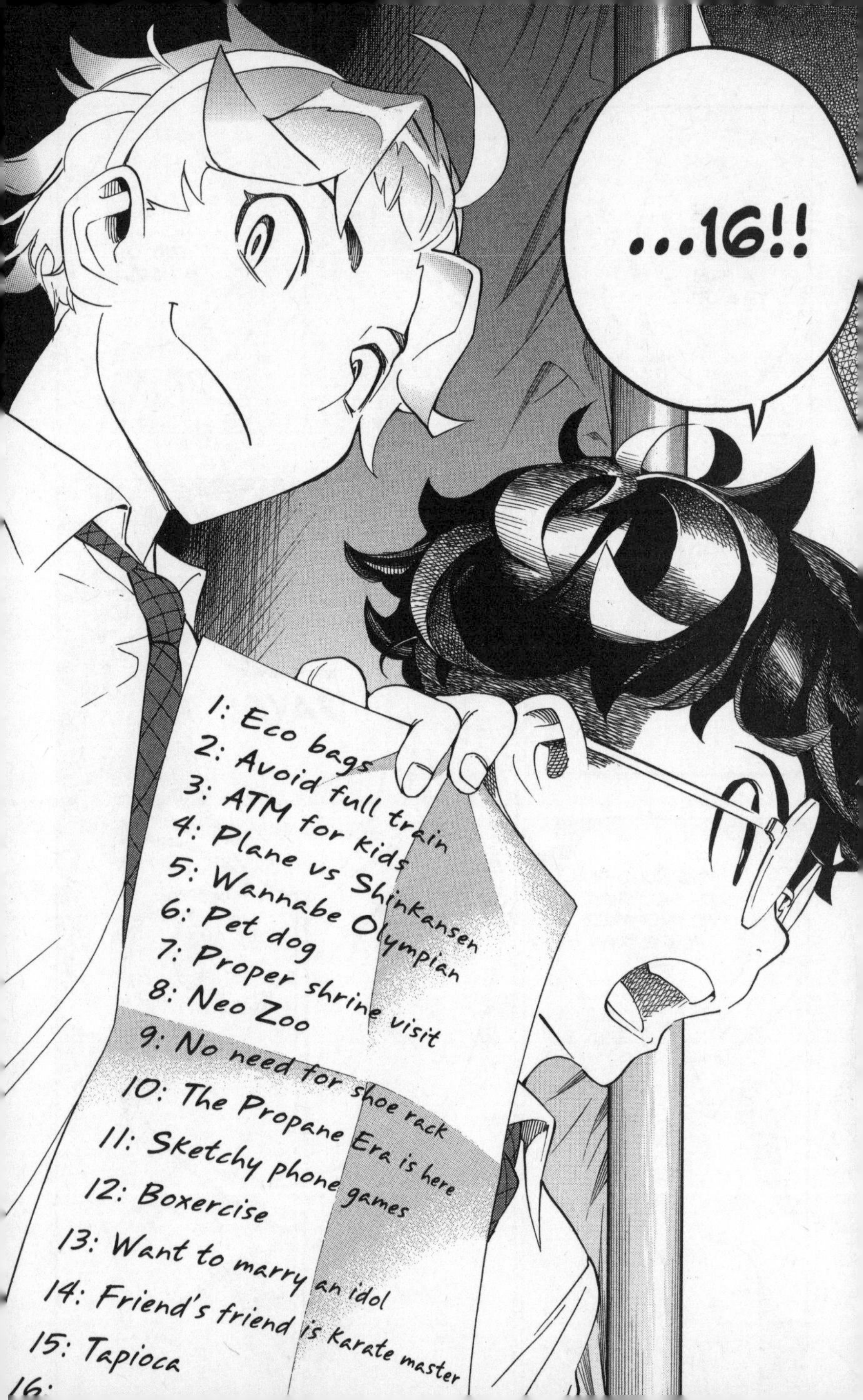
...16!!
1: Eco bags
2: Avoid full train
3: ATM for kids
4: Plane vs Shinkansen
5: Wannabe Olympian
6: Pet dog
7: Proper shrine visit
8: Neo Zoo
9: No need for shoe rack
10: The Propane Era is here
11: Sketchy phone games
12: Boxercise
13: Want to marry an idol
14: Friend's friend is karate master
15: Tapioca
16:

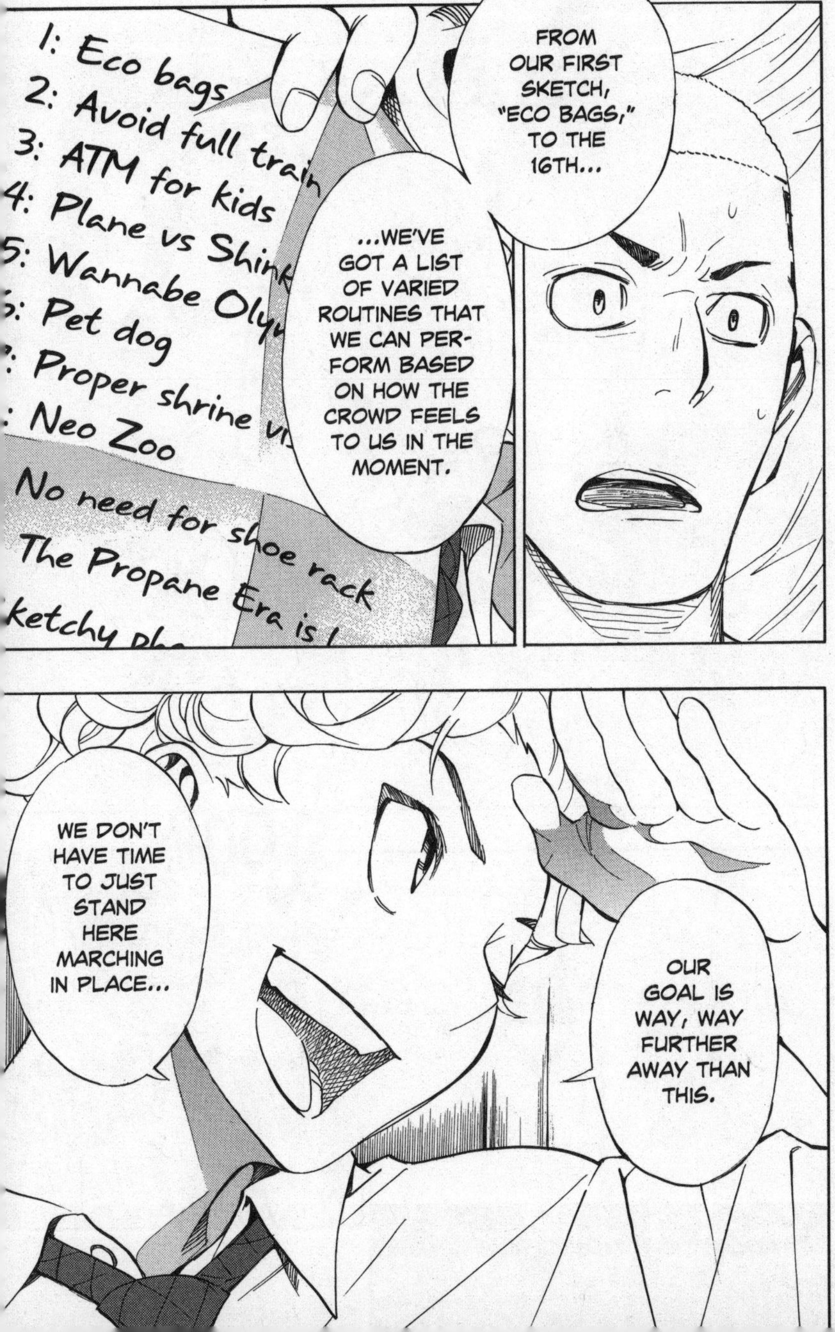
FROM OUR FIRST SKETCH, "ECO BAGS," TO THE 16TH...
...WE'VE GOT A LIST OF VARIED ROUTINES THAT WE CAN PER-FORM BASED ON HOW THE CROWD FEELS TO US IN THE MOMENT.
1: Eco bags
2: Avoid full trai
3: ATM for kids
4: Plane vs Shink
5: Wannabe Oly
: Pet dog
: Proper shrine vi
: Neo Zoo
No need for shoe rack
The Propane Era is
ketchy
WE DON'T HAVE TIME TO JUST STAND HERE MARCHING IN PLACE...
OUR GOAL IS WAY, WAY FURTHER AWAY THAN THIS.

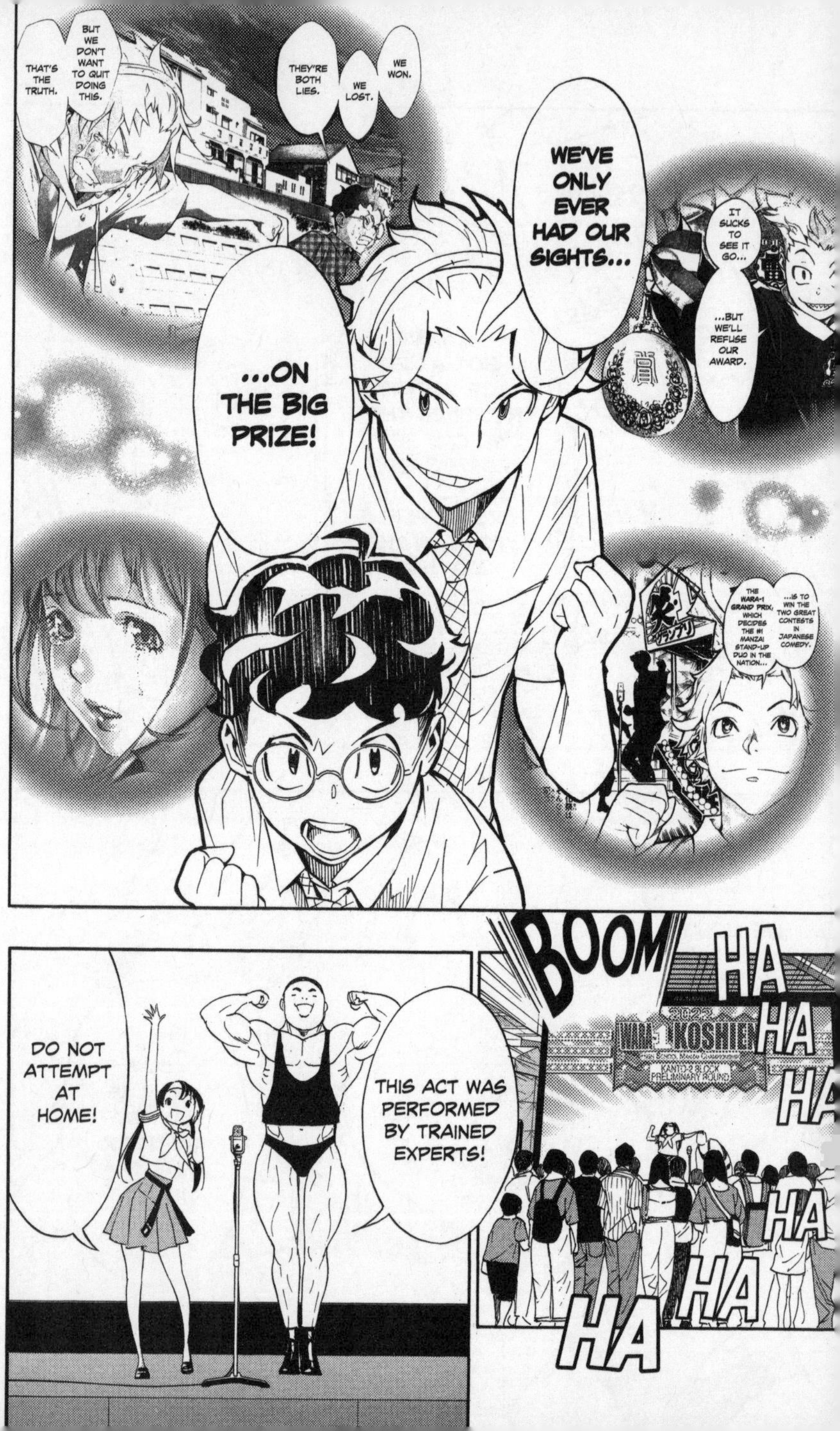
WE WON.
WE LOST.
THEY'RE BOTH LIES.
BUT WE DON'T WANT TO QUIT DOING THIS.
THAT'S THE TRUTH.
WE'VE ONLY EVER HAD OUR SIGHTS...
IT SUCKS TO SEE IT GO...
...BUT WE'LL REFUSE OUR AWARD.
...ON THE BIG PRIZE!
THE WARA-1 GRAND PRIX, WHICH DECIDES THE #1 MANZAI STAND-UP DUO IN THE NATION...
...IS TO WIN THE TWO GREAT CONTESTS IN JAPANESE COMEDY.
BOOM
HA HA HA
WARA-1 KOSHIEN
HIGH SCHOOL MANZAI CHAMPIONSHIP
KANTO-2 BLOCK PRELIMINARY ROUND
HA HA HA
THIS ACT WAS PERFORMED BY TRAINED EXPERTS!
DO NOT ATTEMPT AT HOME!

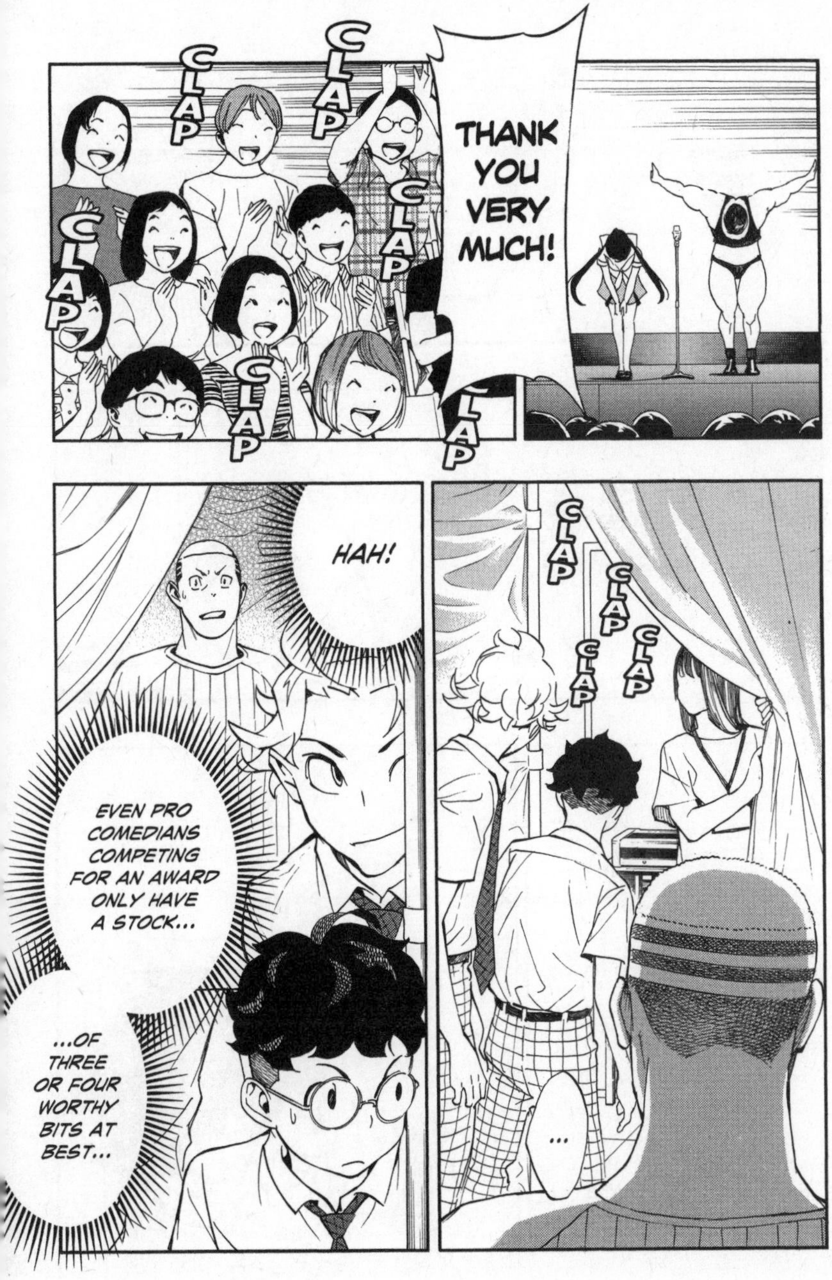
THANK YOU VERY MUCH!
CLAP
CLAP
CLAP
CLAP
CLAP
CLAP
CLAP
CLAP
CLAP
CLAP
CLAP
...
HAH!
EVEN PRO COMEDIANS COMPETING FOR AN AWARD ONLY HAVE A STOCK...
...OF THREE OR FOUR WORTHY BITS AT BEST...

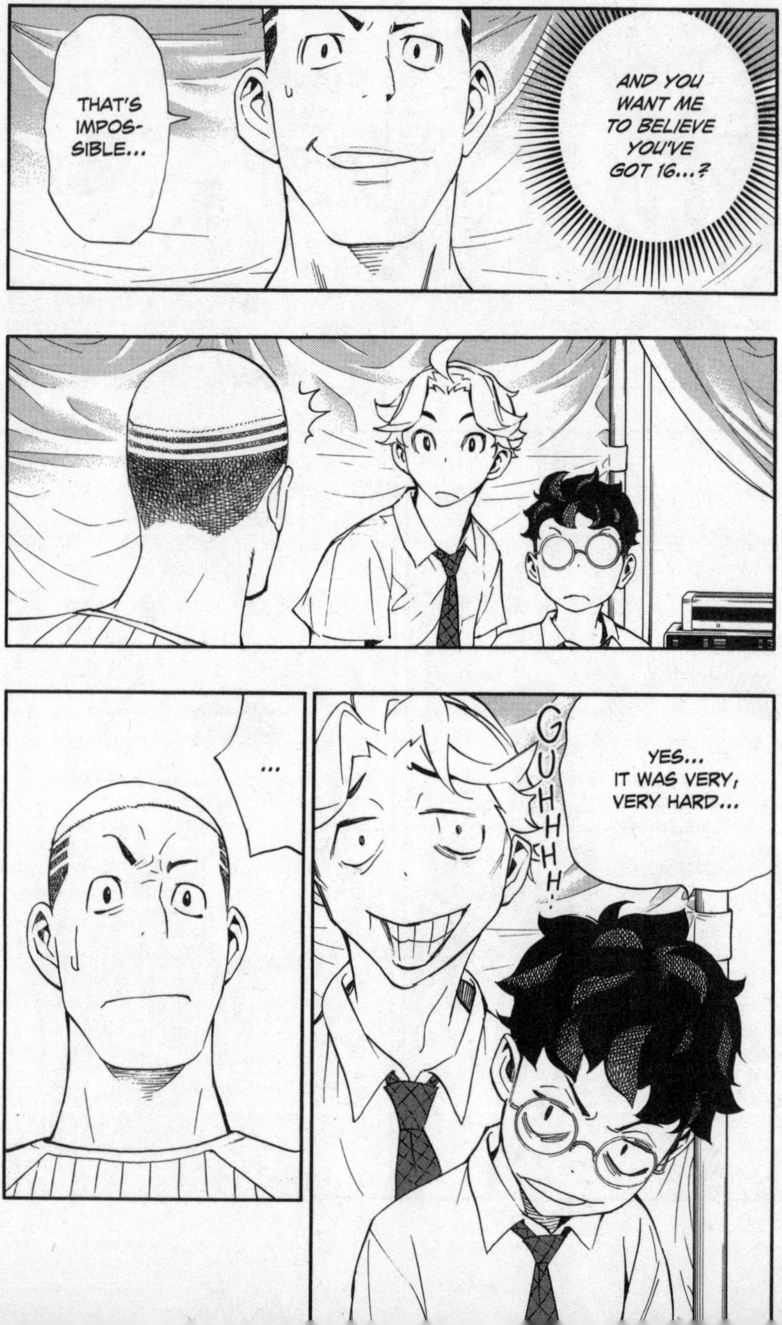
AND YOU WANT ME TO BELIEVE YOU'VE GOT 16...?
THAT'S IMPOS-SIBLE...
YES... IT WAS VERY, VERY HARD...
GUHHHH!
...

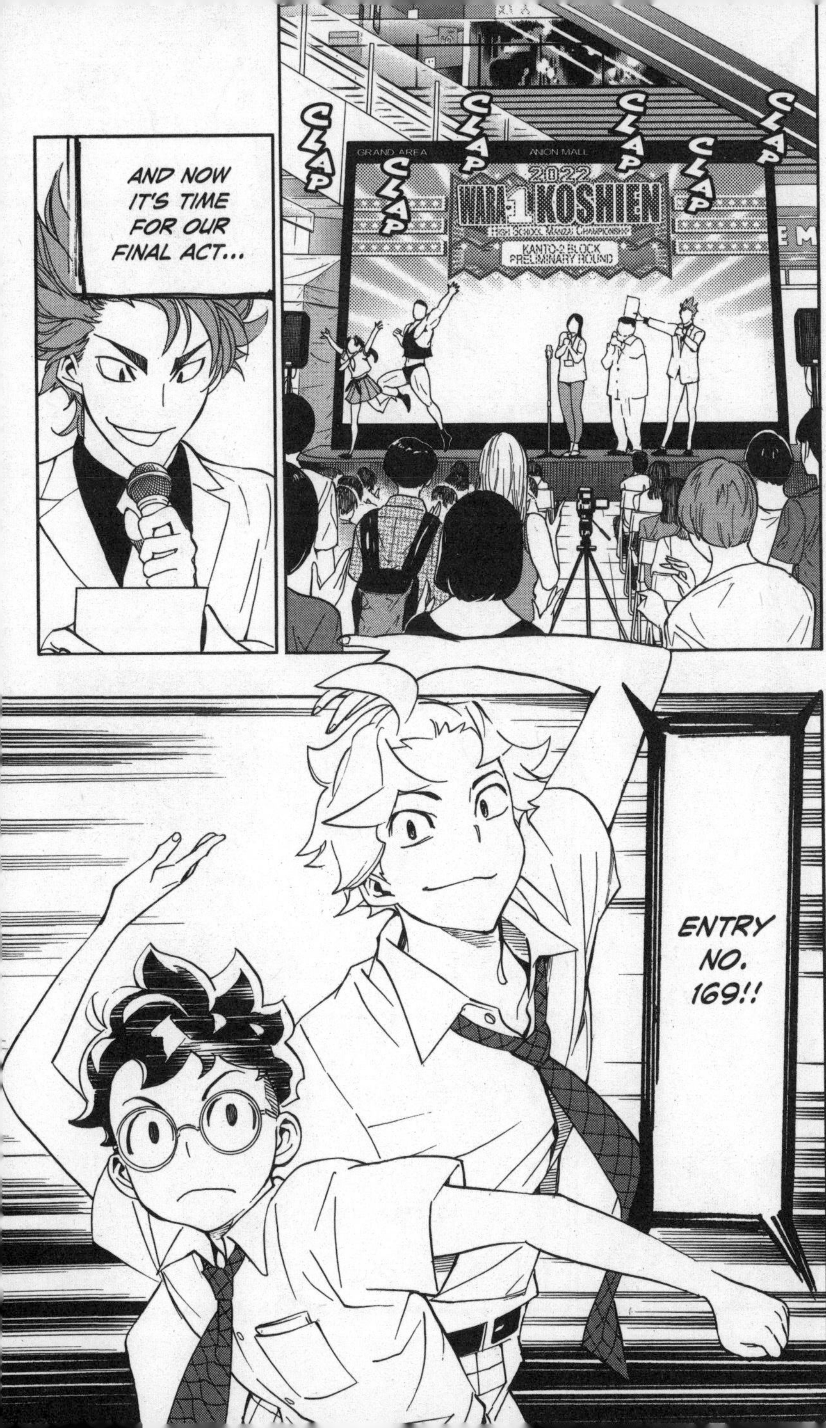
CLAP
CLAP
CLAP
CLAP
CLAP
CLAP
GRAND AREA
ANION MALL
2022
WARA-1 KOSHIEN
HIGH SCHOOL MANZAI CHAMPIONSHIP
KANTO-2 BLOCK
PRELIMINARY ROUND
AND NOW IT'S TIME FOR OUR FINAL ACT...
ENTRY NO. 169!!

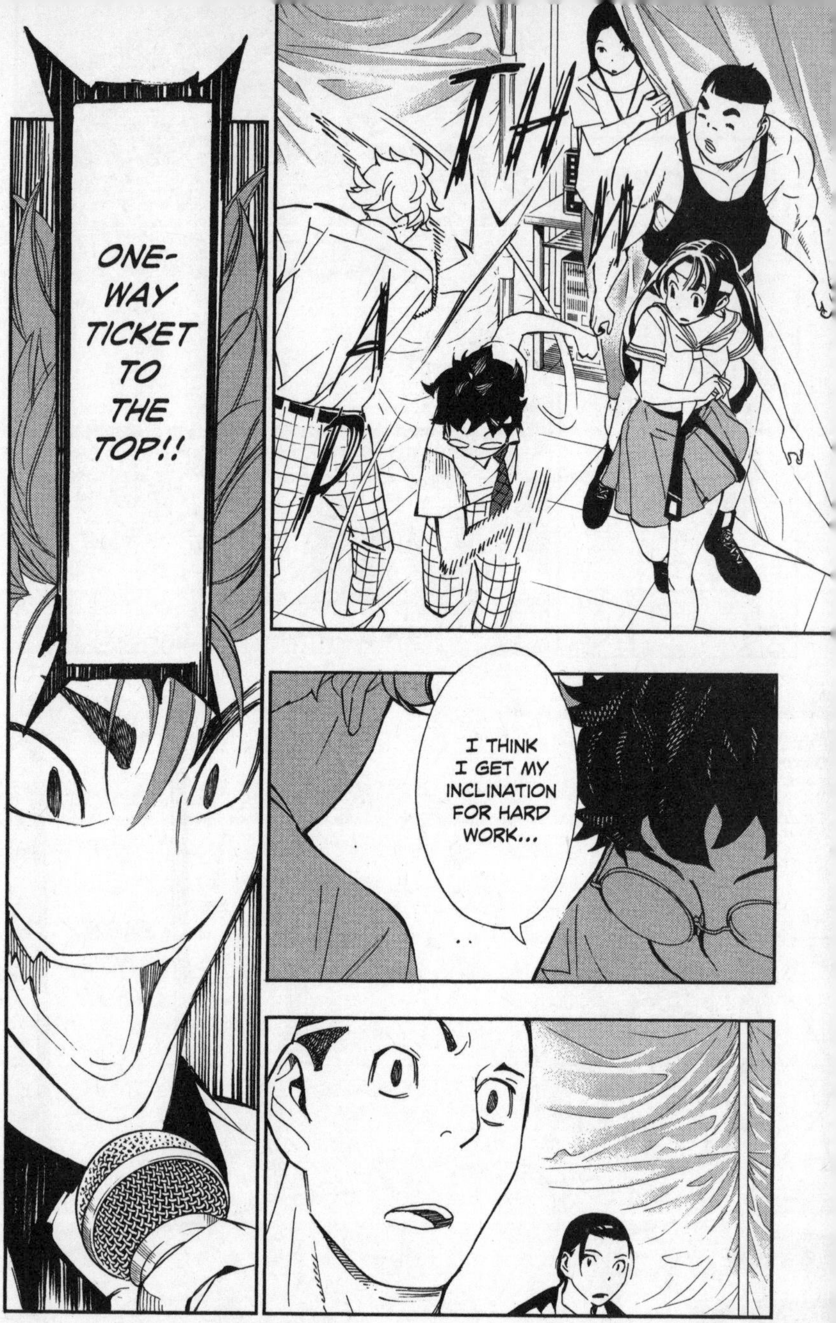
THWAP
I THINK I GET MY INCLINATION FOR HARD WORK...
ONE-WAY TICKET TO THE TOP!!

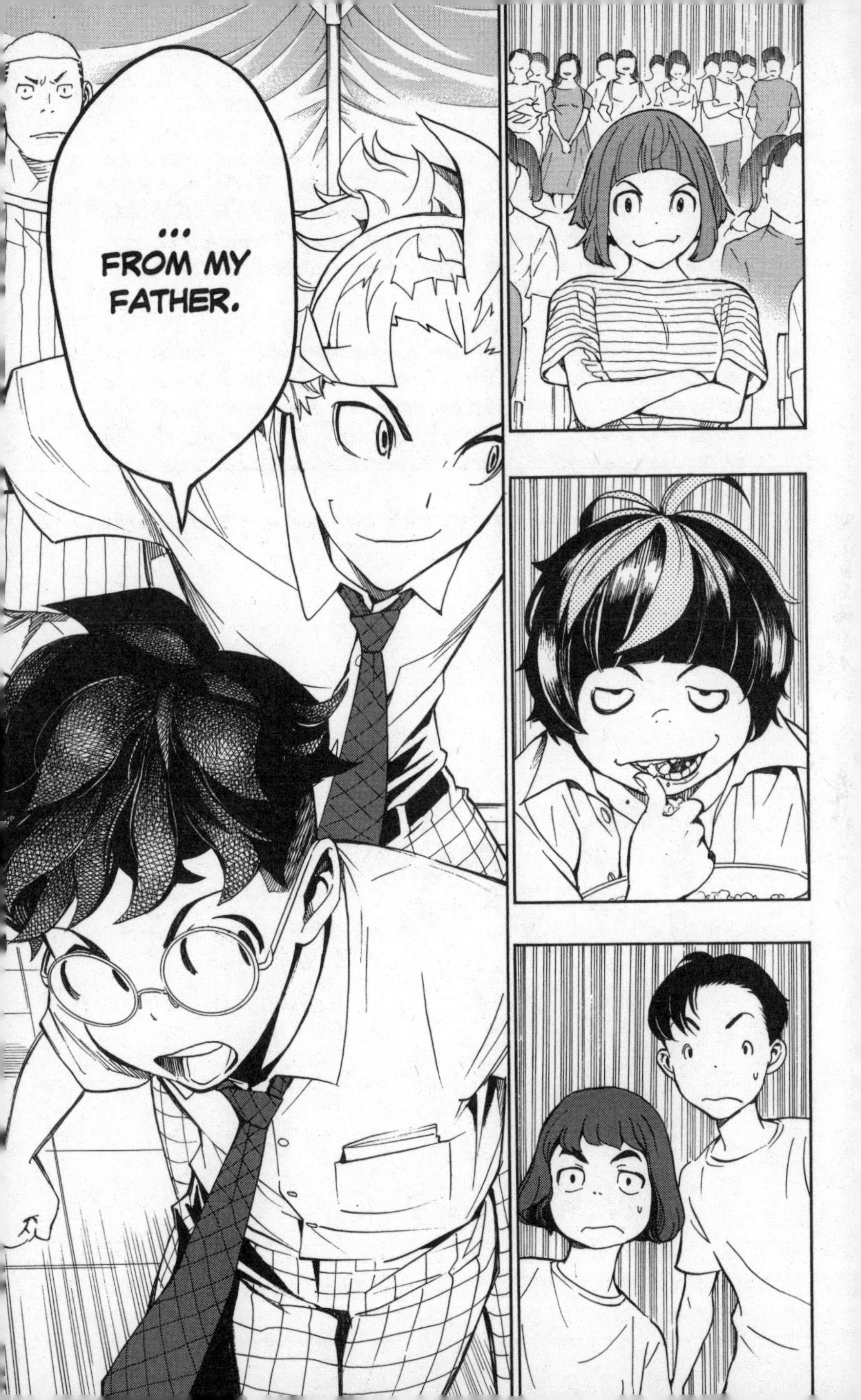
... FROM MY FATHER.

We were extraordinarily confident, but when they read the winning duo's name, my mind went blank. That's right--we just plain lost. (LOL). And the winners were the guys who had just been telling us, "You're geniuses!" minutes earlier. The level of our humiliation could have reached the top of Mt. Everest. I was mortified.

Later, Jicchan suggested that maybe our choice of topic was bad (a skit about drinking alcohol at an izakaya), but maybe we just got beat on fundamentals. We may never know the truth. It's a bitter memory for us both, but the odd feeling of accomplishment it gave us spurred us on to our next goal.

Thanks for reading so far. We'll continue our story in the next volume...

I thought to myself, "This must be why adults drink."

I still remember the name of the pair that won.

WINNER

Akinari Asakura

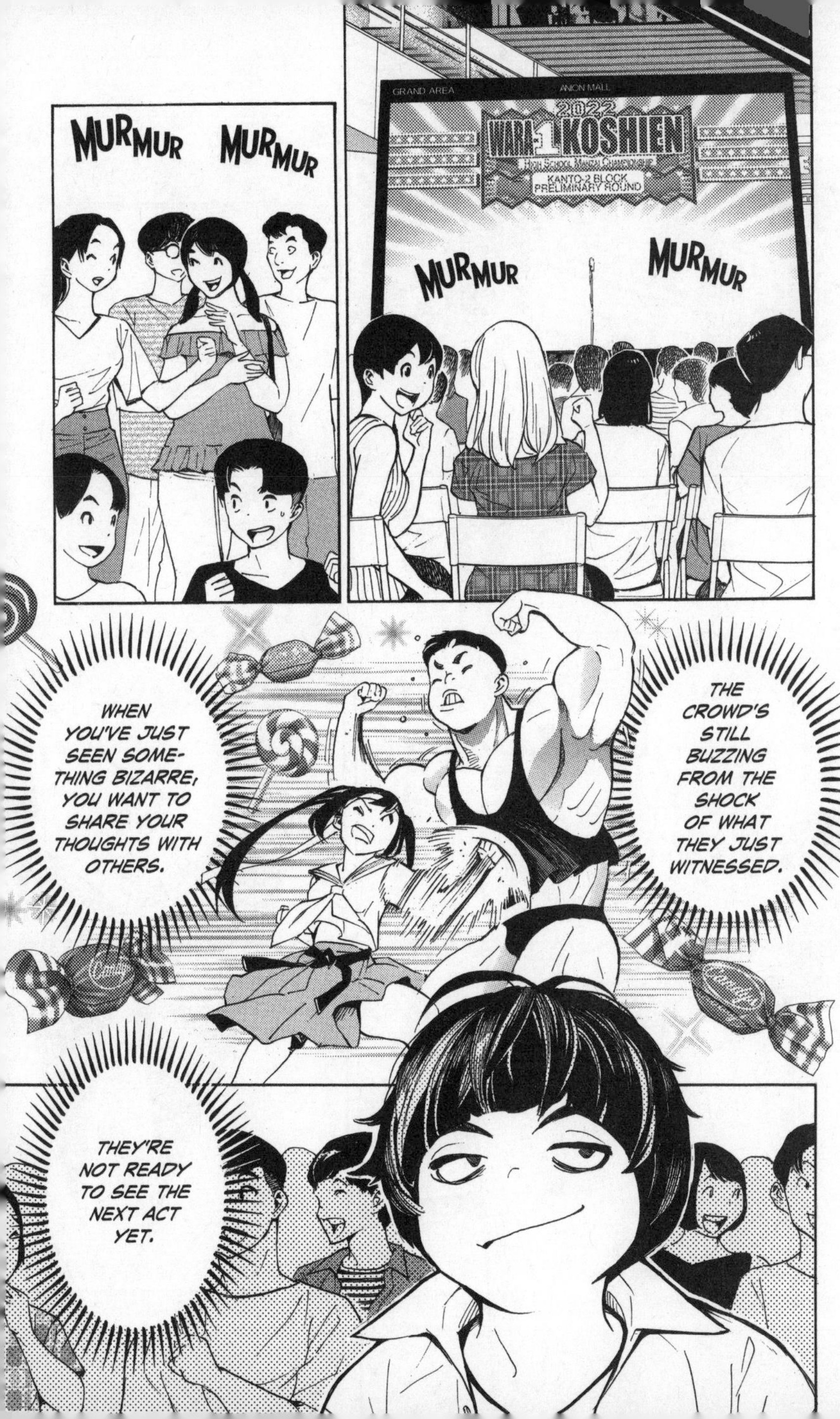
GRAND AREA
ANION MALL
2022
WARA-1 KOSHIEN
HIGH SCHOOL MANGA CHAMPIONSHIP
KANTO-2 BLOCK PRELIMINARY ROUND
MURMUR
MURMUR
MURMUR
MURMUR
THE CROWD'S STILL BUZZING FROM THE SHOCK OF WHAT THEY JUST WITNESSED.
WHEN YOU'VE JUST SEEN SOME-THING BIZARRE, YOU WANT TO SHARE YOUR THOUGHTS WITH OTHERS.
THEY'RE NOT READY TO SEE THE NEXT ACT YET.

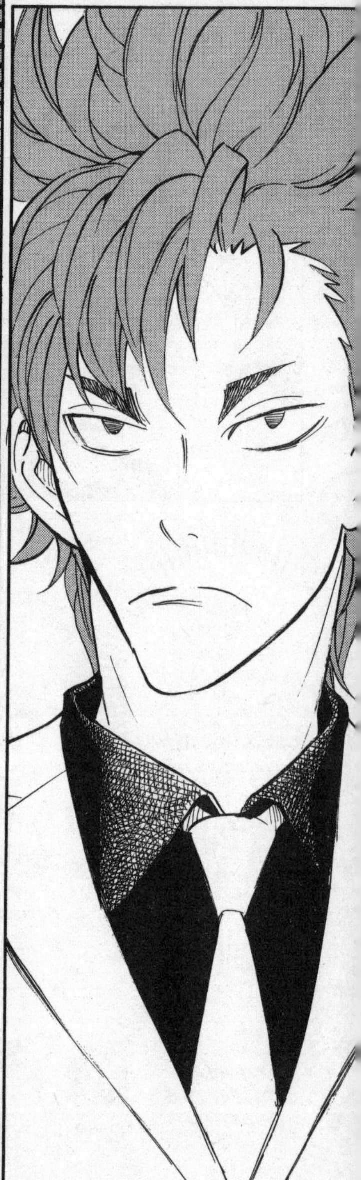

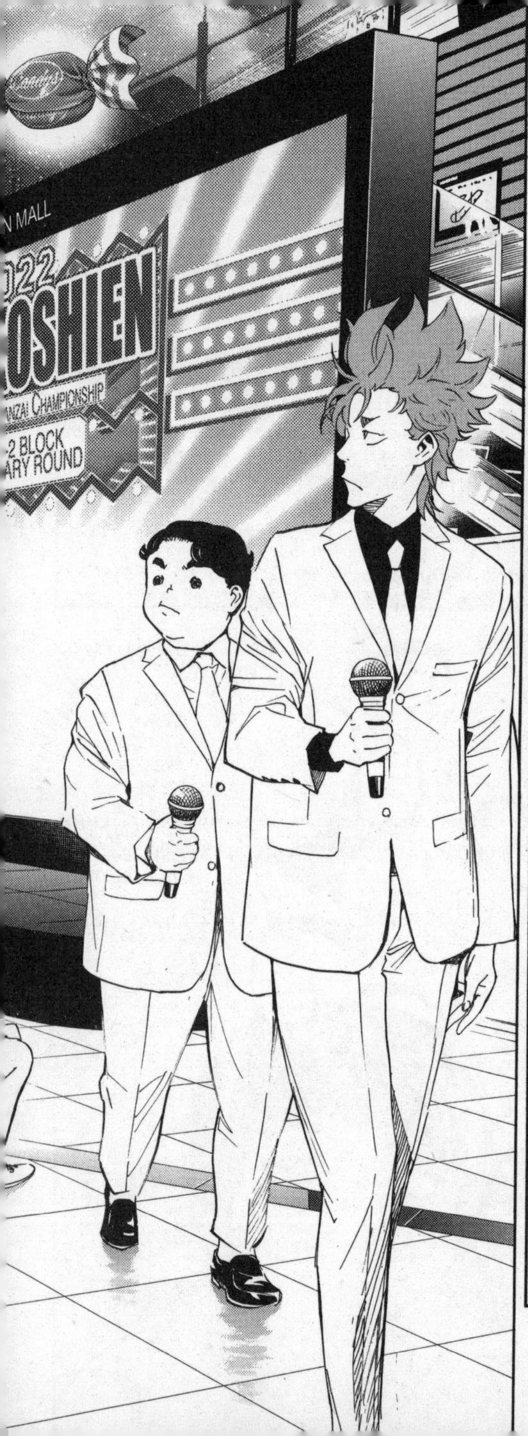
N MALL
022
OSHIEN
ANZAI CHAMPIONSHIP
2 BLOCK
ARY ROUND

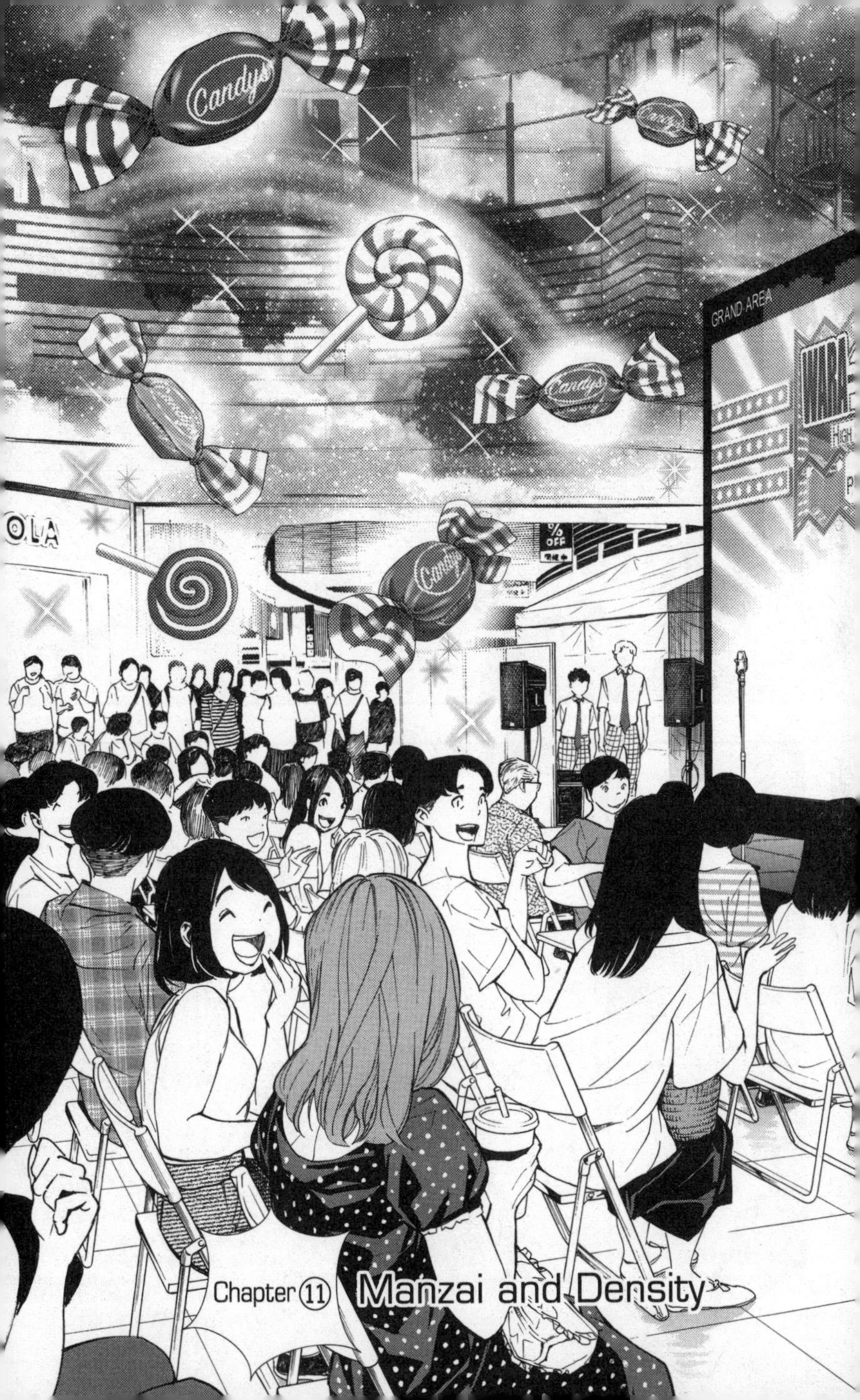
Candys
Candys
Candys
GRAND AREA
OLA
% OFF

Chapter 11 Manzai and Density

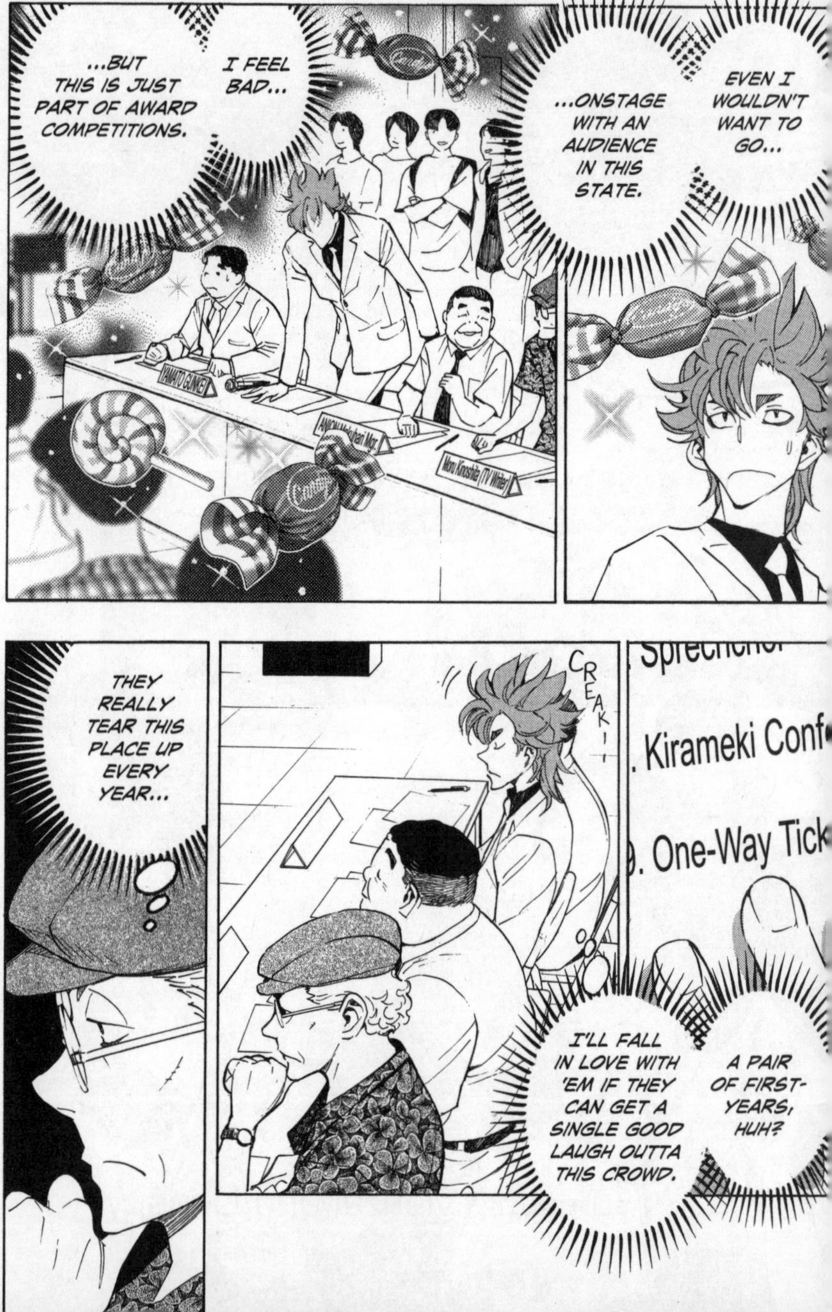

EVEN I WOULDN'T WANT TO GO...
...ONSTAGE WITH AN AUDIENCE IN THIS STATE.
I FEEL BAD...
...BUT THIS IS JUST PART OF AWARD COMPETITIONS.
YAMATO GUNKEI
Maru Kinoshita (TV Writer)
Kirameki Conf
One-Way Tick
A PAIR OF FIRST-YEARS, HUH?
I'LL FALL IN LOVE WITH 'EM IF THEY CAN GET A SINGLE GOOD LAUGH OUTTA THIS CROWD.
CREAK!
THEY REALLY TEAR THIS PLACE UP EVERY YEAR...

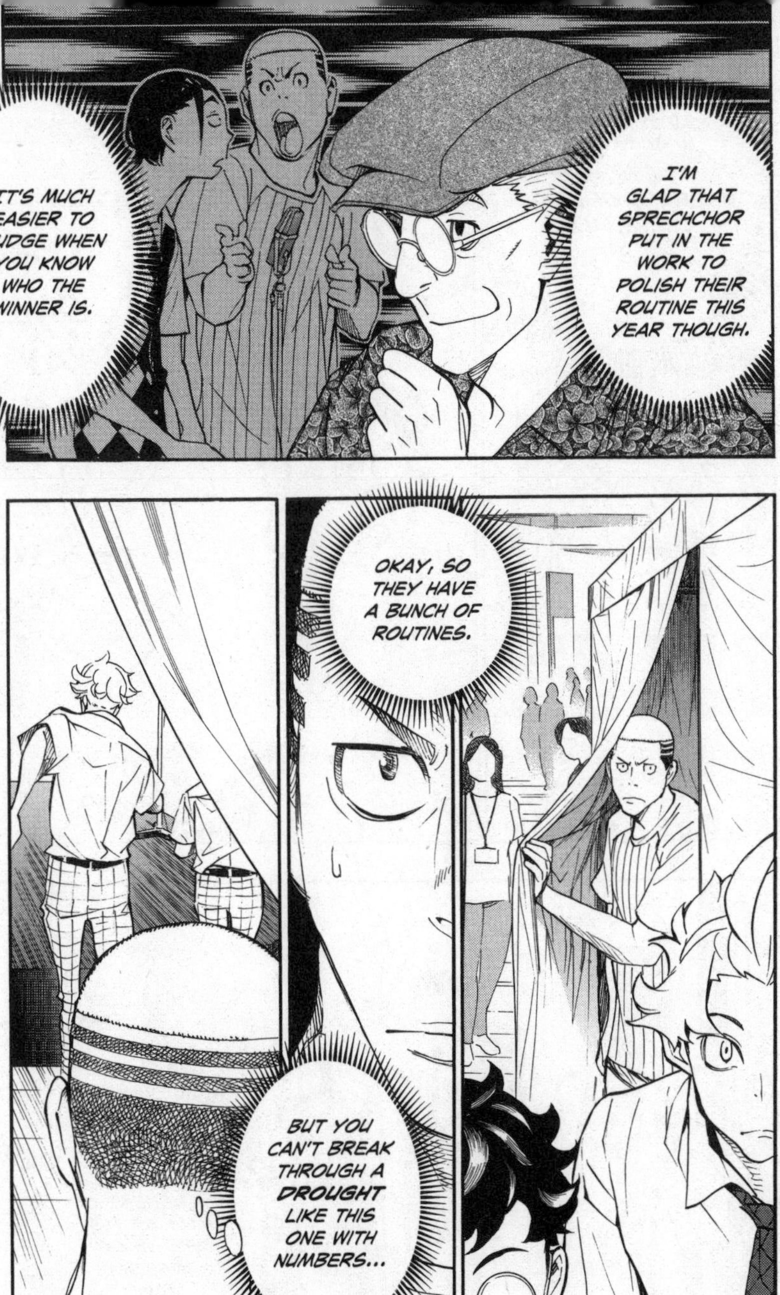
I'M GLAD THAT SPRECHCHOR PUT IN THE WORK TO POLISH THEIR ROUTINE THIS YEAR THOUGH.
IT'S MUCH EASIER TO JUDGE WHEN YOU KNOW WHO THE WINNER IS.
OKAY, SO THEY HAVE A BUNCH OF ROUTINES.
BUT YOU CAN'T BREAK THROUGH A DROUGHT LIKE THIS ONE WITH NUMBERS...

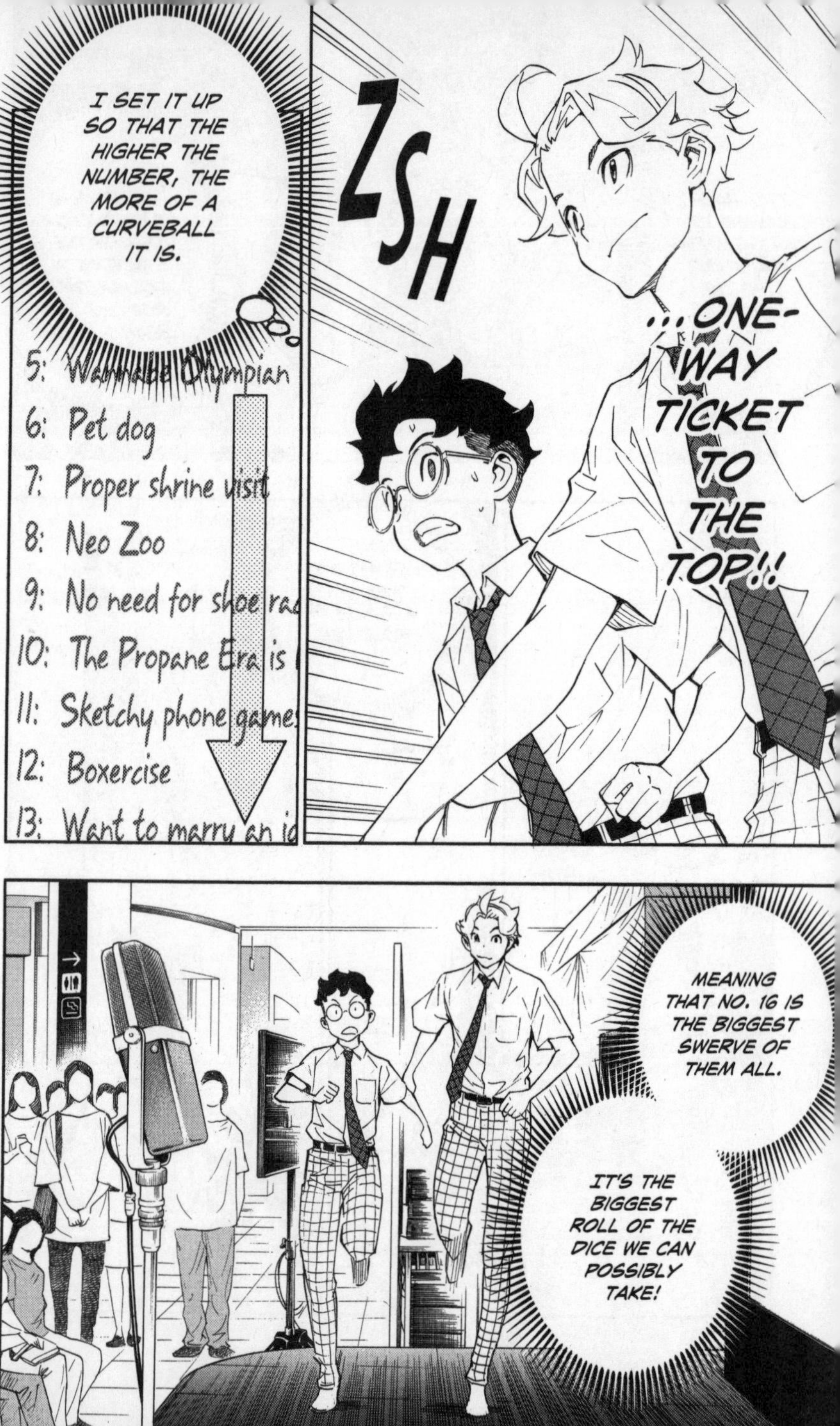
ZSH
...ONE-WAY TICKET TO THE TOP!!
I SET IT UP SO THAT THE HIGHER THE NUMBER, THE MORE OF A CURVEBALL IT IS.
5: Wannabe Olympian
6: Pet dog
7: Proper shrine visit
8: Neo Zoo
9: No need for shoe
10: The Propane Era is
11: Sketchy phone games
12: Boxercise
13: Want to marry an
MEANING THAT NO. 16 IS THE BIGGEST SWERVE OF THEM ALL.
IT'S THE BIGGEST ROLL OF THE DICE WE CAN POSSIBLY TAKE!

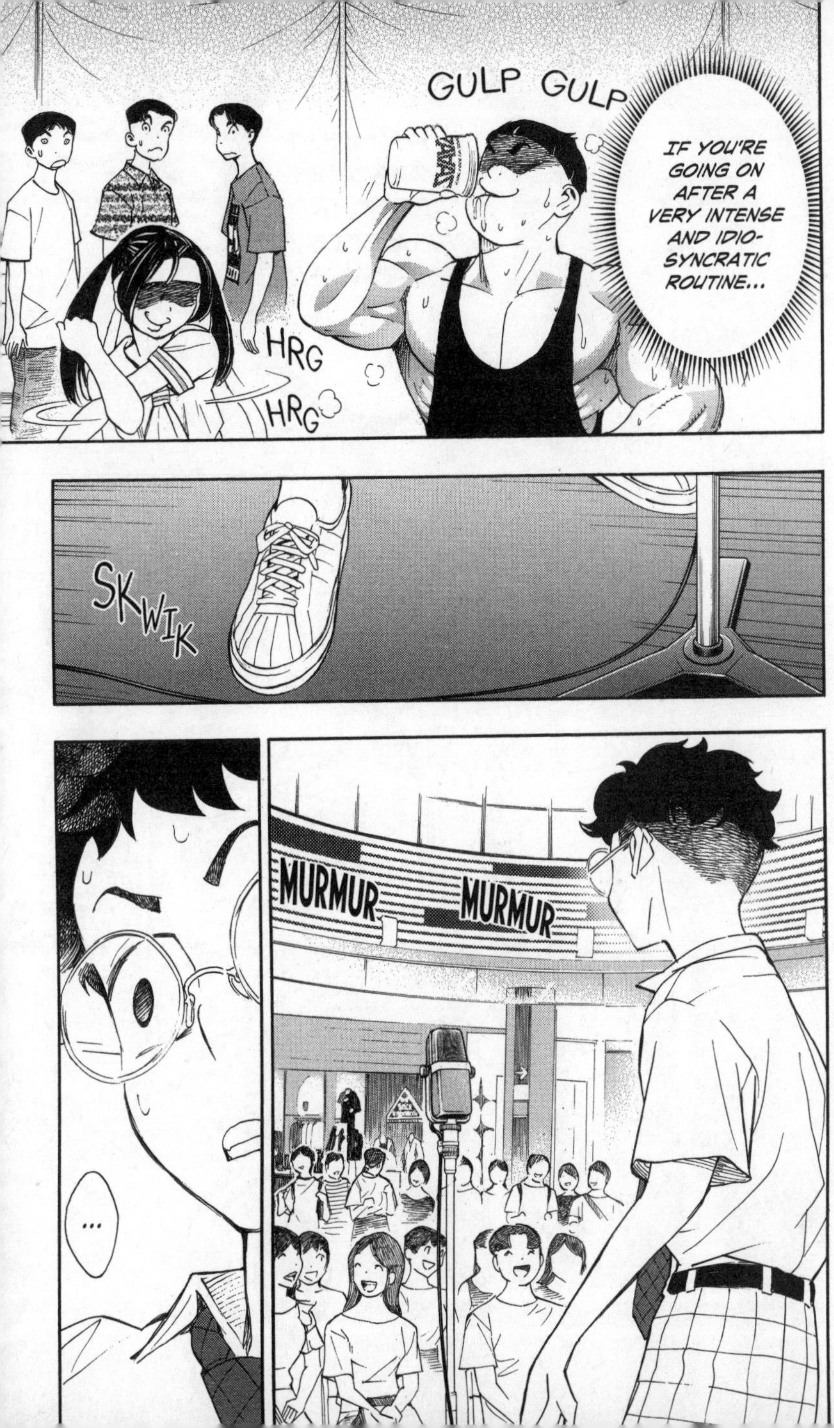
IF YOU'RE GOING ON AFTER A VERY INTENSE AND IDIO-SYNCRATIC ROUTINE...
GULP GULP
HRG
HRG
SKWIK
MURMUR
MURMUR
...

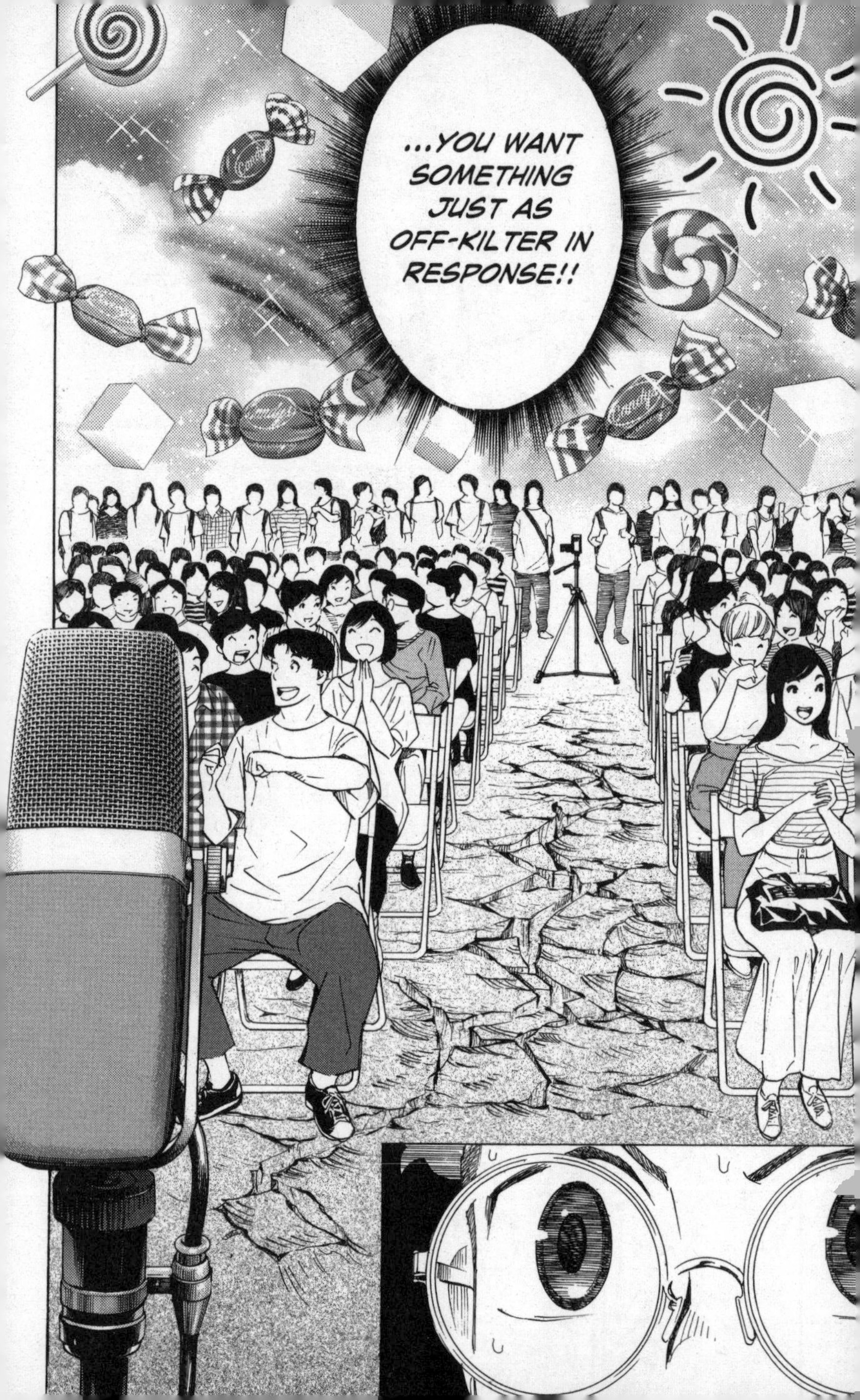
...YOU WANT SOMETHING JUST AS OFF-KILTER IN RESPONSE!!

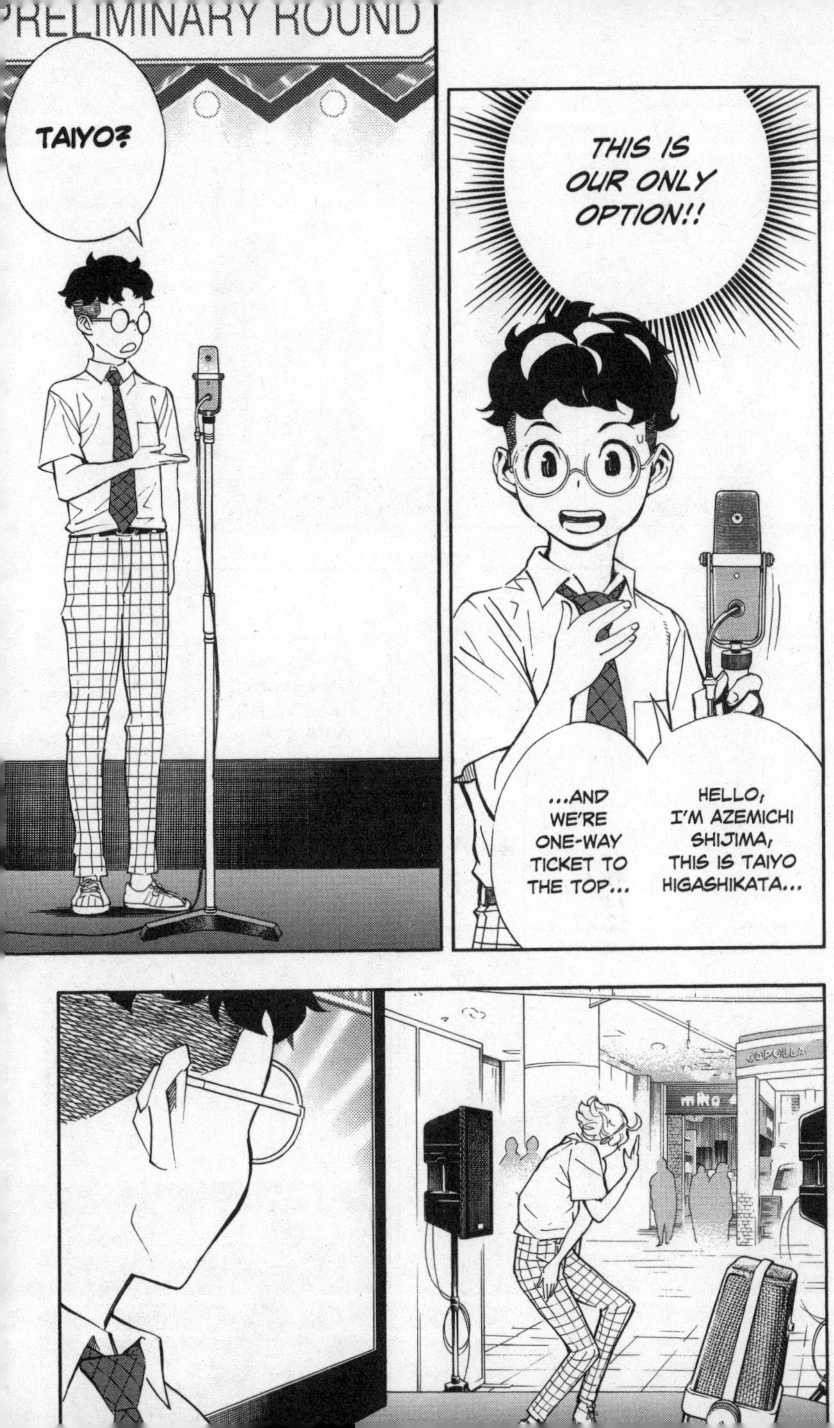
THIS IS OUR ONLY OPTION!!
HELLO, I'M AZEMICHI SHIJIMA, THIS IS TAIYO HIGASHIKATA...
...AND WE'RE ONE-WAY TICKET TO THE TOP...
PRELIMINARY ROUND
TAIYO?
COPOLLA

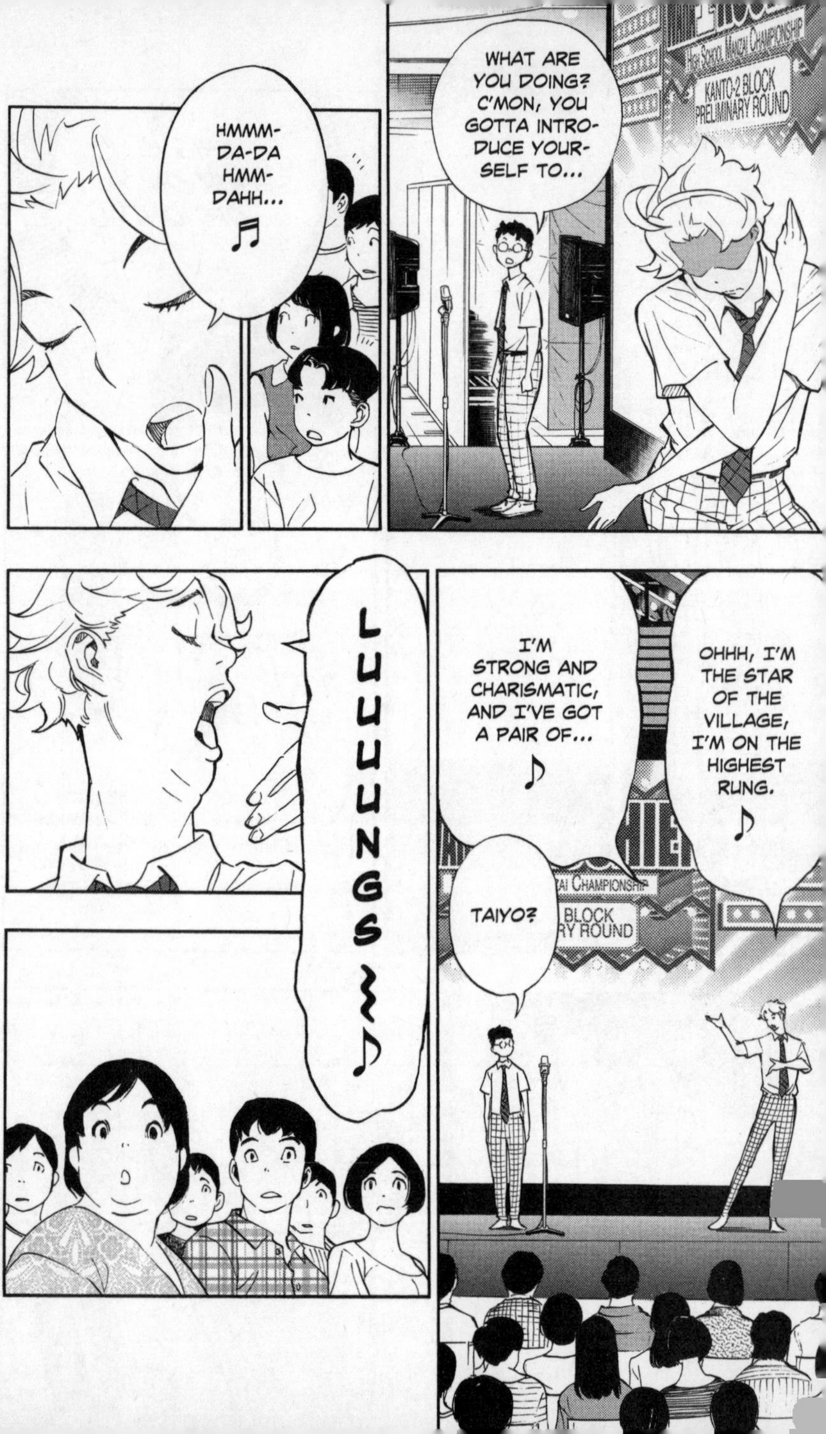
HIGH SCHOOL MANZAI CHAMPIONSHIP
KANTO-2 BLOCK PRELIMINARY ROUND
WHAT ARE YOU DOING? C'MON, YOU GOTTA INTRODUCE YOURSELF TO...
HMMM-DA-DA HMM-DAHH... ♬
OHHH, I'M THE STAR OF THE VILLAGE, I'M ON THE HIGHEST RUNG. ♪
I'M STRONG AND CHARISMATIC, AND I'VE GOT A PAIR OF... ♪
TAIYO?
LUUUUNGS ~♪

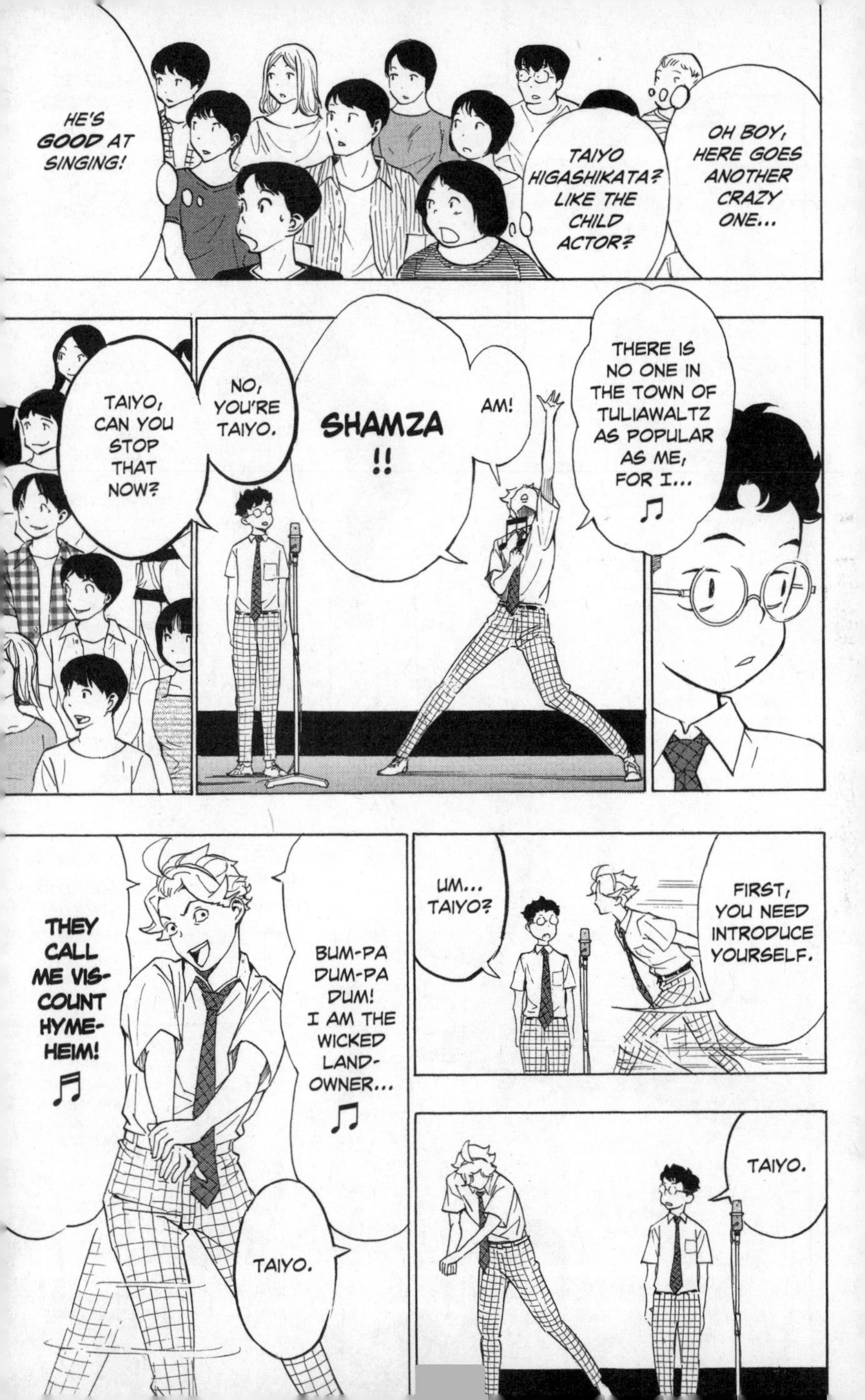
OH BOY, HERE GOES ANOTHER CRAZY ONE...
TAIYO HIGASHIKATA? LIKE THE CHILD ACTOR?
HE'S GOOD AT SINGING!
THERE IS NO ONE IN THE TOWN OF TULIAWALTZ AS POPULAR AS ME, FOR I... ♫
AM!
SHAMZA !!
NO, YOU'RE TAIYO.
TAIYO, CAN YOU STOP THAT NOW?
FIRST, YOU NEED INTRODUCE YOURSELF.
UM... TAIYO?
TAIYO.
BUM-PA DUM-PA DUM! I AM THE WICKED LAND-OWNER... ♫
THEY CALL ME VIS-COUNT HYME-HEIM! ♫
TAIYO.

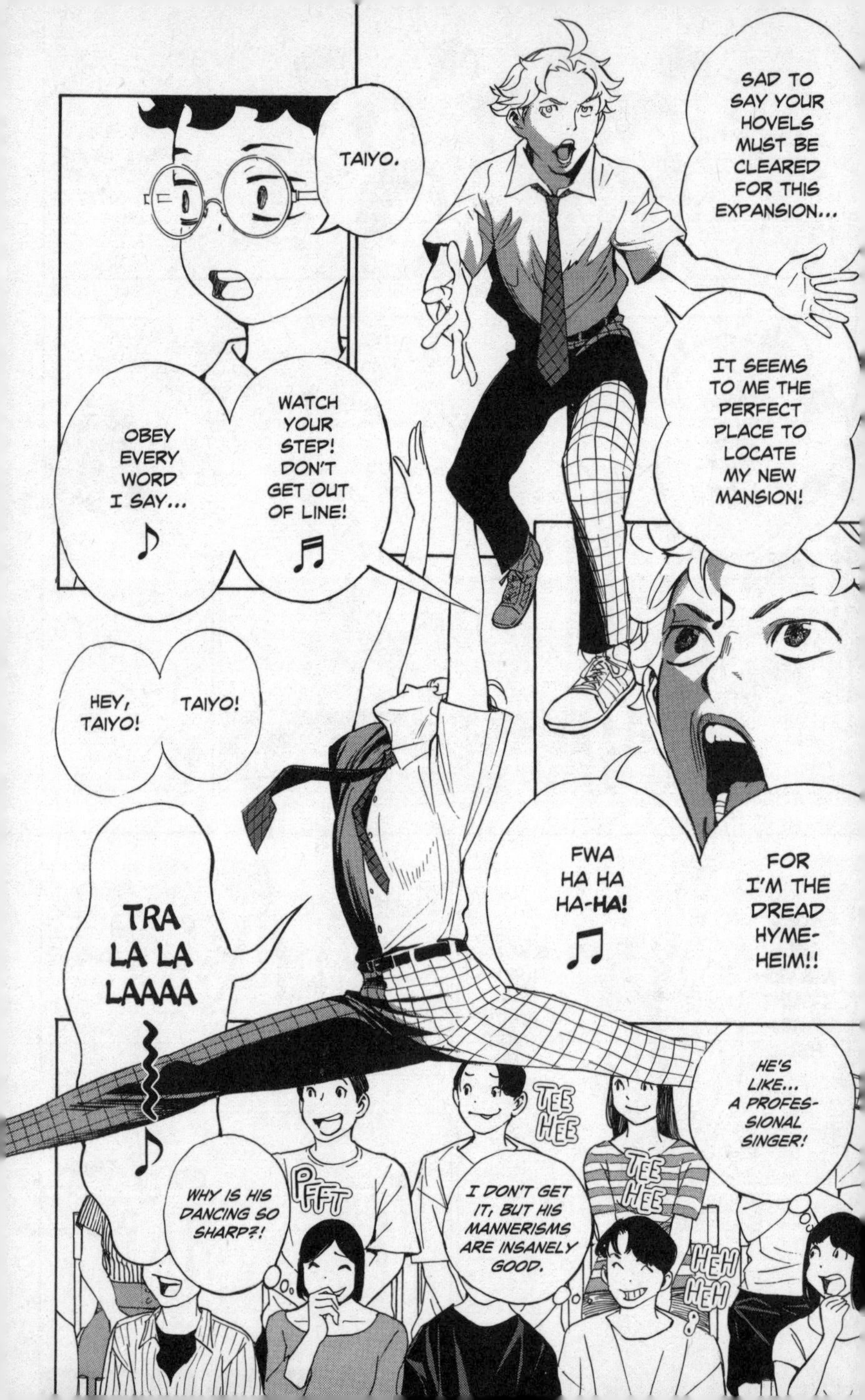
SAD TO SAY YOUR HOVELS MUST BE CLEARED FOR THIS EXPANSION...
IT SEEMS TO ME THE PERFECT PLACE TO LOCATE MY NEW MANSION!
TAIYO.
WATCH YOUR STEP! DON'T GET OUT OF LINE! ♫
OBEY EVERY WORD I SAY... ♪
FOR I'M THE DREAD HYME-HEIM!!
FWA HA HA HA-HA! ♫
TAIYO!
HEY, TAIYO!
TRA LA LA LAAAA ♪
HE'S LIKE... A PROFES-SIONAL SINGER!
TEE HEE
TEE HEE
HEH HEH
I DON'T GET IT, BUT HIS MANNERISMS ARE INSANELY GOOD.
PFFT
WHY IS HIS DANCING SO SHARP?!

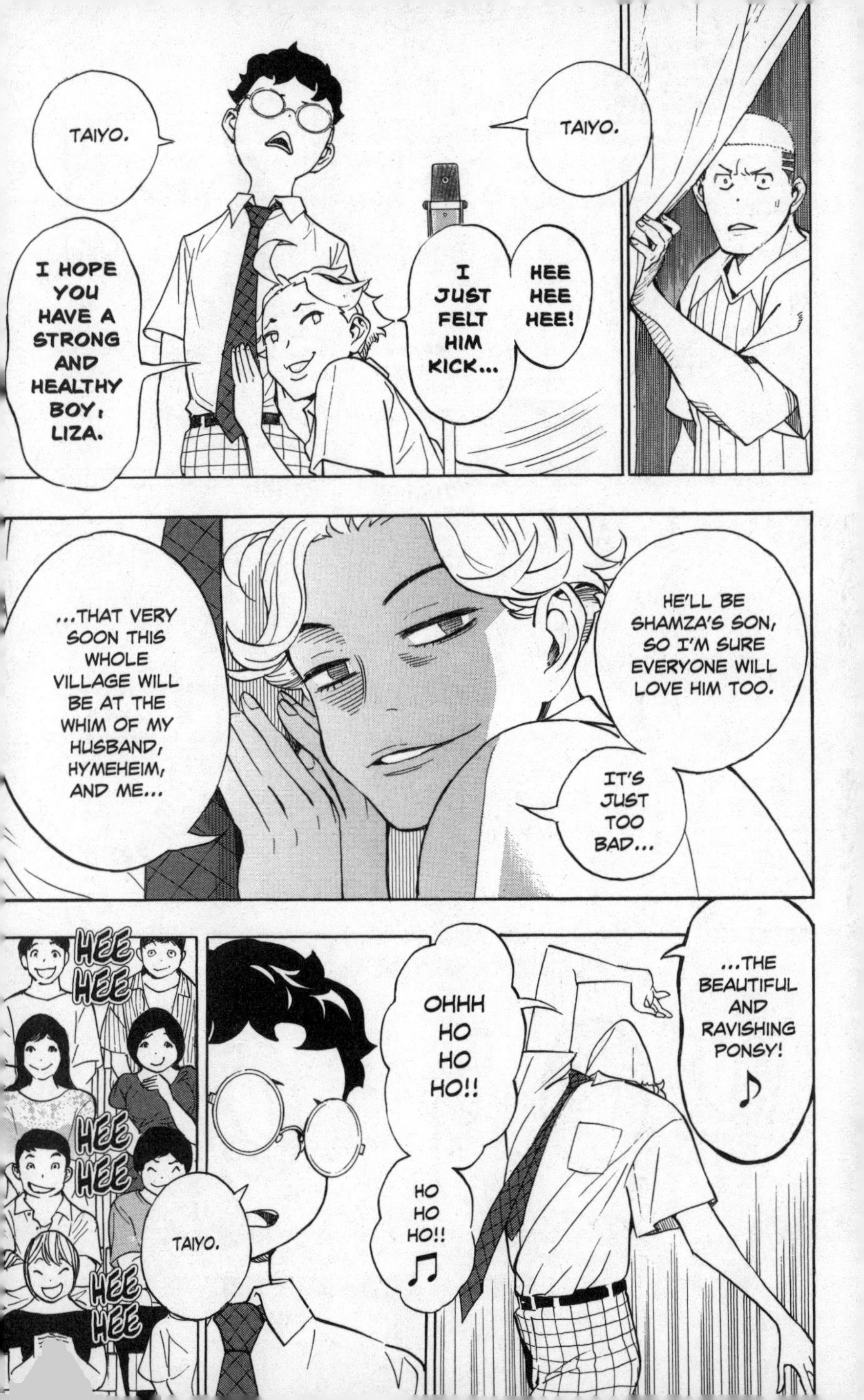
TAIYO.
TAIYO.
HEE HEE HEE!
I JUST FELT HIM KICK...
I HOPE YOU HAVE A STRONG AND HEALTHY BOY, LIZA.
HE'LL BE SHAMZA'S SON, SO I'M SURE EVERYONE WILL LOVE HIM TOO.
IT'S JUST TOO BAD...
...THAT VERY SOON THIS WHOLE VILLAGE WILL BE AT THE WHIM OF MY HUSBAND, HYMEHEIM, AND ME...
...THE BEAUTIFUL AND RAVISHING PONSY! ♪
OHHH HO HO HO!!
HO HO HO!! ♫
TAIYO.
HEE HEE
HEE HEE
HEE HEE

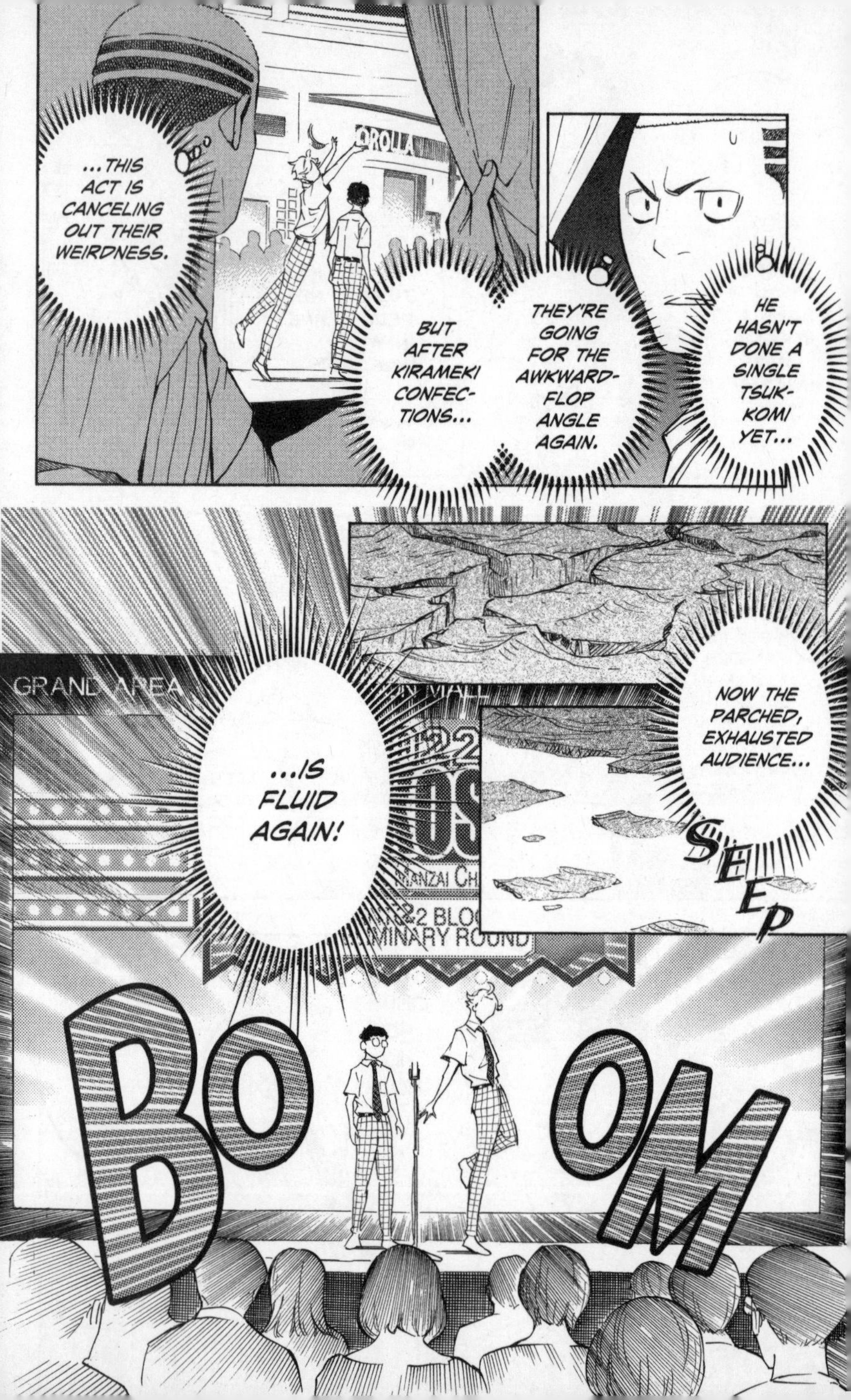
HE HASN'T DONE A SINGLE TSUKKOMI YET...
THEY'RE GOING FOR THE AWKWARD-FLOP ANGLE AGAIN.
BUT AFTER KIRAMEKI CONFECTIONS...
...THIS ACT IS CANCELING OUT THEIR WEIRDNESS.
NOW THE PARCHED, EXHAUSTED AUDIENCE...
SEEP
GRAND AREA
...IS FLUID AGAIN!
BOOM

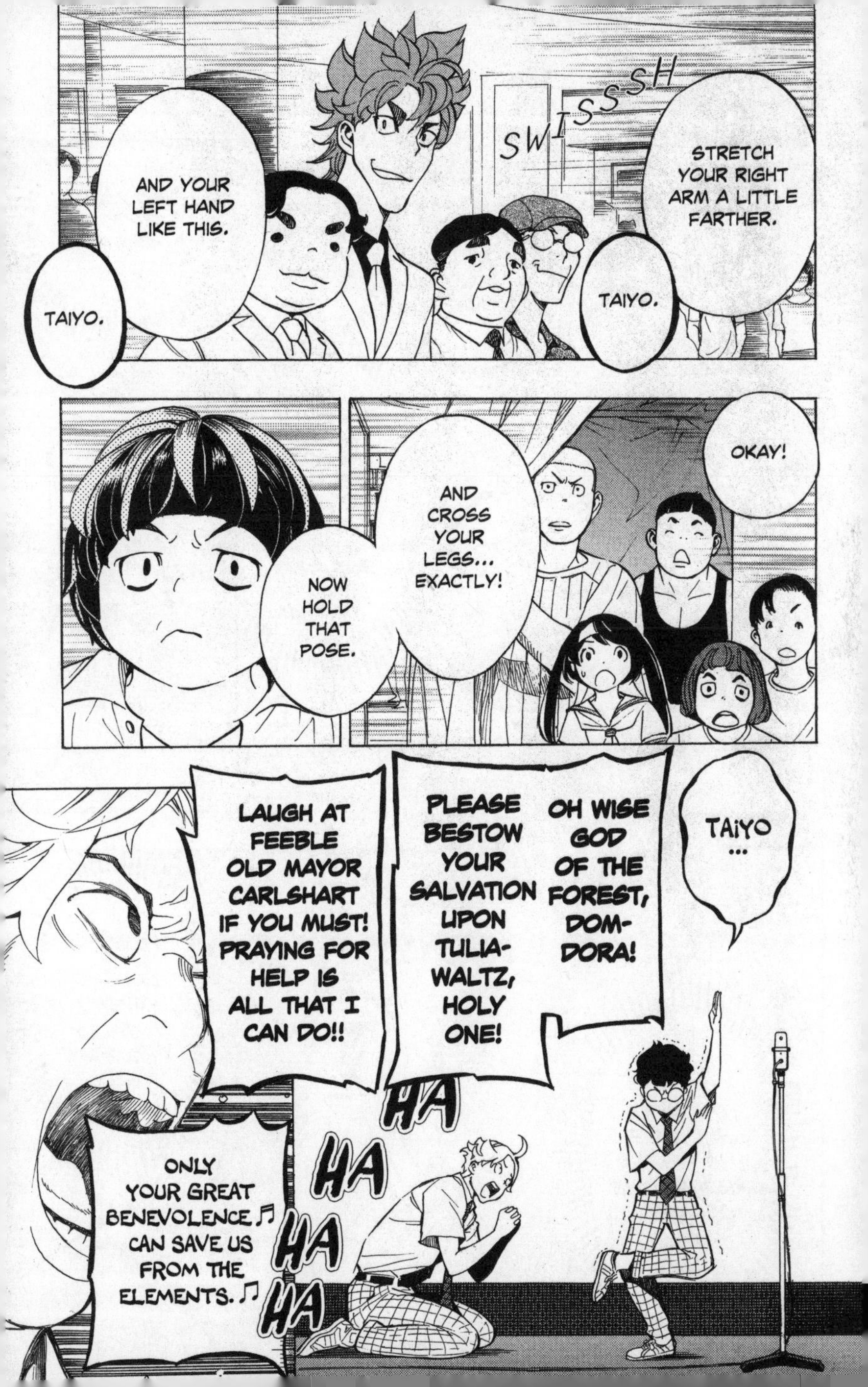
STRETCH YOUR RIGHT ARM A LITTLE FARTHER.
SWISSSH
TAIYO.
AND YOUR LEFT HAND LIKE THIS.
TAIYO.
OKAY!
AND CROSS YOUR LEGS... EXACTLY!
NOW HOLD THAT POSE.
TAiYO ...
OH WISE GOD OF THE FOREST, DOM-DORA!
PLEASE BESTOW YOUR SALVATION UPON TULIA-WALTZ, HOLY ONE!
LAUGH AT FEEBLE OLD MAYOR CARLSHART IF YOU MUST! PRAYING FOR HELP IS ALL THAT I CAN DO!!
HA
HA
HA
HA
ONLY YOUR GREAT BENEVOLENCE ♫ CAN SAVE US FROM THE ELEMENTS. ♫

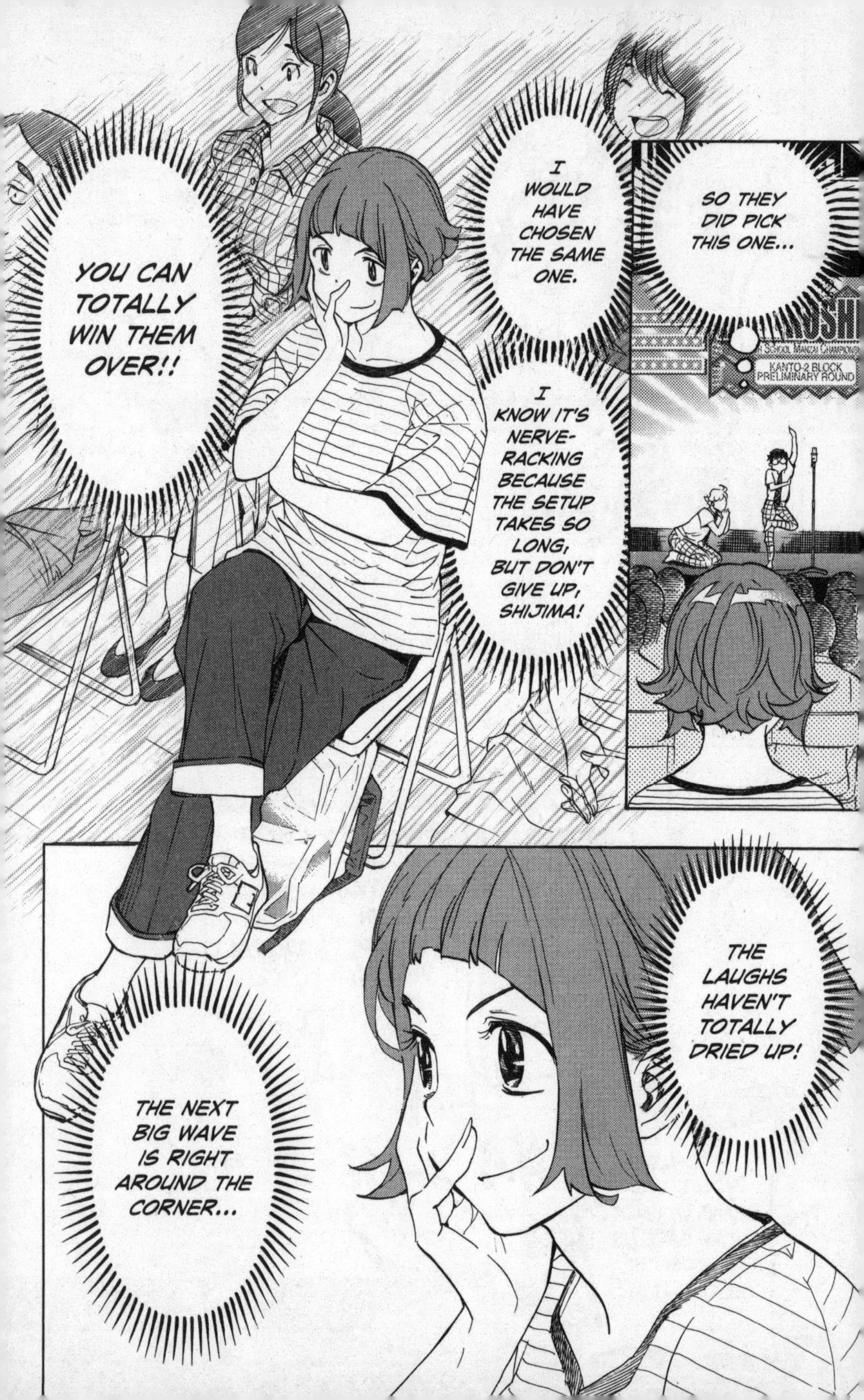
KANTO-2 BLOCK PRELIMINARY ROUND
SO THEY DID PICK THIS ONE...
I WOULD HAVE CHOSEN THE SAME ONE.
I KNOW IT'S NERVE-RACKING BECAUSE THE SETUP TAKES SO LONG, BUT DON'T GIVE UP, SHIJIMA!
YOU CAN TOTALLY WIN THEM OVER!!
THE LAUGHS HAVEN'T TOTALLY DRIED UP!
THE NEXT BIG WAVE IS RIGHT AROUND THE CORNER...

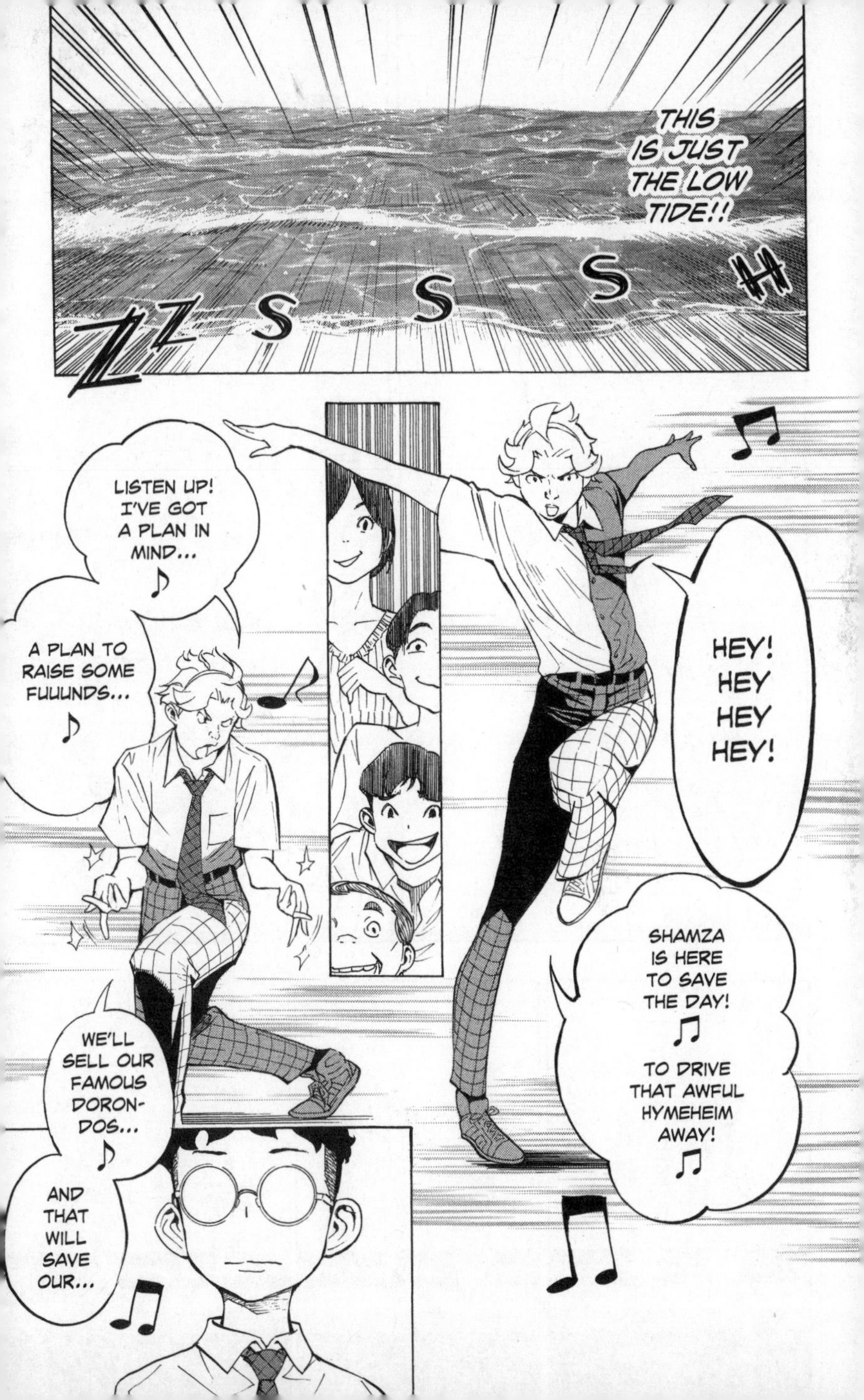
THIS IS JUST THE LOW TIDE!!
ZZSSSH
HEY! HEY HEY HEY!
SHAMZA IS HERE TO SAVE THE DAY! ♫
TO DRIVE THAT AWFUL HYMEHEIM AWAY! ♫
LISTEN UP! I'VE GOT A PLAN IN MIND... ♪
A PLAN TO RAISE SOME FUUUNDS... ♪
WE'LL SELL OUR FAMOUS DORON-DOS... ♪
AND THAT WILL SAVE OUR...

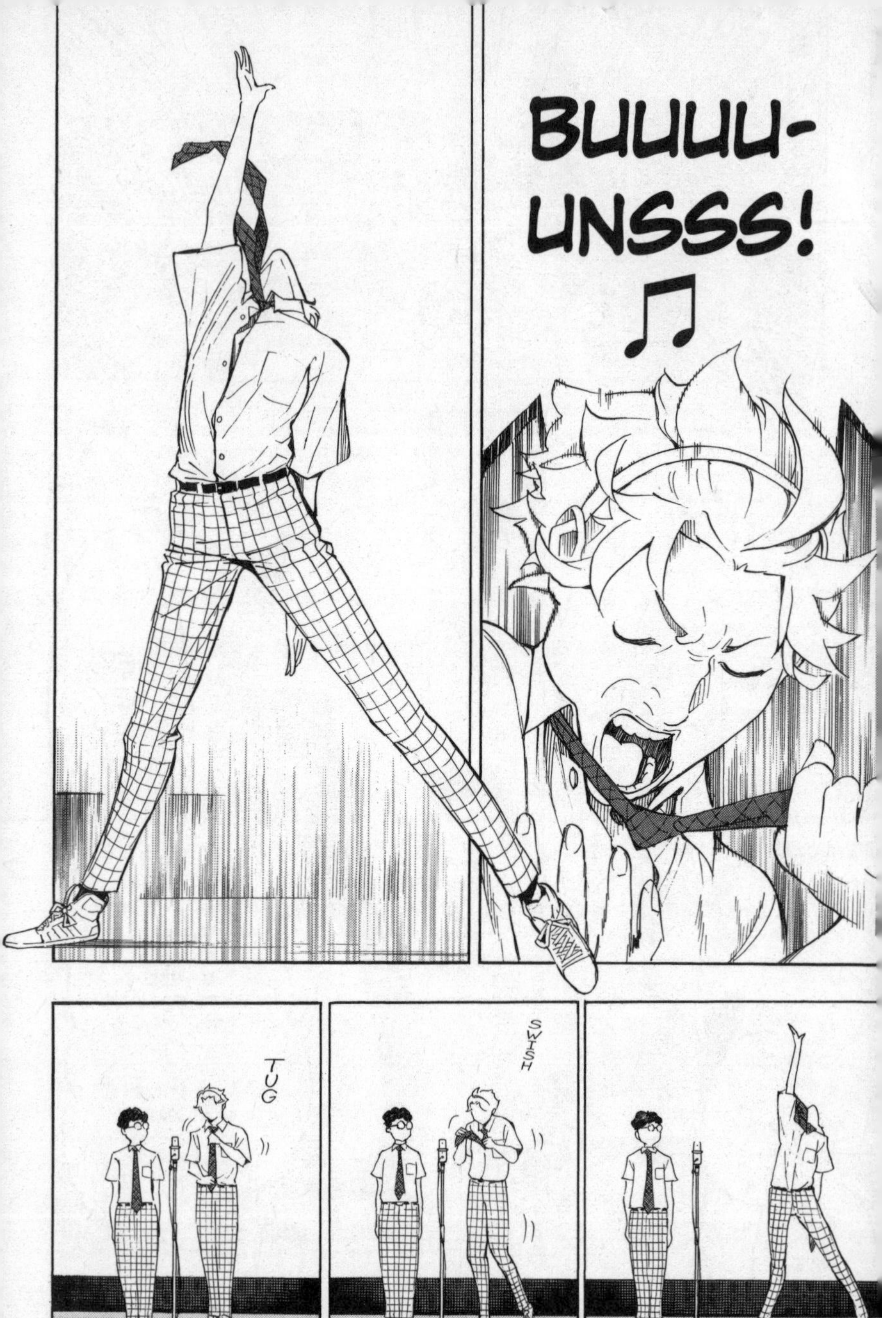
BUUUU-UNSSS! ♫
SWISH
TUG

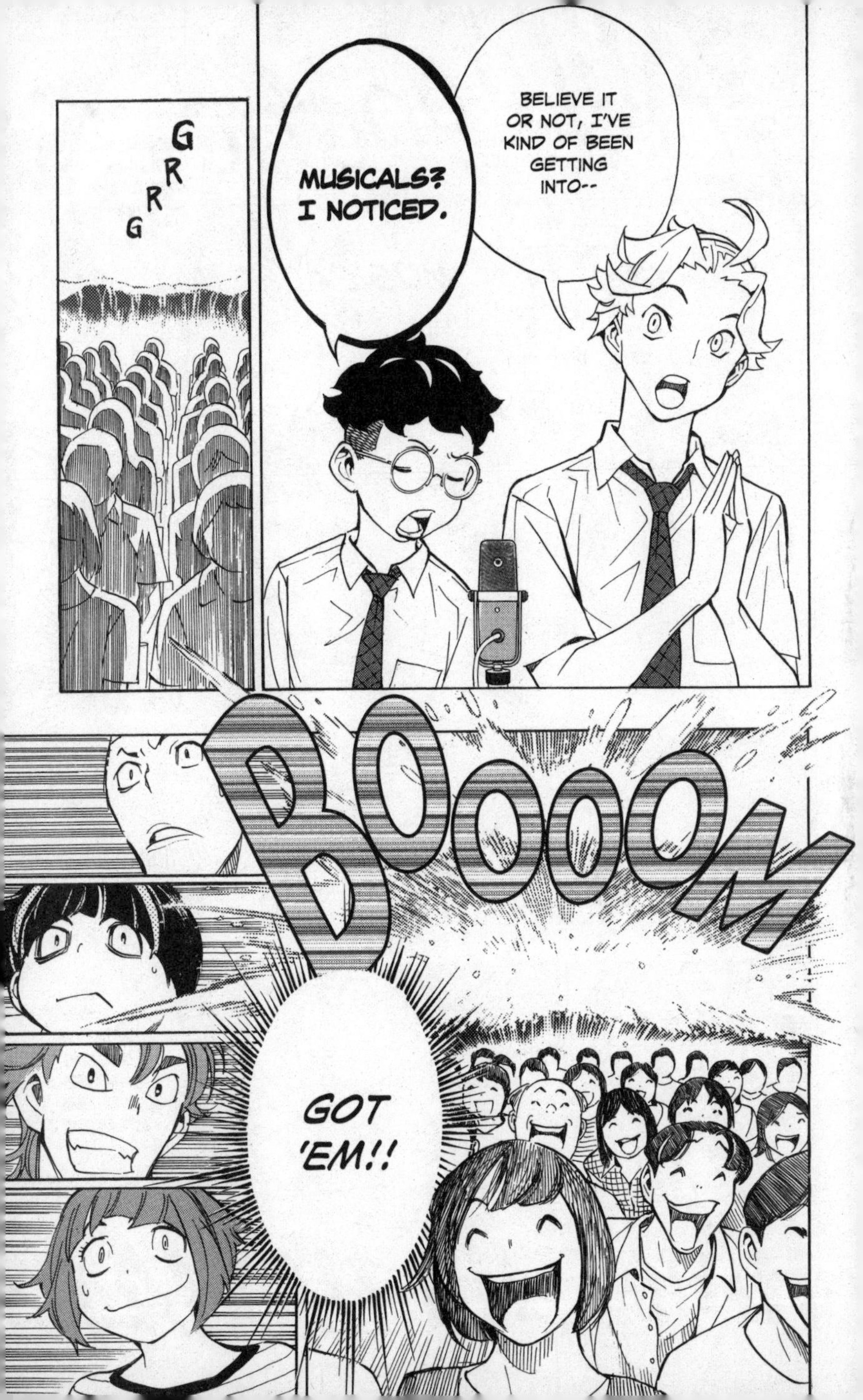
BELIEVE IT OR NOT, I'VE KIND OF BEEN GETTING INTO--
MUSICALS? I NOTICED.
GRRG
BOOOOM
GOT 'EM!!

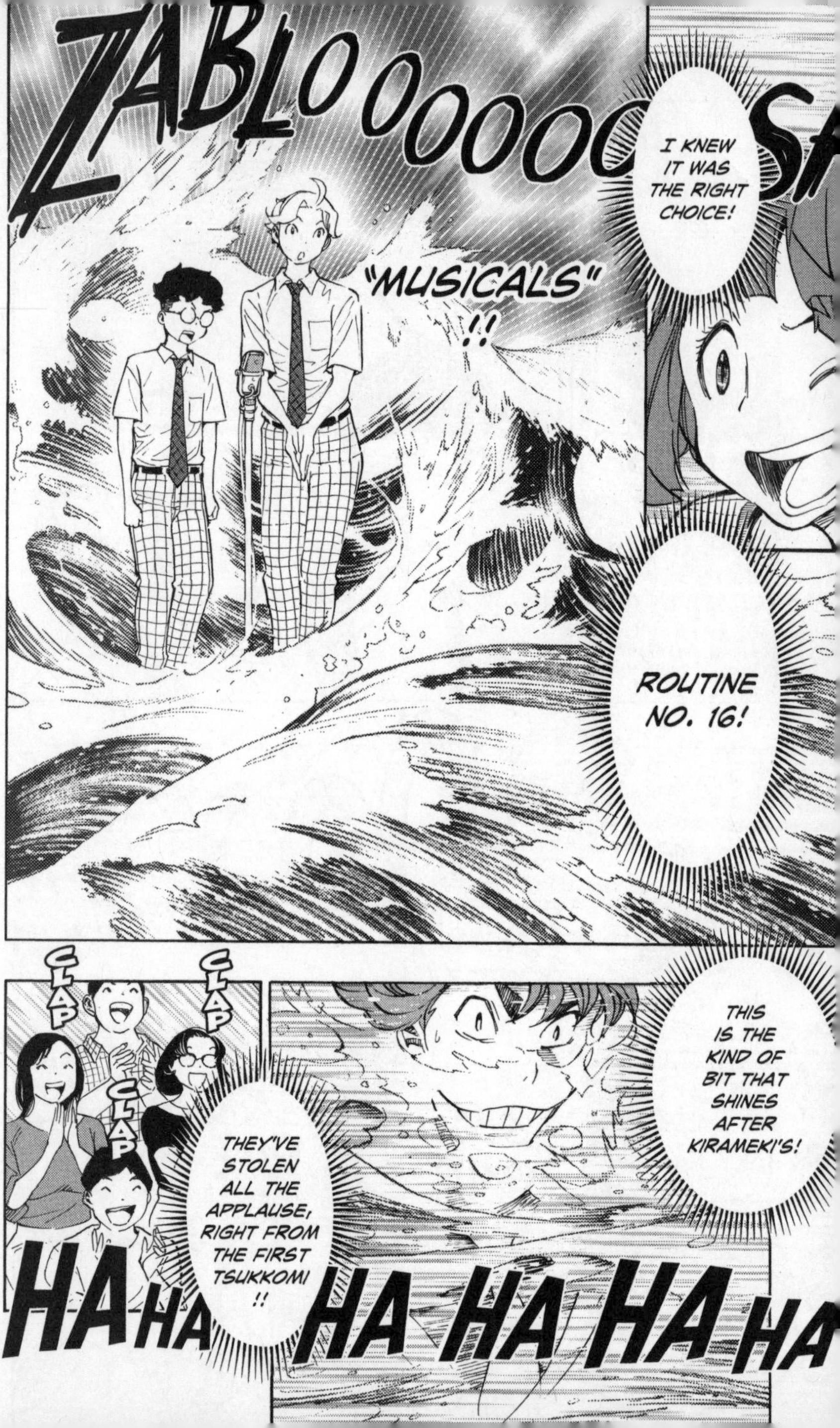
I KNEW IT WAS THE RIGHT CHOICE!
ROUTINE NO. 16!
ZABLOOOOOSH
"MUSICALS" !!
THIS IS THE KIND OF BIT THAT SHINES AFTER KIRAMEKI'S!
THEY'VE STOLEN ALL THE APPLAUSE, RIGHT FROM THE FIRST TSUKKOMI !!
CLAP CLAP CLAP
HA HA HA HA HA HA HA

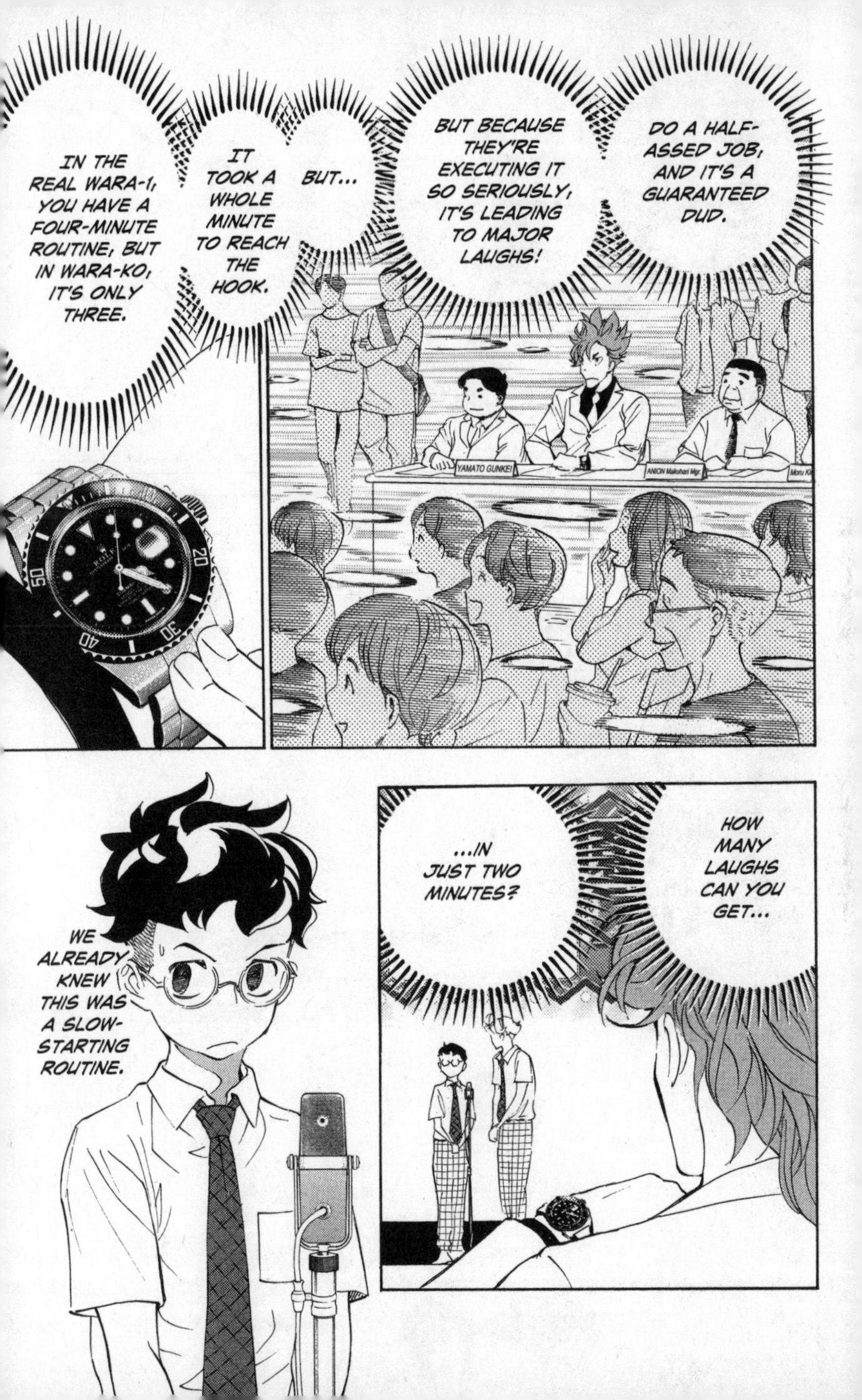
DO A HALF-ASSED JOB, AND IT'S A GUARANTEED DUD.
BUT BECAUSE THEY'RE EXECUTING IT SO SERIOUSLY, IT'S LEADING TO MAJOR LAUGHS!
BUT...
IT TOOK A WHOLE MINUTE TO REACH THE HOOK.
IN THE REAL WARA-1, YOU HAVE A FOUR-MINUTE ROUTINE, BUT IN WARA-KO, IT'S ONLY THREE.
ANION Makuhari Mgr.
YAMATO GUNKEI
HOW MANY LAUGHS CAN YOU GET...
...IN JUST TWO MINUTES?
WE ALREADY KNEW THIS WAS A SLOW-STARTING ROUTINE.

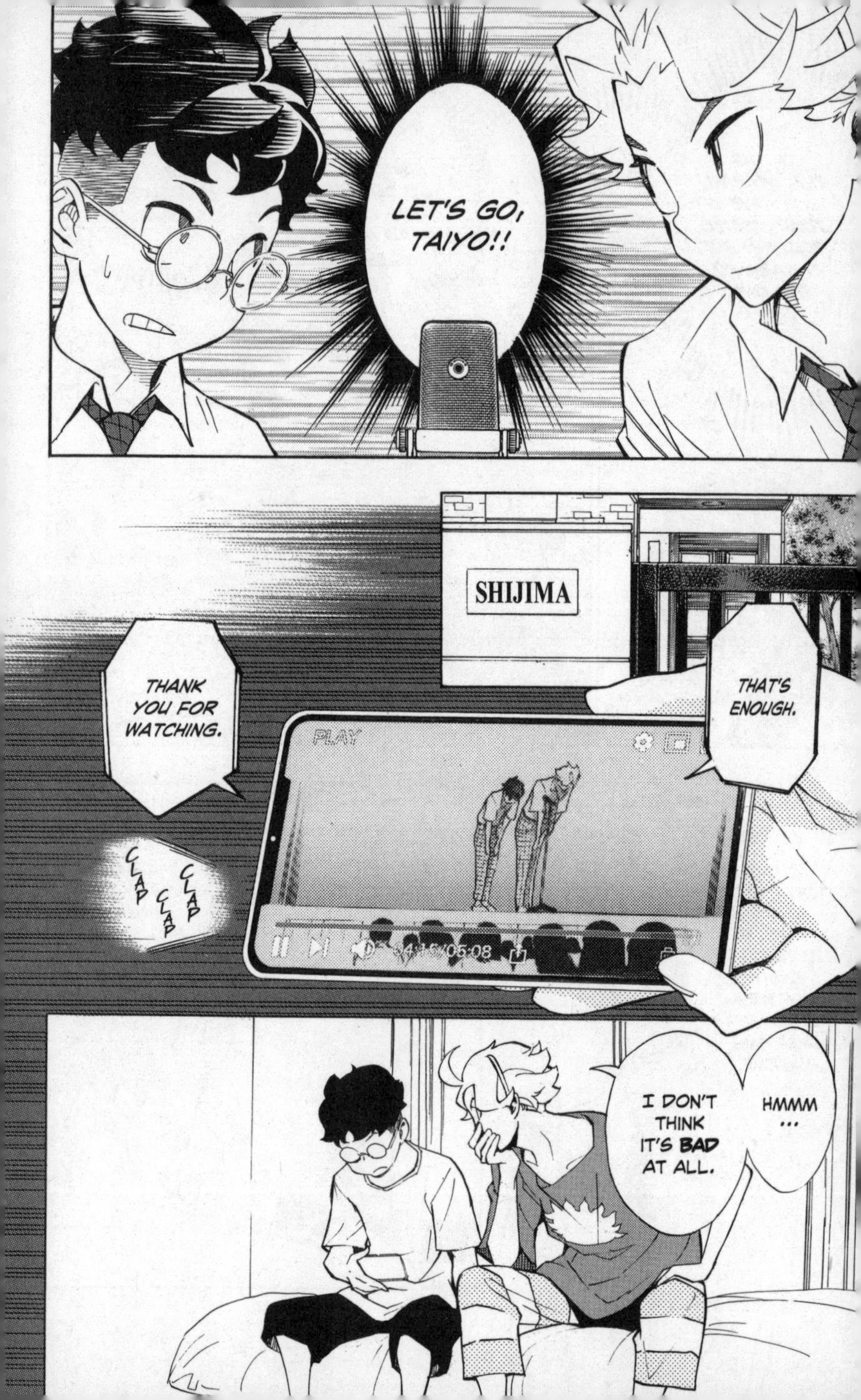
LET'S GO, TAIYO!!
SHIJIMA
THAT'S ENOUGH.
THANK YOU FOR WATCHING.
PLAY
CLAP CLAP CLAP
HMMMM...
I DON'T THINK IT'S **BAD** AT ALL.

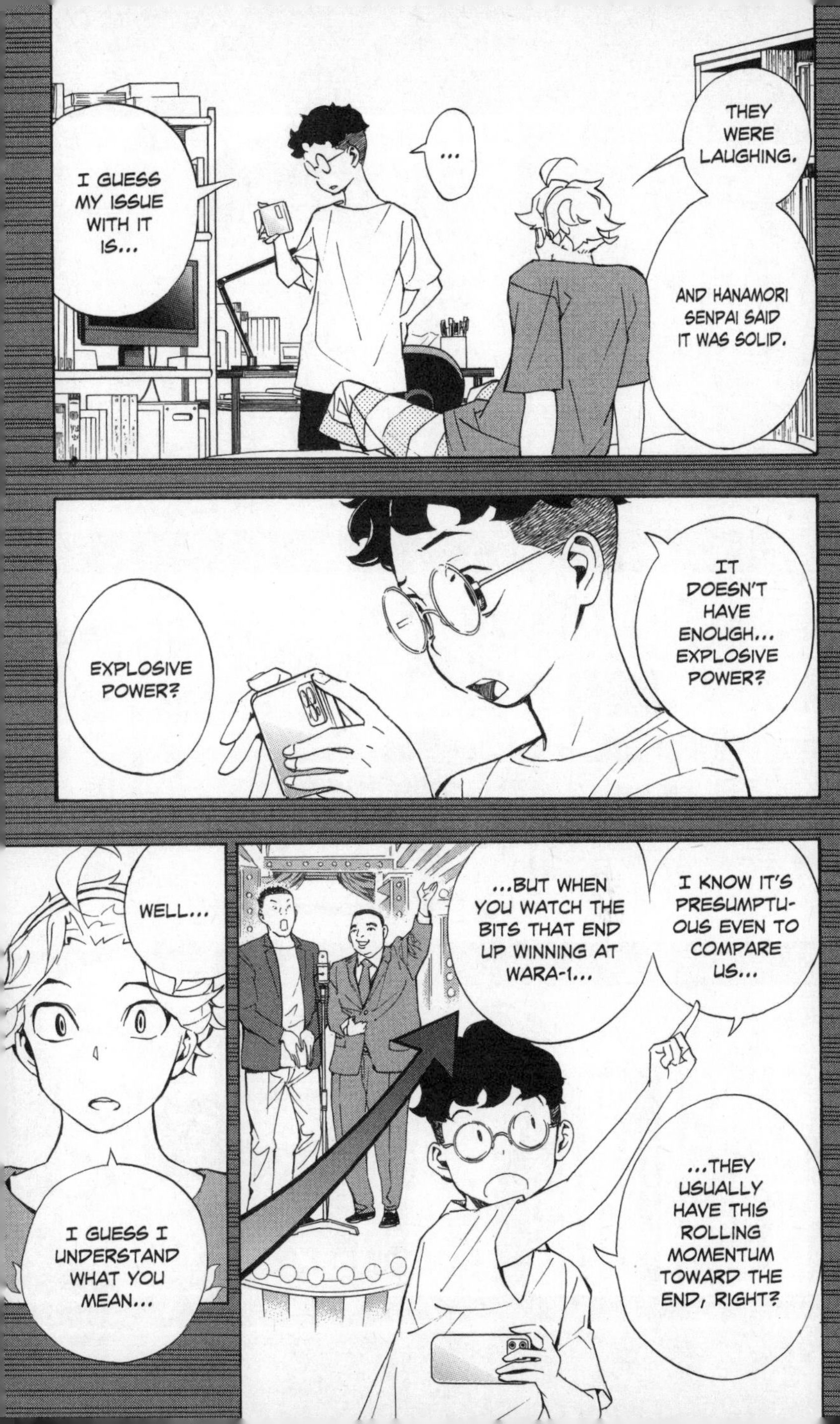
THEY WERE LAUGHING.
AND HANAMORI SENPAI SAID IT WAS SOLID.
...
I GUESS MY ISSUE WITH IT IS...
IT DOESN'T HAVE ENOUGH... EXPLOSIVE POWER?
EXPLOSIVE POWER?
I KNOW IT'S PRESUMPTU-OUS EVEN TO COMPARE US...
...BUT WHEN YOU WATCH THE BITS THAT END UP WINNING AT WARA-1...
...THEY USUALLY HAVE THIS ROLLING MOMENTUM TOWARD THE END, RIGHT?
WELL...
I GUESS I UNDERSTAND WHAT YOU MEAN...

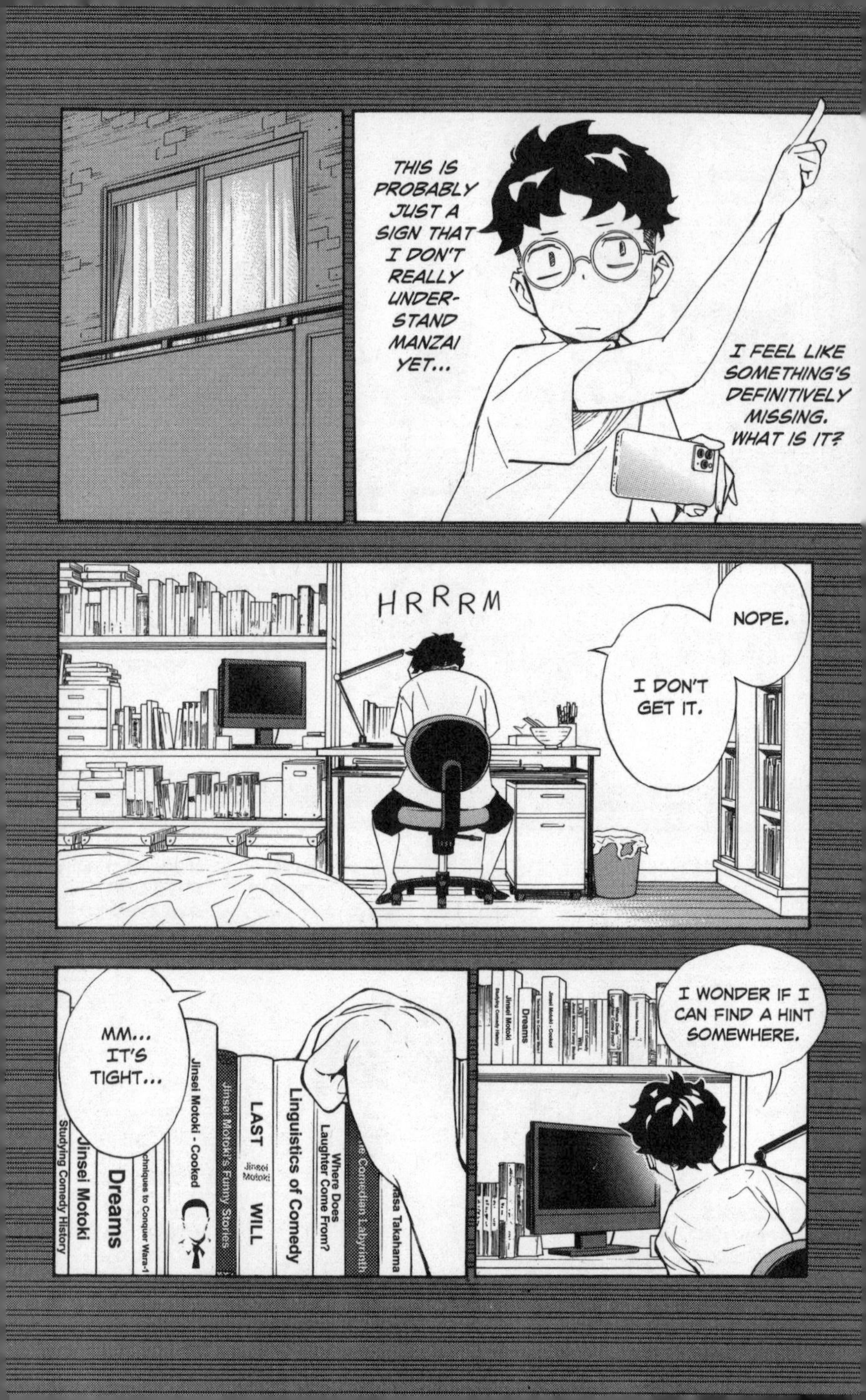
THIS IS PROBABLY JUST A SIGN THAT I DON'T REALLY UNDER-STAND MANZAI YET...
I FEEL LIKE SOMETHING'S DEFINITIVELY MISSING. WHAT IS IT?
HRRRM
NOPE.
I DON'T GET IT.
I WONDER IF I CAN FIND A HINT SOMEWHERE.
MM... IT'S TIGHT...
Where Does Laughter Come From?
Linguistics of Comedy
LAST WILL
Jinsei Motoki
Jinsei Motoki's Funny Stories
Jinsei Motoki - Cooked
Dreams
Jinsei Motoki
Studying Comedy History

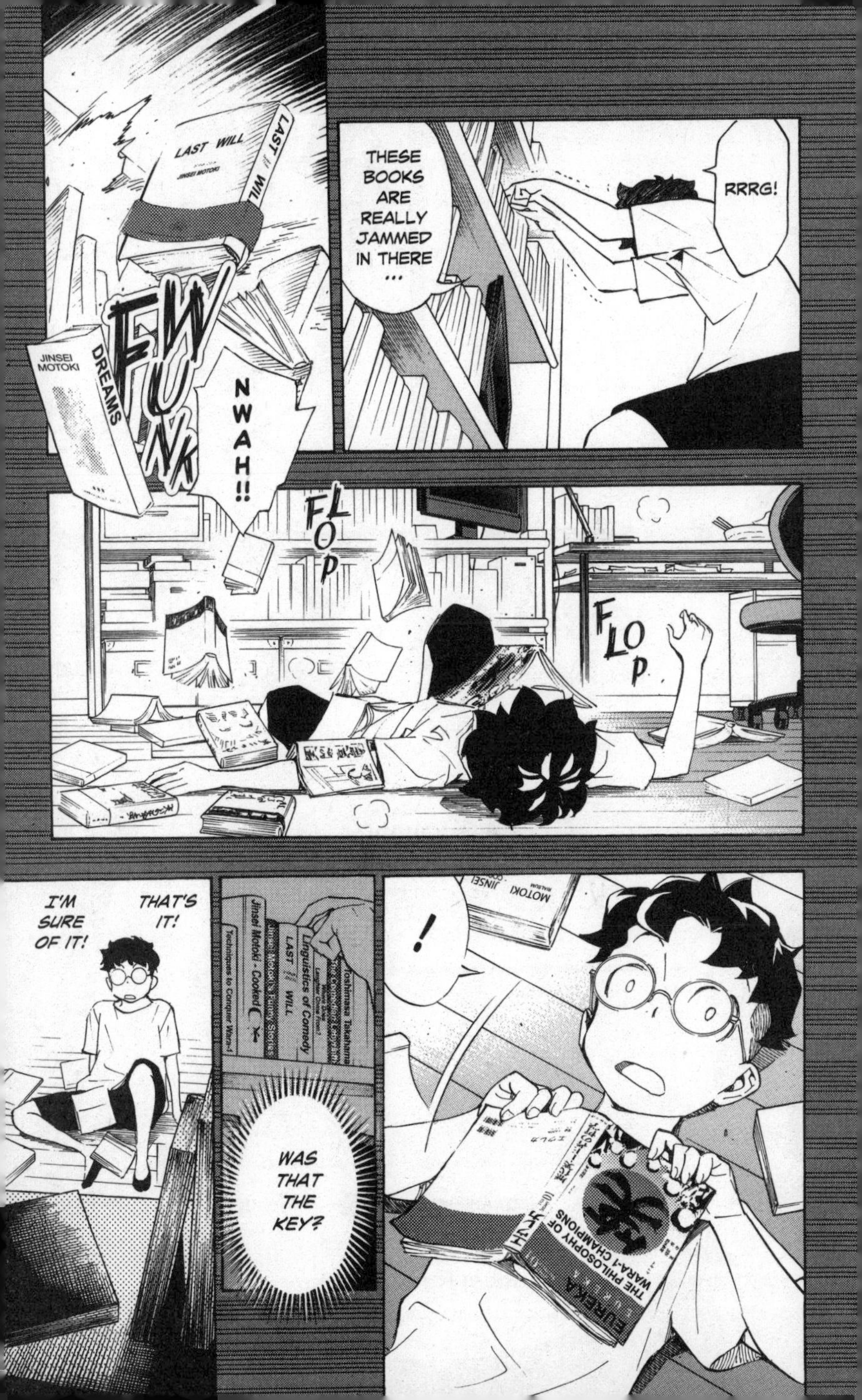
RRRG!
THESE BOOKS ARE REALLY JAMMED IN THERE ...
LAST WILL
JINSEI MOTOKI
LAST WILL
FWUNK
NWAH!!
JINSEI MOTOKI
DREAMS
FLOP
FLOP
!
JINSEI MOTOKI
ALBUM
EUREKA
THE PHILOSOPHY OF WARA-1 CHAMPIONS
Jinsei Motoki
LAST WILL
Linguistics of Comedy
Jinsei Motoki: Cooked
Techniques to Conquer Wara-1
WAS THAT THE KEY?
THAT'S IT!
I'M SURE OF IT!

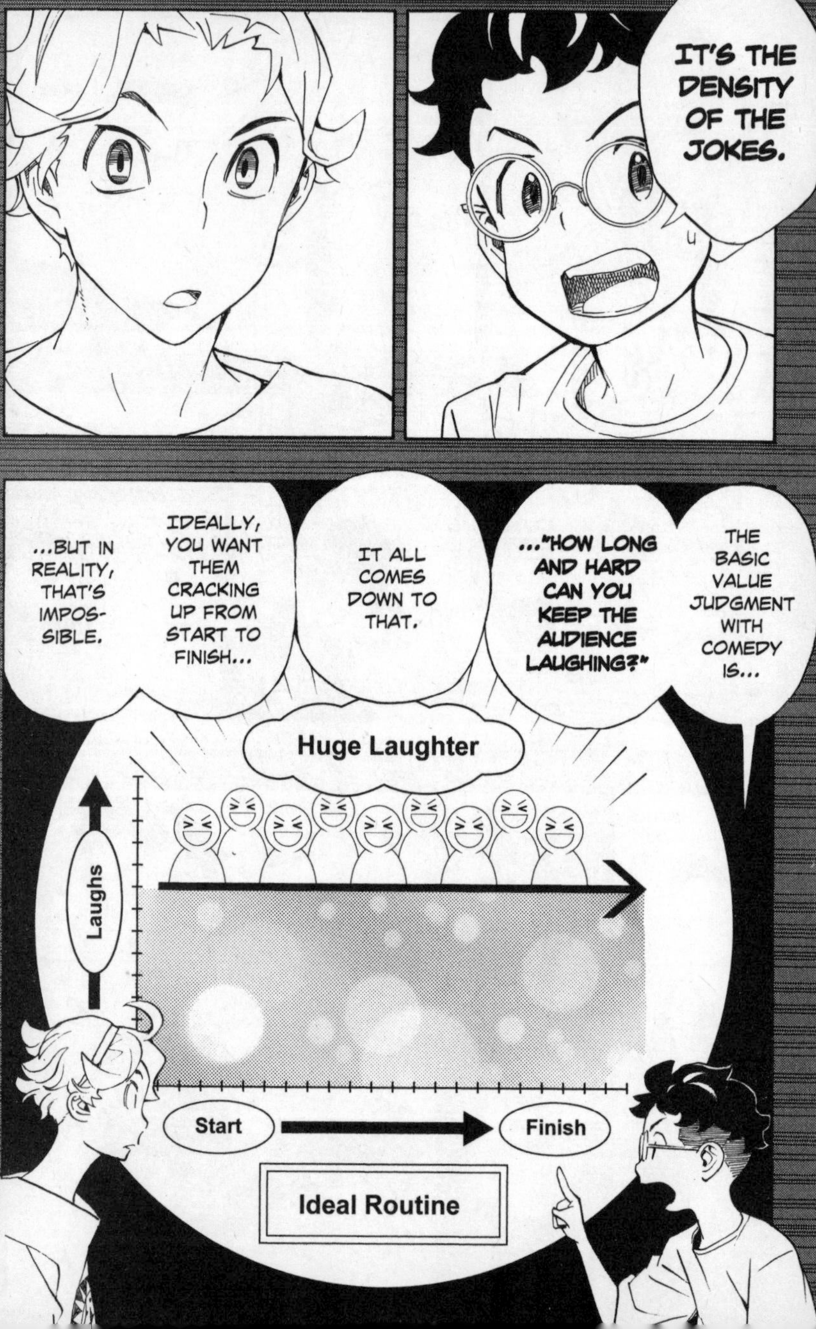
IT'S THE DENSITY OF THE JOKES.
THE BASIC VALUE JUDGMENT WITH COMEDY IS...
..."HOW LONG AND HARD CAN YOU KEEP THE AUDIENCE LAUGHING?"
IT ALL COMES DOWN TO THAT.
IDEALLY, YOU WANT THEM CRACKING UP FROM START TO FINISH...
...BUT IN REALITY, THAT'S IMPOS-SIBLE.
Huge Laughter
Laughs
Start
Finish
Ideal Routine

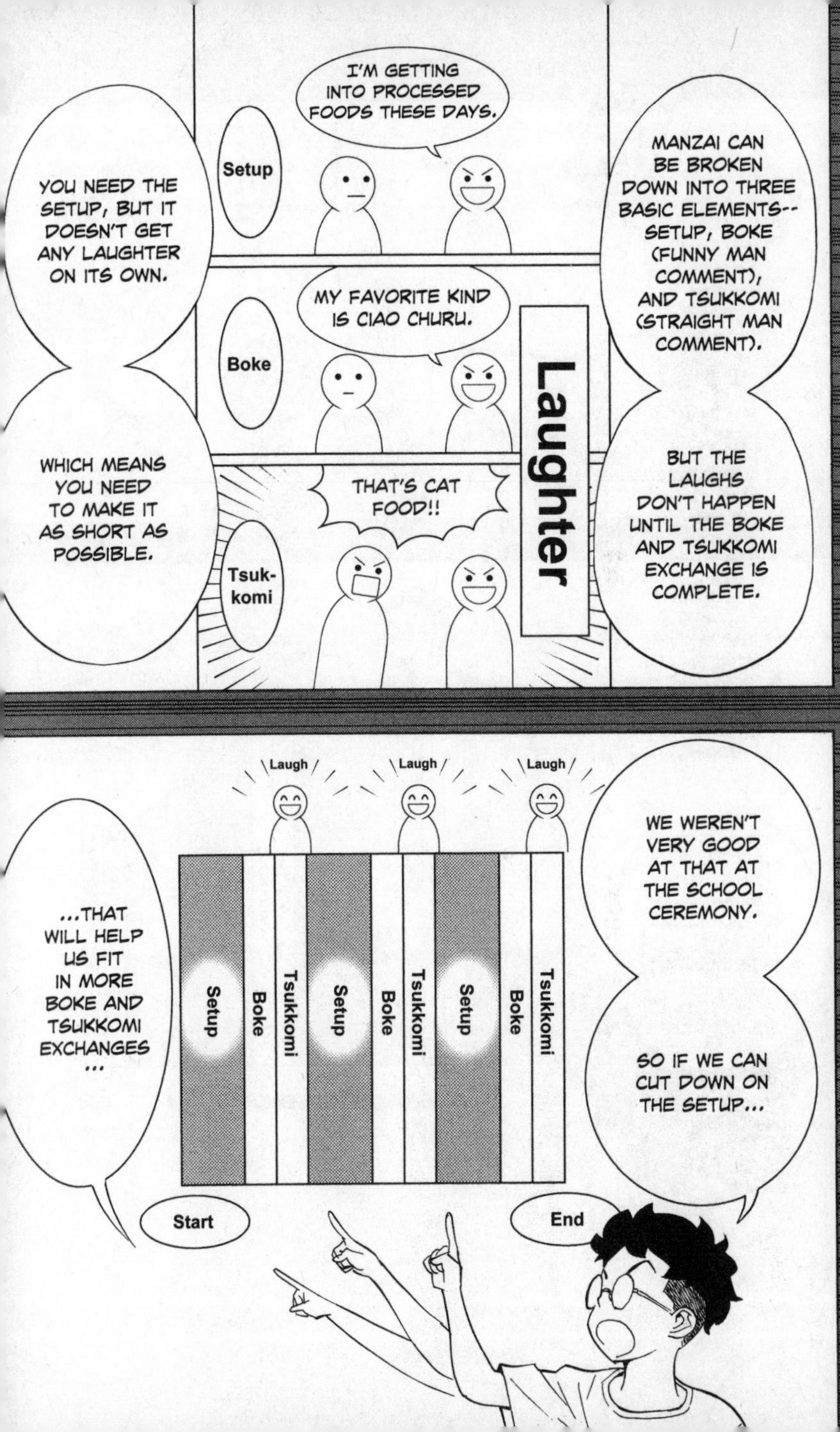
MANZAI CAN BE BROKEN DOWN INTO THREE BASIC ELEMENTS--SETUP, BOKE (FUNNY MAN COMMENT), AND TSUKKOMI (STRAIGHT MAN COMMENT).
BUT THE LAUGHS DON'T HAPPEN UNTIL THE BOKE AND TSUKKOMI EXCHANGE IS COMPLETE.
I'M GETTING INTO PROCESSED FOODS THESE DAYS.
Setup
MY FAVORITE KIND IS CIAO CHURU.
Boke
THAT'S CAT FOOD!!
Tsuk-komi
Laughter
YOU NEED THE SETUP, BUT IT DOESN'T GET ANY LAUGHTER ON ITS OWN.
WHICH MEANS YOU NEED TO MAKE IT AS SHORT AS POSSIBLE.
WE WEREN'T VERY GOOD AT THAT AT THE SCHOOL CEREMONY.
SO IF WE CAN CUT DOWN ON THE SETUP...
Laugh
Laugh
Laugh
Setup
Boke
Tsukkomi
Setup
Boke
Tsukkomi
Setup
Boke
Tsukkomi
Start
End
...THAT WILL HELP US FIT IN MORE BOKE AND TSUKKOMI EXCHANGES...

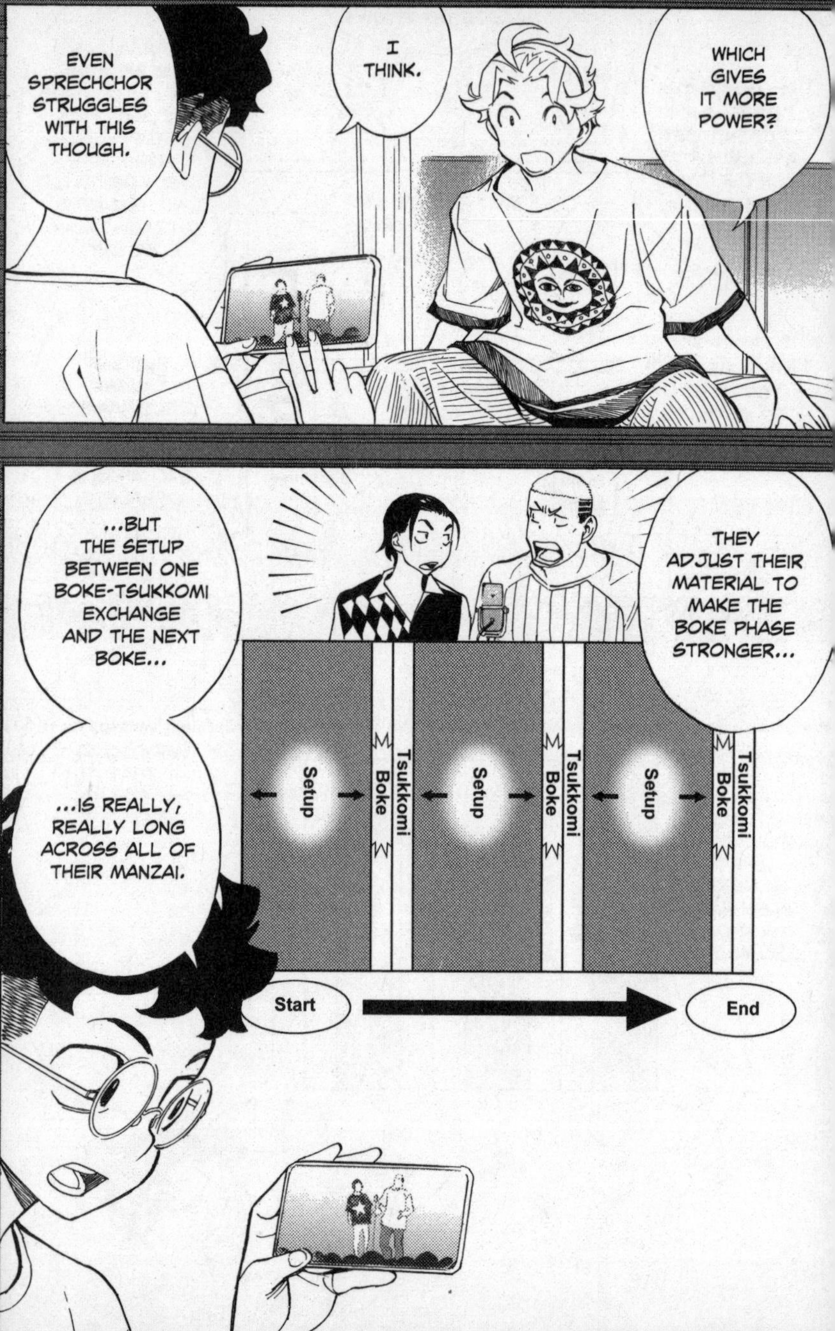
WHICH GIVES IT MORE POWER?
I THINK.
EVEN SPRECHCHOR STRUGGLES WITH THIS THOUGH.
THEY ADJUST THEIR MATERIAL TO MAKE THE BOKE PHASE STRONGER...
...BUT THE SETUP BETWEEN ONE BOKE-TSUKKOMI EXCHANGE AND THE NEXT BOKE...
...IS REALLY, REALLY LONG ACROSS ALL OF THEIR MANZAI.
Setup
Boke
Tsukkomi
Setup
Boke
Tsukkomi
Setup
Boke
Tsukkomi
Start
End

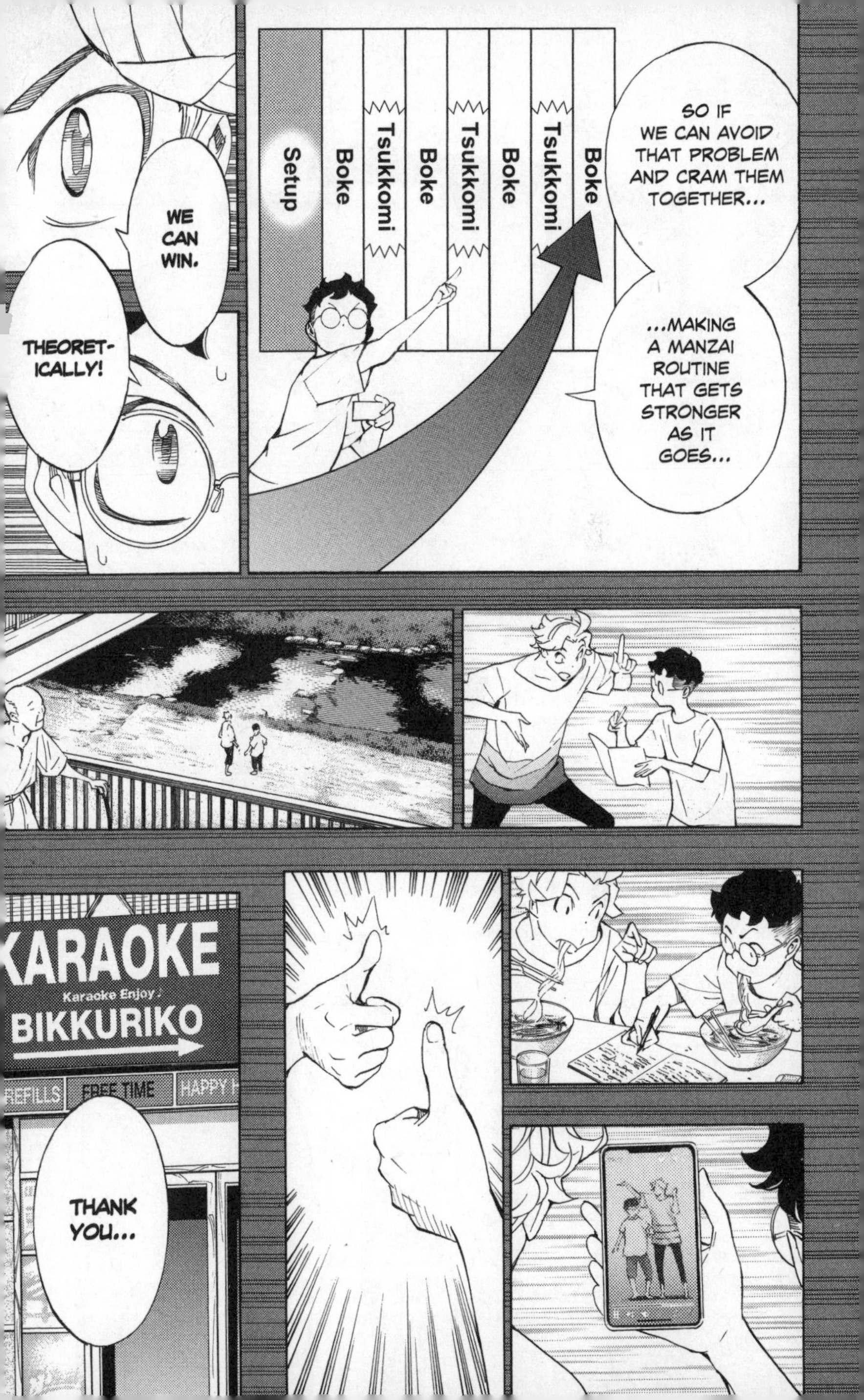
SO IF WE CAN AVOID THAT PROBLEM AND CRAM THEM TOGETHER...
Boke
Tsukkomi
Boke
Tsukkomi
Boke
Tsukkomi
Boke
Setup
...MAKING A MANZAI ROUTINE THAT GETS STRONGER AS IT GOES...
WE CAN WIN.
THEORET-ICALLY!
KARAOKE
Karaoke Enjoy
BIKKURIKO
REFILLS
FREE TIME
HAPPY H
THANK YOU...

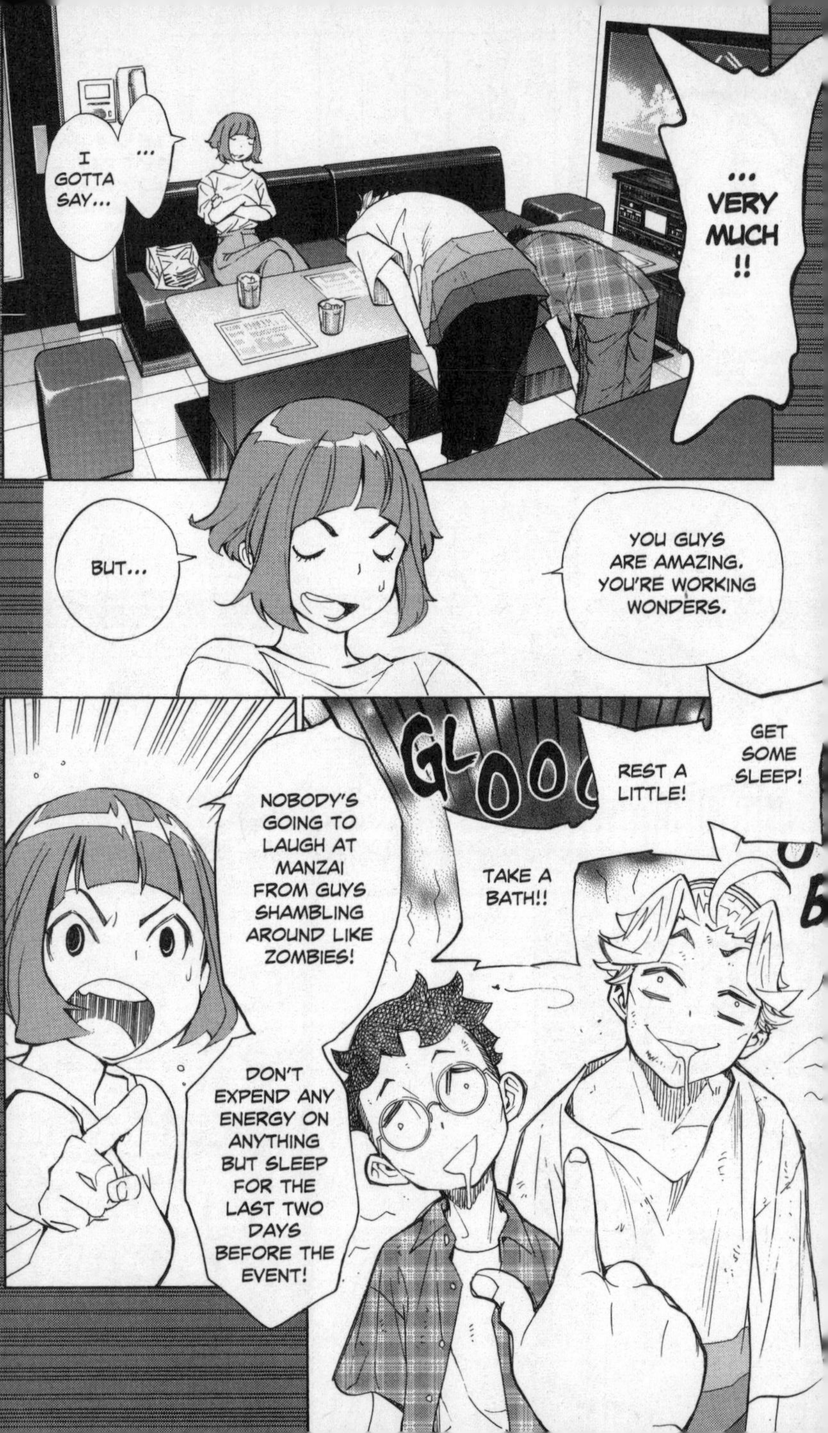
...
VERY MUCH !!
...
I GOTTA SAY...
YOU GUYS ARE AMAZING. YOU'RE WORKING WONDERS.
BUT...
GET SOME SLEEP!
REST A LITTLE!
GLOOO
NOBODY'S GOING TO LAUGH AT MANZAI FROM GUYS SHAMBLING AROUND LIKE ZOMBIES!
TAKE A BATH!!
DON'T EXPEND ANY ENERGY ON ANYTHING BUT SLEEP FOR THE LAST TWO DAYS BEFORE THE EVENT!

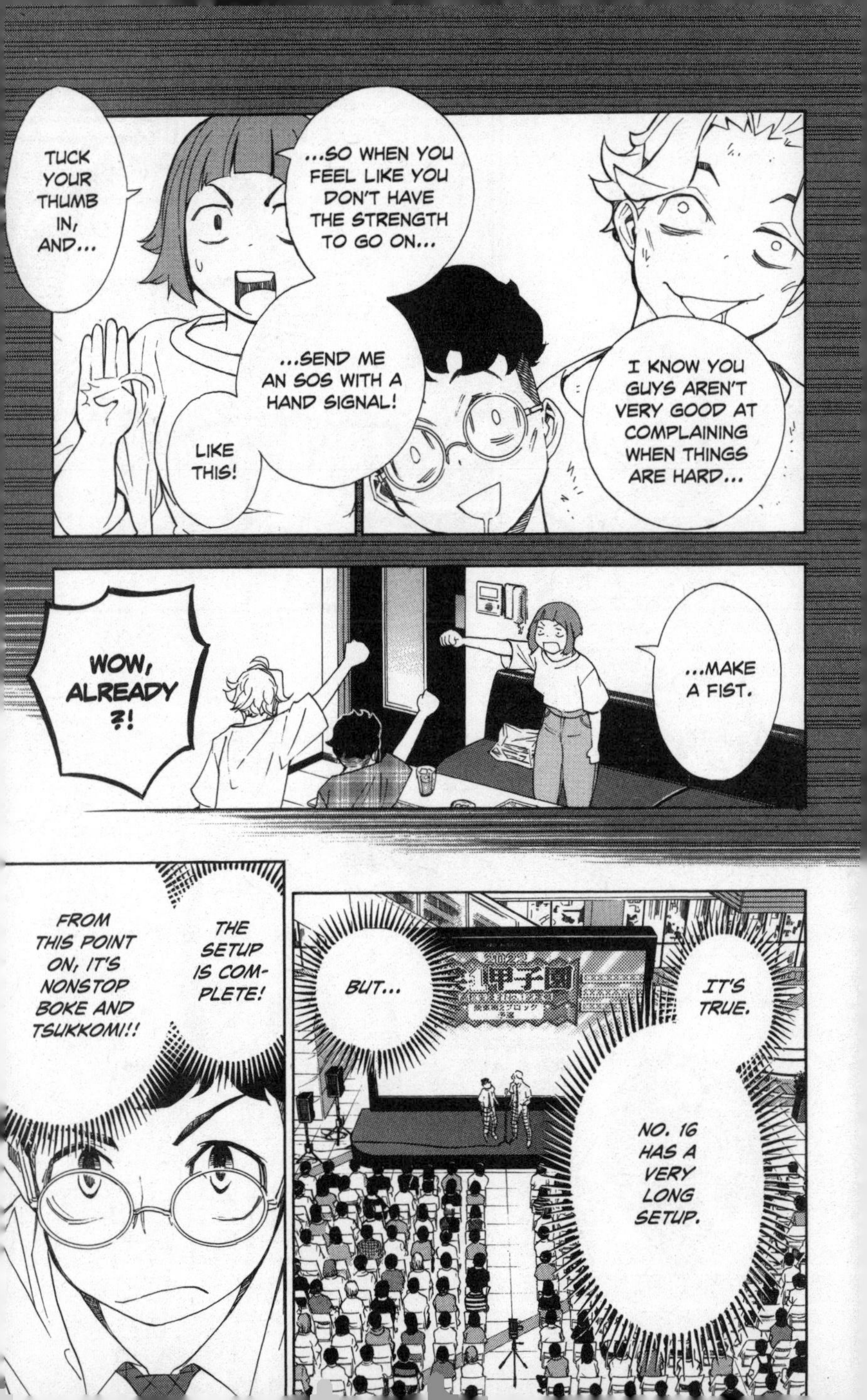
I KNOW YOU GUYS AREN'T VERY GOOD AT COMPLAINING WHEN THINGS ARE HARD...
...SO WHEN YOU FEEL LIKE YOU DON'T HAVE THE STRENGTH TO GO ON...
...SEND ME AN SOS WITH A HAND SIGNAL!
TUCK YOUR THUMB IN, AND...
LIKE THIS!
...MAKE A FIST.
WOW, ALREADY?!
IT'S TRUE.
BUT...
NO. 16 HAS A VERY LONG SETUP.
THE SETUP IS COM-PLETE!
FROM THIS POINT ON, IT'S NONSTOP BOKE AND TSUKKOMI!!

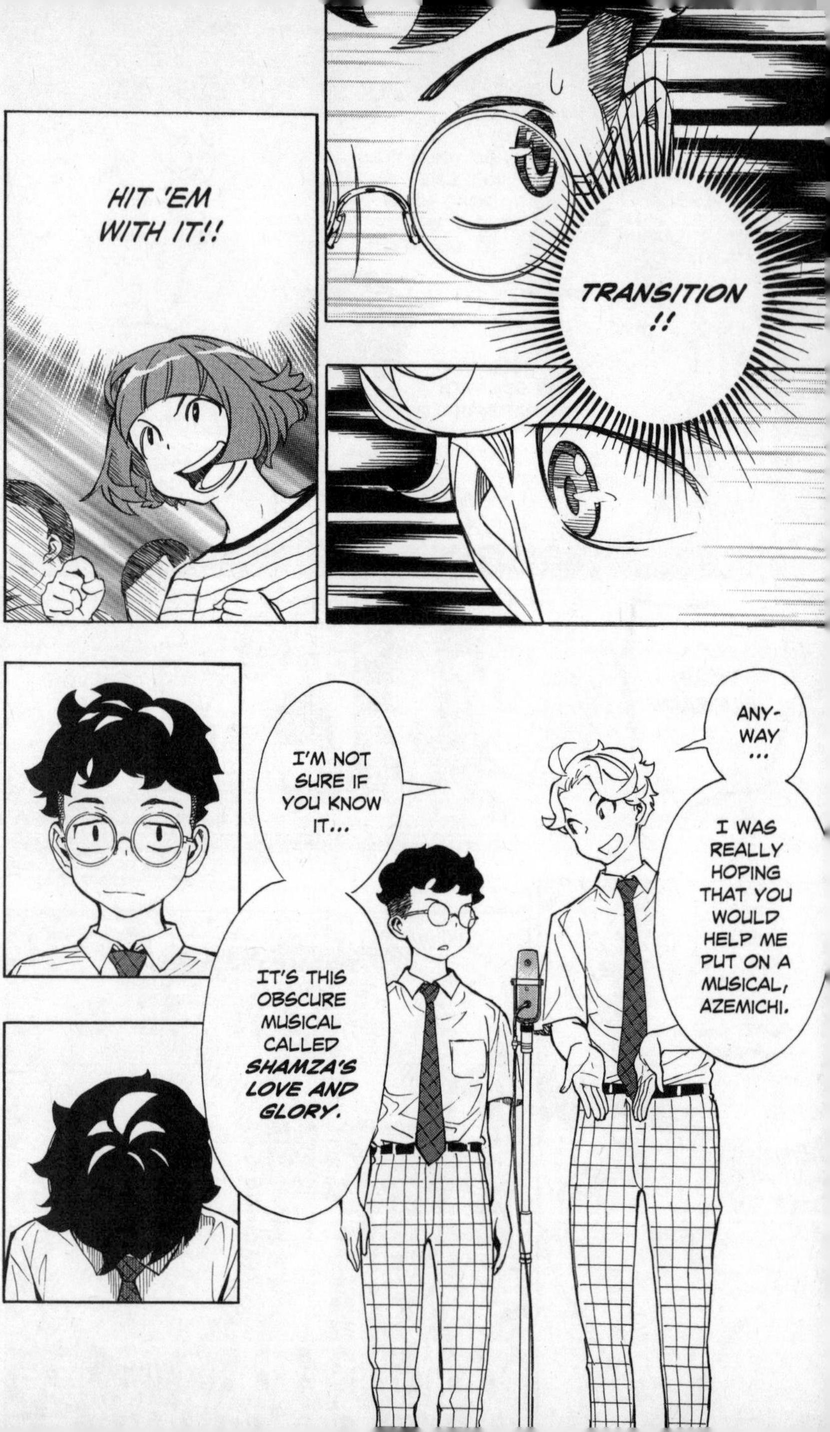
TRANSITION !!
HIT 'EM WITH IT!!
ANY-WAY...
I WAS REALLY HOPING THAT YOU WOULD HELP ME PUT ON A MUSICAL, AZEMICHI.
I'M NOT SURE IF YOU KNOW IT...
IT'S THIS OBSCURE MUSICAL CALLED *SHAMZA'S LOVE AND GLORY*.

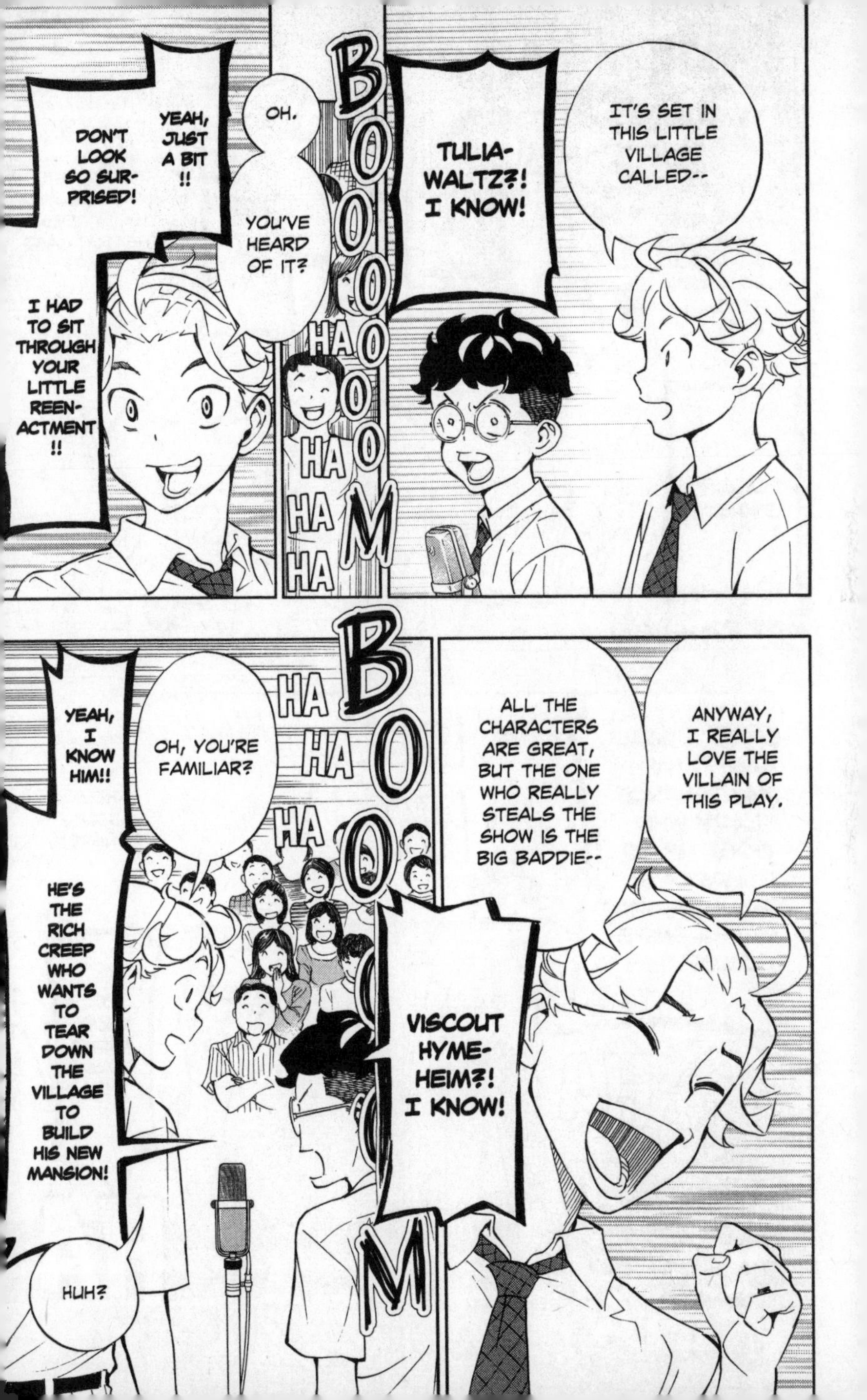
IT'S SET IN THIS LITTLE VILLAGE CALLED--
TULIA-WALTZ?! I KNOW!
BOOOOOOM
HA HA HA HA
OH.
YOU'VE HEARD OF IT?
YEAH, JUST A BIT!!
DON'T LOOK SO SURPRISED!
I HAD TO SIT THROUGH YOUR LITTLE REENACTMENT!!
ANYWAY, I REALLY LOVE THE VILLAIN OF THIS PLAY.
ALL THE CHARACTERS ARE GREAT, BUT THE ONE WHO REALLY STEALS THE SHOW IS THE BIG BADDIE--
VISCOUT HYME-HEIM?! I KNOW!
BOOM
HA HA HA
OH, YOU'RE FAMILIAR?
YEAH, I KNOW HIM!!
HE'S THE RICH CREEP WHO WANTS TO TEAR DOWN THE VILLAGE TO BUILD HIS NEW MANSION!
HUH?

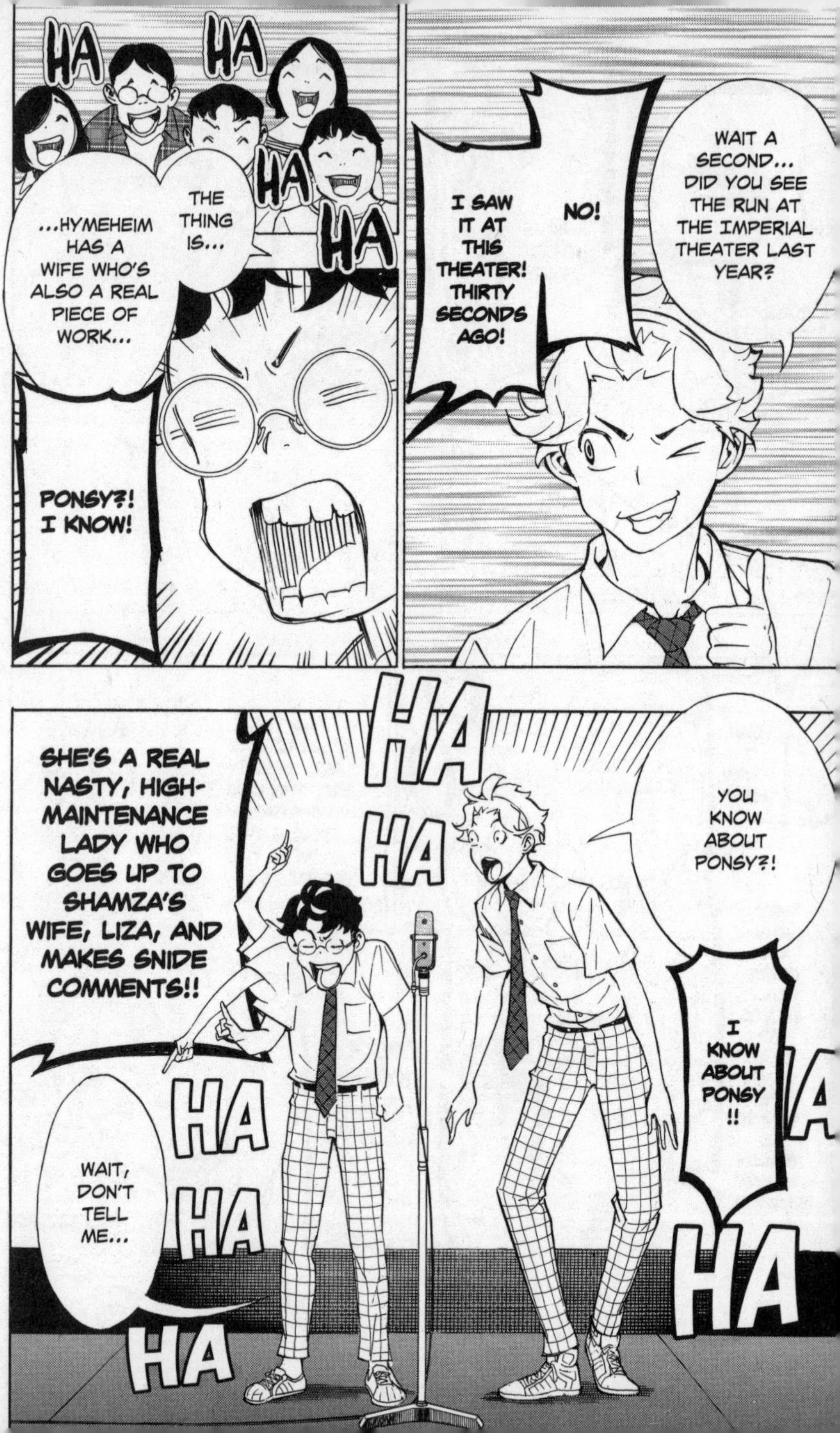
WAIT A SECOND... DID YOU SEE THE RUN AT THE IMPERIAL THEATER LAST YEAR?
NO!
I SAW IT AT THIS THEATER! THIRTY SECONDS AGO!
HA
HA
HA
HA
THE THING IS...
...HYMEHEIM HAS A WIFE WHO'S ALSO A REAL PIECE OF WORK...
PONSY?! I KNOW!
YOU KNOW ABOUT PONSY?!
I KNOW ABOUT PONSY !!
HA
HA
HA
SHE'S A REAL NASTY, HIGH-MAINTENANCE LADY WHO GOES UP TO SHAMZA'S WIFE, LIZA, AND MAKES SNIDE COMMENTS!!
HA
HA
WAIT, DON'T TELL ME...
HA

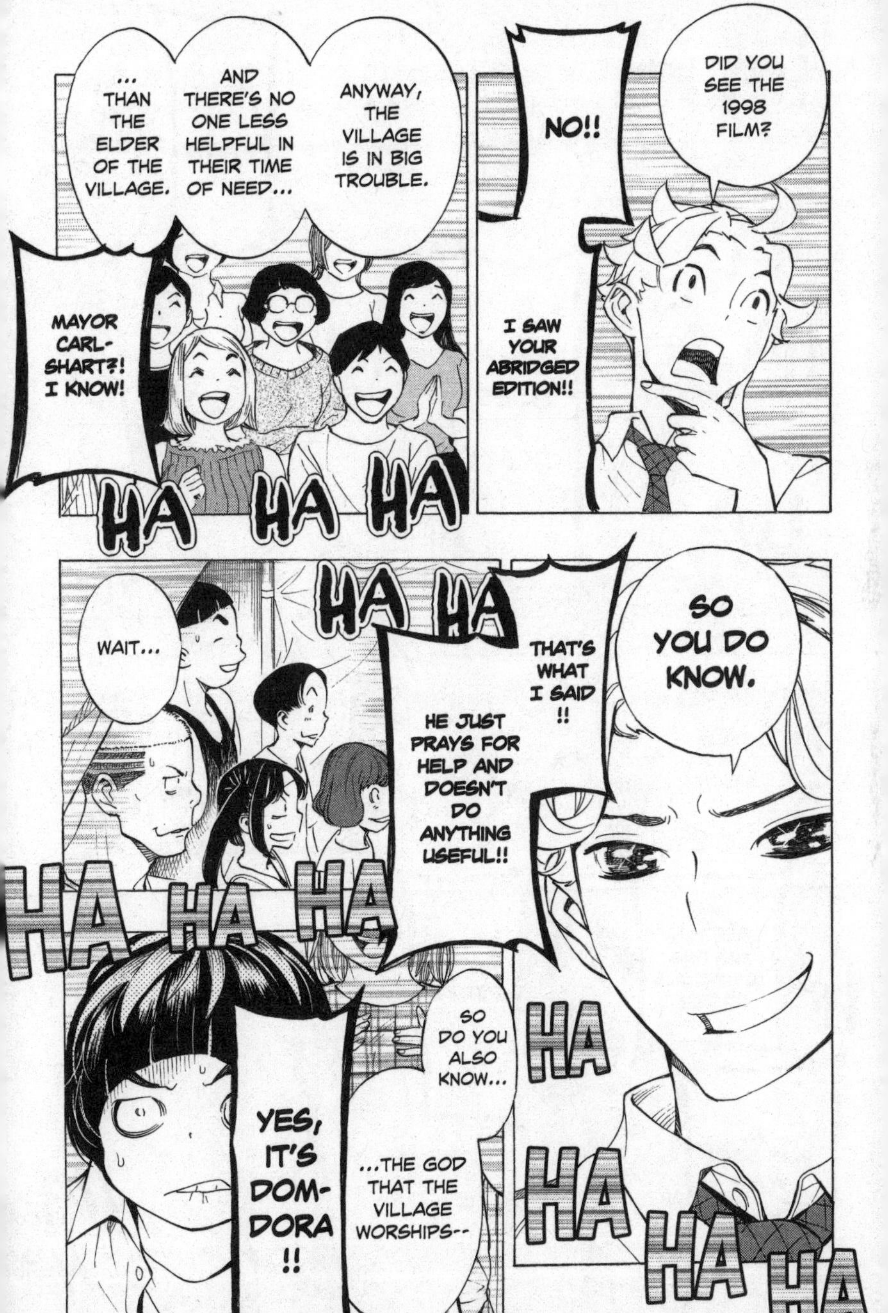
DID YOU SEE THE 1998 FILM?
NO!!
I SAW YOUR ABRIDGED EDITION!!
ANYWAY, THE VILLAGE IS IN BIG TROUBLE.
AND THERE'S NO ONE LESS HELPFUL IN THEIR TIME OF NEED...
... THAN THE ELDER OF THE VILLAGE.
MAYOR CARL-SHART?! I KNOW!
HA HA HA
SO YOU DO KNOW.
THAT'S WHAT I SAID!!
HE JUST PRAYS FOR HELP AND DOESN'T DO ANYTHING USEFUL!!
HA HA HA HA
HA HA
WAIT...
HA HA HA
SO DO YOU ALSO KNOW...
...THE GOD THAT THE VILLAGE WORSHIPS--
YES, IT'S DOM-DORA!!

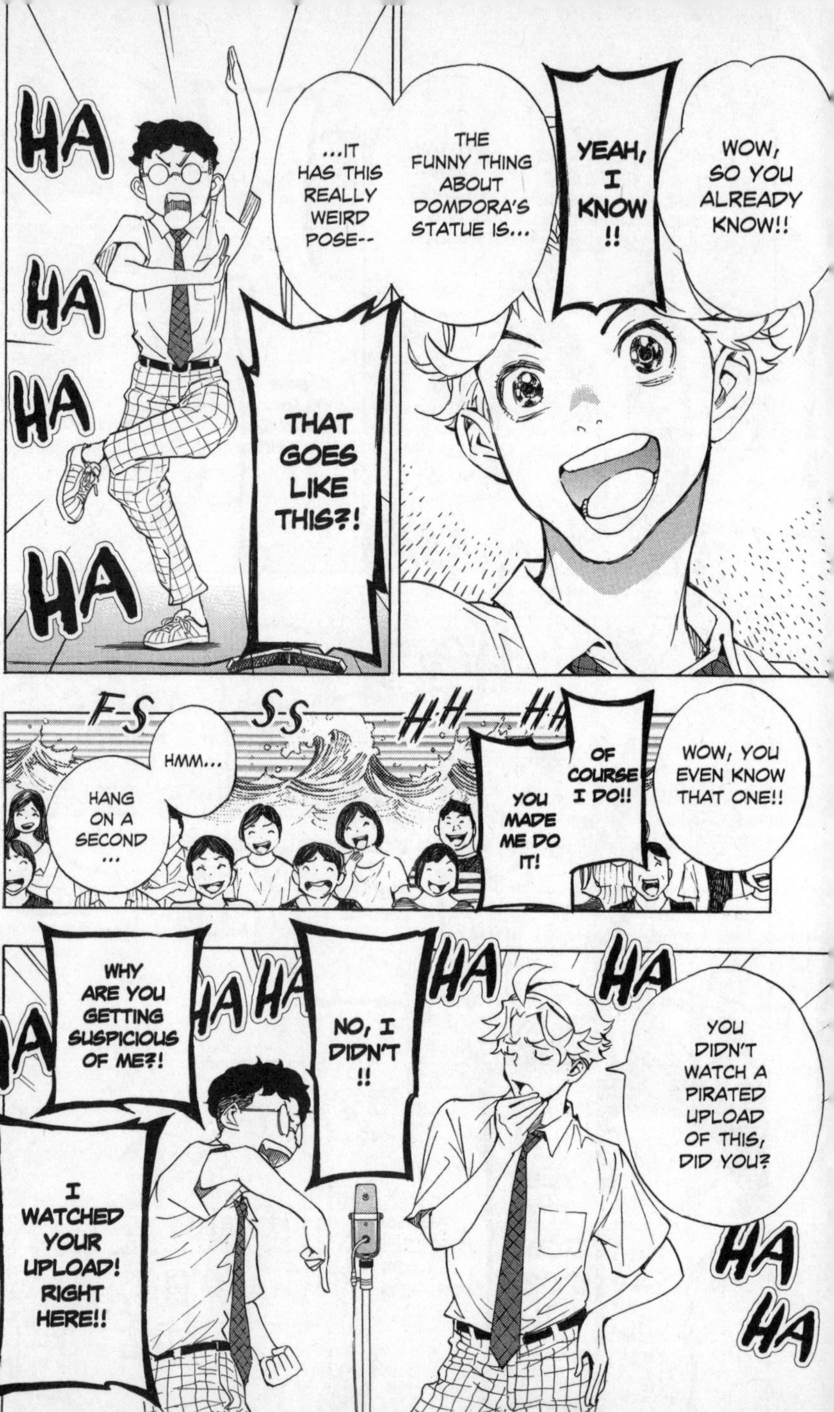
WOW, SO YOU ALREADY KNOW!!
YEAH, I KNOW!!
THE FUNNY THING ABOUT DOMDORA'S STATUE IS...
...IT HAS THIS REALLY WEIRD POSE--
THAT GOES LIKE THIS?!
HA HA HA HA
WOW, YOU EVEN KNOW THAT ONE!!
OF COURSE I DO!!
YOU MADE ME DO IT!
H-H H-H
S-S
F-S
HMM...
HANG ON A SECOND...
YOU DIDN'T WATCH A PIRATED UPLOAD OF THIS, DID YOU?
HA HA
HA HA
NO, I DIDN'T!!
WHY ARE YOU GETTING SUSPICIOUS OF ME?!
I WATCHED YOUR UPLOAD! RIGHT HERE!!
HA HA HA HA

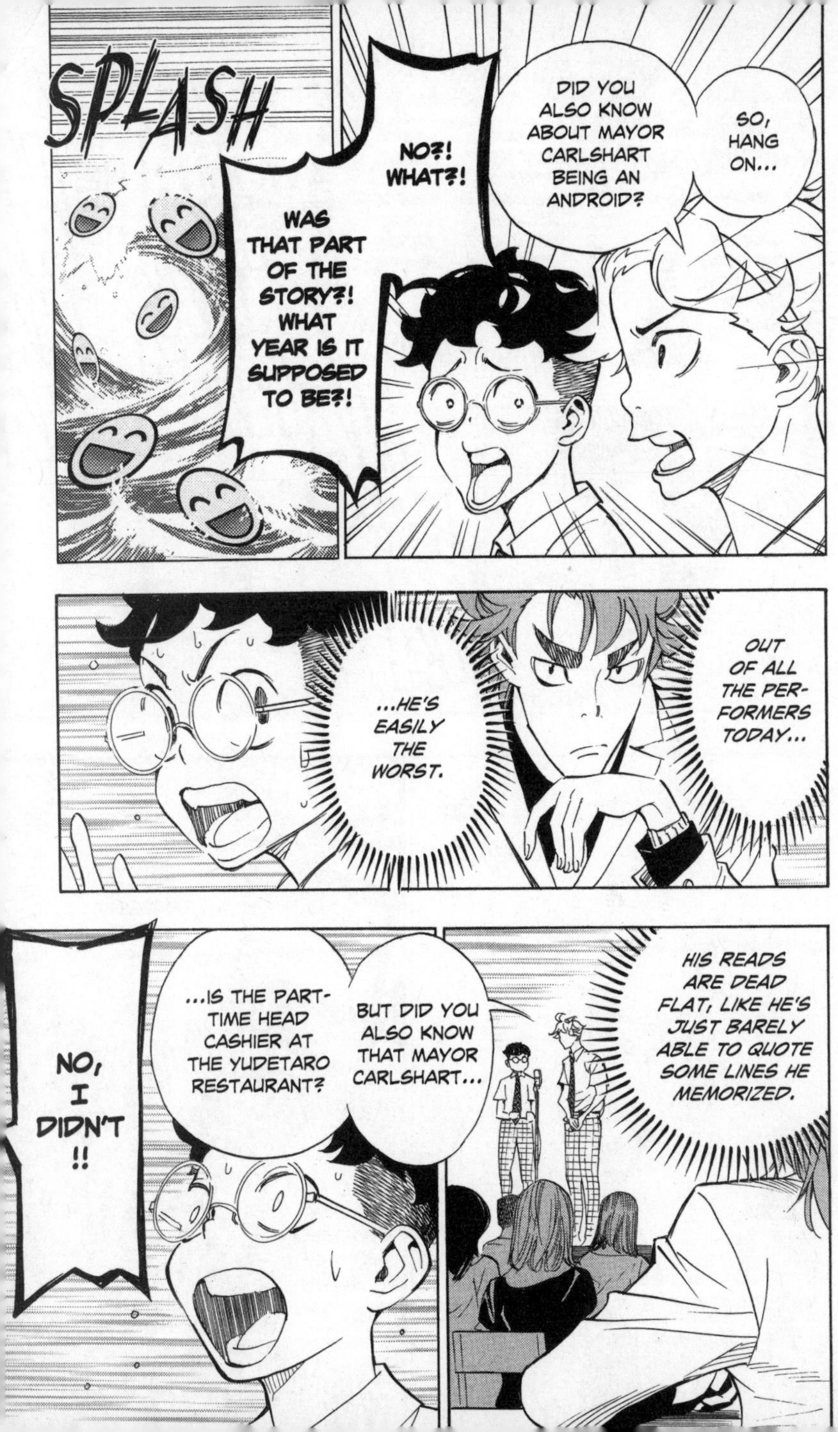
SO, HANG ON...
DID YOU ALSO KNOW ABOUT MAYOR CARLSHART BEING AN ANDROID?
NO?! WHAT?!
WAS THAT PART OF THE STORY?! WHAT YEAR IS IT SUPPOSED TO BE?!
SPLASH
OUT OF ALL THE PERFORMERS TODAY...
...HE'S EASILY THE WORST.
HIS READS ARE DEAD FLAT, LIKE HE'S JUST BARELY ABLE TO QUOTE SOME LINES HE MEMORIZED.
BUT DID YOU ALSO KNOW THAT MAYOR CARLSHART...
...IS THE PART-TIME HEAD CASHIER AT THE YUDETARO RESTAURANT?
NO, I DIDN'T!!

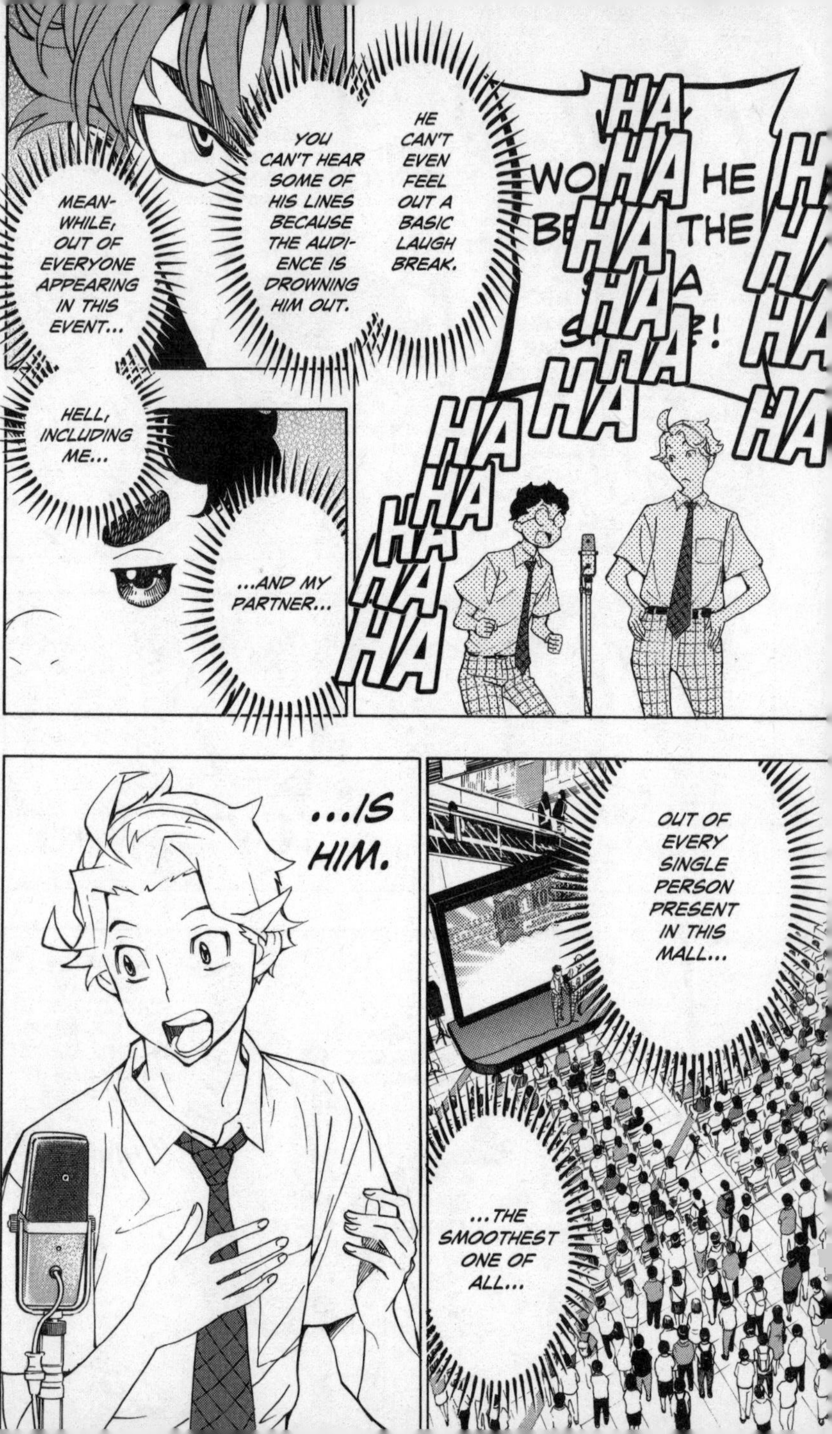
HA HA HA HA HA HA HA HA HA
HE CAN'T EVEN FEEL OUT A BASIC LAUGH BREAK.
YOU CAN'T HEAR SOME OF HIS LINES BECAUSE THE AUDI-ENCE IS DROWNING HIM OUT.
MEAN-WHILE, OUT OF EVERYONE APPEARING IN THIS EVENT...
HELL, INCLUDING ME...
...AND MY PARTNER...
OUT OF EVERY SINGLE PERSON PRESENT IN THIS MALL...
...THE SMOOTHEST ONE OF ALL...
...IS HIM.

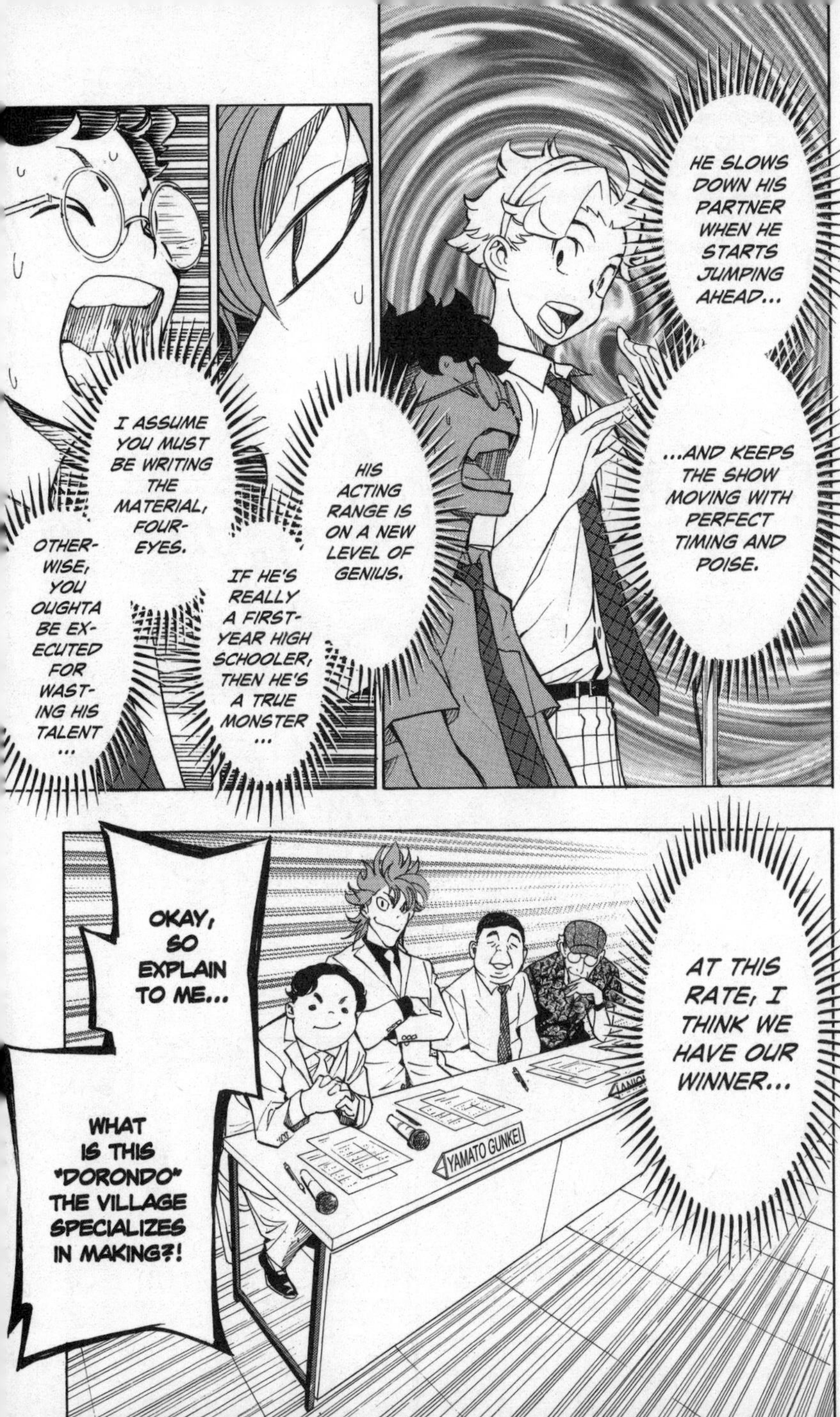
HE SLOWS DOWN HIS PARTNER WHEN HE STARTS JUMPING AHEAD...
...AND KEEPS THE SHOW MOVING WITH PERFECT TIMING AND POISE.
HIS ACTING RANGE IS ON A NEW LEVEL OF GENIUS.
IF HE'S REALLY A FIRST-YEAR HIGH SCHOOLER, THEN HE'S A TRUE MONSTER...
I ASSUME YOU MUST BE WRITING THE MATERIAL, FOUR-EYES.
OTHERWISE, YOU OUGHTA BE EXECUTED FOR WASTING HIS TALENT...
AT THIS RATE, I THINK WE HAVE OUR WINNER...
OKAY, SO EXPLAIN TO ME...
WHAT IS THIS "DORONDO" THE VILLAGE SPECIALIZES IN MAKING?!
YAMATO GUNKEI

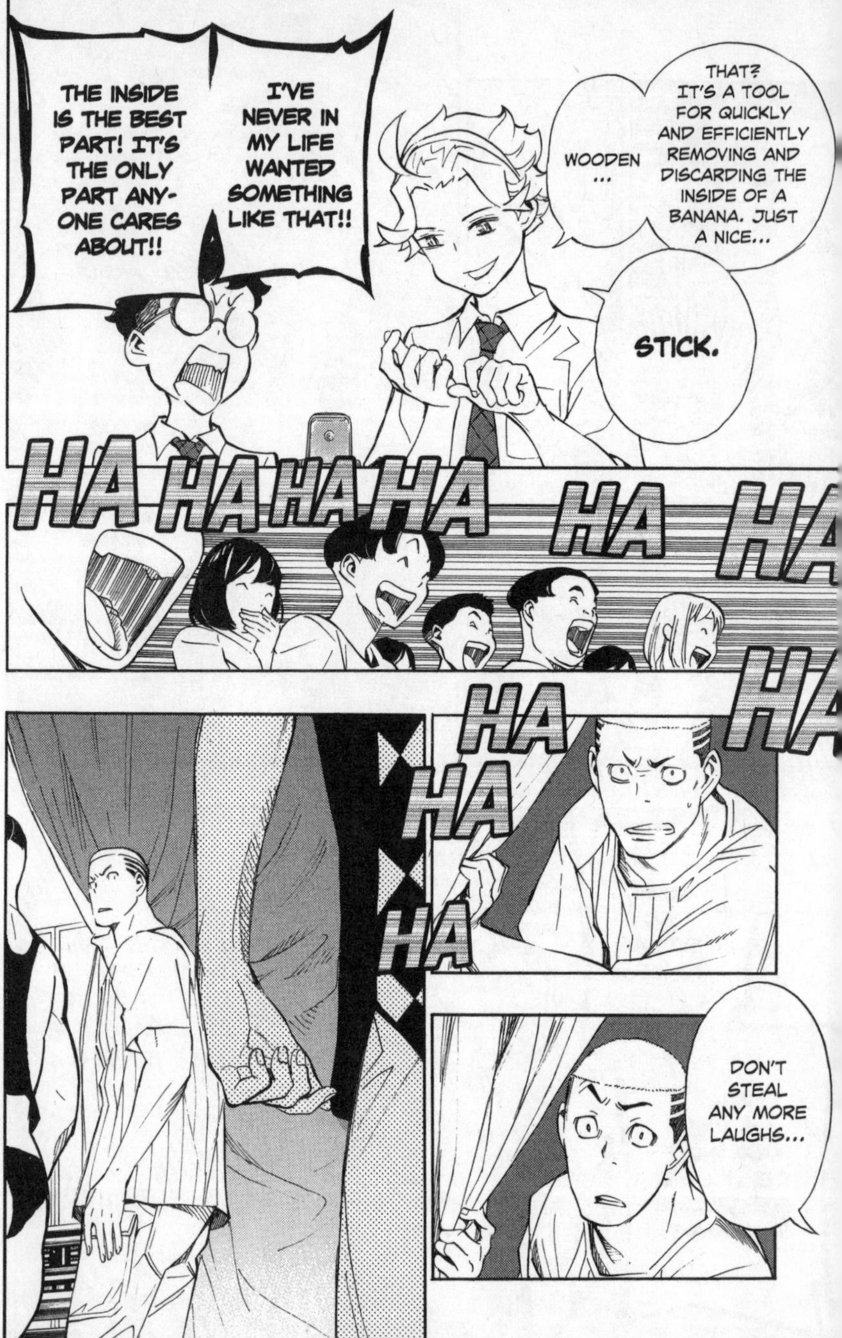
THAT? IT'S A TOOL FOR QUICKLY AND EFFICIENTLY REMOVING AND DISCARDING THE INSIDE OF A BANANA. JUST A NICE...
WOODEN ...
STICK.
I'VE NEVER IN MY LIFE WANTED SOMETHING LIKE THAT!!
THE INSIDE IS THE BEST PART! IT'S THE ONLY PART ANY-ONE CARES ABOUT!!
HA HA HA HA HA HA HA
HA
HA HA HA
DON'T STEAL ANY MORE LAUGHS...

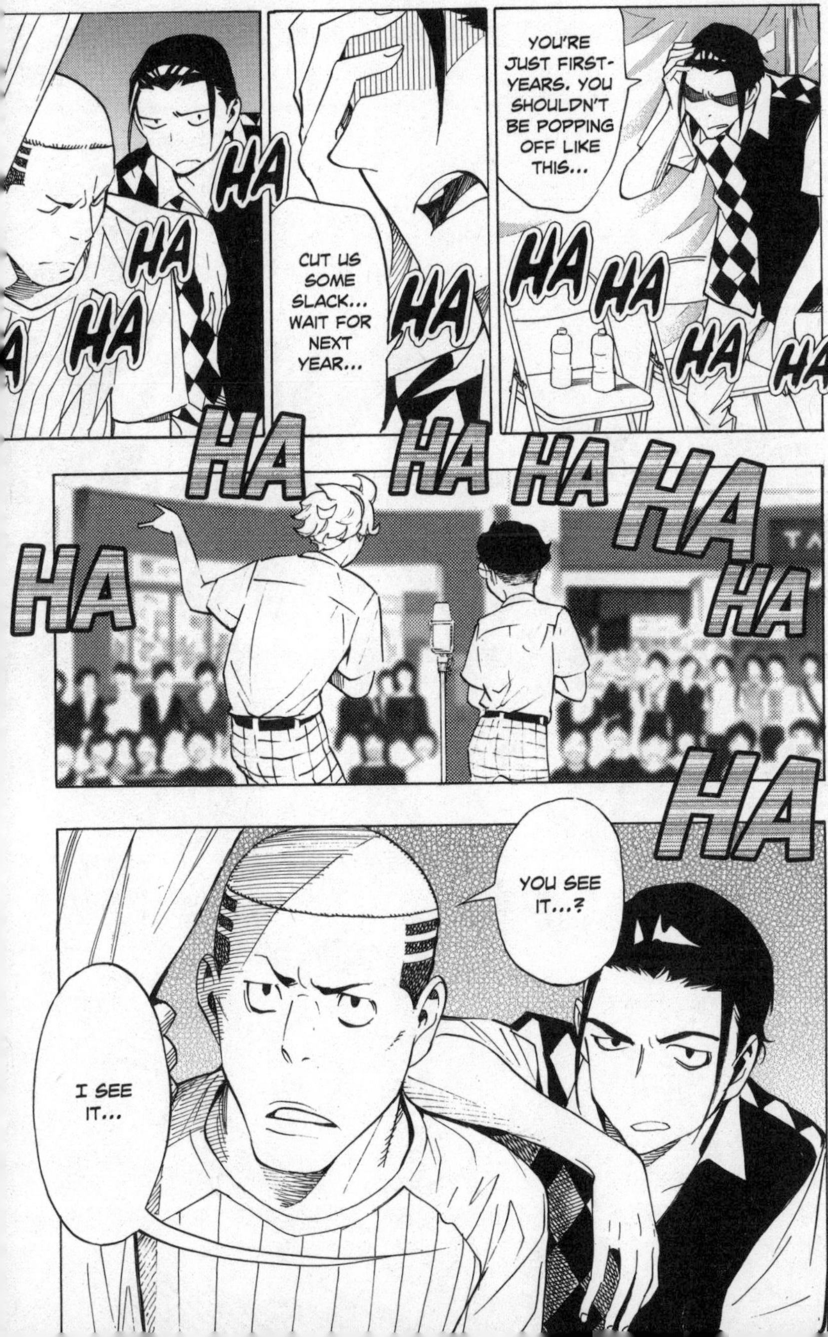
YOU'RE JUST FIRST-YEARS. YOU SHOULDN'T BE POPPING OFF LIKE THIS...
HA HA HA HA
CUT US SOME SLACK... WAIT FOR NEXT YEAR...
HA
HA HA HA
HA HA HA HA HA HA
HA
YOU SEE IT...?
I SEE IT...

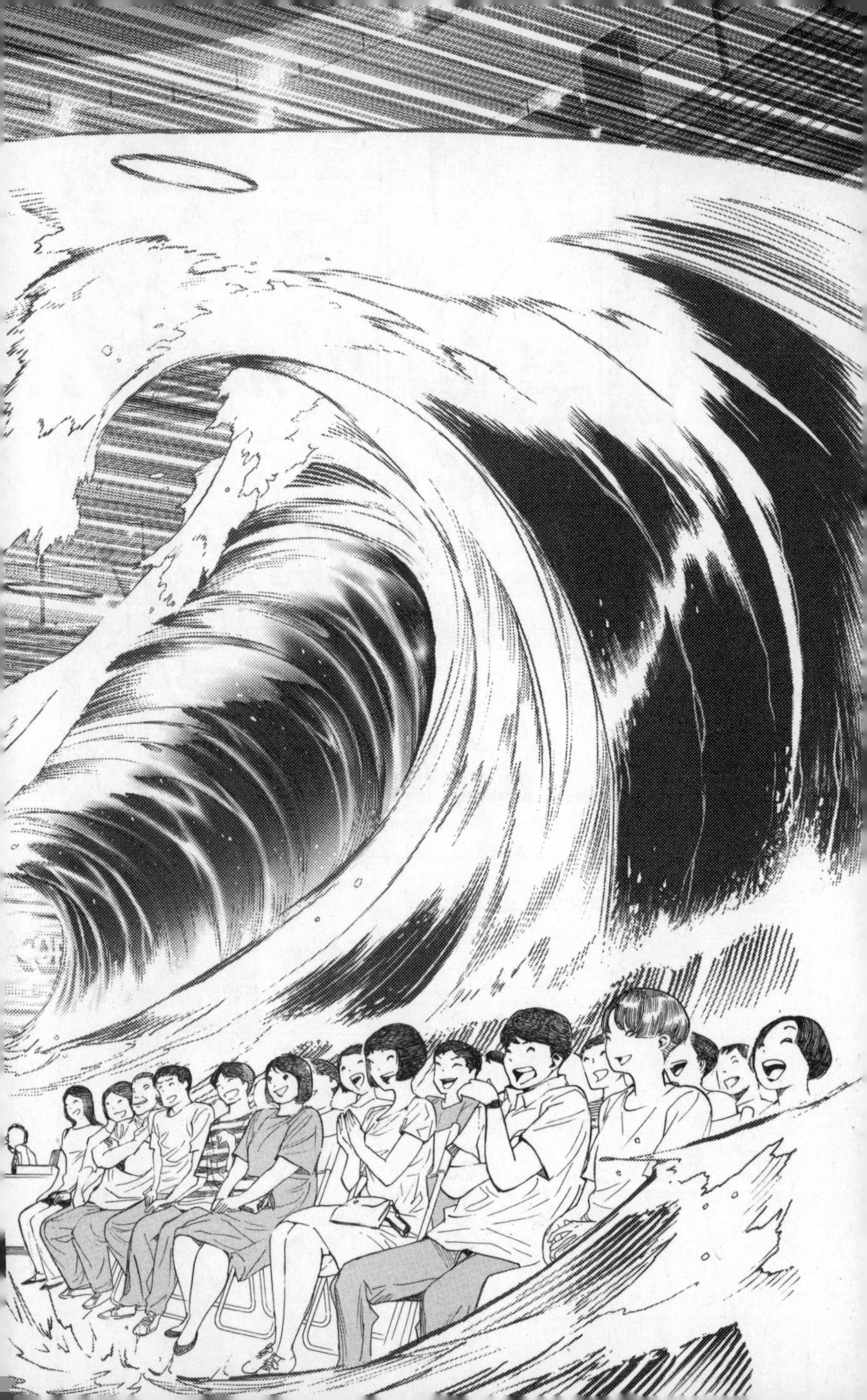

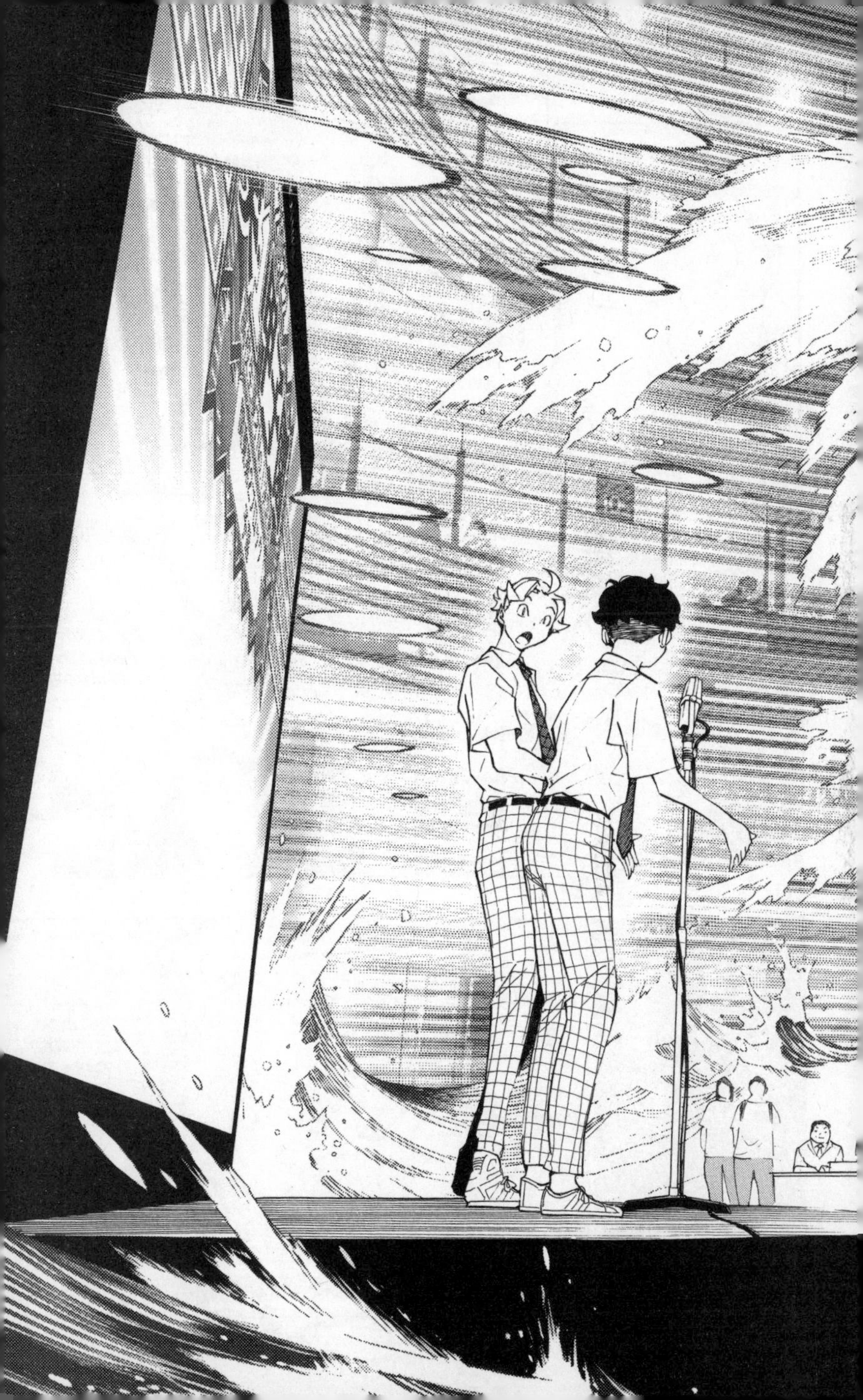

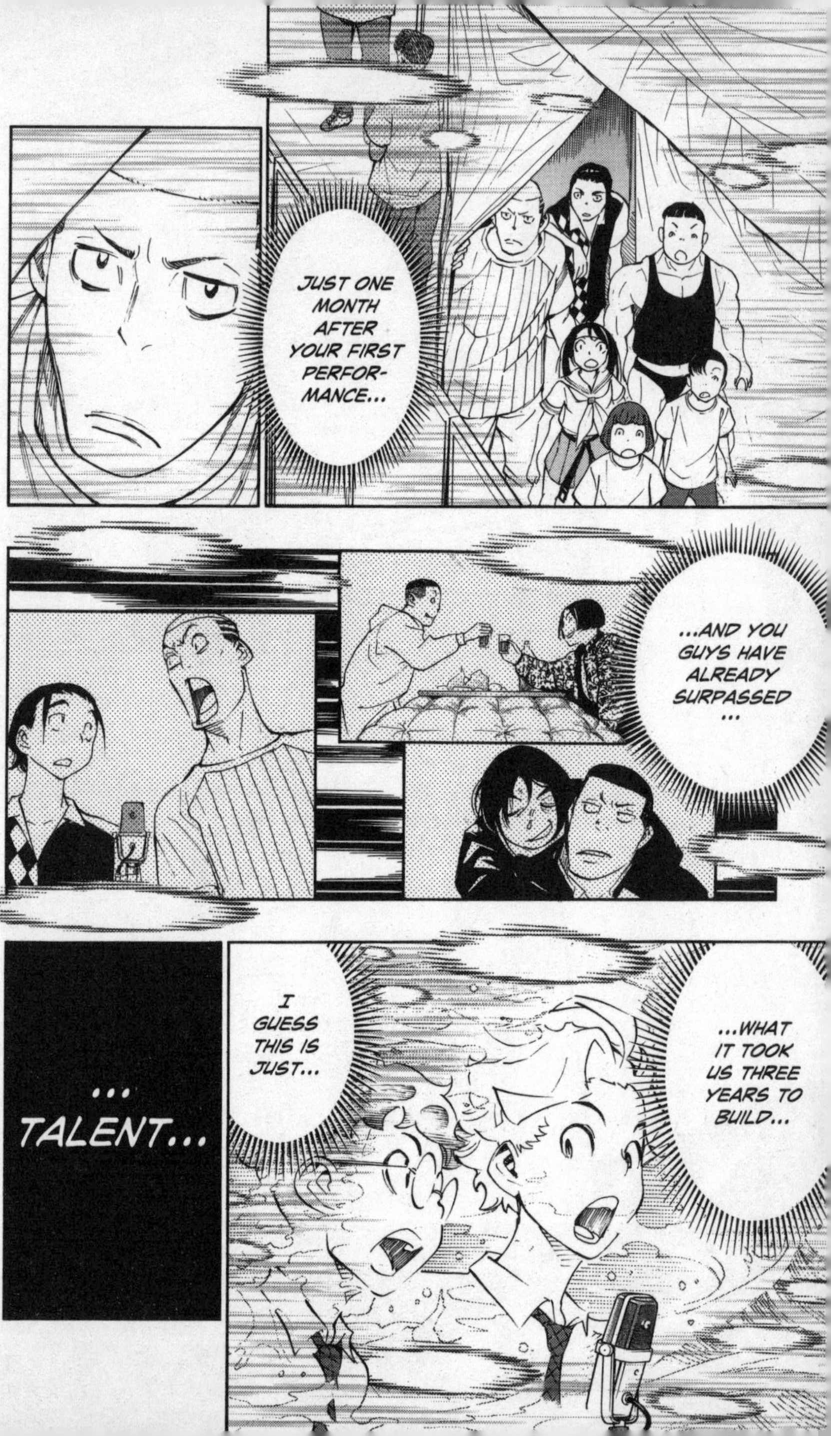
JUST ONE MONTH AFTER YOUR FIRST PERFORMANCE...
...AND YOU GUYS HAVE ALREADY SURPASSED ...
...WHAT IT TOOK US THREE YEARS TO BUILD...
I GUESS THIS IS JUST...
...TALENT...

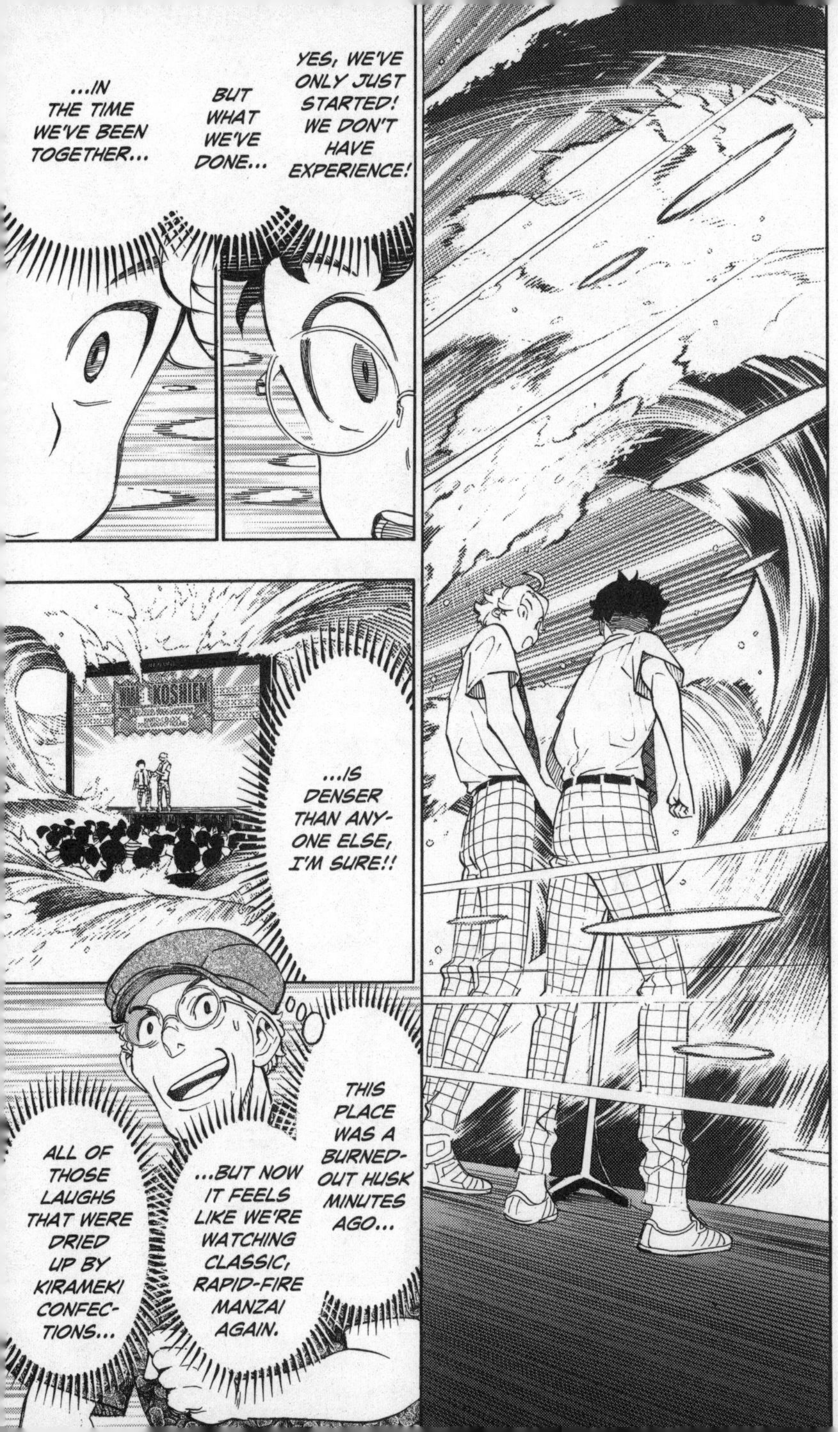
YES, WE'VE ONLY JUST STARTED! WE DON'T HAVE EXPERIENCE!
BUT WHAT WE'VE DONE...
...IN THE TIME WE'VE BEEN TOGETHER...
...IS DENSER THAN ANYONE ELSE, I'M SURE!!
THIS PLACE WAS A BURNED-OUT HUSK MINUTES AGO...
...BUT NOW IT FEELS LIKE WE'RE WATCHING CLASSIC, RAPID-FIRE MANZAI AGAIN.
ALL OF THOSE LAUGHS THAT WERE DRIED UP BY KIRAMEKI CONFECTIONS...

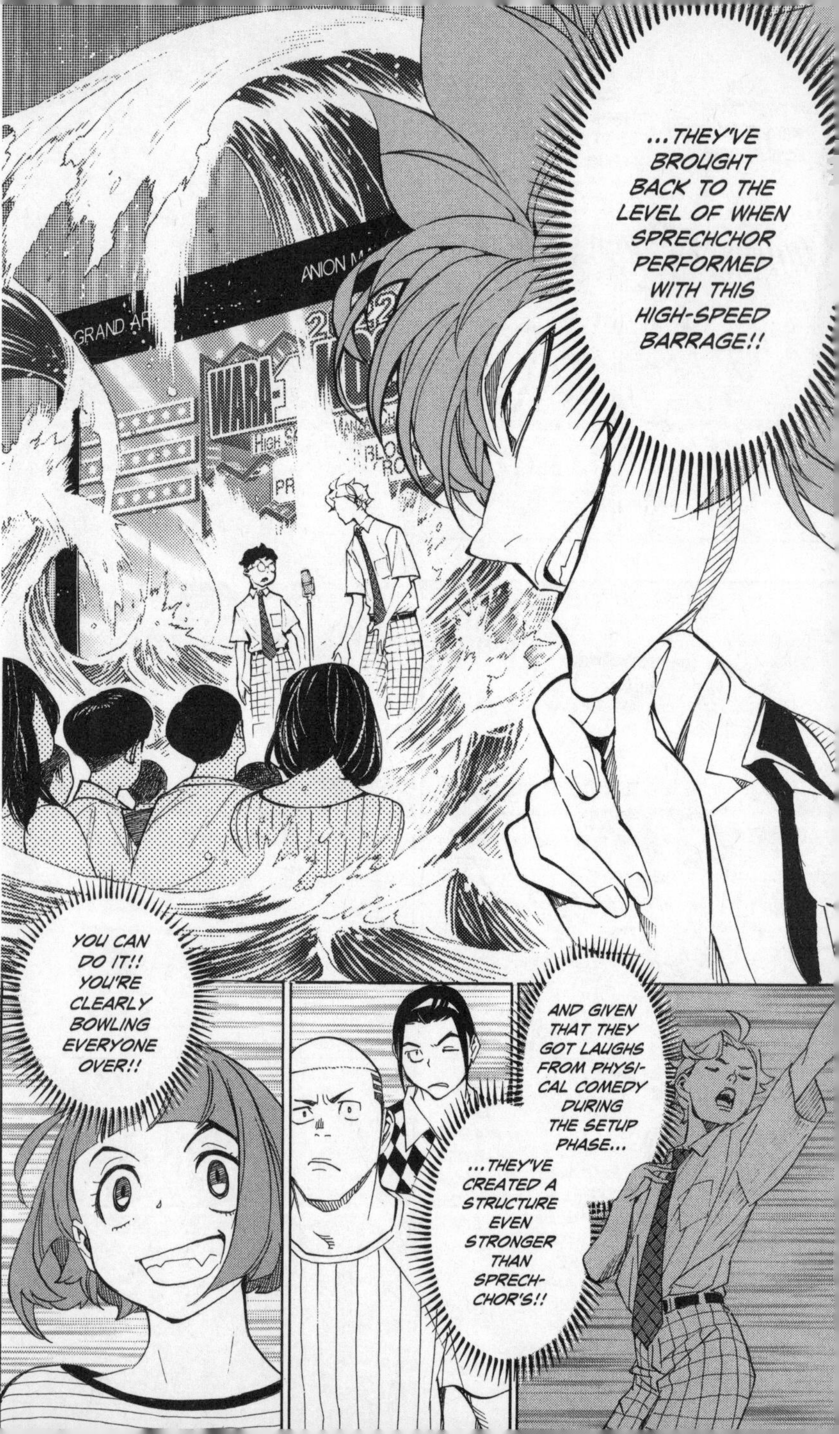
...THEY'VE BROUGHT BACK TO THE LEVEL OF WHEN SPRECHCHOR PERFORMED WITH THIS HIGH-SPEED BARRAGE!!
AND GIVEN THAT THEY GOT LAUGHS FROM PHYSI-CAL COMEDY DURING THE SETUP PHASE...
...THEY'VE CREATED A STRUCTURE EVEN STRONGER THAN SPRECH-CHOR'S!!
YOU CAN DO IT!! YOU'RE CLEARLY BOWLING EVERYONE OVER!!

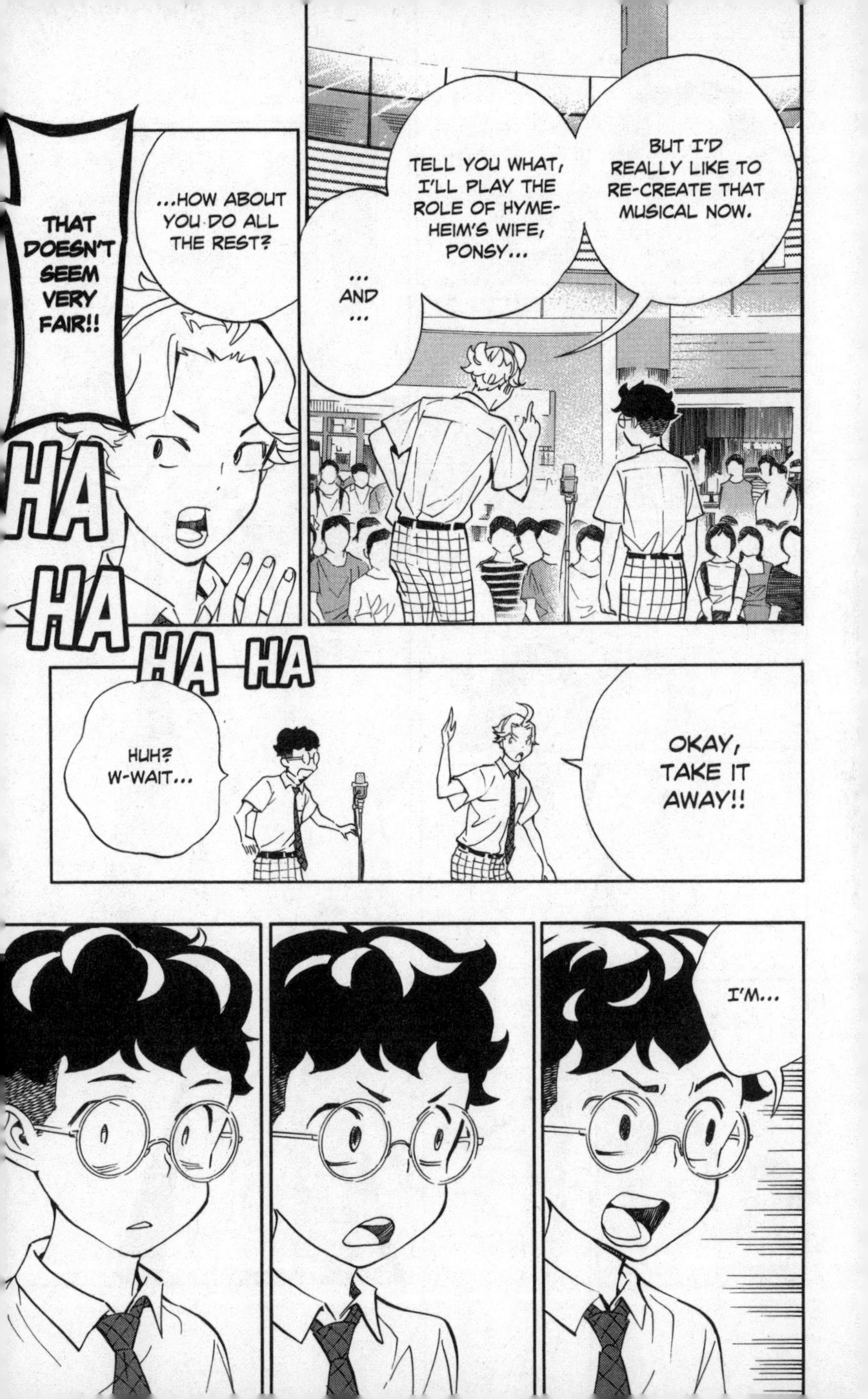
BUT I'D REALLY LIKE TO RE-CREATE THAT MUSICAL NOW.
TELL YOU WHAT, I'LL PLAY THE ROLE OF HYME-HEIM'S WIFE, PONSY...
... AND ...
...HOW ABOUT YOU DO ALL THE REST?
THAT DOESN'T SEEM VERY FAIR!!
HA HA HA HA
OKAY, TAKE IT AWAY!!
HUH? W-WAIT...
I'M...

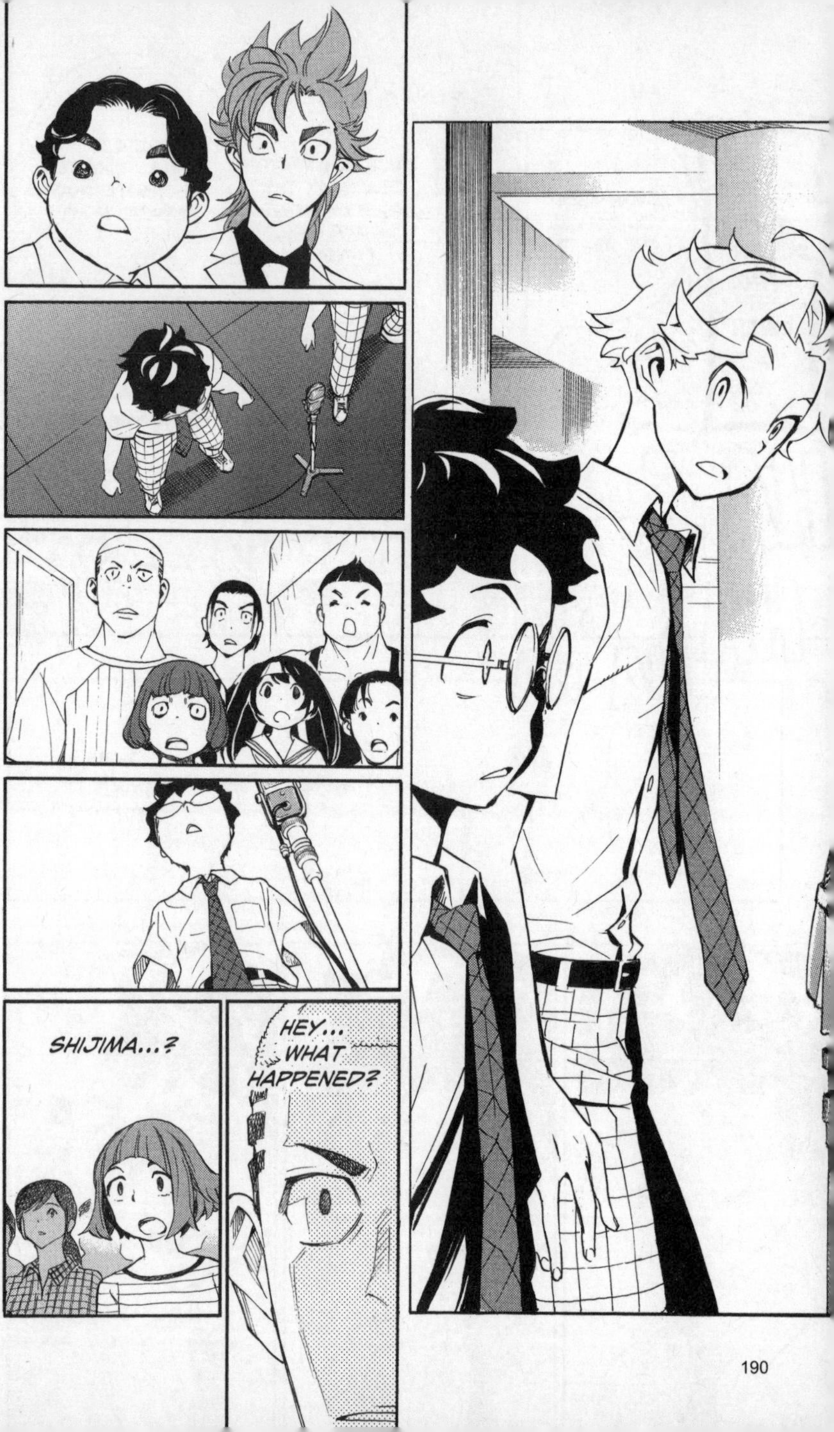
HEY... WHAT HAPPENED?
SHIJIMA...?

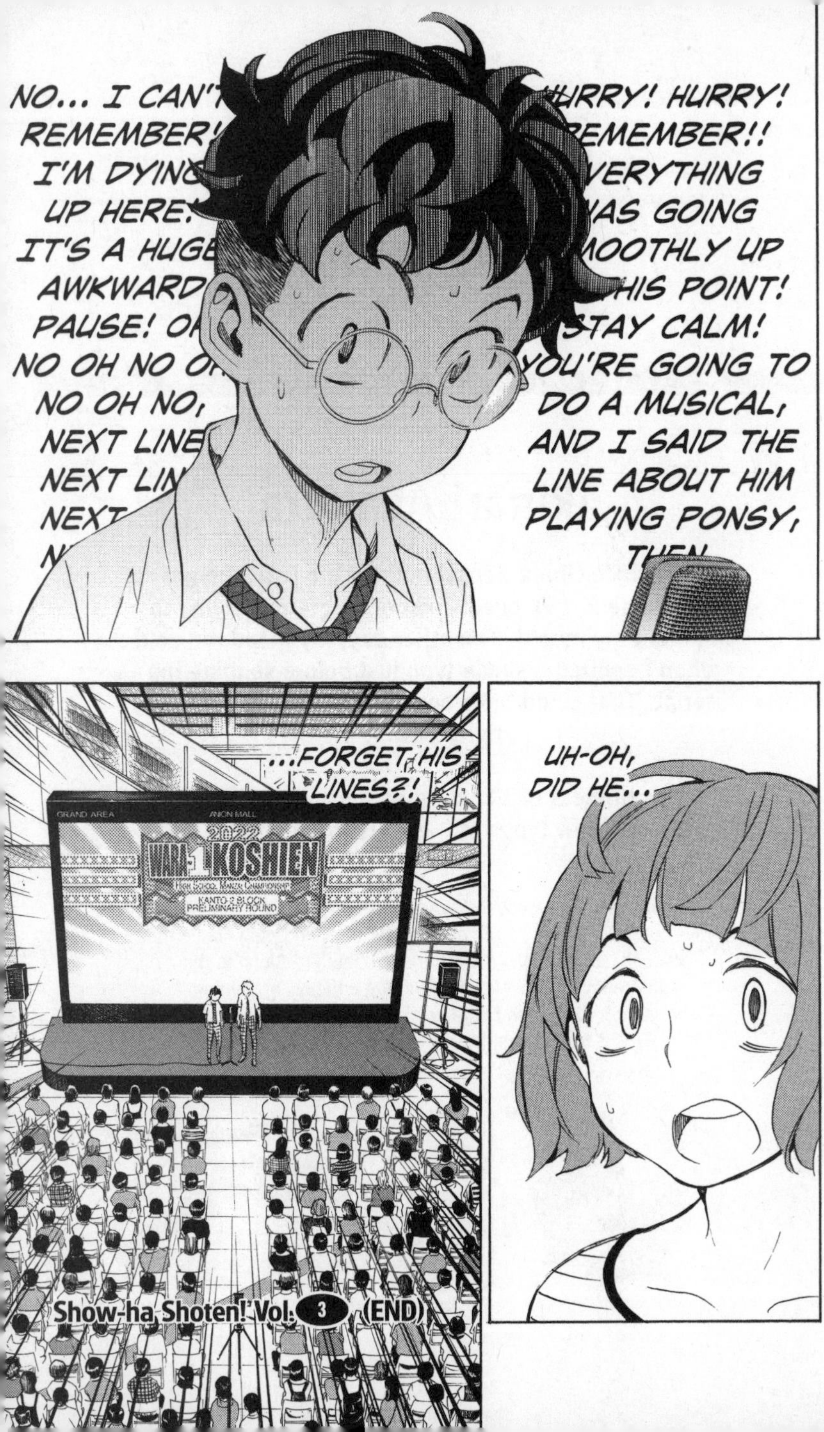

HURRY! HURRY! REMEMBER!! VERYTHING AS GOING MOOTHLY UP HIS POINT! STAY CALM! YOU'RE GOING TO DO A MUSICAL, AND I SAID THE LINE ABOUT HIM PLAYING PONSY, THEN
NO... I CAN'T REMEMBER! I'M DYING UP HERE! IT'S A HUGE AWKWARD PAUSE! OH NO OH NO OH NO OH NO, NEXT LINE NEXT LIN NEXT
UH-OH, DID HE...
...FORGET HIS LINES?!
GRAND AREA
ANION MALL
2022 WARA-1 KOSHIEN
HIGH SCHOOL MANZAI CHAMPIONSHIP
KANTO 2 BLOCK PRELIMINARY ROUND
Show-ha Shoten! Vol. 3 (END)

About the Writer

Akinari Asakura

story

Ever since Obata Sensei noticed the lack of typos in volume 2, I've been walking a tightrope trying to maintain my record. The other day, my blood ran cold when I spotted a single typo just before sending the script. That could have been the end of the legend, right there...

This is volume 3 of *Show-ha Shoten!*, the manga with very few typos at the storyboard stage.

Akinari Asakura is a novelist whose previous works include the mysteries *Ore de wa nai Enjou* (I'm Not the One Being Flamed), *Kyoushitsu ga, Hitori ni naru made* (Until I'm Alone in the Classroom), *Noir Revenant*, and the critically acclaimed *Rokunin no Usotsuki na Daigakusei* (Six Lying College Students). This is his first full-length work as a manga writer.

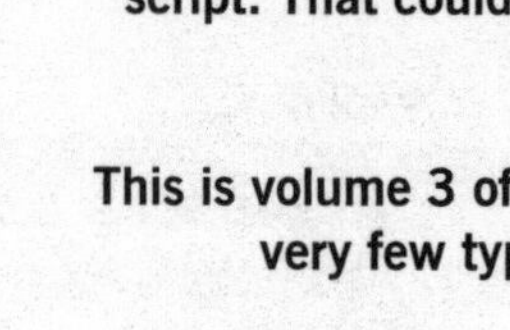
Armor

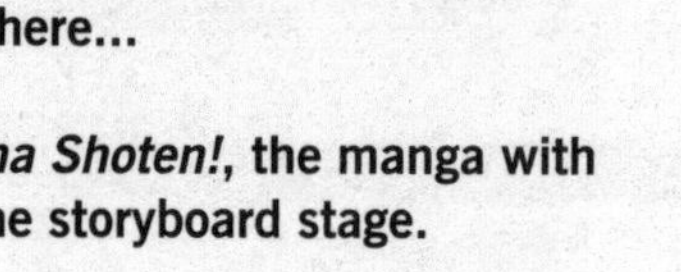
Suzume Kanade
obi

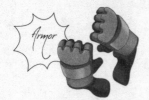

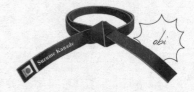

About the Artist

Takeshi Obata

I'm basically incapable of saying anything funny, so it's more often the case that people are laughing *at* me, not *with* me. But I'm used to it, so it's fine.

Takeshi Obata was born in 1969 in Niigata, Japan, and first achieved international recognition as the artist of the wildly popular Shonen Jump title *Hikaru no Go*, which won the 2003 Tezuka Osamu Cultural Prize: Shinsei "New Hope" Award and the 2000 Shogakukan Manga Award. He went on to illustrate the smash hit *Death Note* as well as the hugely successful manga *Bakuman*。 and *All You Need Is Kill*.

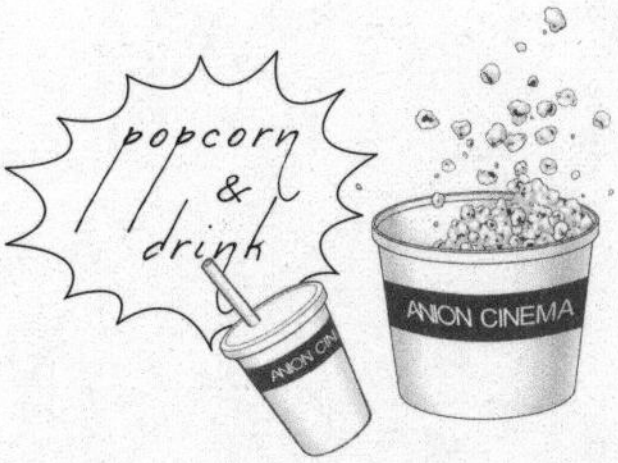
popcorn & drink
ANION CINEMA

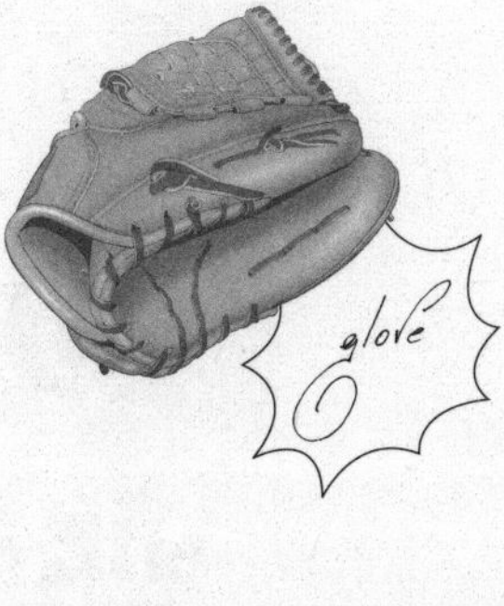
glove

SHOW-HA SHOTEN!

Volume 3
SHONEN JUMP Edition

STORY BY AKINARI ASAKURA
ART BY TAKESHI OBATA

Translation / **Stephen Paul**
Shonen Jump Touch-Up Art & Lettering / **James Gaubatz**
Graphic Novel Touch-Up Art & Lettering / **Elena Diaz**
Designer / **Kam Li**
Shonen Jump Editor / **Alexis Kirsch**
Graphic Novel Editor / **Holly Fisher**

Printed in the U.S.A.

Published by VIZ Media, LLC
P.O. Box 77010
San Francisco, CA 94107

10 9 8 7 6 5 4 3 2 1
First printing, August 2023

PARENTAL ADVISORY
SHOW-HA SHOTEN! is rated T for Teen and is recommended for ages 13 and up. This volume contains mild language.

ratings.viz.com

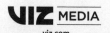

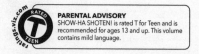

VIZ MEDIA
viz.com

SHONEN JUMP

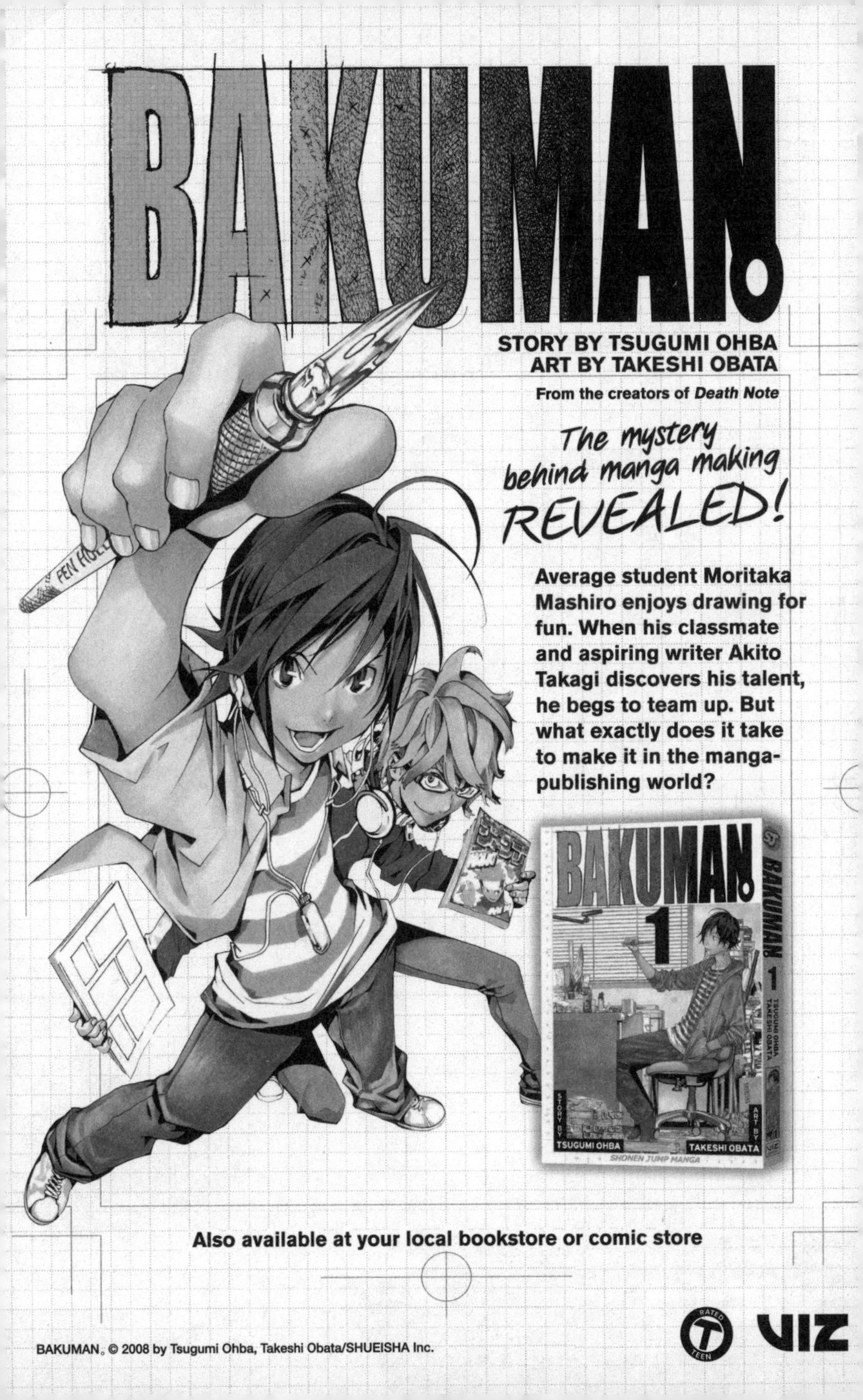

BAKUMAN。
STORY BY TSUGUMI OHBA
ART BY TAKESHI OBATA
From the creators of Death Note
The mystery behind manga making REVEALED!
Average student Moritaka Mashiro enjoys drawing for fun. When his classmate and aspiring writer Akito Takagi discovers his talent, he begs to team up. But what exactly does it take to make it in the manga-publishing world?
BAKUMAN。
1
STORY BY TSUGUMI OHBA
ART BY TAKESHI OBATA
SHONEN JUMP MANGA
Also available at your local bookstore or comic store
RATED T TEEN
VIZ
BAKUMAN。© 2008 by Tsugumi Ohba, Takeshi Obata/SHUEISHA Inc.

SHOYO HINATA IS OUT TO PROVE THAT IN VOLLEYBALL YOU DON'T NEED TO BE TALL TO FLY!

HAIKYU!!

Story and Art by **HARUICHI FURUDATE**

Ever since he saw the legendary player known as the "Little Giant" compete at the national volleyball finals, Shoyo Hinata has been aiming to be the best volleyball player ever! He decides to join the team at the high school the Little Giant went to—and then surpass him. Who says you need to be tall to play volleyball when you can jump higher than anyone else?

Kuroko's BASKETBALL

TADATOSHI FUJIMAKI

When incoming first-year student Taiga Kagami joins the Seirin High basketball team, he meets Tetsuya Kuroko, a mysterious boy who's plain beyond words. But Kagami's in for the shock of his life when he learns that the practically invisible Kuroko was once a member of "the Miracle Generation"—the undefeated legendary team—and he wants Kagami's help taking down each of his old teammates!

THE HIT SPORTS MANGA

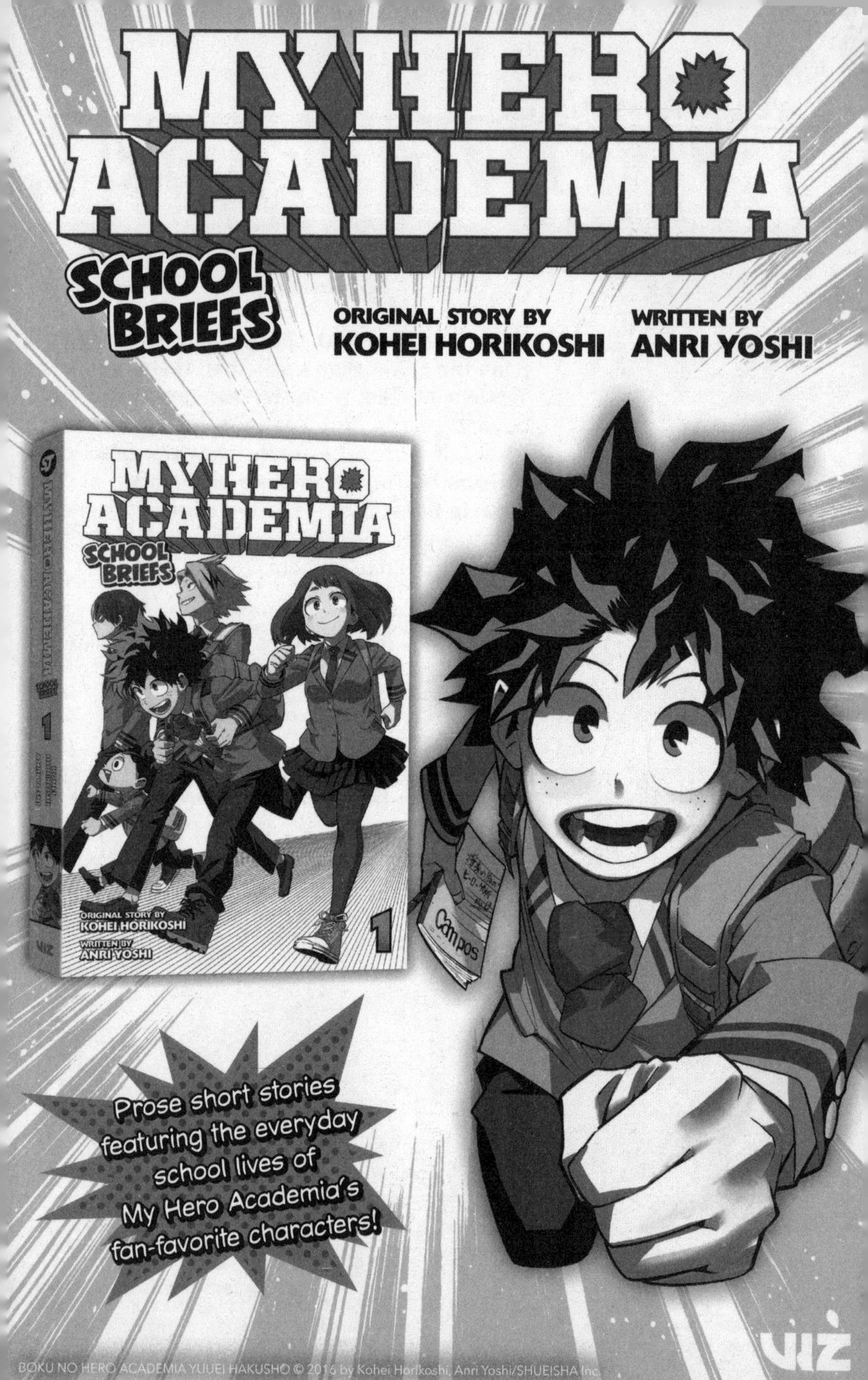
MY HERO ACADEMIA
SCHOOL BRIEFS
ORIGINAL STORY BY
KOHEI HORIKOSHI
WRITTEN BY
ANRI YOSHI
MY HERO ACADEMIA
SCHOOL BRIEFS
ORIGINAL STORY BY
KOHEI HORIKOSHI
WRITTEN BY
ANRI YOSHI
1
Prose short stories
featuring the everyday
school lives of
My Hero Academia's
fan-favorite characters!
VIZ

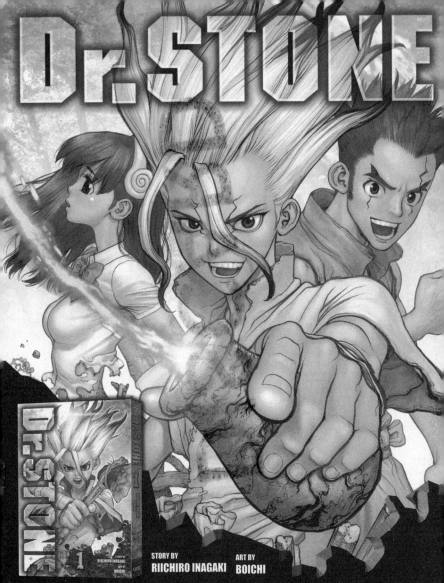

Dr.STONE

STORY BY
RIICHIRO INAGAKI

ART BY
BOICHI

One fateful day, all of humanity turned to stone. Many millennia later, Taiju frees himself from petrification and finds himself surrounded by statues. The situation looks grim—until he runs into his science-loving friend Senku! Together they plan to restart civilization with the power of science!

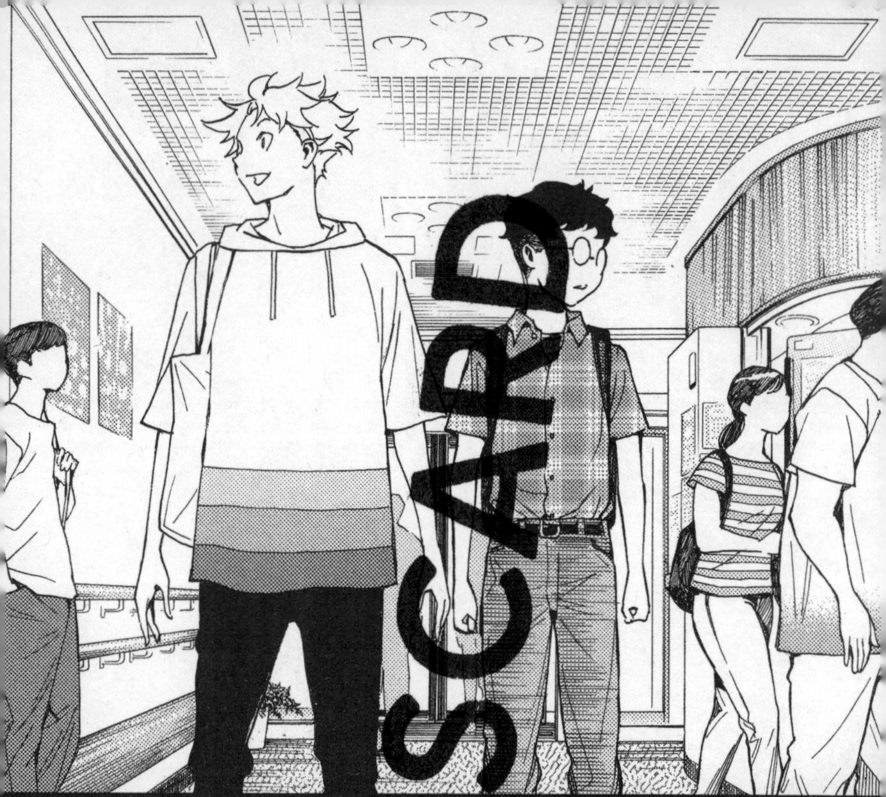

YOU'RE READING THE WRONG WAY!

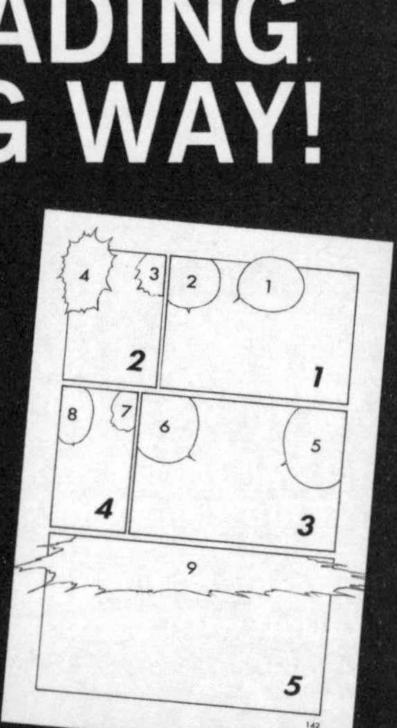
1
2
3
4
1
2
5
6
7
8
3
4
9
5
142

Show-ha Shoten!

reads right to left, starting in the upper-right corner. Japanese is read right to left, meaning that action, sound effects, and word balloon order are completely reversed from English order.

Turn to the other side of the book to get started on the comedy journey!